The Resurgence of Conservatism

in Anglo-American Democracies

The Resurgence of Conservatism in Anglo-American Democracies

Edited by Barry Cooper, Allan Kornberg,

and William Mishler

Duke Press Policy Studies

Duke University Press   Durham and London   1988

© Duke University Press. All rights reserved.
Printed in the United States of America
on acid-free paper ∞
Library of Congress Cataloging-in-Publication Data
appear on the last printed page of this book.

Contents

Preface

The conference from which this publication resulted could not have been held without substantial financial and organizational support. We are grateful to the University of Calgary, Duke University, and the State University of New York at Buffalo for both. We also received financial assistance from the Government of Alberta, the Canadian department of External Affairs, the Social Sciences and Humanities Research Council of Canada, the United States Information Agency, the British Council, the Jackman Foundation of Toronto, and the Brewster Transportation Company of Banff. Ella Wensel, Gloria Folden, and Dorothy Weathers were responsible for the organizational details and Tom Bateman, Janet Harvie, and Martha Lee provided other valuable assistance. Finally, without the collaboration and assistance—both before and after the conference—of some thirty conferees, there would have been no volume.

Barry Cooper
Allan Kornberg
William Mishler

1. The Resurgence of Conservatism in Britain, Canada, and the United States: An Overview

BARRY COOPER, ALLAN KORNBERG, AND
WILLIAM MISHLER

INTRODUCTION

In recent elections in Canada, Britain, and the United States, governments or administrations generally considered conservative, both in their policy agenda and actions, have been elected or reelected with strong and, at times, overwhelming support. In each country the apparent resurgence of conservatism has taken even many informed observers by surprise, not least because it seems to contradict the widespread belief that the expansion of the welfare state is inevitable. As a consequence, it has been derided in some circles as a reactionary denial of progress and lauded in others as a return to traditional values. Still others question whether the election of conservative governments in the three countries really signals a fundamental change in their public philosophies or simply reflects some common short-term ripples in the public mood. In short, the real character and significance of the "resurgence of conservatism" is far from clear.

Better to understand its nature and meaning, the editors of this volume organized a conference on the subject at the Chateau Lake Louise in Alberta, Canada, in May 1986. The conference brought together a group of some thirty scholars from Britain, Canada, and the United States to consider three aspects of the conservative resurgence: the ideological character and meaning of contemporary conservatism; the nature and effectiveness of the policies and programs proposed both by current conservative governments and their political opponents; and the nature, extent, and bases of public and elite support for conservative parties, principles, and leaders in these countries.

Fourteen of the papers that were prepared for the conference are presented in this volume and are divided into four sections. The first section consists of six papers that view the conservative resurgence in comparative perspective. The second section presents three papers that focus on the central themes of the conference as they are reflected in Britain. The third section presents two papers on Canada, and the final section presents three papers concerned with the resurgence of conservatism in the United States.

Not surprisingly, since they were written from different perspectives and employ different methods and approaches, the contributors to this volume do not always agree on the meaning of a particular election, the importance of specific policies, or even what constitutes a "resurgence." Nevertheless, there is remarkable consensus in the essays on fundamental trends and dynamics. On the most general level, for example, there is agreement that something that properly may be called a resurgence of conservatism has occurred in each of these countries, but especially in Britain and the United States. Although the liberal tradition remains deeply rooted and very much alive, the tenor of recent political discourse as well as the direction of political events suggest that the liberalism that has dominated and defined their public philosophies has been infused with important new conservative elements. Philosophically, these conservative elements are hard to define, although a rejection of political abstraction, a renewed emphasis on public morality, especially religion, and an emphasis on private enterprise and initiative in matters both economic and social are among them.

With few exceptions, there also is agreement that the resurgence of conservatism in the three countries has been evolutionary rather than revolutionary in character. Notwithstanding the radical tenor of recent political rhetoric, changes in public policy have been relatively modest to date. Far from producing fundamental upheavals in social or even economic policy, "Thatcherism" and "Reaganism" are widely viewed as having been implemented in piecemeal and incremental fashion and with relatively limited, though certainly significant, effects. This appears to be even more the case in Canada where the policy agenda of the Progressive Conservative party was never as clearly articulated or as ideologically coherent as those of its Conservative and

Republican counterparts. Nor has there been a set of policies that can be labeled "Mulroneyism" to parallel those identified with President Reagan or Prime Minister Thatcher.

Finally, there is agreement that although there has been a resurgence of conservatism in the elite opinion, public policies, and what might be called the public philosophy of the three countries, there is still little evidence of a similar resurgence in public opinion—the recent successes of conservative candidates in national elections to the contrary notwithstanding. We discuss this last point at the end of this overview essay. First, however, we will summarize the several contributions to the volume and attempt to place them within the perspective of Anglo-American political tradition.

THE CONSERVATIVE RESURGENCE IN
COMPARATIVE PERSPECTIVE

The character and significance of the apparent resurgence of conservatism in Britain, Canada, and the United States must be understood and evaluated in the context of the Anglo-American political tradition. This tradition is, of course, generally recognized as liberalism, although what comprises Anglo-American liberalism is much disputed. It can be argued that it encompasses at least three distinct and, at times, antagonistic impulses: the "classical" liberalism of Hobbes, Locke, Adam Smith, and Jefferson; the conservatism of Burke, Churchill, George Grant, or Michael Oakeshott; and the progressive utilitarianism of Bentham, J. S. Mill, T. H. Green, and the social reformers of the twentieth century.

Anglo-American liberalism began as an attempt to open a realm for individual freedom and public happiness by charting a moderate course between the dangers of anarchy and civil war on the one hand and of tyranny and despotism on the other. To this end it argued that men are naturally and, therefore, prepolitically free and endowed with the rights necessary for their preservation and happiness. The state is founded on the basis of individual consent to the adjudication of disputes by a limited and essentially neutral government acting within the framework of a freely enacted code of laws. Man's natural rights, however, limit the scope of political action and public life and turn people's ambitions toward private life and economic enterprise.

Classical liberalism was called into question by the French Revolution and, especially, by the Terror. Of the various reactions to the Revolution, the conservatism of Burke was among the most immediate and ardent. Instead of rights, conservatism saw traditions as the basis of social life. Instead of individuals, it turned to families, communities, and peoples bound together by long-established customs and conventions. Moreover, conservatism looked to the established church and its well-tested moral maxims for a foundation rather than to nature and nature's God. Conservatism understood obligation not as the result of individual consent, but as deference to the wealth of experiences that has shaped communal life in the past. In addition, in Canada, rejection of the tenets of the French Revolution was intensified in Quebec by the clergy and, in Upper Canada, by new elites drawn from the Loyalist tradition. Many of the Loyalists and "Late Loyalists" had been born in the United States. Although they shared the Lockean assumptions governing political life, they also adhered to the views of anti-Lockeans such as Richard Hooker. Conservatism rejected classical liberalism, and since it also praised the feudalistic, agricultural life of the ancien régime, it likewise rejected the capitalist political economy that liberalism engenders.

The conservative impulse aimed at rekindling the harmony of the traditional community, but it also opened the door to a romantic nationalism that all too often replaced reason and moderation with fervor. Consequently, conservatism has been viewed with deep suspicion by many Anglo-American liberals, especially in light of the role romantic nationalism played in fostering the two world wars of this century.

The third element intrinsic to the Anglo-American political tradition is less clearly defined than the first two. It is, in fact, a conjunction of utilitarianism, social idealism, and twentieth-century progressivism. Like conservatism, utilitarianism was in part a reaction to the French Revolution and the doctrine of abstract, universal natural or human rights. It argued that society should pursue the greatest good for the greatest number, even if this meant the sacrifice of the rights of a few of its citizens. In all three countries the reform movements of the late nineteenth century in part were motivated by this concern. Their proponents looked to government and the law as appropriate vehicles for securing the greatest good, and the resulting state intervention in private life was given a positive justification by social idealists such as

T. H. Greene and, in a different way, by John Dewey.

It was only after the First World War, however, that these theories were given serious consideration as practical alternatives in Western societies hitherto largely wedded to the precepts of classical liberalism and conservatism. Economic strife, the war, and the Great Depression seemed to many (e.g., Jane Addams, Arnold Toynbee, Thorstein Veblen, the Webbs, Mackenzie King, and J. S. Woodsworth) to demonstrate the bankruptcy of conservatism as well as individualistic liberalism and the capitalist economy that it engendered and legitimized. Some countries turned toward various forms of collectivism from fascism to socialism. In the Anglo-American states, however, the movement toward such "isms" was constrained by the strong egalitarian strain in the progressive elements of their political tradition. For example, instead of revolution Americans and Canadians were offered the "New Deal" of a Franklin Roosevelt or an R. B. Bennett, a complex of programs that involved large-scale state intervention in the economy as well as the establishment of the basic structure of a welfare state. In Britain the Lloyd George government implemented health insurance following the end of the First World War; during the 1930s social policies were heavily influenced by the research and recommendations of the Beveridge Commission.

The Second World War delayed the full-scale development of these social programs, but the two decades following the war witnessed the installation (irrespective of the label applied to it in individual countries) of a genuine welfare state, the hallmarks of which were a progressive income tax, Keynesian fiscal policies, and large-scale social security, health, and welfare programs. Almost from their inception, welfare state programs came under attack. They were unfair, unjust, inefficient, ineffective, cost too much, didn't go far enough in dealing with basic problems, or went too far and posed an increasing threat to freedom in democratic societies. One reason for such criticisms, according to Joel Smith, Allan Kornberg, and Neil Nevitte, is the mechanism through which the welfare state system is implemented. Although each country's system varies from the others in specifics, in each the great majority of adults are involved continuously in contributing to its funding and only a minority of persons are direct recipients of program benefits at any one time. Since from the perspective of the individual there are long periods when one's only relation to the welfare state is as a financial contributor, the system depends, in a real sense, upon people's generosity and goodwill—which is more likely to be manifested in good rather than bad economic times.

But since criticisms of the welfare state have been made during good and bad times alike, their chapter, "Structural Factors in the Conservative Resurgence," is concerned with identifying the conditions in each country under which the same triggering event—the energy-induced economic crisis of the early 1970s—generated a climate in which the withdrawal of public support for the welfare state and its proponents was severe enough to bring about a conservative electoral triumph. The conditions they point to include (1) a growth of foreign competition for markets; (2) the acquisition of domestic corporations and properties by foreign investors; (3) the withdrawal of support for the national regime by members of both upper and lower economic strata; (4) the emergence of demand overload on the welfare system; (5) strained relationships with foreign powers; and (6) shifts in political participation.

Although they acknowledge that this is not an exhaustive list of factors and that Britain, Canada, and the United States differ in the degree to which a conservative resurgence has occurred, they believe that each country shares these general attributes sufficiently to suggest convergence. They also assert that in each country the resurgence is a product of an electoral coalition of numerous limited-issue groups —disaffected elements of opposition parties who essentially are voting *against* recent prowelfare state incumbents—and the *exit* from the electoral arena of both disaffected partisans of liberal parties and those not identified with any party. Since there have not been massive ideological realignments in the three electorates and since neither the several elements in each country's coalition nor the governments they have brought to office support *every* conservative position, these governments have been unwilling or unable to implement a thoroughgoing conservative agenda. Instead, until now they have restricted themselves largely to rhetoric, the promotion of ancillary policies and programs, and to partial implementation of what has been called "fiscal responsibility." In short, the authors contend that it is more appropriate to view the conservative resurgence in Britain, Canada, and the United States during the 1970s as a rejection by their publics of political parties and officials traditionally associated with the welfare state and its programs rather than as a massive and fundamental conversion to conservative ideals and goals.

As its skeptical subtitle suggests, in "Hunting the Snark: Or Searching for Evidence of That Widely Touted but Highly Elusive Resurgence of Public Support for Conservative Parties in Britain, Canada, and the United States," William Mishler, Marilyn Hoskin, and Roy Fitzgerald find little systematic evidence to support the rich variety of anecdotal evidence regarding the resurgence of public support for conservative parties. Indeed, what Smith, Kornberg, and Nevitte interpret as a rejection by the public of political parties and officials associated with the welfare state, Mishler, Hoskin, and Fitzgerald maintain is simply one part of a more general decline in public support (or dealignment) for all political parties, conservative and liberal alike.

To test this proposition, the authors use time series analyses of data gathered quarterly since 1964 on the relative share of public support for the more conservative of the two major political parties in each country. Although they find some evidence of significant conservative gains in public support during the late 1970s and early 1980s, their analyses indicate the gains generally were short-lived and well within the range of normal fluctuations in public opinion across the past twenty years. Moreover, conservative gains usually were followed closely by a countervailing shift in public support of comparable magnitude toward the liberal party. Based on this evidence, the authors argue that recent trends in public support for conservative parties are simply part of the normal ebb and flow of partisan politics and that the "much-heralded resurgence of conservatism is largely myth."

Proceeding with a detailed examination of the *causes* of recent fluctuations in conservative party support, the authors also find little evidence to support the conventional wisdom that recent conservative gains in the three countries are linked or stem from certain shared social, economic, or political experiences. To the contrary, variations in public support for conservative parties appear to be best explained by idiosyncratic factors, including the popularity of Ronald Reagan, the leadership of Margaret Thatcher, the charisma (both positive and negative) of Pierre Trudeau, and the impact of events such as the Falklands and Grenada invasions, the Watergate scandal, and the patriation of the Canadian Constitution.

What seems initially to be a contradiction between their conclusions and those of Smith, Kornberg, and Nevitte appears, on closer scrutiny, to be a difference largely of focus and perspective. Although the latter chapter demonstrates convincingly that the bankruptcy of liberal policies has become increasingly evident to conservative political actors and opinion leaders in the three countries, the essay by Mishler, Hoskin, and Fitzgerald argues that this bankruptcy has been considerably less obvious to average citizens in the three countries. Their interpretation is consistent with an extensive literature demonstrating the volatility of mass opinion in the Anglo-American democracies and the relative lack of ideologues among mass publics as compared to political elites. It also is consistent in part with the analysis by Norman Thomas of the resurgence of conservatism in the public policies of the three countries.

In "Public Policy and the Resurgence of Conservatism in Three Anglo-American Democracies," Thomas attributes the erosion in support for parties and candidates identified in the public's mind with the focus and functions of the welfare state to a breakdown in the effectiveness of Keynesian countercyclical regulation of the economy. The Keynesian welfare state has proved simply to be ineffective in sustaining economic growth at a high enough level to finance social service programs while at the same time controlling inflation. In that context, conservatives undertook their criticism of the liberal and social democratic arguments that had sustained the Keynesian public policy initiatives. The American, British, and Canadian examples, which are sufficiently distinct to constitute separate variations on the general theme just indicated, are each discussed in detail in this chapter. In each country the government responded to the problems of inflation, slow economic growth, and system overload by changing economic and social policies. The most visible common consequence has been support for the principle of insuring a smaller and less intrusive government. The results, however, have been mixed save for one incontestable consequence: the liberal monopoly of public discourse, which has governed a generation of political debate, has been broken.

The conservative alternative has been more extensively developed in Britain and the United States than in Canada. In the latter country it is neither as ideologically defined nor as contemptuous of welfare state liberalism. Nor have policy changes under the Mulroney government been as sweeping as those under Thatcher and Reagan, although the emphases have been similar—monetarism, free markets, and competition.

Thomas asks whether a "new politics" with an accompanying public philosophy has been produced by rationalizing policies adopted in the three countries. He concludes that in Britain, the United States, and to a lesser degree in Canada there have been substantial changes in the form of modified political agendas, a reduced role for the state, and the development of viable alternatives to established liberal and social democratic public philosophies. In this sense, rather than in the sense of a radical political and economic transformation of their societies, the impact of the conservative resurgence on the policies of the three countries has been profound.

Although it was reasonable to assume that the election and reelection of conservative governments in the three countries would have a profound and salutary effect on their foreign policies and the policies of the Western Alliance more generally, this has not been the case. Indeed, in his chapter, "Gulliver and the Lilliputians: Conservatism, Foreign Policy, and Alliance Relations," William James Booth observes that in some respects the underlying sources of tension within the Western Alliance not only have not been significantly eased, but in some respects they have been exacerbated.

Booth argues that the enduring source of tension in the Alliance is to be found in the frictions generated by the often uneasy relationship of the superpower and its smaller but independent allies. That relationship has been characterized, on the one side, by the superpower's demands for foreign policy cohesiveness (demands often extending beyond those that would be consistent with a narrow construction of the Alliance's purposes) and its tendency to measure its allies' good faith by their fidelity to its leadership across a broad range of international concerns. On the other side, this relationship has as its second principal feature the desire of the smaller and middle powers to maintain sovereignty and influence consistent with the requirements of Alliance membership. The clash of these two guiding threads to foreign policies lies at the root of much of the friction within the Alliance.

Drawing his evidence principally from the 1980–85 period, Booth maintains that the nationalism and unilateralism of key components of Reagan's foreign policy, coupled with a suspicion of Europe's steadfastness, clashed powerfully in this period with the policy agendas of otherwise like-minded governments. In short, despite shared basic perceptions of East/West relations and of the nature of the Soviet threat, and in spite of a common declaratory policy calling for a reinvigorated Alliance, Anglo-American conservatives have found themselves at odds with one another. They have been divided by that long-standing fault line inherent in the relationship between Gulliver and the Lilliputians. Both Gulliver and the Lilliputians, Booth suggests, require the kind of *courage civile* that would recognize the implications of the Alliance and its place in maintaining the democratic regimes of free societies on both sides of the Atlantic.

Turning from the content of policy to a key institutional actor in the policy process, two essays examine the role of the courts in the conservative resurgence in the United States and Canada. In his chapter, "Conservatives and the Courts in the United States and Canada," F. L. Morton observes that the recent electoral successes of conservative political parties in the United States and Canada have had very different effects on the political roles of their courts. The political role of federal judges—especially those on the Supreme Court—has become a highly partisan issue in American politics. The 1980 election of Ronald Reagan culminated two decades of growing conservative resentment toward the Supreme Court and its liberal-activist decisions in policy areas such as abortion, court-ordered busing, and the procedural rights of criminal defendants. The 1980 and 1984 Republican party platforms called for the appointment of federal judges who would respect states' rights and "who respect the traditional family values and the sanctity of innocent human life." Further, since 1981, Senate Republicans initiated more than two dozen bills designed to end judicial policymaking in controversial areas.

Although their court-curbing efforts have not been successful, Reagan's use of the presidential power of appointment has been. Reagan's 1986 appointment of William Rehnquist as chief justice installs the most conservative member of the Court as its new leader. Reagan's two other Supreme Court appointments—Sandra Day O'Connor (1981) and Antonin Scalia (1986)—are both proven judicial conservatives. Together, these appointments may well shift the balance of power on the new Rehnquist Court to the right. Indeed, if Mr. Reagan is given the opportunity to make one or more additional appointments during his presidency, the result may be the overturning of some of the more controversial decisions of the Warren and Burger Courts.

Reagan has had even greater influence on the composition and ideological perspective of lower federal courts. By the end of his second term it is estimated that he will have appointed more than half of all federal judges, a record equaled by only two other modern presidents. Moreover, he has exercised the appointment power in the most partisan fashion since Woodrow Wilson and Warren Harding. He also has reversed the trend toward appointing more black and women judges that was initiated during the Carter administration. Finally, the decisions rendered by Reagan appointees have been faithful to the Reagan criteria of judicial self-restraint and "strict construction" of the Constitution.

Conservative-judicial relations in Canada stand in sharp contrast to recent American experience. In the 1984 federal election that brought the Mulroney Conservatives to power, there was no mention of judicial appointments or court-curbing. Historically, the role of the courts in Canada has been a political nonissue. Nonetheless, there are indications this may change. In the summer that the Conservatives swept to power the Supreme Court of Canada embarked on a series of activist and libertarian charter decisions, which suggest that "American-style" issues such as censorship of pornography, sexual equality, abortion, and education policy have emerged as potential new areas of political conflict. "Single-issue" interest groups in Canada have been quick to learn from their American counterparts the advantages of turning to the courts when they fail in the legislature. If Canadian judges —especially those of the Supreme Court—accept this new invitation to act as an agency of law reform, the Charter of Rights may serve as a catalyst for re-creating a northern version of the "social issues" that have reshaped the American political landscape in recent years.

A. Kenneth Pye's chapter, "Conservatism and the Courts: A Comparative Analysis of Canada and the United States," also views the conservative resurgence in the United States and Canada from the perspective of Supreme Court decisions. There are jurisdictional differences between the two courts and some jurisprudential incompatibilities regarding statutory and common law interpretations. Nevertheless, there are sufficient similarities regarding basic rights, especially criminal procedure, to make a comparison worthwhile.

The differences involved in ordering court decisions along a liberal-conservative continuum are greater and more complex than undertaking the same exercise with legislative or executive decisions. Courts have different purposes and undertake different tasks in democratic regimes than their legislative and executive counterparts, so that their "liberalism" or "conservatism" often is confused with activism or restraint. Yet a conservative court can be an activist court by striking down liberal or progressive legislation. Similarly, a liberal court can exercise restraint by upholding liberal or progressive lower court decisions or by declining to hear appeals. In determining the liberalism or conservatism of a court, therefore, both substantive criteria and criteria of review must be employed.

Despite the problems such distinctions pose for systematic comparative analysis, some generalizations about the behavior of the Canadian and American Supreme Courts can be offered. Pye's analysis and arguments indicate that, as compared to the Warren Court, the Burger Court is basically conservative, although more covertly than overtly. The Canadian Court, especially regarding Charter cases, presents a different picture. Compared to their American colleagues, Canadian Supreme Court justices have been more activist and liberal. Pye suggests several reasons for this, the most intriguing of which is that they have not restrained their urge to assert institutional power. In this respect the current Canadian Court should be compared not with the Burger Court but with the Court of Chief Justice Marshall. Both Chief Justice Marshall and Chief Justice Dickson may be seen as leaders of institutions whose status as supreme arbiters of their respective polities has not yet been secured. Accordingly, they both have used subtle political and judicial strategies to insure an increased political role for their courts in the governing processes of the two countries. To date, the Canadian court has proved (and promises to continue to be) especially complex both because it is a relative novice in deciding constitutional cases arising from the Charter of Rights and Freedoms and because it has the long jurisprudential history and abundant case law of the U.S. Supreme Court to draw on for guidance.

GREAT BRITAIN

The belief persists that the policies of two Margaret Thatcher–led Conservative governments have been anything but moderate and that the renaissance of the British economy is the best evidence of their success. The key supposedly is "Thatcherism," a package of fiscal and monetary austerity with tight restraints on government spending and borrowing aimed at curbing inflation and reducing interest rates and able to overcome the electoral burden of an unemployment rate that had more than doubled to 13 percent. In fact, Thatcherism is more than a set of mechanical principles applied to the instruments of economic policy. It includes both an underlying philosophy about the values of competitiveness and the advantages of private sector efficiency and an old-fashioned liberal political philosophy of individualism.

Nevertheless, as James Alt argues in his chapter, "New Wine in Old Bottles: Thatcher's Conservative Economic Policy," a closer look suggests that the renaissance has not yet taken place. Thus, while Thatcher may have communicated a new philosophy and convinced many to accept its tenets, the acceptance is capricious and, in the absence of evidence of a real payoff, may disappear with changes in intellectual fashion. Indeed, it is not even clear that Thatcherism represents a resurgence of conservatism. In support of this view Alt describes what the Thatcher government did, what it wanted to do, what happened, and why. This enables him to delineate which aspects of Thatcher's policies are conservative, and, of the latter, which are familiar and which are novel in the context of the British Conservative tradition.

Thatcherism has brought about a variety of policy changes closely linked to taxation and public expenditure, the nuts and bolts of economic policies. Some of these changes are familiar Conservative aspects of interparty competition, such as the shift in expenditure priorities toward defense and law and order. Others are conservative but decisive reversals of earlier Conservative policies, such as the increase in profits relative to wages and the reduction of housing expenditures. Still other changes, such as the increased burden of taxes borne by corporations rather than households, are populist rather than conservative. And in some respects there is little change to be observed, reflecting the passive effect of constraints rather than active decisions.

Equally important, the largest departure of the Thatcher years (the persisting high level of unemployment) does not appear to be an obvious consequence of any of these domestic policy changes. Instead, high unemployment originates in two external problems: the dramatic loss of trade competitiveness in Britain over the last decade (mostly before 1981) and the world recession. This loss of competitiveness and its effects on employment do not result from a resurgence of conservatism. They are a consequence of the collision of persisting, traditional British practice with changes in international markets in which exchange rates were determined by the discovery and exploitation of North Sea oil and subsequent oil-based speculation in sterling. Alt concludes that the novel features of these markets (the new wine) interacted with the familiar constraints of British political ideas and institutions (the old bottles) to produce current British conditions.

Another perspective on Mrs. Thatcher and Thatcherism is offered by Ivor Crewe and Donald D. Searing. In their chapter, "Mrs. Thatcher's Crusade: Conservatism in Britain, 1972–1986," the authors note that in 1979 and 1983 the Conservative party won successive elections that broke long-standing electoral records. The first was won by the largest "swing" of the vote recorded since 1945. The second produced the largest difference between two major parties in votes and seats won since 1935. Despite these victories, the authors contend that there has been no renaissance of the Right and no resurgence of conservatism in Britain—at least insofar as it is reflected in such aspects of public opinion and political behavior as the magnitude of the Conservative party vote, partisan identification, party membership, or the popularity of Conservative leaders. What must be explained, then, is why the Conservative party moved so sharply to the right between 1974 and 1983 without any substantial electoral incentive to do so and also why the party did not lose electoral support for having made the move. The reason, the authors argue, is found in the quality of leadership supplied by the Thatcherites.

Their essay investigates the origins and ideological character of Thatcherism, the force that pushed the party to the right by virtue of the convictions and determination of a surprisingly small number of Conservative party leaders. The authors show that Thatcherism was at the time of its emergence a minority outlook characterized chiefly by its unusual combination of the Liberal Whig's free enterprise doctrines with the traditional Tory's attraction to statecraft. They also demonstrate that public support for the package was focused mainly on its third component, Victorian morality. Crewe and Searing argue that Mrs. Thatcher did not develop her ideological crusade primarily for electoral reasons. Rather, she developed her doctrines because she became convinced that they were the medicine Britain badly needed at the time. Indeed, she believed it necessary to set out to convince the public as well as her party of these fundamental facts. Since the nation was not a particularly good pupil, the question arises as to how it was that her party triumphed in 1979 and 1983.

The principal reason, as noted above, appears to have been the Thatcherite style of leadership with its emphases on discipline, free enterprise, and statecraft. Indeed, the Thatcherite leadership style has proved appealing even to many members of the electorate who did not share Thatcherite positions on major issues. This is because the Thatcherites are self-assured, aggressive, and explicit where their predecessors were hesitant, defensive, and mealymouthed. They are combative and resolute where earlier Conservatives were diplomatic and conciliatory. Thatcherism, then, has proved a successful formula.

In the final chapter in this section, "The Resurgence of Conservatism in British Elections After 1974," Mark N. Franklin also considers the significance of the two Conservative electoral victories under Mrs. Thatcher's leadership and the role that issues played in bringing them about. Specifically, Franklin considers three hypotheses about party support and issues: first, that there has been a true resurgence of public support for traditional conservative issues; second, that the Conservatives have been the beneficiaries by default of growing public rejection of socialist issues and ideas; and third, that the conservatives have benefited from the emergence of a wholly new set of issues not traditionally associated with either party.

Of particular interest here is Franklin's careful distinction between issues that divided the "old" right and left (e.g., welfare, law and order, and race) and those that distinguish the "new" right (e.g., cutting taxes, privatizing industry and medicine, and supporting the Common Market). In addition to finding that new issues have emerged, Franklin also argues that the distinctiveness of the new dimension and its increasing importance between 1979 and 1983 lend support to the third interpretative possibility indicated above. Comparing Conservative electoral support between 1979 and 1983, he finds Conservative gains were much higher among voters of the new right and new left quadrants than the old left. Moreover, the Conservatives *lost* support from the old right, "abundant proof that Mrs. Thatcher's victory was not a victory of the right as conventionally conceived." Indeed, Franklin suggests that many of the voters who supported Mrs. Thatcher did so despite her conservatism rather than because of it. That is, British politics have a new dimension that Franklin tentatively characterizes as "particularist" or "postcollectivist." Whatever the label applied to it, it is not a traditional conservative dimension, although the party relied on it for its victories.

CANADA

English-speaking Canada historically has located itself somewhere between the political culture of Britain and the United States. From its beginnings Canada has been fundamentally Lockean, as has been the United States, but conservative rather than liberal. Canadian conservatives are in William Christian's words, "business liberals," indistinguishable from what Americans call "business conservatives." The original conservative heritage, born of the Loyalists' refusal to join the American Revolution, has contributed to both the moralizing independence of Canadian foreign policy (as William James Booth demonstrates) and the conceptual ambiguity of Canadian conservatism.

This conceptual ambiguity is currently reflected in the very name of the Conservative party (i.e., Progressive Conservative). It was selected by party leaders during the Second World War in the hope that it would broaden the appeal of the party enough to supplant the incumbent Liberals in the postwar period. Unfortunately for the party, the Liberals were notoriously difficult to supplant. Indeed, as Roger Gibbins notes in his chapter, "Conservatism in Canada: The Ideological Impact of the 1984 Election," the Liberal party held national office for all but seven of the fifty years preceding the 1984 election, winning eleven of fifteen general elections. Gibbins asks whether their overwhelming electoral victory in 1984 and similar victories by the British Conservative and American Republican parties will inspire Canadian Conservatives to move right both ideologically and in their public policies. In his view such a shift is unlikely. He acknowledges that the national agenda has shifted, but he contends that elements of this shift already were under way during the latter years of the Trudeau government.

More specifically, the proclamation of the Constitution Act of 1982 set in motion a fundamental transformation of the Canadian political agenda. Economic issues have moved to the top, whereas the older concerns of national unity have moved down, although by no means off, the national agenda. Of primary importance has been the emergent issue of free trade that serves, although perhaps only temporarily, as the centerpiece for the new Conservative national agenda. At the same time, however, the ideological temper of the national government and of Canadian public policy has not changed to any dramatic extent. In part this can be traced to the nonideological character and conciliatory style of the new Progressive Conservative prime minister, Brian Mulroney.

The essay goes on to argue that the most dramatic changes stemming from the 1984 election have occurred within the federal Conservative party rather than within the government of Canada. The adoption of free trade, the selection of a Quebec leader, the subsequent capture of Quebec, and the shift in the party's electoral center of gravity from the West to central Canada signify major changes in the Conservative party, changes that dwarf those in national public policy stemming from the 1984 election. Gibbins concludes that although 1984 was a landmark election, it did not signify a resurgence of conservatism in Canada. Progressive Conservatism, yes, but not conservatism as manifested in Margaret Thatcher's Britain or Ronald Reagan's United States.

In their chapter, "Canada's Tory Tide: Electoral Change and Partisan Instability in the 1980s," Allan Kornberg and Harold D. Clarke conduct an in-depth examination of whether 1984 really was a landmark election signaling a basic redistribution of partisan forces in the country. Their analyses of national panel survey data gathered in 1980, 1983, and 1984 indicate that the Conservatives profited significantly from widespread public dissatisfaction with the Liberal government's handling of the country's economic affairs and a diffuse but nonetheless real sentiment that it was "time for a change" after two decades of virtually uninterrupted Liberal rule. The latter party's difficulties were compounded by the lukewarm reception the public accorded the new Liberal leader, John Turner. Indeed, in the struggle for the "hearts and minds" of the Canadian voting public, both Mr. Mulroney and the Conservatives were easy winners over both Messrs. Turner and Broadbent and their respective parties, the Liberals and New Democrats.

Despite the high regard in which both Mulroney and the Conservative party were held, the congruence between voters' positions on important issues and the positions they ascribed to the party, and their negative judgments about the Liberal administration's handling of the economy, the 1984 Conservative victory does not appear to have resulted in a genuine partisan realignment. In fact, postelection survey evidence reveals that fourteen months after the election the Tory tide seems to have ebbed, with fully one-fifth of the electorate not identifying psychologically with any party.

Kornberg and Clarke conclude that despite the uncertainty engendered by such a large number of nonidentifiers and the sensitivity of the public's partisan attachments to short-term political forces, it appears that popular postelection predictions of the Liberals' imminent demise and of a new era of Tory dominance were both greatly exaggerated. The Canadian electorate, they argue, remains a volatile entity, with the fortunes of the Conservatives and other parties hostage to the often fast-flowing and unpredictable currents generated by short-term political forces.

UNITED STATES

Political philosophy and even the affairs of intellectuals can be located without too much difficulty in terms of liberal and conservative opinion. Conservative intellectuals traditionally have entertained doubts about the ability of the intellect to grasp society as a whole and remake it according to plan. In the United States this doubt has taken the form not of romantic Burkean reverence or religious revivalism but of libertarian calculations of small and personal things. The romantic and reverential conservative, a distinct type, preaches rather than teaches, and preachers are not intellectuals. Nevertheless, they do see in the destruction of the family the connection between libertarian individualism and dependency: when individuals are given rights against the family they are made deeply dependent upon the state. That is why the romantic conservative preachers appeal to pride and especially the pride to become an individual and so share that pride in one's own individuality as patriotism. Other obvious sources of conservative opinion in the United States are elected officials who approach their responsibilities with Burkean prudence and that tribe of recent converts called "neoconservatives."

When the focus shifts from elite or intellectual opinion to policy issues and the intentions and results of public action, it becomes more difficult to determine just what conservatism is. In their chapter, "The Economic Conservatism of the Reagan Administration: Notes for a Theory of Party Differences, Partisan Change, and Electoral Accountability," Henry W. Chappell, Jr., and William R. Keech address the question of the conservatism of the macroeconomic policies of the Reagan administration. Their discussion is cast in terms of more general questions about party differences, electoral change, and the accountability of public officials. They develop an explanation for short-term electoral change out of the ideas that parties differ in their goals, that voters retrospectively evaluate the performance of incumbents, and that economic constraints limit what policymakers can do. Parties differ in the ways in which they misjudge or violate the constraints, and therefore in the type of performance for which the electorate may find them wanting. Republicans are more likely to be rejected at the polls for a recession, whereas Democrats are more likely to be defeated after overstimulating the economy. Macroeconomic performance during the Reagan administration has been largely consistent with what might be expected from a Republican administration, with unemployment somewhat higher than in the Carter administration and inflation substantially lower.

Chappell and Keech argue that President Reagan was first elected as a result of public rejection of the Carter administration, not because the voters wished to endorse conservative views. Although Reagan may not have been elected because of his ideology, he did demonstrate —notwithstanding the Goldwater experience in 1964—that a distinctly conservative candidate can win the presidency. His reelection in 1984 owed much to the fact that stabilization policy had avoided short-term problems. In several respects the economic performance of the Reagan administration has been praiseworthy in the short term. However the massive deficits that have been incurred during its stewardship may have purchased current consumption at the expense of future well-being. Chappell and Keech conclude that even though the administration's stabilization policy may reflect the successful implementation of conservative goals, the deficits also reflect an orientation that is not at all conservative.

On a different topic, "Religion and the Resurgence of Conservatism," Michael Gillespie and Michael Lienesch come to a somewhat related conclusion. They argue that although conservative religious groups have been able to influence both the election of Republicans and the public policies they have pursued, American religion generally is at odds with traditional conservatism. They begin by arguing that religion has been a decisive factor in the resurgence of conservatism, but only in the United States. They attribute this not to the level of religious practice, which is similar in Canada, or to the intensity of religious belief, or disestablishment, but to a peculiar ideological affinity of American liberalism and religion.

Religion has given a peculiarly moralistic cast to American conservatism that is absent in both Britain and Canada. This moralism has been most evident in the concern that America's religious conservatives have shown for social reform, a concern manifested in debates over abortion, creationism and evolution, school prayer, sex education, pornography, and the like. In the United States, unlike in Canada or Great Britain, support for economic and foreign policies has often been solicited through appeals both to biblical imagery and to substantive biblical teachings. More recently, they point out, the pluralistic order advocated by Madison has been eroded by factors such as single-issue campaigns and direct-mail lobbying. This kind of focused political action has made bargaining and compromise more difficult to achieve because of the intensity religious sentiments invariably add to political issues.

The authors' historical examination of the relationship of the roles of Protestantism, Catholicism, and Judaism in American political life indicates that although religion has always played a moralistic role in U.S. politics, it has not always been on the side of conservatism. Indeed, the authors suggest that it is the millenialist strain of all three groups that has been responsible for religion's social activism in the United States, in large part because of the resonance between this millenialism and the implicit millenialist impulse in the prevailing American ideology of progress. They thus conclude that the present conservative cast of religion in American political life is only in part a response to secular humanism and is in fact more generally the result of the fortuitous conjunction of conservative ideological impulses idiosyncratic to the various religious groups themselves. Consequently, despite their initial limited success in forming coalitions to influence public policy, it seems unlikely that either those coalitions or their influence will endure for any extended time because, as just noted, the millenialist bases of both American religion and American ideology in general are fundamentally at odds with traditional conservatism.

In the final chapter in this volume, "The Reagan Years: Turning to the Right or Groping Toward the Middle," Morris Fiorina observes that despite Ronald Reagan's impressive electoral victories, the larger significance of the 1980 and 1984 elections remains ambiguous. Existing data provide no great support for the view that the American electorate has shifted to the right, nor do the data show conclusively that an electoral realignment has occurred—whether based on ideology, leadership, or other factors. In particular, the continuing strength of the Democratic party in elections to the House of Representatives and to state offices confounds simple arguments about electoral realignment and conservative resurgence. This interpretation has been given additional force by the results of the 1986 midterm elections. Fiorina argues that national elections in the 1980s can be understood on the basis of familiar arguments about retrospective voting and incumbency, augmented with a notion of sophisticated ticket-splitting. The latter rests on the premise that much of the electorate is not fully comfortable with the positions and goals of either party. This generates a rational preference for divided government on the part of some voters. A simple model of sophisticated ticket-splitting is developed, and preliminary tests suggest that it contributes to our understanding of the outcome of the 1984 election.

RETROSPECT

In the Anglo-American democracies political life is animated by the interactions among individuals and groups within and outside major political institutions, interactions that generally reflect differences that are less fundamental than the division between liberalism or socialism and conservatism. Indeed, it has occasionally been a source of regret by those who would like to reform institutions such as political parties that there is a lack of congruence between what most parties do and what might loosely be termed their putative ideologies.

It is hard to assign precise weight to such criticisms because in democracies such as Britain, Canada, and the United States conservatism and liberalism or socialism are movements of opinion that cohere not as logically integrated doctrines but as pragmatic equilibria. They work, more or less well, as guides for public policies despite the internal intellectual tension that seems to be inevitable when the reflective capacities of human beings abstract the world in order to see it as it is.

Some of these tensions were manifested at the conference among participants and are reflected in their papers. There was, for example, continuing discussion and frequent disagreement among conference participants concerning the degree to which the quantitative studies that were presented substantiated the conservative resurgence. Generally speaking, papers prepared by political theorists were more clear about what the recent changes meant, and they were more convinced that those changes in fact constituted a conservative resurgence. The policy analysts argued that changes in policy were more or less in the expected direction. In contrast, the studies of mass opinion, and especially of *changes* in mass opinion, were much more ambiguous. Such was the gravamen of the futile hunt for the snark by Mishler, Hoskin, and Fitzgerald, but a similar skepticism marks some of the other papers, notably those by Crewe and Searing, Gibbins, and Chappell and Keech.

There appear to be two reasons for this. First, mass opinion—as students of the phenomenon are aware—may be loud on occasion, but frequently it is indistinct. It changes at variable rates and often is riddled with inconsistency. Public policy, in contrast, at least must aim at consistency, or else it is unlikely to work. And since ideology seeks to persuade its audience on the basis of its reasonableness, it will appear the most coherent of all. By way of illustration we may note that several of the papers and a number of conference participants argued that the resurgence of conservatism is a consequence in various degrees of the failure of the welfare state: what was supposed to make us free has made us less free or has made us dependent. This has been articulated most emphatically by political practitioners such as David Stockman and Keith Joseph who formulated coherent analyses of the problem. In office they tried, with mixed success, to put into practice policies that were consistent with their insights. However, as Chappell and Keech observed, liberals and conservatives make *characteristic* mistakes, which means, not simple mistakes. For their part, voters may have recognized that something was wrong with the welfare state and turned to those who criticized it. It was unnecessary for them to reject the welfare state utterly and completely as did Stockman and Joseph. But it is significant that they were sufficiently persuaded by *something* to vote for people who were *not* promising further liberal experiments.

There is a second reason for some of the different conclusions reached in these papers. The theorists consider conservatism as an opinion. Opinions are not simply mistakes or errors; they can be more or less reasonable, refined, or elevated. Indeed, the characteristic approach (or "mistake," in the parlance of Chappell and Keech) of the theorists is to refine and elevate opinions into something called conservatism, which then may be studied on its own by looking at the texts of men such as Edmund Burke or Adam Smith. Their goal is to help us better understand what is *meant* by voting conservative. This understanding includes a judgment as to whether voters did well or were reasonable in voting conservative.

For their part, conference participants taking an empirical approach to the question were unimpressed by this perspective. One cannot account, they argued, for the conservative resurgence (if, indeed, there was or is one) by disputing whether it was reasonable. You do not begin the study of political change with an analysis of opinion but at what is prior to opinion, which may be termed attitude or interest or something else. As James Alt said, in interpreting his own data: "people are as generous as they can afford to be." Alt's is a statement of interest, not an analysis of whether the attitude or interest is reasonable.

What we have, therefore, is a contrast in approach. The political theorists refine opinions or inflate them into philosophies and ideologies, whereas the quantitative analysts reduce opinions to attitudes and interests. As one of the participants, a political philosopher, observed, "although the characteristic mistake of theorists may be to turn voters into philosophers, that of quantifiers may be to make them into robots."

One reason why both accounts have a degree of plausibility and amount to limited understandings of the phenomena is "overidentification"; there are many variables to consider but only three cases with which to work. In short, the problem may be that you either explain what conservatism is or how it came to be, but not both. Or, perhaps, not both at the same time. Yet one must try to do both at the same time: one must try to know what conservatism is before undertaking quantitative/empirical accounts of how it came to be. And no account of what it is will avoid utopian dreaming if it ignores how it came to be. That some of the chapters in this volume came to differing conclusions and provide differing understandings is, as we suggested above, not surprising. Taken together, however, they provide a much-needed and illuminating account of what recent changes in the Anglo-American democracies mean and how they came to be.

2. Structural Factors in the Conservative Resurgence

JOEL SMITH, ALLAN KORNBERG, AND NEIL NEVITTE

Pat's communication skills and his commitment to conservative political beliefs have been an important part of my administration for the last two years. I will miss his leadership and support but I count on his voice to remain a beacon for our political agenda.—Ronald Reagan on the resignation of his communications director, Patrick Buchanan, February 3, 1987

INTRODUCTION

The electoral triumphs of the Progressive Conservatives in Canada in 1979 and 1984, the Conservatives in Britain in 1979 and 1983, and the Republicans in the United States in 1980 and 1984 can be seen as part of a trend that has touched many Western industrialized democracies. The electoral cutting edge of that trend has been the widespread replacement of relatively "liberal" incumbents by candidates espousing positions considerably more "to the right." We shall argue, however, that the electoral results that have produced these changes may well reflect a loss of support for liberal parties and candidates rather than a growth of conservative support. Nonetheless, the fact that these electoral "triumphs of the right" have been both temporally coincidental and sustained has enabled the victorious candidates and other leaders of their parties and associated movements to promote agendas that imply the occurrence of a fundamental reorientation of public priorities. And it is easy to cite evidence for such a claim by contrasting the increasingly interventionist government policies of the last fifty years with the asserted intentions of conservative governments since the late

1970s. There is no question that since the time of the Great Depression newly elected parties of the left or liberalizing incumbent parties embarked on sustained efforts to improve the lot of the working and middle classes by developing a network of agencies and pursuing increasingly comprehensive programs that together came to be called the welfare state. It is significant that until the 1970s both "liberal" and "conservative" governments in each country had presided over the state's expansion.

Perhaps the most widely accepted explanation of this long-term trend in many Western democracies is that it was a product of the party system, for it was during this period that political parties, "mass" and "cadre" alike, matured and became competitive. Competition encourages brokerage politics, and under brokerage politics, especially in the types of two-party systems typical of Anglo-American democracies, parties simultaneously tend to expand their ideological reach and to search for the policy middle ground. Under these conditions competing parties of whatever label tend to produce similar policies,[1] and scholars who study elections tend to generate analytical models that emphasize "politics as usual."

If, however, the recent electoral results in the three Anglo-American democracies indicate a significant loss of support for the strategy of social amelioration and even a willingness on the part of some leading politicians to consider dismantling many of the structures that have been put in place since the Great Depression, then the problem becomes one of explaining potential discontinuity rather than continuity in partisan policies and programs. In this chapter we consider the merits of three types of explanations for such discontinuity—historical, electoral, and structural—and argue that the structural explanation is the most promising. More specifically, we will take some aspects of the thesis that the welfare state is intrinsically unstable and in incipient decline as a point of departure, and we will employ several types of data to examine one variant of this thesis.

THREE APPROACHES

The resurgence of conservatism, as manifested in a new willingness of major political parties and their leaders to include attacks on welfare state policies and their attendant programs in their platforms, has been signaled by election outcomes that have shifted in a conservative direction. Therefore, it would seem reasonable to turn to election studies for an explanation of the political transformation. That literature has several prima facie advantages. Most election studies have been conducted in Organization for Economic Cooperation and Development (OECD) countries; the data from them are relatively reliable and at times are amenable to cross-national comparisons. The relative socioeconomic homogeneity of those electoral democracies has prompted scholars with different country interests to ask similar sorts of questions about their electoral politics. As a result, it is not surprising to find that the concepts, theories, and analyses that shape our understanding of elections and electoral behavior are generally quite similar regardless of the country or election studied (e.g., Belknap and Campbell, 1952; Campbell, Converse, Miller, and Stokes, 1960; Butler and Stokes, 1976; Aitken, 1977; Clarke, Jenson, Leduc, and Pammett, 1979; Niemi and Weisberg, 1976; Barnes and Kaase, 1979; and Dalton, Flanagan, and Beck, 1984). The theoretically sophisticated literature ranges broadly across observable abstract and transcendent collective and individual aspects of electoral politics. It includes such concerns as left-right orientations; orientations to parties, leaders, and issues; and citizen participation, interest, and efficacy; and it considers specific expressions of these phenomena that vary with time and space. Analytical styles run the gamut from popular journalism to the most elegant formal social science, while the modes of analysis range from speculation, to investigative reporting, to surveys, to experimentation, modeling, and simulation. All have been employed in the effort to understand individual voting behavior and the transformations in political forms and meanings that may be found in democratic polities. In this sense it is a literature that is well developed, but it tends to be oriented to the explanation of "normal" election outcomes.

We have characterized the fifty-year period that witnessed the development of the welfare state as one of continuity, notwithstanding the fact that at various times in each of the three countries nominally liberal and conservative parties have alternated in office. This is because it has been a period marked by few concerted attempts to activate such radically conservative programs as extensive privatization, significant deregulation, or the withdrawal of various forms of government financial support from large sectors of the population. To the extent that there have been any efforts to deviate from this policy direction they have been marginal and short-lived. In brief, the period was archetypically one of "normal" politics. The implications of the literature on election and voting behavior, therefore, is that elections will continue to be won by candidates who do not threaten the tradition of government intervention or the termination or serious weakening of essential constituent elements of the welfare state. Such an inference is consistent with dominant modes of thought concerning electoral politics and their outcomes, for the explanation of even qualitative changes in electoral support as, for example, the role of critical elections in "realigning" the distribution of partisan forces in an electorate is structured in evolutionary rather than revolutionary terms.

Given this orientation, even increasingly sophisticated theories of electoral behavior are not really well equipped to provide systematic explanations of the simultaneous resurgence of conservatism cross-nationally for at least two reasons. The first has to do with the *extent* of the change in the electoral orientations of each country's citizens. Electoral outcomes generally are explained by some combination of two factors. Either voters change their minds about their usual electoral choices, i.e., conversion occurs, or, alternatively, there may be a shift in the composition and character of the electorate, i.e., replacement. In the latter case, if the same voters do not change, then some must stop voting, or die, or new voters or nonvoters with specific clusters of attributes must enter the electorate in numbers sufficient to change previously "normal" election outcomes (Nie, Verba, and Petrocik, 1976:74–95). There is no indication of such dramatic replacement processes occurring in the electorates, so the resurgence of conservatism as we understand it to be manifested in these countries must reflect substantial individual changes in electoral behavior.

If the resurgence of conservatism is largely a product of conversion, then theories of voter behavior are not entirely appropriate for explaining these recent electoral trends, for they tend to share a common weakness even though they tend to be of two different types. Many of the older versions of such theories tend to be static in the sense that they predict for different elections from such relatively unchanging attributes of individuals as gender, race, educational level, and occupation (Berelson et al., 1954; Campbell et al., 1954, 1960); many of the newer versions tend to be psychologistic, e.g., rational choice theories (Fiorina, 1981; Kiewiet, 1983). To compensate for their weakness in explaining major changes (without making it explicit and regardless of their form) some argue that external structural conditions, perceived or not, shape the manner in which personal attributes will have an impact on behavior, but they treat these external factors as exogenous. Others do not even recognize the role of external factors. This is our point of departure, for we shall argue that without giving at least equal attention to these structural conditions neither replacement nor conversion models of electoral behavior can provide a satisfactory account for the kind of changes that have occurred in the three countries.

The second reason theories of electoral behavior are not well equipped to explain the conservative resurgence is that the shifts to the right occurred at approximately the same time not only in all three countries but also in several other Western countries (e.g., Germany, Sweden, Norway). This implies that the three cases in question are not and should not be treated largely as idiosyncratic events accountable only in terms of unique local circumstances.[2] The occurrence of this many idiosyncratic cases within such a brief period is improbable, particularly since Western European communist parties were also losing support at the same time, and even parties of the left that did win elections were tempering their traditional programs and actions (e.g., in France). Moreover, conventional models of comparative voting behavior contain no theoretical bridge directly linking shifts in individual voting behavior in one country to comparable shifts in another (for example, through contagion by some "learning" or "demonstration" or "imitation" process). In the absence of a compelling account for either the temporal coincidence of similar electoral changes across different countries or the extent of individual changes in electoral preferences within these countries, some more general explanation is required.

Another frequently employed type of explanation is historical. It is tempting to account for occurrences by reaching back to rediscover the logic behind the events and actions that precipitated them. For example, some scholars trace the origins of the welfare state to the Great Depression and/or the carnage of World War I and the subsequent social unrest they spawned (Dyson, 1980; Flora and Heidenheimer, 1981; Guest, 1985). Others, working at a higher level of abstraction, see it as an inevitable consequence of the economic transformations of the eighteenth and nineteenth centuries (Rimlinger, 1974; Titmus, 1958), transformations that induced conditions of extreme individualization and stress that intellectuals of the 1920s and 1930s captured in the concept of mass society (Kornhauser, 1959).

As explanations, both of these accounts may be aesthetically satisfying and psychologically persuasive. Yet it is in the nature of historical analysis that the differences between two such positions cannot be resolved definitively. The putative precipitating events occurred in a particular sequence, and, having happened, there is no way to reconstruct them experimentally. We cannot know, for instance, whether the leftward shift and the welfare state would have occurred had either or both World War I and the Great Depression not occurred, or instead, whether, perhaps, it was the "lessons" of the Russian Revolution that persuaded Western leaders to try to redress, in part, long-standing power and resource imbalances between capital and labor. The tests of these arguments involve counterfactuals. Moreover, historical explanations are seriously limited to the extent that they neither identify the general conditions that would lead to those or similar occurrences nor the conditions that would have very different outcomes. These limitations of historical explanation would apply to any effort to account for the convergence of recent conservative political triumphs by a similar strategy.

An alternative explanation, in this case a structural one, must overcome these weaknesses of conventional electoral historical explanations. It would be a simple matter to appropriate a fully developed structural explanation of the political dynamics and interrelationships of the welfare state if one were available. Ideally such a theory should provide a compelling interpretation of *how* the shifting distribution of power between contending groups is related to changes in the character of the welfare state by addressing such central questions as: Which groups gear the pace and direction of change under different circumstances? How? With what consequences? A comprehensive theory also should enable one to specify the extent to which change is constrained or encouraged by the international environment as well as to identify the nature of state involvement in these processes. But in the absence of a robust and comprehensive structural explanation we take some elements of Claus Offe's partially developed theory as a point of departure because they satisfy three minimal requirements. First, they

contain the kernel of a plausible explanation of how changes in the
social and economic contexts of politics are sufficient to override the
customary impact of the sorts of short- and long-term factors employed
in most conventional models of individual voting behavior.[3] Second,
unlike historical explanations of change, it is possible to specify the
central tenets of Offe's explanation in a form that makes the theory
susceptible to empirical testing—although our work is not such a test
and only illustrates its plausibility. Third, the empirical specification
of the theory is sufficiently general that it can be applied cross-
nationally to all three countries in question. As we shall indicate,
however, what remains problematic is the identification of the conditions that stimulate challenges to the integrity of the welfare state.

For many observers the Western economic recession of the 1970s
was the triggering event. Although that recession may well have been
"the" cause because it destabilized arrangements that were ready to be
destabilized, as an explanation it suffers the same weaknesses as do
historical explanations of the rise of the welfare state.[4] From a structural perspective, however, the economic shock of the recession can be
understood as representing a class of factors capable of placing stress
on an increasingly tenuous set of complex arrangements. Offe (1984)
has argued that the welfare state *is* such a tenuous set of complex
arrangements. But viewed in this light an explanation of the conjunction of recent conservative election victories coupled to a redirected
domestic political agenda requires the identification not just of a triggering cause but also of a set of conditions that, when such a triggering
event occurs, are likely to produce major changes in the policy direction and goals of political leadership and control.

OFFE'S MODEL

Offe argues that although the welfare state can satisfy both the left and
the right in the short run, it can satisfy neither in the long run. In the
short run the welfare state provides amelioration and surcease for the
working class and a sense of release from domination by the capitalist
class; for the latter it reduces the threat of the losses that would accompany a real social revolution. In the long run, however, members of the
capitalist class withdraw support as they come to realize that a substantial share of the resources being taken from them is being used for

the bureaucracy itself. Moreover, what little capital is redistributed does not just ameliorate the immediate stress experienced by workers but also increases workers' ability to control their participation in the process of production (Offe, 1984). To the extent that the welfare state has an impact on the workplace it displaces risk and restructures capital-labor market relations in significant ways. For example, it facilitates workers' ability to strike by providing unemployment insurance, and it enables workers to withhold cheap labor by providing welfare payments as alternative income. Members of the working class also become aware of how much capital is appropriated for administration rather than redistributed. Moreover, they become increasingly sensitive to the fact that to secure the benefits of the welfare state their behavior must conform to ruling-class norms. Accordingly, they too become disillusioned and withdraw support from incumbents who propagate and implement the instrumentalities of the welfare state.

Following from this argument, if the dominant feature of the past twenty years has been the actual or impending failure of the welfare state, and if the propagation and promotion of the welfare state are associated with incumbent "liberals" and their parties, one could expect a serious decline in support for them, albeit for different reasons in different classes. Any prediction as to where support might move will be shaped by the theoretical stance adopted. A Marxist interpretation, for example, might foresee polarization—a shift to the left on the part of members of the working class and a shift to the right on the part of the bourgeoisie. In the absence of a revolution, however, in an electoral contest that offers no viable alternatives on the left, one might expect a sharp decline in electoral participation by members of the working class accompanied by continued high participation by the bourgeoisie. If the numbers are at the proper levels, the result would be a conservative shift. This scenario would be consistent with the observed electoral outcomes, the positions on welfare programs being espoused by politicians, and the continued support for specific welfare programs by the public.

This scenario has at least two weaknesses. It leaves unexplained the failure of revolutionary ferment to develop, and it requires voting shifts to be balanced in precisely the quantities necessary to account for the observed outcomes. Because both the strength of support for incumbent liberal parties and the distribution of voters between the working classes and the bourgeoisie have been quite different in the countries in which conservative politicians have taken power, the similarity in election outcomes (i.e., strong conservative votes) weakens the force of this argument. Moreover, even if by chance the different necessary numerical shifts had occurred in each country, it would not explain the rather passive acquiescence of workers in all these countries to conservative proposals for privatization, deregulation, and even wage reductions and the loss of job security.

The ascendancy of conservatives and their programs, therefore, seems to argue for a simpler explanation—perhaps one along the following lines. Given that in major Western democracies the electoral systems as such have not been called into serious question, support for the parties identified with welfare state programs and policies has eroded for reasons of the sort proposed by Offe. The erosion is the product of a combination of three different types of change. Some voters, out of disappointment or resentment, have curtailed their participation in the activities of electoral politics; some, for similar reasons, have chosen to vote for the only other real option in a two-party system without necessarily being positively supportive of the positions of that party; and, in the absence of viable alternatives on the left, some members of all classes either have moved toward, further to, or remained on the right by actively embracing the positions of its proponents. Seen from this perspective, the recent electoral triumphs of conservatives need not necessarily imply a substantial increase in the public's acceptance and support of conservative philosophies, parties, and candidates. Rather, they could have been the product, to a large extent, of a combination of increased nonvoting and voting to express rejection of the longtime traditional party option. If so, the conservative resurgence more appropriately might be considered the result of extensive citizen disaffection with the incumbent establishment that voters identify with the failures but not the ideals and purposes of the welfare state than of massive conversions to conservative ideals and goals. Such a view would make more reasonable the tendency in each of the countries for citizens to express support of conservative candidates without supporting all their particular proposals and policies. To take one obvious example, it could explain what journalists have come to call Reagan's "teflon presidency." The fact that unpopular proposals and scandals in his administration fail to diminish support for him is more comprehensible if he is the recipient of the benefits of disillusionment with the administration of welfare and other programs by previous incumbents from the opposition party.

This explanation finesses the questions of why workers should *continue* to support their electoral systems—indeed, their regimes —and, relatedly, under what conditions they might withdraw support and seek to replace them (Dalton, Flanagan, and Beck, 1984). Although in the long run those probably are the central questions, in the short run our focus will be on the general conditions that, for various reasons, may trigger public acceptance of arguments to the effect that welfare state policies and programs cost too much, are not working, cannot be relied upon, are unfair and unjust, and, at a minimum, that options like the free market have to be given a new chance. Following this line of argument, the central question becomes: What sorts of systemic changes would have to be widely perceived and interpreted as sufficiently threatening to generate public support for politicians who propose substantial changes in a welfare state system that had been developing for more than forty years? This is the question to be addressed in the remainder of this chapter.

SPECIFYING THE ARGUMENT

The above discussion should clarify the sense in which we understand the idea of a resurgence of conservatism. A clear statement of that understanding is desirable because the phenomenon to which the concept refers can have very different manifestations (e.g., shifts in public opinion, changes in governmental policies, electoral victories for challengers to incumbents, alterations in individuals' party identifications). It also is useful to specify one's referent because scholars often differ in the manifestations of the resurgence they have in mind when they use the phrase. They may find themselves in apparent disagreement because they have not been explicit about what it is they are referring to and, also, because judgments as to the directionality, meaning, and significance of a change reflect the individual's political position. One thing that we do not mean is that there has been a demonstrable fundamental shift in public attitudes and party alignments that has brought earlier political forces back into power and earlier political programs back into currency. We have not tried to demonstrate that they have returned, nor are we convinced that it could be demonstrated. If nothing else, the concept of conservatism and its specific implications have changed considerably during the period in which we are interested.[5]

Our position is that there has been a distinct change in the terms of the public political (not scholarly or philosophical) debate over the welfare state and that that change has been associated with a new electoral competitiveness on the part of conservative politicians. For approximately a forty-year period (i.e., from the mid-1930s to the mid-1970s) politicians might have questioned such things as the level of a minimum wage or the age at which children might work or the level of unemployment benefits or all the specifics of a social security program. They might even, though less frequently, question whether there ought to be a particular program. But with few and limited exceptions they did not suggest that large numbers of programs and regulatory agencies charged with protecting the public's interests ought not to exist. Even more fundamentally, no serious politician seeking broad support from a relatively large electorate would argue publicly that the state, nationally or locally, should not be addressing issues of welfare. (Recall the firestorm of criticism that followed Senator Goldwater's suggestion during the 1964 presidential campaign that the Social Security system might be privatized.) Recently, however, conservative politicians with realistic expectations of widespread public support have been willing to espouse openly and with vigor positions that call for termination of a spectrum of long-established programs associated with the welfare state, and even to appeal to such hoary sentiments as "let's get the government off our backs" or "that government governs best that governs least." In sum, our sense of events is that since that period there has been increasing questioning and debating of these commitments in terms embedded in philosophic and social as well as economic critiques of public welfare and the state's role in providing it.

The convergence of these several recent electoral results not only signifies the reality of these trends but also has increased the political power of individuals and groups committed and willing to try to implement many of the more radical implications of their critiques. As a consequence, there has been an increase in explicit public statements of and proposals for conservative and antiwelfare changes in state policy, even though it has not always been possible to implement those policies in specific actions. In summary, then, the converging resurgence of conservatism that we accept as having occurred in the three countries and as being necessary to explain is constituted, among other things, in: (a) mounting criticism of both the very concept of the welfare state and its particular manifestations; (b) the withdrawal of commitments to enlarge or even to sustain its recent scope; (c) the ability of parties and candidates committed to decreasing support for and even terminating welfare programs and policies to win public office and control governmental institutions; and (d) the willingness of these new governments to promote ancillary programs and policies related to other values that have been invoked to motivate the attack on the forms and functions of the welfare state and its proponents. *In short, the terms of and participants in public political debate have changed drastically since the mid-1970s. Although we grant that the three countries differ in the degree to which such a conservative resurgence has occurred, we believe that each shares these general attributes sufficiently to suggest a convergence in a conservative resurgence.*

Having specified the sense in which we mean that there has been a resurgence of conservatism, it also is useful to summarize and clarify three other core assumptions. First, we have defined the problem as particular to Western-style political systems in a period that roughly spans events since World War I. Second, we consider the present resurgence of conservatism the first instance since the Great Depression of relatively sustained political success for conservative groups espousing positions that directly attack policies and programs that have had majority support during most of that period. Finally, our allusion to the present political trend as in part a response to the OPEC-induced recession of the 1970s indicates that we view the three countries as components of an inclusive world system.

We have argued that the period since the Great Depression has been shaped and dominated by the rise of the welfare state. The maintenance as distinct from the development of welfare state programs and the organizations that implement them requires the accumulation of economic resources that can be put at the disposal of the state. Although this can be accomplished by drastic appropriation tactics (e.g., extremely high taxes, requisition of private properties and other resources), except for periods in which general socioeconomic conditions are severely disrupted such draconian state actions in liberal democracies are unlikely to be widely tolerated for any substantial length of time. Therefore, in the longer term the maintenance of a welfare state requires a healthy economy—one that is growing, shows strong signs of growing, or, at least, does not seem to be in imminent danger of long-term serious decline.

Given its ties to the economy, the question of when the welfare state is likeliest to lose its broad base of support would appear to have two answers. One would be in long periods of economic boom during which, for various reasons, many members of the populace can lose sight of the circumstances that created the need for the welfare state and can develop a (perhaps false and misplaced) sense of confidence in their own ability to look after their needs (Dryzek and Goodin, 1986). We shall not dwell on this, however, because the 1970s were not a period of long economic boom in these countries. The second answer would be during periods of economic bust—depressions and severe recessions. In such periods the tax base collapses, government income contracts severely, and the funds necessary to pay for welfare state programs are severely diminished. Although this is a plausible answer, we shall argue that the continuation of welfare state programs may be threatened as much, or more, by the *prospects of* as by an *actual* long-term economic decline.

The negative impact of the prospects of a weak economy on the welfare state is a seeming paradox, given its historical roots in a major economic dislocation. The paradox, however, is only apparent because it is the anticipation rather than the actuality of a major economic disaster that is most likely to spur the motivation to end the diversion of resources needed to fund the welfare state. One of the ironies of the situation is that Western countries responded to the experience of the Great Depression not only by elaborating the welfare network but also by authorizing systematic government intervention to monitor the economy and to avoid and insure against the catastrophes that can occur when it is uncontrolled. For these reasons attacks on the welfare system probably are less likely during severe downturns[6] (for that is when the system is needed) than they are when there are threats of such downturns.

Our reasons for this assertion have to do with the mechanisms through which the welfare state is implemented. Although each country's system varies from the others' in specifics, in each case almost every adult is involved continuously in contributing to its funding, even though at any given time only a minority of people are direct recipients of program benefits. Indeed, from the perspective of the individual there are long periods during which one's only relation to the welfare state is as a financial contributor. In a very real sense, then, such a system clearly must be premised on the assumption of, and depend upon, people's generosity and goodwill. Such altruism is much more likely to be manifested when times are good, and to be suspended when the basic wherewithal that enables one to contribute appears to be on the verge of being lost.

A wide variety of trends and events, many of them visible in the 1970s, signify the sort of weakening economy and prospective fiscal drains that could lead to a suspension of generosity and goodwill on the part of the majority and a willingness at least to consider the withdrawal of support for the structures and processes of the welfare state.

(1) *A growth of foreign competition for markets.* This threatens the income of corporations and other economic actors who pay the wages of important segments of the national labor force and share the costs of many major welfare programs.

(2) *The acquisition of domestic corporations and properties by foreign investors.* During economic boom periods foreign investors seek opportunities in advanced capitalist economies because in a troubled world they seem reasonably safe. However, an influx of foreign owners can create fears of situations that are new to advanced capitalist economies, for example, a flight of capital, a movement of assets out of the country with an attendant loss of jobs, and management decisions by foreign owners that will violate long-established local standards and cause a deterioration in working conditions and income (Vernon, 1977).

(3) *The withdrawal of support for the national community by members of both upper and lower economic strata.* For the former this might take the form of capital flight, often through the mechanism of participation in transnational corporations. The consequences can be manifested in a variety of ways, including a loss of interest

in national politics and a consequent withdrawal of monetary support for and personal interest in national political actors, as well as the withdrawal of capital investments that are no longer available to be treated as taxable property that can help in meeting governmental fiscal commitments. Presumably this could happen if dissatisfaction with the costs and consequences of the welfare state (discussed above) combine with shifting "comparative advantages" and the appearance of more attractive opportunities outside the country. Coupled with assertions of a loss of support for the welfare state, such withdrawal of support could generate strong pressures to stop or even reverse long-standing state practices. With respect to lower classes, workers also may withdraw support when they suffer losses of their relative shares of jobs and their related income, when inflationary trends devalue their incomes and property, and when the established welfare system seems incapable of redressing these and other grievances.

(4) *The emergence of demand overloads on the welfare system.* Demographic and social changes may require cash payments from specific programs that are greater than was anticipated when they were established. This has been the experience of the American Social Security system, the planning for which never anticipated increases in longevity of the magnitude actually experienced. Similarly, the planning for the program for aid to dependent children also did not anticipate the subsequent explosive growth in single-parent families. In such cases the related burdens of claim processing and oversight required substantial expansions in agency size and associated unplanned for administrative costs. In addition to these sources of unexpected demand, there has been an increase in state responsibilities to the public (e.g., educational loans, regulation of numerous activities that could have a harmful impact on the public) with costs that can outstrip the revenues available to pay for them (Heclo, 1981).

(5) *Strained relationships with foreign powers.* Since World War II the major world powers have coexisted in a state of continuous international tension. As a consequence, there are periodic demands for major investments in armaments and defense. The funding of such programs may require increasing taxes and/or diverting funds from welfare state programs.

(6) *Shifts in political participation.* In virtually every Western electoral democracy participation is a right but not an obligation. Even
though participation may be urged, significant numbers of citizens
do not participate. Although the numbers vary from country to
country, nonparticipants usually come disproportionately from the
working class. When electoral nonparticipation increases, therefore, those who benefit most from the welfare state tend to constitute declining proportions of the voting population, while those
who contribute more to meeting the costs but do not feel they
receive commensurate benefits constitute a growing proportion.
The latter become increasingly willing to turn to radically conservative options to remove or at least to lessen what they consider to
be an unfair financial burden.

DATA AND ANALYSIS

We do not claim that the above events and conditions amount to an
exhaustive list of factors that might produce a withdrawal of support
for parties and leaders associated in the public mind with the welfare
state. But they do constitute a diverse and empirically manageable
array of factors of the sort suggested by Offe's analysis. The expectation is that if these factors are found to covary in a consistent direction,
they could be roughly indicative of the kind of structural transformation sufficient to induce a climate within which—when a triggering
event such as the energy-induced economic crisis of the early 1970s
occurs—conservative forces could be expected to triumph. An empirical exploration of the kind of argument that flows from Offe's analysis
requires the development of indicators of these structural conditions
and the application of those indicators to trend data. Before proceeding, however, it is necessary to inject a cautionary note by addressing
three matters that complicate such an analysis—issues of timing, cross-
national comparisons, and data sources.

(a) *Timing.* Essential to Offe's notion of causality is the condition
that the structural changes precede the elections that produce conservative victories. What is problematic is that no indication is given of
the "proper" timing—of the amount of time that may elapse between
the structural changes and the electoral outcomes. Presumably, there
must be sufficient time for the changed structural conditions to be

perceived, understood, and eventually translated into locally mean-ingful political arguments. Cross-national variations in the electoral rules of the game complicate matters further. In the United States two years must elapse between congressional elections and four years between presidential elections, whereas in parliamentary systems the timing of elections is to a great degree the decision of incumbent governments. Given such factors we can only guess that the total "lag" from all sources might range from one to five years.

(b) *Cross-national comparisons.* The second complication is inher-ent in most cross-national comparative analyses, and it revolves around the question of the extent to which the three Anglo-American democ-racies can be compared. There are substantial national differences in the timing and trajectories of their developmental circumstances. The countries are differentially endowed economically, geographically, and demographically. The complex mix of man-made and natural environ-ments has resulted in their possessing different advantages and capac-ities. To this is added the fact that each country's experience of the catastrophes that precipitated spurts in the development of the wel-fare state was different. And those differences account for differential levels of commitment to the welfare state (Dryzek and Goodin, 1986). (Offe distinguishes, for these reasons, between "mature" and "less committed" welfare states.) Added to this is the fact that we cannot assume that each case is discrete and will vary independently along all relevant criteria. Trade decisions in the United States, for example, affect Canada's economic performance. Similarly U.S. defense policy affects Western Europe and Great Britain.

To recognize these problems is prudent; to regard them as fatal would end most cross-national research efforts. By relying on time series data and by focusing on rates of change we are able to minimize many of the effects of the most serious problems. However, even time series data can mask true rates of change because the statistical pro-cess of standardizing a given indicator (normed at 100) picks a partic-ular year as an equally satisfactory common baseline for a large set of countries, even though conditions in some particular members of the set being singled out for comparisons may have varied significantly during that year.

(c) *Data.* The final reason for caution relates to the nature of the time series data. They derive originally from each country. As is well known, governments have been known to vary in their views as to what is appropriate in the way such data are collected and reported. In all instances the data provided were then assembled and organized by such international agencies as OECD, Interpol, WHO, and UNESCO. Not surprisingly, the type of data they assemble and the way they summarize and present them reflect the particular interests of each agency, so we do not have enough relevant information to fully address the problem at hand. Despite these limitations we were able to draw on more than one hundred time series that included data on the economy, political participation, social problems, demographic structure, quality of life, and similar relevant facets of the collective experience of each country. Nonetheless, because of the aforementioned underlying measurement problems, rather than trying to subject Offe's theoretical formulation to a rigorous test, we instead will assess the data impressionistically to see whether they are consistent with a pattern of structural transformation of the sort we have inferred from his analysis. (All relevant data are available to interested readers upon request to the authors.)

To begin with, the material on voting in national elections since the 1950s is consonant with the premise that electoral participation has declined. In Canada 80.6 percent of the eligible electorate voted in the election of 1958. By 1980, after a pattern of irregular declines, the proportion had dropped to 69.3 percent. In the United Kingdom 83.6 percent of the electorate cast valid votes in the election of 1950. When Mrs. Thatcher won office in 1979 the comparable proportion was 76.0 percent, having increased from 72.8 percent in the previous general election. The rate of voting in the 1983 election was even lower. Again, although the long-term decline obviously has been irregular, in none of the ten elections subsequent to 1950 was the participation rate ever as high. In the United States the trend has been similar, being 63.7 percent in 1952, 61.6 percent in 1956, 65.4 percent in 1960, and declining through the next five elections to a low of 55.1 percent in 1980. There are no data on whether those losses were concentrated in the working class as our argument would have it. However, an analysis of support for a mildly socialist party, the New Democratic party, in one Canadian election demonstrates that where its candidates were likely to be perceived as having little chance of winning, working-class nonvoting was higher (Zipp and Smith, 1982).

Although our examination of the other data series yielded nothing conclusive, several trends consistent with our arguments were observed. Perhaps the most impressive data were those summarizing trends in gross domestic product and industrial production during the decade of the seventies. In each of the three countries the first half of the decade began with sluggish economic conditions. These gradually improved, but then collapsed in 1975. The second half of the decade —the years immediately prior to the conservative resurgence—was again marked by gradual rather than sharp improvements. By 1979 the upward thrust had waned, and by the beginning of 1980 a downward slide had resumed. The repetition of an unpromising economic trend is quite consistent with our suggestions that support for parties identified with the welfare state would decline during periods of some growth, when there also would be reasons to anticipate severe economic problems.

It also should be noted that records for the twenty-one-year period from 1963 to 1983 show that in Great Britain, Canada, and the United States, government final consumption expenditures (i.e., current purchases of goods and services for public administration, defense, health, and education, excluding all transfer payments) constituted a very high proportion of the gross domestic product (GDP). Only in 1973, at the beginning of the second decade of that period, did West Germany reach as high a level. Except for the Scandinavian countries, which long have been wedded to a pattern of high taxes and high government expenditures, these are the only consistently high ratios. The data indicate that there has been a long-term opportunity for the citizens of the three countries to become sensitive to a pattern in which their governments, rather than they themselves, spend a substantial portion of their hard-won income and wealth. (The fact that West Germany also elected a more conservative government in this period is consistent with the pattern.) The impact of a high component of government spending in the GDP may well have been exacerbated by the rise in consumer prices throughout the decade, although no more so in Canada, Great Britain, and the United States than in other OECD countries.

One possible reason for a loss of voter confidence in incumbent liberal governments during the second half of the 1970s (in addition to the fact that the pattern of recovery from 1975 seemed to repeat the insufficient gains of the first five years of the decade but at an even lesser magnitude) were sharp increases in the unemployment rates of all three countries between 1974 and 1975—from 3.1 to 4.6 percent in Britain, from 5.3 to 6.9 percent in Canada, and from 5.5 to 8.3 percent in the United States. Moreover, aside from some minor decreases, those rates were sustained into the 1980s. By 1980, except for Italy, they had become the highest of any of the major members of the OECD. It can be argued that the concatenation of high levels of unemployment with rising prices, increased governmental expenditures, and GDP growth that was even less sufficient to avoid a recession than it had been in the early 1970s would have done little to sustain the confidence of voters in incumbent parties, their leaders, and their programs.

During the decades of the 1960s and 1970s the distribution of gainful employment in all three countries shifted dramatically. The proportion of civilian employment in agriculture, already the lowest of the large OECD countries, declined by 60 percent in the two North American countries and by almost 45 percent in Great Britain. Only the Low Countries were as low. Moreover, there were continuous although not as extreme declines in the proportions of gainfully employed workers engaged in manufacturing. Again, the three countries were in the vanguard of the Western and other OECD countries. The basic restructuring of the economies indicated by these declines also was reflected in continued complementary gains in service employment during the two decades—the proportionate increases at the end of the period ranging from a little under 20 percent for the United States to almost a third for Britain. Service activities are tertiary, however, and do not signify a relatively tangible and lasting wealth in the same way that primary and secondary activities based on land and property may. For populations brought up on traditional economic values, increasingly service-based economies that employ large numbers of poorly paid, low-skilled personnel (as well as well-paid white-collar managers and professionals) as human capital and that lack the sense of security conveyed by wealth based on real property also would do little to inspire public confidence in incumbent political authorities. If nothing else, even if the significance of these shifts was not understood by most people, the fact that these changes required drastic changes in a labor force geared to another type of economy would be enough to generate massive apprehension on the part of traditional skilled and semiskilled workers with the way things were going. This, again, may be the sort of structural shift that would be conducive to breaking long-established political habits.

Throughout most of this same period, 1960–82, net savings as a percentage of the GDP were lower in the three countries than in any of the other OECD member nations, although toward the end of the period some of the Scandinavian countries had declined to the same levels. In the critical 1975–79 period the three were the lowest of the large members, and for the entire period from 1960 to 1982 they had the three lowest averages of the twenty-three member nations (i.e., 10.1 percent in Canada, 8.7 percent in Britain, and 7.9 percent in the United States, as opposed to an average of 11.7 percent for the OECD countries). Inasmuch as the level of savings relative to GDP is an aggregate phenomenon that may not be easily recognized by individuals as an indication of weakness in the economic system, it also should be noted that, aside from the Scandinavian nations, during the period from 1960 to 1982 the three countries also had the lowest proportions of net household savings as a component of disposable household income. Because many Americans, Britons, and Canadians subscribe to a norm of saving 10 percent of their income, we may note that the yearly average in each case was well under that—8.6 percent in the United States, 8.4 percent in Canada, and 6.7 percent in Great Britain. As compared to the Scandinavian countries, the three countries were incomplete welfare states, so it is plausible that low saving rates were disturbing for citizens who knew that they would have to provide for many of their needs themselves.

The major industrial democracies all showed increases in output per hour and compensation per hour during the 1970s. However, again, for the critical second half of the decade the three countries had the lowest rates of increase, whether indexed against a norm of 1967 or averaged as an annual percentage change. Compensation gains also were lowest in the two North American countries, a condition unlikely to contribute to worker optimism. In contrast, compensation gains were unusually high in Great Britain, a factor that could have raised anxiety levels in an economy with visibly disintegrating markets and physical plant.

SUMMARY AND DISCUSSION

In this chapter we have argued that the recent ascendancies of aggressively conservative governments in Canada, the United States, and Great Britain, as well as in several other Western electoral democracies, are individual manifestations of some common basic structural conditions in those countries. The same circumstances that led us to that position also led us to conclude that neither conventional theories of electoral behavior nor historical analyses of social change are adequate to account for this conjunction. In the first instance we argued that in order for theories of electoral behavior to account for shifts they must explicate and employ an account of changing structural conditions that would make it possible to use relatively fixed qualities of the same individuals to explain their changing behavior.[7] In the latter instance we argued that historical accounts are untestable, even though they may be plausible. Instead of adopting either of these approaches, our point of departure was Offe's analysis of the basic contradictions inherent in the welfare state and the implications of those contradictions for democratic electoral politics.

Starting from Offe's analysis of these contradictions we have tried to identify the conditions in which members of electorates would experience various sentiments (e.g., this is not the time for goodwill and to be generous in taking care of other people's needs, welfare programs are inefficient and ineffective, welfare programs don't go far enough or don't even deal with the basic problems, welfare programs have gone too far and threaten our freedoms, the programs are unfair and unjust) that would lead them to withdraw support from parties and candidates traditionally associated with the welfare state and its programs. Such withdrawal might take any of three forms. People either might stop voting, vote for opponents of those they previously had supported largely as an act of resentment, or embrace those who would terminate or cut back many of the programs and agencies that constitute the welfare state. The most likely structural condition for explaining the recent resurgence of conservatism (i.e., political events that have put aggressively conservative parties in control of governments and their programs high on the agenda for public debate and consideration) would be a period of incipient major economic difficulty. Sensitivity to that possibility could be heightened by such

other conditions as increased foreign political and economic competition and intrusion, increased signs of loss of control of the domestic
economy, ominous threats of major international conflicts, demand
overloads on the welfare system, and increasingly visible signs of the
withdrawal of support for the extant national community by members
of both upper and lower socioeconomic strata. The empirical part of
our analysis examined time series data for the three countries to
ascertain whether any of these conditions had developed or increased
in the period prior to the recent elections in which the reality of an
anti-welfare conservative turn was manifested.

Our view of the significance of the recent electoral victories of
Conservatives in Great Britain and Canada and Republicans in the
United States is that they have provided an opportunity for leading
conservatives to redirect public political debate to the welfare state, its
particular programs, and the assorted conservative social, political,
and economic values that underlie their critiques. Moreover, our view
of the present conservative resurgence does not see it as the result of
an integrated mass movement with broad popular support for *all* of its
positions but as the product of a coalition of numerous limited-issue
groups that have united in support of the successful candidates and
parties. The total number of voters represented by these groups alone
may well have been insufficient to bring conservatives to office. Neither these voters nor the administrations they have put in place support every component of what has come to be recognized as a total
conservative platform (i.e., all the issues of interest to the coalition of
groups that have aligned themselves with the candidates of the parties
on the right). Moreover, recent conservative electoral victories have
required, and future victories will continue to require, the support of
two types of voters, the less ideological elements of their own parties
and disaffected elements of opposition parties who essentially are
voting *against* recent pro-welfare state incumbents. They also have
required and will require that disaffected partisans of liberal parties
and those not identified with any party who have chosen to exit from
the electoral arena continue to do so. Further, as the other chapters in
this book reveal, because there have not been massive ideological shifts
in the three electorates, not only have these new conservative governments been unable or unwilling to try to implement a total conservative agenda but also, until now, they have had to restrict themselves

largely to rhetoric and partial implementation of what is being called "fiscal responsibility."

Earlier we discussed at some length the limitations of the available data for our purposes. One thing that we did not mention, however, is that the restriction of the analysis to Britain, Canada, and the United States raises a question of the generality of our basic argument. In this regard we might again remind the reader of Offe's distinction between mature and incompletely realized welfare states. He does not develop the distinction in sufficient systematic detail to permit one to categorize Western electoral democracies along the implied underlying continuum. Nonetheless, it is clear that these three electoral democracies are not fully developed welfare states to the degree that the Scandinavian states are; neither are they as incompletely realized as are Portugal, Spain, and Greece (Heidenheimer, Heclo, and Adams, 1983). Because we were unable to categorize the OECD countries in this regard and because of the aforementioned problems in contrasting time series data that may be comparable only in surface appearance, we have not tried to test our arguments comparatively across all the OECD states. We note, however, that the three countries may be unique in one regard that could affect the sensitivity and responsiveness of their domestic politics to the conditions that we have suggested might be pertinent.

We have in mind the conjunction of two conditions. One is that each of the three countries had and continues to have what is essentially a "brokering" two-party system. Thus, even though the NDP provides a third alternative in Canada, the Liberal-SDP alliance has been building a potentially viable third choice in Britain, and an expanding group of nonvoters may be on the way to becoming a recognized third option that cannot be neglected by politicians in the United States, voters in the three countries effectively have only two viable options in choosing a governing party or chief executive. The second is that since 1960 each of the three countries has had to deal with major social paroxysms stemming from deep cleavages—the French-English and center-periphery splits in Canada, the black-brown-white and regional splits in the United States, and the black-brown-white and North-South splits as well as separatist Welsh, Scottish, and Northern Irish movements in the United Kingdom. This is not to deny that Spain has major separatist movements, that Flemings and Walloons battle in Belgium, that religious conflict is deep in the Netherlands —and one could go on. What may be distinctive for Canada, Britain, and the United States, however, is the conjunction of internal domestic cleavages with a basically two-party electoral system oriented toward brokerage politics.

This may be particularly pertinent to our analysis. The aforementioned cleavage structures demonstrate both the extent of each country's welfare needs and the insufficiencies of the entrenched system for meeting them. Recognition of this failing can be presumed to have eroded support for the political party and actors most closely associated with the deficient system. But, given the essentially two-option character of each country's electoral system, those disaffected from incumbents either can refrain from voting or vote for the opposition, regardless of whether they feel positive about the opposition's program. Sufficient numbers have opted for the latter despite the fact that the conservative program may offer little in the way of positive alternatives to resolve the principal complaints of both disaffected voters and nonvoters alike. Therefore, it is because of the conjunction of cleavages among unequals and a two-party electoral system that it may be that a full comparative analysis would show that our argument is most appropriate for the three predominantly English-speaking states.

Obviously an exploratory analysis of this sort also is valuable for highlighting future research needs and strategies. In the preceding paragraphs we raise questions that suggest the desirability of including a wider range of countries in a more extensive study. That range should include countries with both more and less fully developed welfare states. Furthermore, it would be important—as the range of countries widened—to make sure that the concepts of liberalism and conservatism appropriate to Canada, Great Britain, and the United States were equally appropriate, and, furthermore, to specify empirically how liberalism and conservatism are manifested in each particular national case.

With respect to time series indicative of structural conditions that should be examined, the ideal of equally valid and reliable comparable series available for all countries being contrasted is probably unattainable. This is especially the case for data derived from international organizations that convert them to standard forms dictated by organizational purposes. The implication is that it would be preferable to take each country as a case and ask how the sorts of structural conditions that we have discussed in general and abstract terms would be manifested in that particular context. Taking that approach, it would not be necessary to deal with the issue of convergence, for convergence could be expected whenever comparable structural conditions conducive to a conservative resurgence happened to occur in different countries at the same time. In view of the increased level of international dependencies generated by transnationals and world trade, however, more widespread convergence is to be expected.

Our argument involved not only the premise that certain structural conditions upset long-standing but tenuous political arrangements, but also the premise that these arrangements increasingly are tenuous because the impact of the welfare state now seems as questionable to labor as it is unsatisfactory to capital. Our analysis emphasized workers both because they make up the largest share of the eligible electorates in Western-style democracies and because, purely on the basis of rational self-interest, they might be expected to be staunch supporters of the parties and candidates that created and implemented the welfare state and its programs. Our analysis, however, does not assert that large numbers of workers had actually embraced the programs and policies of conservative political leaders and parties, only that many of them either stopped voting or voted for the opposition out of protest or resentment or, simply, out of loss of conviction. These aspects of our argument can and should be studied in detail in each country; available election studies with longitudinal panel designs can be very useful for these purposes. Furthermore, there is Offe's argument that workers find that the welfare state, though it may cushion against severe economic blows, has done little to restore economic equity or even to accomplish any meaningful redistribution of capital, and that securing the benefits of the programs often generates resentment because the welfare state intrudes into areas of behavior traditionally considered private. Studies in each country of skilled and unskilled workers' responses to work and class relations and of their attitudes toward welfare programs and their rules and regulations also are relevant for more formal and stringent tests of this analysis. By implication, then, to the extent that our argument is causal and involves a combination of structural and individual mechanisms, it is important to understand that no single set of data is available or can be created readily to test it. Rather, it is necessary to combine a variety of approaches to test as many of its facets and links as possible.

The data that we did review and summarize are selected and illustrative. Although spotty at some times and difficult to interpret at others, we did not observe any data series that would contradict the two main components of our argument. One is that the recent electoral trends characterized as a resurgence of conservatism should be explained on a structural rather than an individual voter level. The second is that the structural changes have been of a sort that would undermine confidence in and electoral support for the more liberal parties and politicians that developed and promoted the welfare state as an accommodation to the problems of Western free market economies. If the sources of dissatisfaction and anxiety that beset citizens of the three countries continue to be unresolved, the forces behind political change will remain strong and unsatisfied. Without structural changes the next political alternative would seem to be a shift left and/or the withdrawal of additional citizens from participation in electoral politics. If conditions at that future time continue to be unresolved, the argument would suggest a new shift to the right, and so on, ad infinitum. A continuing series of pendulumlike swings between left and right without any effective resolution of basic systemic difficulties appears highly unlikely. In the longer run, therefore, basic structural changes in the conditions that give rise to the anxieties of modern life, and not mere cosmetic reinterpretations of socioeconomic reality, are possible, even probable.

NOTES

1   A classic illustration of this tendency was provided by George Wallace during his third-party campaign for the American presidency when he remarked that "there was not a dime's worth of difference between the Democratic and Republican parties."

2   For this same reason several chapters in this volume that explain election outcomes in the individual countries do not directly address our concerns.

3   This is not to suggest that historical approaches cannot be structural (for example, see Charles Tilly, 1975). The point is that structural explanations involve an explicit search for and specification of underlying social and economic factors.

4   In fact, at any time since the 1930s a cogent explanation of the loss of voter support for the welfare state could have been presented. For example, although there was some small redistribution of capital and power from the upper to the lower classes, it

was quite gradual, being seriously constrained by the entrenched pyramidal class structures of the industrial democracies. Further, although there was progress in assuaging the more extreme deprivations of the working class, welfare programs only cushioned but never have prevented the impact of economic dislocations on the employment and income of workers. Given the ideals of its proponents, the problems that sparked the development of the welfare state could be neither completely nor permanently resolved. Indeed, Marxists seem to argue that the welfare state is like a Band-Aid on the internal contradictions of capitalism. Therefore, given that the welfare state and its goals never have been completely realized, the question is to identify structural factors that could precipitate the reorientation that only recently produced the conservative resurgence.

5   See, for example, Norman Thomas's argument elsewhere in this volume regarding the shift to the right of the political center of the several major political parties in each of the three countries.

6   It is appropriate to note that one of the consequences of these measures is that they are now called "recessions" rather than "depressions" or "crashes."

7   A life-course theory of political behavior could serve the same function, but we are unaware of any beyond the weak proposition that people become more conservative as they get older.

REFERENCES

Aitken, Donald. 1977. *Stability and Change in Australian Politics.* New York: St. Martin's Press.

Barnes, Samuel H., and Max Kaase. 1979. *Political Action: Mass Participation in Five Western Democracies.* Beverly Hills: Sage Publications.

Belknap, George, and Angus Campbell. 1952. "Political Party Identification and Attitudes Toward Foreign Policy." *Public Opinion Quarterly* 15: 601–23.

Berelson, Bernard R., Paul F. Lazarsfeld, and William N. McPhee. 1954. *Voting: A Study of Opinion Formation in a Presidential Campaign.* Chicago: University of Chicago Press.

Butler, David, and Donald Stokes. 1976. *Political Change in Britain,* 2nd ed. New York: St. Martin's Press.

Campbell, Angus, Philip Converse, Warren Miller, and Donald Stokes. 1960. *The American Voter.* New York: John Wiley and Sons.

Campbell, Angus, Gerald Gurin, and Warren E. Miller. 1954. *The Voter Decides.* Evanston, Ill.: Row, Peterson.

Clarke, Harold, Jane Jenson, Larry Le Duc, and John Pammett. 1979. *Political Choice in Canada.* Toronto: McGraw-Hill Ryerson.

Dalton, Russell, Scott Flanagan, and Paul Beck, eds. 1984. *Electoral Change in Advanced Industrial Societies.* Princeton, N.J.: Princeton University Press.

Dryzek, John, and Robert E. Goodin. 1986. "Risk-sharing and Social Justice: The Motivational Foundations of the Post-War Welfare State." *British Journal of Political Science* 16: 1–34.

Dyson, K. 1980. *The State Tradition in Western Europe*. New York: Oxford University Press.

Fiorina, Morris P. 1981. *Retrospective Voting in American National Elections*. New Haven, Conn.: Yale University Press.

Flora, Peter, and Arnold J. Heidenheimer. 1981. *The Development of the Welfare State in Europe and America*. New Brunswick, N.J.: Transaction Books.

Guest, Dennis. 1985. *The Emergence of Social Security in Canada*. Vancouver: University of British Columbia Press.

Heclo, Hugh. 1981. "Towards a New Welfare State?" In Peter Flora and Arnold J. Heidenheimer, eds., *The Development of the Welfare State in Europe and America*. New Brunswick, N.J.: Transaction Books, pp. 383–407.

Heidenheimer, A. J., Hugh Heclo, and C. T. Adams. 1983. *Comparative Public Policy: The Politics of Social Choice in Europe and America*, 2nd ed. New York: St. Martin's Press.

Kiewiet, D. Roderick. 1983. *Macroeconomics and Micropolitics: The Electoral Effects of Economic Issues*. Chicago: University of Chicago Press.

Kornhauser, William A. 1959. *The Politics of Mass Society*. Glencoe, Ill.: Free Press.

Nie, Norman H., Sidney Verba, and John R. Petrocik. 1976. *The Changing American Voter*. Cambridge, Mass.: Harvard University Press.

Niemi, Richard, and Herbert Weisberg, eds. 1976. *Controversies in American Voting Behavior*. San Francisco: W. H. Freeman.

Offe, Claus. 1984. *Contradictions of the Welfare State*, ed. John Kennedy. Cambridge, Mass.: MIT Press.

Rimlinger, Gaston V. 1974. *Welfare Policy and Industrialization in Europe, America and Russia*. New York: John Wiley and Sons.

Tilly, Charles, ed. 1975. *The Formation of National States in Western Europe*. Princeton, N.J.: Princeton University Press.

Titmus, Richard H. 1958. "War and Social Policy." In *Essays on the Welfare State*. London: Allen and Unwin, pp. 75–88.

Vernon, Ray. 1977. *Storm Over the Multinationals: The Real Issues*. Cambridge, Mass.: Harvard University Press.

Zipp, John, and Joel Smith. 1982. "A Structural Analysis of Class Voting." *Social Forces* 60: 738–59.

3. Hunting the Snark: Or Searching for Evidence of That Widely Touted but Highly Elusive Resurgence of Public Support for Conservative Parties in Britain, Canada, and the United States

WILLIAM MISHLER, MARILYN HOSKIN, AND ROY E. FITZGERALD

INTRODUCTION

"Just the place for a Snark!" the Bellman cried,
As he landed his crew with care;
Supporting each man on the top of the tide
By a finger entwined in his hair.

"Just the place for a Snark! I have said it twice:
That alone should encourage the crew.
Just the place for a Snark! I have said it thrice:
What I tell you three times is true."[1]

The theme of this volume requires that we consider seriously the possibility that the election since 1979 in Britain, Canada, and the United States of a series of governments generally considered conservative reflects a fundamental resurgence of conservatism in the Anglo-American democracies. To be sure, conservatism is an elusive concept and one whose ambiguity and susceptibility to different interpretations have allowed various political analysts to choose indicators to suit their particular points of view. Still, the view that there has been a renaissance of support for conservative principles, policies, and leaders is one that is repeated frequently in the conventional wisdom of each nation and can be supported as well by a wealth of anecdotal evidence.

In Great Britain, for example, the election in 1979 appears to have been a watershed event signaling a number of changes in government which have committed that nation to a conservative course. The election of Margaret Thatcher as prime minister, her institution of the rigid monetarist and austerity policies known popularly as "Thatcherism," the hemorrhaging of popular support for the opposition Labour party, the success of the Conservative government's confrontations with the unions, the popularity of that government's decision to wage war to preserve British control of the Falkland Islands, and, of course, the landslide reelection of Thatcher in 1983, all point in the direction of a surge of conservatism both in government and among the public.

In the United States a number of events appear to suggest a similar trend. The election of Ronald Reagan as president in 1980 and the Republican party's victory in the Senate elections of the same year, the institution of a radical program of tax and domestic spending cuts now variously praised or decried as "Reaganomics," the unprecedented peacetime buildup of the armed forces, the increased use of force in foreign policy exemplified by the invasion of Grenada and the bombing of Libya, and the landslide reelection of Reagan in 1984 lend credence to the argument that a conservative tide is in progress.

Finally, although Canadian evidence of a swing to conservatism at the federal level[2] is both more recent and less pronounced, the election of Brian Mulroney in 1984 and the early conservative tenor of his government certainly accord with the thesis and appear at least superficially to parallel trends in Britain and the United States. Perhaps of even greater significance for the rebirth of conservatism in Canada in the long run, however, may be the resignation of Prime Minister Pierre Trudeau, who before his retirement from public life dominated Canadian national politics in a way that may have insulated that nation from some of the political trends occurring elsewhere.

At least as interesting as the possibility that a resurgence of conservatism is under way in these countries is the frequent suggestion by conservative pundits and politicians that the separate conservative victories in Britain, Canada, and the United States may be linked—the common result of a series of shared social, economic, and political experiences and conditions. On the international front, for example, the nagging reality of continued Soviet animosity and adventurism despite Western efforts at détente is widely credited with promoting public support for conservatism throughout the West, though especially in the United States. Similarly, the increased incidence of

terrorism worldwide and the putative "loss" over the last twenty years
of pro-Western regimes in Vietnam, Iran, Nicaragua, Ethiopia, Angola,
Mozambique, and Rhodesia, to name but a few, has produced widespread public frustration, if not outright humiliation, over the apparent impotence of the West in the face of sundry challenges from the
Soviet Union and its client states. Such common dilemmas, it is argued,
have contributed to a resurgence of support for conservative parties
and principles not only in Britain, Canada, and the United States but
among Western democracies more generally.

On the domestic front, as well, the commitment to broadly similar
social welfare policies characteristic of the three nations during most
of the 1950s and 1960s has come under increasing attack since the
early 1970s. More than simply failed experiments in governmental
intervention, welfare state policies have been blamed by conservatives
in each country as having contributed to lawlessness, economic leth-
argy, and the deterioration of basic social values.[3]

A somewhat more subtle version of this argument traces the apparent resurgence of conservatism in the West to changes in social class
structures brought about by the transition to postindustrial society.
According to this perspective, institutionalization of the welfare state
has combined with the increasing affluence of the working classes to
obscure traditional class differences. This, in turn, has allowed conservatives to make inroads among former supporters of liberal parties
by appealing to values associated with life-style, social order, and
protection of property. Thus, for example, increasingly satisfied with
the status quo and anxious to protect recent economic gains, members
of the growing lower-middle class are held to have responded to labor
disputes (especially by well-established and highly paid unions),
domestic violence and disorder, and other threats to domestic order
and stability by rallying to the conservatives. The logic of this argument applies equally to threats of economic disruption whether from
foreign imports, migrant labor, or the twin economic threats of unemployment and inflation (Cain, 1980; Conover, 1983; Himmelstein and
McRae, 1984).

One of the problems with anecdotal evidence, of course, is that its
supply is inexhaustible and rarely limited to one side of a debate.
Skeptics who doubt the reality of a conservative renaissance in the
Anglo-American democracies can find numerous examples that accord

with their views, among them: the recapture by the Democratic party of the U.S. Senate, the continuing control by the Democrats of the House of Representatives and a majority of statehouses and state legislatures in the United States,[4] the internal discord in the British Conservative party and its fluctuations in public opinion polls, and the continuing series of political blunders, scandals, and resignations that have plagued the Progressive Conservative government in Canada. Perhaps more telling from this perspective, despite the apparent popularity of their appeals, ardent conservatives have yet to mount serious legislative assaults on established liberal welfare commitments in any of these three nations.

Unlike the Bellman in Lewis Carroll's poem, we are reluctant to accept as true the claim that a fundamental resurgence of conservatism is under way simply because the claim has been repeated so often. Anecdotes and wishful thinking aside, remarkably little systematic evidence has been produced that gives credence to the claim. Even less evidence supports the thesis that recent conservative victories in the three countries are related and stem from common experiences. Moreover, to the extent the scholarly literature has addressed these concerns, it has done so only indirectly, from several different perspectives, and with inconsistent if not contradictory results.

The research reported here begins to correct this neglect. Specifically, we employ time series methods and data on public support for political parties in Britain, Canada, and the United States since 1964 to examine whether and to what extent recent events reflect a fundamental resurgence of conservatism in each country and to determine, as well, the extent to which changes in conservatism across the countries have similar dynamics and common origins.

PREVIOUS RESEARCH

He had brought a large map representing the sea,
Without the least vestige of land:
And the crew were much pleased when they found it to be
A map they could all understand.
                              •••
"Other Maps are such shapes, with their islands and capes!
But we've got our brave Captain to thank"

(So the crew would protest) "that he's brought us the best———
A perfect and absolute blank!"

Although little systematic research has directly considered the possibility of a resurgence of public support for conservative parties,
principles, and leaders in the Anglo-American democracies, our "map"
is not completely blank. Several discrete bodies of literature bear indirectly on the question and provide a useful point of departure.

That which addresses ideology most directly relies heavily on
survey data and focuses variously on (1) public and elite support for
democratic principles (Stouffer, 1955; McClosky and Brill, 1983; Sullivan et al., 1982; Jackman, 1972; Prothro and Grigg, 1960), (2) public
attitudes on political, social, and economic issues (Page, 1978; Marks,
1983; Carmines and Stimson, 1981; Miller et al., 1976; Chafetz et al.,
1983; Davis, 1980; Conover, 1983), or (3) the structure and content of
individual belief systems or "ideologies" (Converse, 1964; Stimson,
1975; Marcus et al., 1974). Despite widely different approaches and
continuing controversies over concepts, methods, and implications, a
small number of consistent patterns emerge from this work. Of particular interest is the suggestion that except in those few instances where
individual self-interest on issues is direct, immediate, and abundantly
clear, issue orientations and ideological commitments tend to be
extremely volatile and epiphenomenal—reflections of specific election campaigns or of support for particular candidates rather than of
abiding principles (Hibbs, 1982b; Piereson, 1978; Sniderman et al.,
1974). Nevertheless, although there is little in this literature (most of
which focuses on the United States) to support the thesis of increasing
conservatism, the absence of good time series data on public attitudes
combined with unresolved debates about the conceptualization and
measurement of ideology limit the utility of this research for assessing
ideological change or resurgence.

More useful in this regard is the literature concerned with the
possibilities of partisan realignment or dealignment in Western democracies. Beginning with attempts to determine whether U.S. elections
in 1968 and 1972 signaled the emergence of a Republican majority,
studies of changes in party loyalty have demonstrated what appears to
be a gradual decline in public attachments to political parties of all
ideological hues in a number of Western democracies, including all

three in our study. Clarke and Stewart (1984) refer to this as "dealignment by degree." Since there is little evidence anywhere of party realignment or a shift of public attachments from parties of one ideological type to those of another (Crewe, 1983; Dalton et al., 1984; LeDuc, 1985; Hibbs, 1982b), the clear thrust of this research runs contrary to the resurgence hypothesis.[5]

Nevertheless, there is some evidence in this literature that dealignment may occur more rapidly among some parties within a system than others and that, of late, dealignment has occurred more rapidly among more liberal parties (LeDuc, 1985; Wattier, 1983; Berrington, 1983; Norton, 1984; Cain, 1980). This suggests that we cannot preclude the possibility of a shift in the *aggregate balance* of partisanship from liberalism to conservatism as a result of a process that might be called "dealignment by different degrees." Such a pattern might occur, for example, if the erosion or dealignment of support for the Republican party in the United States proceeded at a slower pace than the erosion of support for the Democratic party. Although both parties would lose supporters, the more rapid decline in Democratic support would have the practical effect of producing a shift in the *balance* of public support away from the Democrats and toward the Republican party. Such an occurrence could result in Republican electoral victories without reflecting any fundamental realignment of public ideologies.

Two other bodies of literature have less to say about the nature and extent of partisan or ideological change than about the potential causes of such change. The largest and most obvious literature in this regard is that which seeks to describe and explain individual behavior in discrete elections. Although continuing to debate the relative importance of parties, candidates, issues, and events—especially individual judgments of the performance of the economy—there is virtual consensus that a fully and properly specified model of political support needs to take each of these various categories of factors into account (on the United States: Pomper, 1975; Hibbs, 1982a; Ranger, 1980; Abramson et al., 1982; Himmelstein and McRae, 1984; Nie et al., 1979; on Britain: Butler and Stokes, 1976; Butler and Kavanagh, 1984; Penniman, 1979; Ranney, 1985; Miller, 1984, among many; on Canada: Clarke et al., 1979; Penniman, 1975 and 1981; LeDuc et al., 1984).

A second approach to explaining political change in these countries, and the one closest to that followed in this chapter, uses aggregate time series data to examine patterns of political support for political parties or chief executives. Building on an extensive but disparate literature,[6] a virtual cottage industry has developed utilizing time series methods to identify the impact of economic factors (principally unemployment, inflation, and real income) on public support for political parties or chief executives over extended periods (typically a decade or more). Although a variety of measurement and methodological disagreements have produced conflicting evidence (Norpoth, 1984), there appears to be consensus in this literature that (1) economic factors affect support; (2) inflation exerts a greater impact than unemployment; and (3) the public tends to punish poor economic performance but not necessarily reward good performance (for the United States: Kiewiet, 1983; Kinder and Kiewiet, 1981; Hibbs, 1982a; Fiorina, 1981; Lau and Sears, 1981; Klorman, 1978; Tufte, 1978; for Britain: especially the works of Whiteley, 1984a, 1984b, 1986; Richardson and Moon, 1984; Hibbs, 1982a; for Canada: Clarke and Stewart, 1984; Monroe and Erickson, 1985).

A few studies have extended this approach to consider political variables as well. Most such efforts, however, concentrate on a small number of relatively crude, composite political indicators (such as Mueller's "rally" variable and Norpoth's threat to national security measures) intended primarily as controls to clarify economic effects rather than explore the effects of political personalities and events per se. Others, such as Stimson (1976) and MacKuen (1983) include more political variables but concentrate solely on their impact on presidential popularity. A notable exception is the work of Clarke et al. (1985), which incorporates a somewhat larger number of more refined political indicators (including leader satisfaction, internal party disputes, strikes, by-elections, war, and new party formation) and demonstrates that both "normal" and "crisis" political events had significant influence on short-term fluctuations in support for the British Conservative party (also Clarke and Stewart, 1984).

Although these studies are limited in what they can tell us about long-term effects of political factors, they underscore the importance of including political and event variables as potential sources of change, especially in light of the relatively small explanatory power of economic variables. In addition, the concerns of this volume require that we consider not only the *idiosyncratic* causes of partisan change in each nation but also the effects of those experiences and events thought to be *common* to the Anglo-American democracies. In short, we need to examine the validity of claims that potent political variables — Soviet challenges, domestic unrest, labor strikes, and others discussed earlier — have inspired a genuine rebirth of enthusiasm for conservatism across nations.

METHODS AND MEASURES

" 'You may seek it with thimbles — and seek it with care;
You may hunt it with forks and hope;
You may threaten its life with a railway-share;
You may charm it with smiles and soap — '"

("That's exactly the method," the Bellman bold
In a hasty parenthesis cried,
"That's exactly the way I've always been told
That the capture of Snarks should be tried!")

Before proceeding to consider the extent to which there has been a resurgence of conservatism in Britain, Canada, and the United States or to ascertain its causes, several conceptual and methodological issues require brief attention. Important among these "thimbles and cares" are the measurement of conservatism and the treatment of time. As indicated previously, conservatism is an elusive concept and one subject to multiple and conflicting interpretations. Rather than join the philosophical debate over fundamental meanings, we employ a pragmatic measure that we believe taps in a rough and ready way relative changes in political ideology over time. Specifically, *our assumption is that if a resurgence of conservative ideology has occurred in the Anglo-American democracies, it ought to be reflected over time in greater support for conservative principles and policies and, ultimately, in greater public support for those political parties most closely identified with them.*

With this in mind, we measured conservatism in terms of the level of public support for what is conventionally considered the more conservative of the two major parties in each country (e.g., Republicans in the United States, Conservatives in Britain, and Progressive

Conservatives in Canada).[7] Because of the possibility, noted earlier, that the overall dealignment of party attachments in Western democracies in recent decades may conceal important shifts in the *relative* strength of liberal versus conservative support (what we have called dealignment by different degrees), we did not believe it sufficient to examine support for conservative parties in isolation. Instead, we measure support for the more conservative major party in each country *relative* to the percentage of the public who supported either of the two largest parties (i.e., percent major conservative party supporters/ percent major conservative + major liberal party supporters). In this way we effectively ignore political independents and third-party supporters and concentrate on changes in the *balance of support* between the more liberal and more conservative major party in each country over time.[8]

As indicated above, our measure of conservatism is based on the assumption that a resurgence of conservatism in the Anglo-American democracies is likely to result, at least in the short run, in a shift in public support from the more liberal to the more conservative of the electorally viable political parties in each nation. This assumption, of course, follows closely the logic of voting advanced by Downs (1957: 99), which holds quite simply that voters compare party ideologies and support the party whose ideology is closest to their own. Beginning with this premise and assuming a two-party system with a unimodal distribution of voters along an ideological continuum on which the parties are in equilibrium at the center, then a shift in the distribution of voters toward the conservative end of the ideological distribution should produce a sharp, albeit temporary, shift in public support toward the more conservative of the two parties and away from the more liberal party. However, the shift in public support toward the conservative party should be temporary. According to Downs, the dynamics of party ideologies are such that any rightward shift in the ideological distribution of voters should precipitate a rightward shift in the positions of both political parties as they adjust to the change in public opinion, eventually reaching new (and adjacent) equilibrium positions at the center of the new ideological distribution.

At first glance the second part of this dynamic appears to contradict the logic underlying our measure of conservatism. After all, if both parties respond identically, then there is no reason to expect that ideological change will produce a net shift in the relative balance of public support for the two parties. To the contrary, if both political parties move *simultaneously* to the right in response to ideological change, we might expect them to retain their relative shares of public support even as they both pursue increasingly conservative public policies. Indeed, in another essay in this volume Norman Thomas suggests that this is what has happened in the Anglo-American democracies in recent years.

Our assumption, however, is that parties respond *sequentially* rather than *simultaneously* to changes in the ideological distribution of the public. Again following the logic advanced by Downs, our expectation is that as a rightward shift in public opinion occurs the conservative party will benefit but will be forced to adopt even more conservative policies in order not to lose supporters to "extremist" minor parties on the right. As the conservative party moves right, the gap between the major parties widens. This creates opportunities and incentives for the more liberal party to follow the conservative party to the right in order to close the gap and thereby regain the liberal's previous share of public support. This suggests, then, that in the short run a shift to the right in the ideological distribution of voters ought to be reflected in increased support for the conservative party, but in the long run the dynamics of party ideologies probably work to mitigate these effects.

This leaves the questions of how long is "long-term" and what is the "short run." We would argue that the time required for a substantial ideological change to produce a new, more conservative party equilibrium is substantial and certainly is measured in years not months. Although highly adaptable, political parties are not ideological chameleons. Institutional factors insure that the pace of ideological adjustment and adaptation is relatively slow and probably requires significant losses in at least one and more often successive elections to overcome institutional inertia and resistance to ideological change. Consequently, since we use quarterly measures of party support and are searching for evidence of a resurgence of conservatism whose electoral effects are first apparent in the late 1970s we are confident in our assumption that if a genuine resurgence of conservatism has occurred it ought to be reflected over a period of at least one election cycle (and probably longer) in substantial and sustained shifts in public support toward the more conservative party in each of the three countries under consideration.

The data used in the study consist of quarterly measures of conservative support, economic performance, and political events in Britain, Canada, and the United States.[9] The specific indicators are described in the appendix. In Canada and Britain the conservative support data are derived from surveys that asked respondents variants of the question, "If the federal/general election were held today, which party would you support." In the United States the political support data are derived from periodic Gallup polls that ask respondents, "All things considered, do you generally consider yourself to be a Democrat, a Republican, or what?" Because the British and Canadian questions solicit immediate vote intentions while the U.S. questions tap more fundamental partisan loyalties, the two are not strictly comparable. In particular, we suspect, political support in the United States probably is less sensitive in the short term to the effects of political and economic conditions and events, whereas the British and Canadian support data should manifest greater sensitivity to short-term effects and greater volatility as a result. Despite these differences, however, it is reasonable to believe that both measures of party support will be sensitive to ideological trends and enable us to identify a conservative renaissance if one has occurred since 1964.

With respect to time, our decision to begin the analysis in 1964 is prompted by a desire to identify a period both sufficiently long to allow us to distinguish fundamental ideological trends from temporary partisan drift and sufficiently varied to include a range of plausible economic and political sources of change. The 1964–84 period fits both criteria. During these years each of the three countries experienced both economic growth and recession, survived periods of domestic and international disorder as well as relative stability, and witnessed a broad array of political leaders and events. Moreover, because 1964 arguably represents a high water mark of enthusiasm for liberal governments and their policies in the three countries, the period since then should provide maximum opportunities to observe the conservative resurgence if it has occurred.

Although vital for understanding change, the use of time series data introduces special problems. In particular, such analyses are complicated by the tendency of time-related observations to be autocorrelated in such a way that the value of a variable at one time is dependent at least partly upon one or more earlier values of the same variable.[10] A number of strategies have been developed to cope with this problem. Most attack it by eliminating the time dependencies in a series prior to analysis. The strategy we employ is a variant of this approach developed by Box and Jenkins (1976) and elaborated by Box and Tiao (1975). Greatly simplified, it involves the development of an Auto-Regressive Integrated Moving Average (ARIMA) model to identify the nature and extent of time-dependent trends in an input series (or independent variable) and then proceeds to estimate statistically whether and to what extent hypothesized interventions (independent variables) are associated with significant changes in the input series after time dependencies are removed. Specifically, we use ARIMA procedures to eliminate time-dependent trends in conservatism in each country so we can better assess the impact on conservatism of fluctuations in the economies of each country and of various political personalities and events.[11]

RESULTS

And the Banker, inspired with a courage so new,
It was matter for general remark,
Rushed madly ahead and was lost to their view
In his zeal to discover the Snark.

But while he was seeking with thimbles and care,
A Bandersnatch swiftly drew nigh
And grabbed at the Banker, who shrieked in despair,
For he knew it was useless to fly.

Figures 3.1, 3.2, and 3.3 display the raw trends in the conservative share of major party support in Britain, Canada, and the United States since 1964. To help assess the significance of the fluctuations we have drawn lines on each graph representing the mean level of conservative support across the twenty-one-year period and the first and second standard deviations above and below the mean as previously indicated. If the past decade has witnessed a fundamental resurgence of conservatism, we would expect to find not only that there is a trend toward increased support for conservative parties in each of the three nations, but also that the trend in each country is *sustained* (i.e., lasting more than a year or two) and *substantially greater than the normal fluctuation in conservative support across the twenty-one-year period* (defined somewhat arbitrarily as within one standard deviation of the mean).

Inspection of the trends in figures 3.1–3.3 provides limited support at best for the basic resurgence thesis. Perhaps the strongest case for resurgence occurs in the United States, where the conservative share of major party support has risen in twelve of the nineteen quarters since 1980 and has increased from a low of approximately 31 percent in the first quarter of 1980 (at the beginning of President Carter's last year in the White House) to a high of nearly 48 percent with the reelection of President Reagan in the last quarter of 1984.

Even here, however, the evidence of long-term resurgence is far from clear. Although by the end of 1984 the Republicans' share of major party support was more than three standard deviations above the twenty-one-year mean, it reached that pinnacle very suddenly and late in the period—evidence suggestive more of a sudden spurt of

Figure 3.1. Conservative (Republican) Share of Major Party Support in the United States, 1964 to 1984 (in percentages).

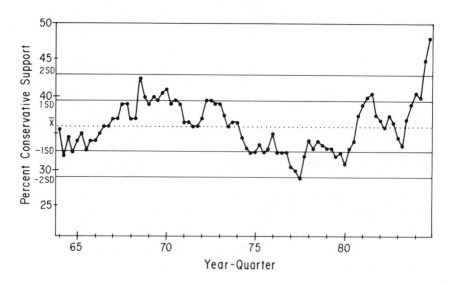

Figure 3.2. Conservative Share of Major Party Support in Canada, 1964 to 1984 (in percentages).

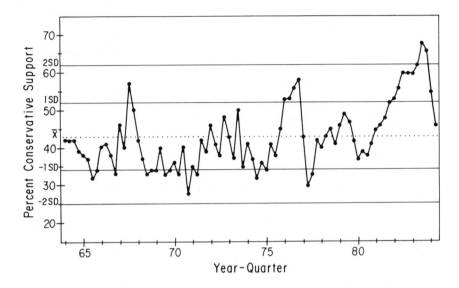

party popularity in response to contemporaneous events than of a sustained surge of conservative ideology. Indeed, as recently as the second quarter of 1983 the conservative share of two-party support was nearly a full standard deviation *below* the twenty-one-year average and did not exceed the mean by much more than one standard deviation until the third quarter of 1984—or about the time of the nomination of Walter Mondale and the renomination of Ronald Reagan.

In Canada, in contrast, the pattern appears to have been one of a conservative resurgence during the late 1970s and early 1980s that faltered and then collapsed just at the time that the Progressive Conservatives returned to power. From a low of 30 percent in the second quarter of 1977 conservative support increased in nineteen of the next twenty-five quarters to peak at nearly 70 percent (more than 2.5 standard deviations above the mean) in the third quarter of 1983, about the time that Liberal Prime Minister Pierre Trudeau retired from public life. Thereafter, conservative support declined precipitously, falling nearly 25 percentage points in three quarters to end the period only slightly above the twenty-one-year mean.

Support for the resurgence hypothesis is even more tenuous in the British case. Although the late 1970s and early 1980s witnessed two separate surges in conservative support (from 1975 to 1977 and from 1981 to 1983), neither of these advances was sustained for more than two years; neither returned conservative support to the level it enjoyed in 1968 and 1969; and both were followed by a precipitous regression in conservative support toward the long-term mean. The available evidence clearly suggests that recent increases in British conservatism have been of relatively short duration and generally within the normal range of variation in partisan support.

It is possible, of course, in looking for evidence of recent and fairly steep increases in conservative support that we might have overlooked the possibility that conservatism has increased gradually and episodically over longer periods—proceeding, essentially, two steps forward and one step back. Not surprisingly, given the volatility of the time series, evidence of longer, more gradual, and intermittent trends is even more difficult to discern. Nevertheless, those dedicated to the resurgence thesis will be able to find at least hints of such a pattern in the data for Canada and the United States.

In Canada, for example, inspection of the entire time series reveals three very clear peaks in conservative support spaced about equally across the period (in 1967, 1976, and 1983). Interestingly, each peak is slightly higher than the previous one, thus hinting at the possibility of a cyclical pattern of increasing amplitude. Also interesting in this regard is the observation that each surge in conservatism is followed by a sharp decline, coincident in each case with events related to Quebec or to Prime Minister Trudeau. As noted previously, the sharp decline in conservative support in 1983 coincided with Trudeau's resignation as prime minister. The decline in 1976 began with the victory of the separatist Parti Quebecois in provincial elections, and the drop in conservative support in 1967–68 was associated both with a period of heightened tensions in Quebec (highlighted by the visit to Quebec of French President Charles de Gaulle) and with the selection of Pierre Trudeau to succeed Lester Pearson as leader of the Liberal party.

For the United States the data in figure 3.1 could be interpreted as indicating a conservative resurgence beginning in the wake of the Goldwater debacle of 1964 and culminating in the election of President Nixon in 1968. Although this pattern owes more to a decline in support for the Democratic party than an increase in Republican loyalty (data not shown), the conservative *share* of major party support increased by more than 10 percent in the period between the defeat of Goldwater and the election of Nixon. Then, following four and one-half years of relative equilibrium, conservative support plummeted in 1973 (in the wake of the Watergate scandal) and continued to languish with only minor fluctuations until the emergence of Ronald Reagan as the front-runner for the Republican nomination in 1980. Although plausible, the suggestion of a long-term resurgence of conservatism in Canada and the United States that was derailed or delayed in the United States by Watergate and interrupted in Canada by threats to national unity or the appeal of "Trudeau-mania" is highly speculative and supported by little evidence.

Even less evidence supports the contention that the variations in conservatism across the three countries follow a common pattern or

Figure 3.3. Conservative Share of Major Party Support in Great Britain, 1964 to 1984 (in percentages).

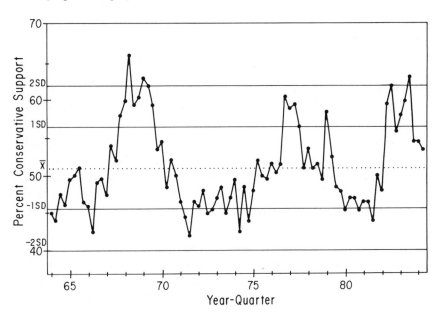

reflect global trends. To examine this possibility systematically, cross-correlations were calculated between the conservative support measures for each of the three nations.[12] The cross-correlations were lagged up to a maximum of sixteen quarters or four years in each direction, thereby allowing for the possibility that conservative trends in one country mirror those in another but with a lead time or lag time of anywhere between three months and four years. The results, presented in table 3.1, suggest that variations in conservative support across the three countries have followed independent paths.

As might be expected, given their close geographic proximity, substantially integrated economies, and the pervasiveness of American media in Canada, the most similar patterns of conservative support are those in Canada and the United States. The unlagged (zero order) correlation between variations in conservative support in these countries is .20 compared with correlations of −.04 between both Canada and Britain, and Britain and the United States. However, none of the correlations is substantial, and none is statistically significant.

Examination of the lagged cross-correlations yields similarly negative results. For example, none of the lagged cross-correlations between the British and Canadian series is statistically significant. The largest (−.19) occurs when the British data follow the Canadian data (i.e., are "lagged forward") by seven quarters. In addition to being nonsignificant, however, the sign of the relationship is in the wrong direction, suggesting that conservative trends in the two countries have been antagonistic. There is only one significant cross-correlation between the British and U.S. series, which occurs when the British data follow the U.S. data by fourteen quarters. However, the sign of this relationship also is in the wrong direction, and nothing in the overall pattern of cross-correlations suggests this is anything other than a statistical aberration.[13] Three of the cross-correlations between the U.S. and Canadian series are significant. All are quite small, and two are in the wrong direction. The third, which occurs when the U.S. data are lagged forward ten quarters, also runs contrary to expectations. It indicates that fluctuations in Canadian conservatism have anticipated those in the United States by about two and one-half years. However, there are compelling reasons, as we have suggested, to believe that whatever resurgence of conservatism has occurred in these two countries began earlier in the United States.

Table 3.1.   Cross-Correlations of Conservative Support Variables in Britain, Canada, and the United States.

Number of quarters lagged[a]	Britain/ Canada	Britain/ United States	United States/ Canada
−16	.02	.17	−.18
−15	.04	−.11	−.07
−14	−.01	.10	−.23*
−13	−.04	−.01	.08
−12	−.06	−.05	.06
−11	.07	−.08	−.06
−10	−.03	−.00	.25*
− 9	.09	−.02	.00
− 8	−.09	.07	−.00
− 7	−.19	.14	.07
− 6	.01	−.07	−.02
− 5	−.07	.14	−.04
− 4	.14	−.12	−.02
− 3	−.10	−.02	−.12
− 2	−.05	−.01	−.12
− 1	.02	.03	.09
0	−.04	−.04	.20
1	.10	−.14	−.12
2	.11	−.00	−.04
3	.13	.13	.05
4	−.07	.04	−.01
5	.16	−.01	.07
6	−.06	.21	−.09
7	−.01	−.20	−.03
8	−.05	.18	−.06
9	−.09	−.11	−.03
10	.06	−.06	.14
11	−.13	−.05	−.03
12	.10	−.03	.20
13	.05	.10	−.27*
14	−.09*	−.28	.11
15	−.08	.15	−.03
16	.15	−.13	.01

Key:
* p≤.05; one-tailed test.
[a] Negative numbers reflect backward lags, positive numbers forward lags.

MODELS OF CONSERVATIVE SUPPORT

> "We have sailed many months, we have sailed many weeks,
> (Four weeks to the month you may mark),
> But never as yet ('tis your Captain who speaks)
> Have we caught the least glimpse of a Snark!"

Although it does not appear from the evidence presented thus far that anything like a conservative tide is sweeping the Anglo-American democracies, it is clear there has been considerable ebb and flow in the balance of public support for conservative parties over the past two decades in each of the countries examined. To understand more clearly the causes of these trends, ARIMA procedures were used to analyze variations in conservative support in each of the three countries. As indicated previously, ARIMA procedures permit assessments of the effects of multiple independent variables on a time series while controlling statistically for the possible distortions caused by nonstationarity and autocorrelation.[14] Greatly simplified, the procedure involves the identification of a "noise model" that describes the time dependencies in the data and that, when applied to the time series, produces residuals that are "white noise" (i.e., uncorrelated).

Once the proper noise model is identified, intervention terms are added to the model and their parameters estimated. Since ARIMA models are highly sensitive to specification error we developed them in stages, building separate univariate models for each independent variable before proceeding to develop multivariate models. This enabled us to experiment with different time lags and intervention functions for each hypothesized intervention and to select the most promising formulation for inclusion in the initial multivariate models. Although clearly exploratory, this approach is justified by the absence of good theory with respect to most of the independent variables in our analyses.[15]

The initial multivariate models are reported in tables 3.2, 3.3, and 3.4, respectively, for Britain, Canada, and the United States. Table 3.5 reports the coefficients for the final (revised and reestimated) multivariate models that include only the statistically significant or otherwise important predictors of conservatism from the initial models.[16] The W coefficients in these models are impact coefficients and can be interpreted roughly as regression coefficients. They indicate the unit change

Table 3.2.   Economic and Political Predictors of Conservative Support
in Great Britain. Initial Multivariate Models (All Variables)

Predictor		W	t
Economic predictors			
Unemployment		$(.83)^1$	$(4.21)^*$
Inflation		$(.48)^1$	$(5.25)^*$
Common political predictors			
Disorder		−.66	−1.49*
Strikes		−.74	−1.56*
Soviet adventurism		.34@	.61
Major patriotic event		1.36	.43
International crises		−3.46	−1.69*
Major liberal event		5.31	2.36*
National humiliating events		1.88	2.57*
Nation-specific predictors			
Thatcher government		.42 +	1.79*
Kinnock leadership		−2.43 +	−1.51*
Foot leadership		−.25	−.25
SDP events		1.07	.72
Falklands War		5.74	1.57*
Noise Model			
	MA (1)	.52	4.84
	MA (10)	.84	19.57
RMS		7.79	
Q (25 lags)		23 (NS)	
R^2		49%	

Key:
* p≤.10, one-tailed test.
@ lag = 1 quarter.
+ ramp effect (all other variables are pulse effects).
1 Because of multicolinearity between inflation and unemployment separate models
were estimated for the two economic variables in Britain. All figures refer to the
"Inflation" model except those in parentheses.

in the conservative share of major party support associated with a unit
change in the intervention variable. The t coefficients are traditional
measures of statistical significance. The statistics at the bottom of the
tables indicate the overall performance of the models[17] and demon-

Table 3.3.   Economic and Political Predictors of Conservative Support in Canada. Initial Multivariate Models (All Variables)

Predictor		W	t
Economic predictors			
Unemployment		−.94	−.64
Inflation		1.44	1.38*
Common political predictors			
Disorder		1.75	.78
Strikes		−3.68	−2.23*
Soviet adventurism		−1.18	−.92
Major patriotic event		−2.79	−1.04
International crises		−2.35	−.93
Major liberal event		7.03	4.72*
National humiliating events		NA	
Nation-specific predictors			
Mulroney selection		5.78	1.26
Trudeau selection		−9.81	−2.44*
Trudeau resignation		−17.68	−3.95*
Clark government		2.72	.75
Quebec events		−14.62	−4.39*
Sovereignty association		5.00	1.07
New Economic Policy		11.85	2.63*
Constitutional accord and proclamation		5.22	1.24*
Noise model			
	MA (1)	.69	7.50
	MA (8)	.30	2.68
RMS		23.48	
Q (25 lags)		24 (NS)	
R^2		46%	

Key:
* $p \leqslant .10$, one-tailed test.

strate that all of the models perform satisfactorily. Specifically, the Residual Mean Square (RMS) for each model is reasonably low; the LBQ statistics are not statistically significant across twenty-five lags (indicating that model residuals are "white noise" as required); and the pseudo-R^2 statistic[18] indicates that the combination of political and

Table 3.4.   Economic and Political Predictors of Conservative Support
in the United States. Initial Multivariate Models (All Variables)

Predictor	W	t
Economic predictors		
Unemployment	−.30	−1.20
Inflation	.21@	.93
Common political predictors		
Disorder	.88@[1]	3.83*
Strikes	.31	1.05
Soviet adventurism	−.41[1]	−.73
Major patriotic event	.27[2]@	.51
International crises	.49[2]@	.94
Major liberal event	−.26	−.56
National humiliating events	1.37[1]	1.78*
Nation-specific predictors		
Reagan administration	2.89#	3.89*
Carter administration	−1.82#	−1.92*
Ford administration	.24#	.20
Nixon administration	1.63#	1.59*
Watergate	−2.90#	−3.68*
Vietnam (1965−68)	.52#	.66
Vietnam (1969−72)	1.16#	.99
Grenada invasion	1.39	1.30*
Noise model		
RA (1)	.85	50.71
RA (6)	−.34	−27.04
RMS	1.92	
Q (25 lags)	14 (NS)	
R^2	48%	

Key:
* p≤.10, one-tailed test.
@ lag = 1 quarter.
# step level effect.
+ ramp effect (all other variables are pulse effects).
1 coded zero during Republican administrations.
2 coded zero during Democratic administrations.

Table 3.5. Economic and Political Predictors of Conservative Support
in the United States, Great Britain, and Canada. Multivariate
Models (Significant Variables Only)

Predictor	United States	
	W	t
Economic predictors		
Unemployment	−.33	1.52*
Inflation	.20@	.96
Political predictors		
Disorder	.90@	4.43*
Strikes		
International crises	.80^2@	1.71*
Major liberal event		
Humiliating events	1.12^3	1.57*
Nation-specific variables		
Reagan administration	2.79#	4.00*
Carter administration	−1.86#	−2.32*
Nixon administration	1.36#	1.41*
Grenada invasion	1.40@#	1.40*
Watergate	−2.71@#	−4.57*
Vietnam (1969−73)	1.56#	1.49*
Thatcher		
Kinnock		
Falklands War		
Mulroney selection		
Trudeau selection		
Trudeau resignation		
Quebec events		
New Economic Policy		
Constitutional accord and proclamation		
[Noise models not shown]		
Reduction in mean square	1.76	
Q (25 lags)	15 (n.s.)	
R^2	47%	

Key:
* p≤.10, one-tailed test.
# Step level effect.
+ Ramp effect (all other variables have pulse effects).

	Great Britain		Canada	
	W	t	W	t
	(.92)[1]	(4.89)*	−2.10	−1.69*
	(.51)[1]	(5.56)*	1.56	1.51*
	−1.02@	−2.48*	−2.48	−1.92*
	−5.03	−2.77*		
	5.45	2.80*	7.03@	5.74*
	1.50	2.80*		
	.40+	1.92*		
	−1.33+	−1.46*		
	9.69	3.12*		
			4.92	1.13
			−9.92	−2.76
			−18.53	−4.62*
			−13.97	−4.87*
			11.96	2.93*
			6.08	1.66*
	7.61		22.38	
	22 (n.s.)		25 (n.s.)	
	46%		44%	

@ lag = 1 quarter.
1 inflation and unemployment estimated in separate models; all coefficients refer to inflation model.
2 Coded zero during Democratic administrations.

economic indicators accounts for between 44 and 50 percent of the variance in conservatism after the time dependencies in the data are removed.

Examination of the impact coefficients in these models provides mixed though generally unencouraging support for the conventional wisdom that recent increases in conservatism in the three countries are rooted in common experiences. Despite our willingness to experiment with different lag structures and alternative intervention and transfer functions, there is little evidence that fluctuations in public support for conservative parties in these countries are influenced by global trends, international events, or common domestic experiences. On the contrary, the evidence presented strongly suggests that the ebb and flow of conservatism in these countries has been influenced much more profoundly by idiosyncratic and country-specific circumstances and events.

Consistent with the rather well-developed body of literature on economic effects and political support, our models indicate that fluctuations in economic performance have had significant effects on the balance of support for conservative parties in each of the three countries. However, the effects tend to be small and inconsistent. As expected, increasing levels of inflation contribute to increased support for conservative parties in each country, although the relationship is not statistically significant in the United States and is small in Britain.[19] Rising levels of unemployment, by contrast, work to the detriment of conservative parties in Canada and the United States, although they work to the disadvantage of the party in power in Britain, regardless of the party's ideology. Again, however, the size of the effects is small. Thus, for example, the impact coefficient for inflation in the British case indicates that an increase of 2 percent in the inflation rate from one quarter to the next—a substantial increase even during recent periods of high inflation—produces a very modest shift (less than 1 percent) in public support from the Labour to the Conservative party. Similarly, a 1 percent quarterly increase in the U.S. unemployment rate diminishes public support for the Republican party by an almost imperceptible .3 percent. Even in Canada where economic effects are most pronounced, profound economic dislocations have relatively small effects on the balance of public support for the two major parties.

Somewhat less support exists in these data for the thesis that variations in conservatism stem from common public reactions to international crises or global threats. For example, although there were numerous instances of Soviet adventurism and aggression throughout the period of study (ranging from the invasions of Czechoslovakia and Afghanistan to the destruction of Korean Airlines Flight 007) there is no evidence that these events influenced the balance of public support for conservative parties in any of the three countries. Not only are the coefficients small and statistically insignificant, but in the United States and Canada they are in the opposite direction to that predicted.

Similarly, although international crises not directly associated with the Soviet Union (such as the OPEC oil embargo) appear to have produced small temporary increases in conservative support in the United States, they have had no significant effect on public opinion in Canada and have substantially hurt the conservative cause in Britain. In the latter case, it happens that most of the major international crises of the period occurred during periods of Conservative government in Britain. Thus it appears that the public has "punished" that party for international crises that occurred on its watch. Why this should be the case, however, when the public usually rallies to the support of the government during periods of international crisis is something we cannot explain.

Finally, international events, such as the loss of colonies or the capture of citizens as hostages abroad, which have the effect of humiliating the nation or calling into question its strength and resolve, have been followed by significant increases in conservatism in Britain and the United States.[20] Here, again, however, the effects are small; humiliating events produced on average only about a 1.5 percent shift in public opinion toward the more conservative party. Moreover, the conservatives' advantage was of short duration, disappearing on average within a quarter of the conclusion of the event.

An equally mixed picture emerges from these data with regard to the several categories of noneconomic domestic events widely believed to contribute to conservatism across the three nations. Instances of domestic violence and disorder are associated with small temporary increases in conservatism in the United States during Democratic administrations (the relationship is negligible during Republican administrations) and in Canada (where the Liberal government has held power for all but the final two quarters of the period under study).[21] In Britain, in contrast, domestic disorder hurt the Conservative party regardless of the government in power at the time. These relationships, however, are very small and are statistically significant only in the United States. Even then, each instance of domestic disorder produced on average only about a 1 percent increase in conservative support, virtually all of which increase was dissipated within three months of the event. Major patriotic events such as the wedding of Prince Charles and Lady Diana in Britain or the bicentennial celebration in the United States had no significant effects on conservatism in any of the countries.

Consistent with the conventional wisdom, the implementation of major liberal policies has benefited the Conservative party in Britain and Canada, though, surprisingly, not the Republican party in the United States. Indeed, the coefficients in the final models indicate that each of the major liberal initiatives we coded produced on average a gain in conservative support of approximately 7 percent in Canada and of nearly 6 percent in Britain. Foremost among these policies in Canada was the National Energy Program (NEP), whose implementation in 1980 resulted in a one quarter shift in support to the Progressive Conservative party of almost 14 percent.

In contrast, labor disorder had no significant effect on conservatism in the United States and, although significant in both Canada and Britain, actually hurt the conservative cause in those nations. Whatever the specific effect of Margaret Thatcher's policy of confrontation with the unions—and there is reason to believe, contrary to the conventional wisdom, that her policies *hurt* the Conservatives' fortunes[22] —the overall effect of labor unrest in Britain has been to help the Labour party at the expense of the Conservatives. The existence of a similar dynamic in Canada suggests that despite apparent public support for the confrontational rhetoric of conservative leaders, the reality of labor discord undermines the conservative position and causes the public to rally to parties of the left as those best able to negotiate with unions and cope with labor crises.

Rather than responding to experiences or events common to the Anglo-American democracies, levels of conservative support over the past twenty years appear to have been influenced to a far greater extent by idiosyncratic or country-specific factors. In Canada, for example, the personality of Prime Minister Trudeau and events linked in various ways to the separatist movement in Quebec have been especially important. Consistent with our earlier suggestion that threats to national unity in Canada serve to rally public support to the Liberals as the only party traditionally able to draw significant support from both French and English Canada, the measure with the greatest impact on conservatism over the past twenty years is a variable recording major separatist events in Quebec (e.g., the visit to Quebec of Charles de Gaulle, the election of the Parti Quebecois, the political kidnappings by the FLQ, etc.). On average, each major disturbance in Quebec has produced an abrupt though short-lived decrease in conservative support of nearly 14 percentage points. Conversely, support for conservatism has increased consistently in the wake of other events such as the defeat of Sovereignty Association, the achievement of federal-provincial agreement on a new constitution, and the subsequent proclamation of the constitution, each of which can be interpreted as reducing the risk of national disintegration.

The personality of Prime Minister Trudeau also has had profound effects on the balance of public support for the major parties in Canada, although it cuts in different directions during different periods of his career. Compare, for example, the impact of Trudeau's arrival on the political scene with that of his departure sixteen years later: his selection as Lester Pearson's successor as leader of the Liberal party in 1968 was followed by a sudden, sharp, and enduring swing in public support from the Progressive Conservative to the Liberal party of nearly 10 percent; his resignation from public life in 1984 and his replacement as party leader and prime minister by John Turner had a similar albeit even stronger effect. Indeed, support for conservatism *fell* by nearly 18 percentage points in the quarter in which Trudeau resigned and remained depressed for the remainder of the period for which we have data. By the end of his career the personality of Pierre Trudeau had become the Liberal party's biggest liability, just as it had been the party's principal strength at the beginning of his tenure.

Significantly, the factors most responsible for the ebb and flow of conservative fortunes in Canada, including the unpopularity of certain Liberal policies, the public's fascination with and fickle attitudes toward Pierre Trudeau, and the rise and decline of separatist sentiments in Quebec are those least susceptible to the direct influence or control of the Conservative party. By comparison, the Conservative government of Joe Clark had only a very small and statistically insignificant impact on the balance of party fortunes in Canada. And although the Conservatives' selection of Brian Mulroney as party leader produced a swing to the party in public support of almost 5 percentage points, the effect of Mulroney's selection is not statistically significant and vanishes in less than a quarter after the event.

Predictably, in Britain, the event that appears to have had the greatest impact on conservatism over the past twenty years is the Falklands War. British success in that relatively brief conflict was associated with an abrupt temporary increase in conservative support of nearly 10 percentage points. Moreover, it is likely that our analysis underestimates both the strength and duration of the Falklands' effect. In a study using monthly data on Margaret Thatcher's popularity and employing fewer control variables, Norpoth (1986) estimates not only that the Falklands War produced an immediate increase in public support for Margaret Thatcher of 16 to 20 percent but also that the Falklands' effect dissipated relatively quickly over the ensuing months, disappearing finally in the aftermath of the British general election of 1983.

Among other idiosyncratic effects on conservatism in Britain, the selection of Margaret Thatcher as Conservative party leader, the rise of the Social Democratic party, and the conflict and disarray characteristic of the Labour party during the period Michael Foot served as party leader appear to have had no appreciable effects on the balance of power between the Labour and Conservative parties. Although the selection of Margaret Thatcher and Neil Kinnock as Conservative and Labour party leaders also appears to have had only a small impact on the balance of public support for their parties, this appearance is misleading. In estimating Thatcher's impact on conservative support we experimented with several different impact specifications including the possibilities that her selection as party leader produced: (a) a sudden temporary increase (or pulse) in conservatism; (b) a sudden permanent increase (step level change) in conservatism; or (c) continuing increases in conservatism across her tenure as leader (a ramp effect). Only the latter specification was statistically significant when other variables were controlled. The resulting impact coefficient indicates that conservative support increased by approximately .4 percent on average during *each* of the quarters since Thatcher's selection as leader in 1976. Overall, therefore, her tenure as Conservative leader has resulted in an increase in Conservative support of nearly 13 percentage points, controlling for other influences in our model. The tenure of Neil Kinnock as Labour party leader was modeled in a similar fashion. The resulting coefficient indicates that an average swing to Labour from the Conservative party of 1.3 percent, on average, for each quarter of his tenure or about 8 percent in all during his first year and a half as leader. Taken together, these data indicate that the effect of Kinnock's selection more than offsets Thatcher's continuing appeal and produces a net shift in public support away from the Conservative party toward Labour.

Finally, consistent with suggestions that recent increases in support for conservatism in the United States are by-products of the "Reagan revolution," the largest surge in American conservatism occurred in the aftermath of Reagan's first presidential nomination. Other things held constant, Reagan's tenure as president has produced a step-level shift in public support from the Democratic to the Republican party of almost 3 percentage points—a figure all the more impressive given that our measure of conservatism in the United States reflects changes in long-term party identification rather than short-term party preferences. Moreover, the impact of the Reagan presidency is independent of and in addition to the effects of the improved economy, the rally effects of international crises, and the variety of other events included in the model that have occurred during his tenure and have contributed to increased Republican support. Among the most significant of these events was the invasion of Grenada, an action that resulted in an additional though temporary increase in conservative support of nearly 1.5 percentage points, controlling for other factors.

Interestingly, the data in the final U.S. model are consistent with and provide at least a small measure of support for the argument, previously discussed, that Reagan's nomination may have revived a gradual and long-term shift in public support from the Democratic to the Republican party that was spawned by the war in Vietnam and nurtured by the presidency of Richard Nixon before being interrupted and reversed by the effects of Watergate. The increase in conservatism that has coincided with Reagan's term as president is almost a perfect mirror image of the decline in conservative support that occurred during the Watergate era beginning with Nixon's resignation in 1974 and ending with Reagan's nomination in 1980. Our model indicates that prior to Watergate the Nixon presidency increased conservative support by more than 1.25 percentage points, other things being equal. Although the Vietnam War does not appear to have helped the conservative cause significantly during the Johnson years (controlling, of course, for the high levels of inflation and domestic disorder during this period), Nixon's conduct of the war produced an overall increase in Republican support of more than 1.5 percentage points over and above the effects of other factors. Watergate reversed these gains, producing a shift in public support to the Democrats that continued through the Carter years. An interesting footnote here is that the Carter presidency, widely viewed as having contributed to the decline in public support for liberalism in America, actually increased support for the Democratic party, other things being equal. It did so, moreover, by a greater margin than Nixon's presidency helped the Republicans.

Notwithstanding the possibility that the Reagan presidency has revived a conservative renaissance in the United States begun during the Nixon administration but sidetracked by Watergate, the primacy of idiosyncratic explanations of conservative support in Britain, Canada, and the United States clearly contradicts suggestions that recent conservative victories in these nations are the common result of a series of shared social, economic, and political experiences heralding the demise of liberalism generally or of parties associated with liberal policies or values in particular. The primacy of idiosyncratic influences also reinforces our earlier arguments about the episodic and ephemeral nature of recent ideological trends. That the surge of conservative support observed in each of the countries in the late 1970s and early 1980s depends so heavily on the influence of individual personalities and isolated events increases suspicions that recent trends represent temporary deviations in partisan support rather than long-term shifts in political ideology.

SUMMARY

"It's a Snark!" was the sound that first came to their ears,
And seemed almost too good to be true.
Then followed a torrent of laughter and cheers:
Then the ominous words, "It's a Boo—"

Events of the past decade, especially the string of election victories by political leaders committed to conservative policies, have been interpreted widely by political pundits, government leaders, and the media as evidence of an underlying public rejection of liberal values in Britain, Canada, and the United States and of a dramatic shift to the right in the prevailing ideologies of those nations. Although students of public opinion and electoral behavior have expressed skepticism about such claims, the absence of systematic analyses of time series data on trends in public support for conservatism and liberalism in the Anglo-American democracies has allowed the anecdotal evidence to stand largely unchallenged.

Analysis of trends in public support for conservative parties since 1964 suggests the much-heralded resurgence of conservatism is largely myth. Although the evidence clearly documents that conservative parties made significant gains in public support during the late 1970s and early 1980s in Britain, Canada, and the United States, our analyses call into question both the scope and durability of such gains. Indeed, except in the United States, increases in conservative support fall well within the normal range of variation in public opinion over the past twenty years and appear already to be on the wane. Although the conservative tide has risen somewhat higher in the United States, it has done so in a manner suggestive of a short-term shift in the national mood as opposed to a fundamental change in the public philosophy.

Even were there clear evidence of a fundamental resurgence of conservative support in these nations, the importance of idiosyncratic personalities and events in explaining recent changes would raise serious questions about the stability and durability of the trends observed. Despite the fact that several of the leadership variables in our analysis produced step-level increases in conservative support, there is little evidence to suggest that the effects of leaders outlast their administrations. Similarly, with respect to political events, the evidence indicates that, except in unusual cases (Watergate being the most prominent), their effects, though occasionally large at the moment, are extremely short-lived.

This is not to say, of course, that the current upsurge in conservatism in the United States will vanish with Ronald Reagan's retirement from the political scene—though we suspect it will. Republican support already has begun to erode in Reagan's second term, much as occurred in 1981–82. Nor is it to say that the post election decline in British and Canadian conservatism signals an end to Thatcherism or indicates that the revival of Canadian conservatism has been stillborn. It is to say, however, that public support for conservative parties (and for liberal parties, too) is highly volatile in all of the countries studied and is subject to large and very rapid surges and declines in response to relatively ordinary political occurrences. As a consequence, although increases of the moment may give the impression of a fundamental resurgence of conservative ideology if viewed over a very short time, a longer perspective indicates that recent trends are part of the normal ebb and flow of public sentiment in a democracy in response to contemporaneous leaders and events.

> They hunted till darkness came on, but they found
> Not a button, or feather, or mark,
> By which they could tell that they stood on the ground
> Where the Baker had met with the Snark.
>
> In the midst of the word he was trying to say,
> In the midst of his laughter and glee,
> He had softly and suddenly vanished away—
> For the Snark *was* a Boojum, you see.

NOTES

1 With apologies to Lewis Carroll, whose poem, "The Hunting of the Snark," we have appropriated as a leitmotif for this essay. We also wish to thank Ann Palmer for her assistance in preparing the data for analysis; Lynda Erickson, Kristen Monroe, and Harold Clarke for their generosity in making their data available; and Paul Whitely, David Falcone, Mark Franklin, and Michael Maggiotto for their useful criticisms and suggestions.

2 The Conservative party in Canada has long enjoyed greater support at the provincial than federal level and has, in fact, controlled more provincial legislatures than the Liberals for a number of years. The New Democratic party, the Parti Quebecois, and the Social Credit party also have controlled one or more provincial legislatures at different times over the past twenty years. Nevertheless, because we are interested, primarily in national (i.e., federal) patterns of political support, we will rely exclusively upon the aggregate national data.

3 For an elaboration of these arguments, see for example the chapters in this volume by Thomas and by Smith, Kornberg, and Nevitte.

4 For a recent discussion of a broad range of evidence suggesting that the resurgence of conservatism in the United States is largely myth, see Ferguson and Rogers (1986). An anecdotal rejoinder is provided by Will (1986).

5   Despite widespread agreement in the literature that the overall pattern of change observed in these countries is one of dealignment, there is some evidence within individual countries that partisan realignments have occurred in certain regions. The American South is a frequently cited example.

6   This research is reviewed in detail by Monroe (1984).

7   Although minor parties have played important roles in each of these countries and contribute in important ways to ideological trends, their support tends to be small, regionally concentrated, and sporadic. Moreover, support for minor parties in each of the three systems frequently is an expression of protest against one or both of the larger parties rather than an affirmative expression of support for the minor parties' policies, leaders, or principles. We focus on the two major parties in each nation, therefore, to capture long-term national trends in conservative support.

8   Thus, for example, if popular support for the conservative party drops from 40 to 35 percent from one period to the next but support for the liberal party drops from 55 to 40 percent our index will register an *increase* in the conservative share of ideological support from 42 to 46 percent across the two periods.

9   A considerable debate exists in the literature regarding the relative advantages of using monthly versus quarterly measures of political support and economic performance. Although we attempted initially to collect monthly data for these variables, the extreme volatility of the political support measures in Canada and Britain combined with the difficulty and expense of obtaining monthly data on party support in the United States convinced us to aggregate the monthly observations on a quarterly basis. One of the advantages of this procedure is that it tends to smooth some of the sharper spikes in the monthly support data that result variously from measurement error and from random shocks or perturbations. This enables us to better distinguish true change from error and to focus more clearly on longer-term trends in political support and their political and economic causes. For further discussion of this debate, see Norpoth (1984).

10   For a useful introduction to these problems, see Ostrom (1978).

11   For an unusually readable discussion of the procedures involved in identifying, estimating, and analyzing such models, see McCleary and Hays (1980). A good review of the methodological variations found in analyses of political trends is by Norpoth (1984).

12   The conservative support measure for each country was differenced to achieve stationarity before the cross-correlations were calculated.

13   Using a .05 significance level, approximately two of the thirty-two cross-correlations should (falsely) appear statistically significant purely by chance.

14   Although the data on the Republicans' share of public support in the United States were stationary (i.e., the mean and variance of the series are constant over time) in their raw form, the data on the balance of support for the Conservative parties in Britain and Canada were stationary in their variances but unstationary in their means. This indicates, in effect, that the British and Canadian series drifted (upward and/or downward) over time. To correct this problem, the British and Canadian data were differenced. This involved subtracting the observation at time $_{t}-1$ in

each series from the observation at time $_t$. In practical terms, this means the British and Canadian models measure *changes* in the conservatives' share of major party support, whereas the U.S. model measures the *level* of the conservative share.

Following standard procedures ARIMA "noise models" describing the stochastic behavior of each time series were identified for each country. For the United States, an autoregressive model of order (1) (6) was required to remove the time dependencies from the conservatism series and ensure that the residuals from the multivariate model were "white noise" (i.e., without significant autocorrelation). This means that the conservative share of major party support in any quarter is partially dependent on the level of conservative support in the previous quarter and partially the result of a cyclical or seasonal trend every six quarters (or one and one-half years). The noise components of the British and Canadian models were identified as Moving Average processes of order (1) (10) and (1) (8), respectively. Here, again, this means that a cyclical pattern exists with respect to changes in the balance of party support in these nations of approximately two years in Canada and two and one-half years in Britain. Economies of space prevent us from considering in detail the substantive interpretation of these cyclical patterns. However, in another essay we suggest that the pattern in Britain may reflect an electoral cycle (Mishler, Hoskin, and Fitzgerald, 1986).

15   For a justification of this approach, see Yantek (1984). However, see also the note of caution raised by Beck (1985).

16   Consistent with standard techniques, we proceeded incrementally to delete statistically insignificant variables from each of the multivariate models removing at each step the variable with the smallest t value. In doing so we used a .10 level of statistical significance to reduce the possibility of omitting important variables. We proceeded in this fashion, reestimating the models after each step, until only significant variables remained. In one or two cases we also retained nonsignificant political variables in the model where it appeared that their deletion confused the interpretation of other variables or where strong theoretical concerns dictated retaining the variable.

17   The Residual Mean Square (RMS) is a standard "goodness-of-fit" measure and indicates the amount of variance remaining in the data after the model has been applied. In contrast, the Lung-Box Q statistic measures "badness-of-fit," indicating whether significant autocorrelations remain in the model's residuals after the noise components and the interventions have been applied. Finally, the R^2 statistic is a crude measure of the extent to which the intervention terms "explain" variations in conservative support after the effects of the noise model have been removed.

18   The R^2 statistic used in this analysis differs significantly from that employed elsewhere in the literature. Typically in time series analyses R^2 measures the percentage of total variance in an input series "explained" (i.e., accounted for) by the model including both the noise component and the intervention terms. Because the noise component is included, the size of the coefficient is inflated and its interpretation is unclear. To remedy this problem, we modified the R^2 statistic so that it measures only the effect of the intervention terms in the model after the effects of the noise component are removed. Thus the statistic is calculated as 1.0,

minus the ratio of the residual sum of squares from the final model (including both the noise component and the intervention terms) over the residual sum of squares from the noise model only. Or as Carroll explains it in "Hunting the Snark":

"Taking Three as the subject to reason about—
A convenient number to state—
We add Seven, and Ten, and then multiply out
By One Thousand diminished by Eight.

"The Result we proceed to divide, as you see,
By Nine Hundred and Ninety and Two:
Then subtract Seventeen, and the answer must be
Exactly and perfectly true.

"The method employed I would gladly explain,
While I have it so clear in my head,
If I had but the time and you had but a brain—
But much yet remains to be said."

19   The high level of multicolinearity between inflation and unemployment in Britain ($r = .81$) required us to estimate their effects in separate models.

20   No significant national humiliating events were identified for Canada during this period.

21   Among the alternative specifications explored in constructing the models of conservatism is the possibility that economic conditions and events could have very different, even contradictory effects on the balance of party support depending on which party controlled government at the time of the event. Because of this possibility we experimented with univariate models for Britain and the United States that distinguished the effects of a variety of political and economic variables under Labour and Conservative governments in Britain and during Democratic and Republican administrations in the United States. Since Box-Jenkins procedures require the use of continuous, uninterrupted time series measures and cannot be used if there are any gaps in the time series from whatever causes, it is not possible to partition the data, physically, to construct separate ARIMA models of the effects of, say, inflation first under Democratic administrations and then under Republican ones. To circumvent this problem we use the entire time series in constructing separate liberal and conservative models of the effects of inflation. However, in examining the effect of inflation during liberal governments we set the value of inflation equal to zero for all quarters in which the conservatives are in control of government. We reverse the procedure to examine the effects of inflation under conservative administrations. Similar procedures were not applied to the Canadian data since the Liberals were in power there for all except three of the quarters under consideration.

22   See, on this point, Mishler, Hoskin, and Fitzgerald (1986).

REFERENCES

Abramson, Paul R., et al. 1982. *Change and Continuity in the 1980 Election.* Washington, D.C.: Congressional Quarterly Press.

Beck, Nathaniel. 1986. "Estimating Dynamic Models Is Not Merely a Matter of Technique." *Political Methodology* 2: 71–89.

Berrington, Hugh. 1983. "Change in British Politics: An Introduction." *West European Politics* 6: 1–25.

Black, E. R. 1980. "Turning Canadian Politics Inside Out." *Political Quarterly* 51: 141–53.

Box, G. E. P., and G. M. Jenkins. 1976. *Time Series Analysis: Forecasting and Control.* San Francisco: Holden-Day.

Box, G. E. P., and G. C. Tiao. 1975. "Intervention Analysis with Applications to Economic and Environmental Problems." *Journal of the American Statistical Association* 70: 70–79.

Butler, David, and D. Kavanagh. 1984. *The British General Election of 1983.* London: Macmillan.

Butler, David, and Donald Stokes. 1976. *Political Change in Britain.* New York: St. Martin's Press.

Cain, Bruce E. 1980. "Challenge and Response in British Party Politics." *Comparative Politics* 12: 335–48.

Carmines, Edward G., and James A. Stimson. 1981. "Issue Evolution, Population Replacement, and Normal Partisan Change." *American Political Science Review* 75: 107–18.

Chafetz, Janet Saltzman, et al. 1983. "Growing Conservatism in the United States? An Examination of Trends in Political Opinion Between 1972 and 1980." *Sociological Perspectives* 26: 275–98.

Clarke, Harold D., and Marianne C. Stewart. 1984. "Dealignment of Degree: Partisan Change in Britain, 1974–1983." *Journal of Politics* 46: 689–718.

Clarke, Harold D., et al. 1979. *Political Choice in Canada.* Toronto: McGraw-Hill Ryerson.

———. 1985. "Politics, Economics, and Party Popularity in Britain, 1979–1983." Paper presented at the annual meeting of the American Political Science Association, New Orleans, September.

Conover, Pamela Johnston. 1983. "The Mobilization of the New Right: A Test of Various Explanations." *Western Political Quarterly* 36: 632–49.

Converse, Philip. 1964. "The Nature of Belief Systems in Mass Publics." In David Apter, ed., *Ideology and Discontent.* New York: Free Press, pp. 206–61.

Crewe, Ivor. 1983. "The Electorate: Partisan Dealignment Ten Years On. *West European Politics* 6: 183–215.

Davis, James A. 1980. "Conservative Weather in a Liberalizing Climate: Change in Selected NORC General Social Survey Items, 1972–1978." *Social Forces* 58: 1129–56.

Downs, Anthony. 1957. *An Economic Theory of Democracy.* New York: Harper & Row.

Ferguson, Thomas, and Joel Rogers. 1986. "The Myth of America's Turn to the Right." *Atlantic* (May): 42–53.

Fiorina, Morris P. 1981. *Retrospective Voting in American National Elections.* New Haven, Conn.: Yale University Press.

Hibbs, Douglas A., Jr. 1982a. "On Demand for Political Outcomes: Macro-Economic

Performance and Mass Political Support in the United States, Great Britain, and Germany." *Journal of Politics* 44: 426–42.

———. 1982b. "President Reagan's Mandate from the 1980 Elections: A Shift to the Right?" *American Politics Quarterly* 10: 387–407.

Himmelstein, Jerome, and James A. McRae, Jr. 1984. "Social Conservatism, New Republicans, and the 1980 Election." *Public Opinion Quarterly* 48: 592–605.

Jackman, Robert. 1972. "Political Elites, Mass Publics, and Support for Democratic Principles." *Journal of Politics* 34: 353–73.

Kiewiet, D. Roderick. 1983. *Macroeconomics and Politics*. Chicago: University of Chicago Press.

Kinder, Donald R., and D. Roderick Kiewiet. 1979. "Economic Discontent and Political Behavior: The Role of Personal Grievances and Collective Economic Judgments in Congressional Voting." *American Journal of Political Science* 23: 495–527.

Klorman, Ricardo. 1978. "Trends in Personal Finances and the Vote." *Public Opinion Quarterly* 42: 31–48.

Lau, Richard R., and David O. Sears. 1981. "Cognitive Links Between Economic Grievances and Political Responses." *Political Behavior* 3: 279–302.

LeDuc, Lawrence. 1985. "Partisan Change and Dealignment in Canada, Great Britain, and the United States." *Comparative Politics* 17: 1–24.

———, et al. 1980. "Partisanship, Voting Behavior, and Elections: Outcomes in Canada." *Comparative Politics* 12: 401–20.

———, et al. 1984. "Partisan Instability, in Canada: Evidence from a New Panel Study." *American Political Science Review* 78: 470–88.

McCleary, Richard, and Richard A. Hay, Jr. 1980. *Applied Time Series Analysis for the Social Sciences*. Beverly Hills: Sage Publications.

McClosky, Herbert, and Alida Brill. 1983. *Dimensions of Tolerance: What Americans Believe About Civil Liberties*. New York: Basic Books.

MacKuen, Michael B. 1983. "Political Drama, Economic Conditions, and the Dynamics of Presidential Popularity." *American Journal of Political Science* 27: 165–92.

Marcus, George, et al. 1974. "The Application of Individual Differences Scaling to the Measurement of Political Ideologies." *American Journal of Political Science* 18: 405–20.

Marcus, Gregory B. 1982. "Political Attitudes During an Election Year: A Report on the 1980 NES Panel Study." *American Political Science Review* 76: 538–60.

Miller, Arthur, et al. 1976. "A Majority Party in Disarray: Policy Polarization in the 1972 Election." *American Political Science Review* 70: 753–78.

Miller, William. 1984. "There Was No Alternative: The British General Election of 1983." *Strathclyde Papers on Government and Politics*, no. 19. Glasgow: University of Strathclyde.

Mishler, William, Marilyn Hoskin, and Roy Fitzgerald. 1986. "British Parties in the Balance: A Time Series Analysis of Long-Term Trends in Public Support for Major Parties." Paper presented at the annual meeting of the American Political Science Association, Washington, D.C.

Monroe, Kristen R. 1984. *Presidential Popularity and the Economy*. New York: Praeger.

————, and Lynda Erickson. 1985. "The Economy and Political Support: The Canadian Case." Unpublished manuscript.

Nie, Norman H., et al. 1979. *The Changing American Voter*. Enlarged ed. Cambridge, Mass.: Harvard University Press.

Norpoth, Helmut. 1984. "Politics, Economics, and Presidential Popularity." Paper presented at the Shambaugh Conference, University of Iowa.

————. 1986. "War and Government Popularity in Britain." Paper presented at the annual meeting of the American Political Science Association.

Norton, Philip. 1984. "Britain: Still a Two-Party System?" *West European Politics* 7: 27–45.

Ostrom, Charles W., Jr. 1978. *Time Series Analysis: Regression Techniques*. Beverly Hills: Sage Publications.

Page, Benjamin I. 1978. *Choices and Echoes in Presidential Elections*. Chicago: University of Chicago Press.

Penniman, Howard R., ed. 1975. *Canada at the Polls: The General Election of 1974*. Washington, D.C.: American Enterprise Institute.

————, ed. 1979. *Britain at the Polls, 1979*. Washington, D.C.: American Enterprise Institute.

————, ed. 1981. *Canada at the Polls, 1979 and 1980*. Washington, D.C.: American Enterprise Institute.

Piereson, James E. 1978. "Issue Alignment and the American Party System, 1956–1976." *American Politics Quarterly* 6: 275–308.

Pomper, Gerald M. 1975. *Voter's Choice: Varieties of American Electoral Behavior*. New York: Dodd, Mead.

Prothro, James W., and Charles W. Grigg. 1960. "Fundamental Principles of Democracy: Bases of Agreement and Disagreement." *Journal of Politics* 22: 276–94.

Ranger, Robin. 1980. "Neoconservatism Sets the Tone for U.S. Presidential Elections." *International Perspectives*: 7–11.

Ranney, Austin, ed. 1985. *Britain at the Polls, 1979*. Durham, N.C.: American Enterprise Institute and Duke University Press.

Richardson, J. J., and Jeremy Moon. 1984. "The Politics of Unemployment in Britain." *Political Quarterly* 55: 29–37.

Sniderman, Paul, et al. 1974. "Party Loyalty and Electoral Volatility: A Study of the Canadian Party System." *Canadian Journal of Political Science* 7: 268–82.

Stimson, James A. 1975. "Belief Systems, Constraint, Complexity, and the 1972 Election." *American Journal of Political Science* 19: 393–418.

————. 1976. "Public Support to American Presidents: A Cyclical Model." *Public Opinion Quarterly* 40: 1–21.

Stouffer, Samuel. 1955. *Communism, Conformity, and Civil Liberties*. New York: Doubleday.

Sullivan, John, et al. 1982. *Political Tolerance and American Democracy*. Chicago: University of Chicago Press.

Tufte, Edward R. 1978. *Political Control of the Economy*. Princeton, N.J.: Princeton University Press.

Wattier, M. J. 1983. "Ideological Voting in 1980 Presidential Primaries." *Journal of*

Politics 45: 1016–26.

Whiteley, Paul. 1984a. "Inflation, Unemployment, and Government Popularity: A Dynamic Model for the United States, Britain, and West Germany." *Electoral Studies* 3: 3–24.

———. 1984b. "Perceptions of Economic Performance and Voting Behavior in the 1983 General Election in Britain." *Political Behavior* 6: 395–410.

———. 1986. "Macroeconomic Performance and Government Popularity in Britain —the Short-Run Dynamics." *European Journal of Political Research.* Forthcoming.

Will, George. 1986. "See the Canyon? It Isn't There." *Washington Post*, June 1, C-7, col. 5.

Yantek, Thom. 1984. "Box-Jenkins Transfer Function Analysis." *Political Methodology* 10: 377–411.

APPENDIX

The data analyzed here are drawn from a variety of sources to tap both economic and political variables relevant to the examination of ideological trends. All variables were coded and entered on a quarterly basis. Here we list variables by major category, note their source, and, where appropriate, detail the measurement or coding procedures.

I. Economic variables

All economic data were taken from OECD annual publications, reflecting standard usage in time series research. Major variables in this category include:

unemployment, measured in both absolute numbers and in the percentage of the work force listed as seeking employment.

inflation, measured as the percentage change in the standard OECD consumer price from one quarter to the next.

In order to control for liberal or conservative incumbency, each of these variables was recomputed to create separate measures of those economic data under liberal or conservative governments in Britain and the United States. Similar variables were not constructed for Canada owing to the small number of quarters in which the Progressive Conservatives held power.

II. Political variables

In order to maximize the potential for explaining variations in conservative and liberal support, an extensive list of political variables was developed. Basic is the conservatism measure, described in the text as the conservative share of the support accorded to the two major parties (calculated as the conservative proportion of the sum of the percentages of liberal and conservative identifiers). The data for this measure are taken from Gallup Poll sources in the United States and Britain and from the Gallup Canadian affiliate (Canadian Institute for Public Opinion). Events data have been recorded from a number of annual yearbooks for each nation: the series of Whittaker's Almanacks, the *Canadian Almanac and Directory, Facts on File*, and the Britannica volumes entitled

Book of the Year. In addition, we utilize most of those variables analyzed by Mueller in his major study, *War, Presidents, and Public Opinion,* and use the major political studies of each nation to cross-reference important dates and events. The following common variables were utilized:

Disorder. This variable taps domestic unrest in each of the three nations and, understandably, includes different instances in each. The total number of incidents in a given quarter was recorded. For the United States this included urban riots, large-scale antigovernment protests, civil rights demonstrations, and assassinations. In Britain it consisted almost entirely of incidents of Irish violence, although a few instances of bombings or internal terrorist activities were recorded as well. The Canadian cases were limited to a very small number of ethnic demonstrations, antigovernment protests, or less clearly defined disruptions in major cities.

Strikes is a simple measure of labor unrest, defined as strike activity sufficiently newsworthy to warrant being recorded in the annual events collections noted above.

Soviet adventurism/communist threat is considered a variable whose effects would be felt across all three nations, although they should be most severe in the United States. We include actions directly attributable to the Soviet Union (the invasion of Czechoslovakia and Afghanistan, the downing of a Korean Airlines jet) as well as those seen as communist threats more generally (such as the Gulf of Tonkin incident and the seizures of the *Pueblo* and *Mayaguez* ships).

International crisis events are those dramatic enough to attract attention by more than a single nation but not identified specifically with the Soviet Union—such as the OPEC oil embargo in the early 1970s and nonspecific terrorist incidents.

Patriotic events are those that should be expected to inspire national pride. These are largely subjective judgments. Examples include the adoption of a national flag and return of the Constitution in Canada, the first manned landing on the moon for the United States, and the royal wedding in Britain.

Liberal events are those actions, almost always taken by governments, that advance liberal policies beyond the normal continuation of existing policy. To be coded into this category, therefore, the action would have to be judged to be extraordinary. Examples would be the signing of the 1965 Civil Rights Act, major liberal court decisions such as the *Miranda* or *Roe* judgments, or the imposition of uncommon wage and price controls.

National humiliating events reflect badly on national power or standing. For the United States these included the attack on the U.S. peacekeeping forces in Lebanon and the lengthy hostage crisis in Iran; for Britain the loss of colonies.

Leader variables were defined for each nation. In most cases these simply meant defining the period during which a particular executive was in power. For Britain and Canada, where Opposition leadership is both more important and more clearly defined, we define the beginning of an executive's influence as the point of selection as party leader. In Britain we limit our analysis to the role of Margaret Thatcher and her major opposition leaders (Michael Foot and Neil Kinnock); in Canada we define leadership periods for Brian Mulroney only, since the Liberals were in power for the vast majority of time covered by our study. In Canada we also code the resignation of Pierre Trudeau, the major Liberal figure of this period, to note its effects on support for conservative parties.

Nation-specific events. Several events or experiences specific to one of our three nations were sufficiently important to code individually. For Britain we added the period dating from the formation of the SDP as indicating a significant modification of the party system and, of course, the Falklands War. For Canada we coded instances specific to the Quebec issue and noted the dates of the return of the Canadian Constitution and the Sovereignty Association referendum separately. For the United States we defined a separate variable for Watergate impact (defined as the period beginning in January 1974 and continuing to the first nomination of Ronald Reagan). In addition, we defined Vietnam under separate Johnson and Nixon administrations. The invasion of Grenada was also coded separately.

4. Public Policy and the Resurgence of Conservatism in Three Anglo-American Democracies

NORMAN C. THOMAS

INTRODUCTION

The principal features of political change in the Anglo-American democracies since the early 1970s include the coming to power of conservative governments in each country and the modification or replacement of their liberal or social democratic public philosophies[1] by conservative policies. Three values make up the core of resurgent Anglo-American conservatism: first, a strong commitment to the free market in preference to the state as the means of economic allocations; second, an emphasis on individual and corporate freedom as the key to economic progress and social well-being; and third, a greatly reduced role for the state in the economy and society.

The thesis of this chapter is that this resurgence of conservatism can be understood and explained to a considerable extent as a reaction against the policies of the Keynesian social welfare state, which in turn had emerged in response to the Great Depression. The sustained and substantial growth of government following World War II has produced major changes in the patterns of politics in each country, producing major policy modifications as a result.

THE APPROACH: POLICY AND POLITICS

The principal theoretical assumption underlying this essay is that

I am indebted to Joel D. Wolfe for his helpful advice, suggestions, and comments.

policy affects politics (Schattschneider, 1935:288; Lowi, 1972:229; Brown, 1983:6). Although it is customary and useful to regard policy as the dependent variable, it also enhances understanding to explore the ways in which policy "determines" political patterns. The argument that guides this analysis follows that employed by Lawrence Brown (1983). As adapted to this study, the argument maintains that the post-World War II expansion of the welfare state, in both the scope and scale of its activities, set in motion the following sequence of events:

(1) Major programs such as maintenance and health services produced problems as well as benefits; examples of these problems included uncontrollable expansion of expenditures, red tape, and scandals.

(2) These problems led to efforts to find solutions or "rationalizing policies," Brown's term for government attempts to solve obvious problems in its programs (1983:7).

(3) Regardless of their success or failure, rationalizing policies became increasingly important over time. Unfortunately, the solutions tended to become problems in their own right. As Aaron Wildavsky has observed, this is especially true of big problems, the solutions to which tend to become their own worst problem (1979:63).

(4) Eventually, rationalizing policies result in changes in political patterns, including the public philosophy, that collectively constitute a new politics. The changes usually occur gradually, over a period of years, rather than dramatically.

(5) Ultimately, the new politics results in new policies, and in due course the cycle can be expected to begin again.

In the Anglo-American democracies, two major categories of solutions (rationalizing policies) to the problems of big government emerged from the conservative attack on the liberal welfare state—macroeconomic and microeconomic. The macroeconomic solutions entailed management of the economy primarily by using monetary policy to control the money supply, tight expenditure controls, and stimulation of private investment through tax policy. The microeconomic solutions involved deregulation and privatization and were designed to strengthen markets and reduce the role of government.

This chapter examines the resurgence of conservatism in each of the three Anglo-American democracies as they moved through the sequence of events outlined above in seeking and implementing rationalizing policies. Although there are many similarities in the political economies of the three countries, the differences among them are sufficiently large that it is necessary, in the interest of clarity, to treat them separately. The analysis of each country begins with a description of the development and growth of its welfare state, moves to an examination of conservative efforts to rationalize its welfare state programs, and concludes by exploring the extent to which those efforts altered the public philosophy and changed public policy.

THE CONTEXT: BIG GOVERNMENT
AND INFLATION

The resurgence of conservatism has been a response to the inability of the Keynesian welfare state simultaneously to maintain real economic growth at levels sufficient to finance the rapidly increasing expenditures of its social service programs and to control inflationary forces unleashed by the oil price shocks of 1973–74 and 1979–80. The welfare state had its theoretical foundations in Keynesian conceptions of economic management that involved the use of the state to enhance individual well-being and equality. By the early 1970s the welfare state had reached the full extent of its development with the British variant being the most and the American the least extensively developed (King, 1973:300–309).

Differences between the three welfare states notwithstanding, each was experiencing similar problems by the mid-1970s. Government, as measured by public expenditure, had grown substantially as a result of demographic changes, inflation, and rising unemployment. Control of public expenditure was proving to be increasingly difficult as governments confronted three politically unpalatable options: cutting spending, raising taxes, or borrowing.

The growth of government primarily reflected increased expenditures in four program areas: income maintenance, health, education, and interest on public debt (Rose, 1985:16). Interestingly, according to Rose, the period from 1954 to 1980 witnessed a substantial decline in defense spending, from 8.5 to 4.7 percent of GDP in Britain and from 11.3 to 4.6 percent in the United States. In Canada defense spending fell from 16.2 to 10.5 percent of total government spending between

1969–70 and 1979–80 (Doern and Phidd, 1983:272). In each of the three countries there was a pronounced "welfare shift" in public expenditures during the 1960s and 1970s (Huntington, 1975:11–15). That shift was accompanied by increasing public antipathy to the growing size and cost of government.

The disruptions in the world economy resulting from the oil price shocks of the 1970s brought major difficulties to most national economies. In the Anglo-American democracies these difficulties were symbolized in the term "stagflation," which refers to a combination of low rates of growth, high inflation rates, and unemployment at levels not experienced since the 1930s.

The standard Keynesian response to unemployment growth, increasing public expenditures to stimulate demand, appeared increasingly inappropriate in the face of strong inflationary forces. During the 1970s Britain, Canada, and the United States each attempted to control inflation through exhortation and experiments with incomes policy. Although incomes policies produced some positive short-term results in each country, they were soon abandoned as neither labor nor business was willing to support them on a long-term basis. Each seemed to fear that it would bear a disproportionate share of the cost of controlling inflation.

Efforts to curb inflation by reducing public expenditures encountered strong opposition from interests that benefited from major spending programs. Also, politicians feared the electoral consequences of reducing or rescinding past policy commitments. In each county powerful "distributional coalitions" (Olson, 1982) hampered efforts to adapt public policy to changed economic conditions. Pluralism has served the Anglo-American democracies well in the allocation of resources between the public and private sectors and within the public sector as long as the total economic pie (GNP or GDP) was growing rapidly enough so that all participants received increases every year. However, as economic growth slowed and public expenditures continued to expand, the political economies of the industrial democracies approximated zero-sum conditions (Thurow, 1981). Pluralist democracy appeared to one British observer to have become a "collective trap in which each pursuing his own rational self-interest contributes to harming everyone, himself included, and in which no individual way out is possible" (Pollard, 1982:113).

In this context, conservatives launched a three-pronged attack on the liberal and/or social democratic public philosophies that had provided the rationales for the development of the welfare state. First, control of inflation rather than full employment became the primary objective of public policy. Second, monetary policy replaced fiscal policy as the principal instrument of economic management. Third, the role of government in national economic and social life was to be reduced and that of the free market increased.

THE AMERICAN CASE

The American welfare state developed later and is, with the exception of education, less extensive than the British and Canadian variants. In education the United States led the industrial democracies in expanding public schooling and in making higher education widely available. However, it has generally lagged behind in the development and extension of other social services.[2]

The establishment of the welfare state is usually associated with the New Deal: the most important social services programs (Social Security and unemployment compensation), acceptance of macroeconomic management on the basis of Keynesian economics, and expansion of federal economic regulation involving securities exchange, electric power and natural gas, telecommunications, air transportation, and labor-management relations, all emerged in response to the crisis of the Great Depression. There were, however, important measures enacted in other reformist periods: the populist revolt produced the Interstate Commerce Act (1887) and the Sherman Antitrust Act (1890); progressivism brought the Food and Drug Act (1906), the Federal Reserve Act (1913), and the Clayton and Federal Trade Commission Acts (1914); and the Great Society saw the enactment of Medicare, Medicaid, the Elementary and Secondary and Higher Education acts (all in 1965) and set the stage for subsequent regulation of the environment, traffic safety, occupational safety and health, and consumer product safety. Almost all of the American welfare state programs were established in reformist periods. In most instances enactment followed a protracted period of debate over the appropriateness of the government assuming a role at all, with powerful interest groups leading the opposition. Federal action occurred only as a last resort, after it had been established conclusively that the objectives sought could not be obtained through the private sector or through state and local governments. Even when a federal role was found to be necessary, implementation through categorical grants in aid to state and local governments was preferred to direct federal administration.

The public philosophy of the American welfare state was established during the New Deal, replacing an earlier combination of Jeffersonian liberalism and laissez-faire capitalism. The New Deal public philosophy adapted traditional liberalism to twentieth-century urban-industrial society. Only if the state played a positive and active role, it held, could individual liberty be maximized.

According to Samuel Beer, the New Deal public philosophy had two essential elements, centralization and egalitarianism. This meant national action to meet the economic crisis of the depression and to reduce inequalities of wealth and economic power. Its programs, however, were only mildly redistributive because it concentrated more on achieving a new balance of economic power by strengthening the bargaining position of heretofore ineffectually organized interests. It sought to establish the sense of community associated with small republics on the national level by means of Hamiltonian energetic government (Schambra, 1982:42). It was deeply committed to a capitalism supported by government intervention. Finally, as prosperity and growth returned following World War II, it assumed that by judicious and professional management of the economy affluence could be made permanent. In the affluent society the liberal public philosophy argued increasingly for a more equitable distribution of wealth and income through new and expanded social programs and for additional regulation to enhance environmental quality and safety in the workplace, on the highways, and in the marketplace (Schambra, 1982:44–45). This required more centralization and continued governmental growth.

By the late 1960s, argues William Schambra, liberals had begun to question the assumptions on which prosperity had been built—principally the importance of rational pursuit of economic self-interest in the free market—and governmental programs began to erode economic performance (Schambra, 1982:46). Growth came under attack, and liberals advocated austerity and recognition of limits. The marriage of the Jeffersonian commitment to community and equality and the Hamiltonian commitment to prosperity and energetic government that symbolized the New Deal public philosophy seemed to be dissolving. The reason was that the American people were "not prepared to pay the price of a redistributive tax structure, massive welfare programs, a powerful and intrusive central government, and a no-growth economy" to sustain it (Schambra, 1982:46). That is, by the mid-1970s government appeared to be seriously overloaded.

The concept of "overload" holds that there has been a rapid escalation in the benefits that democratic states can provide, that many of those expectations inevitably and increasingly have been disappointed as resources have not kept pace with them, with the result that public confidence in, and support for, political institutions has declined sharply (King, 1975; Birch, 1984). The overload problem developed in the period from 1965 to 1974. During that decade federal entitlement program expenditures grew rapidly as a result of policy changes that expanded eligibility and the rights of beneficiaries of existing programs, increased benefit levels and tied benefits to the consumer price index, and established major new programs such as Medicare and Medicaid (Weaver, 1985:311–318). Entitlement programs provide benefits to individuals to which they are entitled by statute. Spending on entitlements is highly resistant to control because reductions in authorized benefit levels require new legislation rather than mere reduction in appropriation levels; beneficiaries of several large programs, such as Social Security and Medicare, are well-organized and able to protect those programs; and ethical constraints limit support for reducing benefits to the elderly and the truly needy. Between 1970 and 1976 entitlement payments to individuals increased from $151 billion to $286 billion and as a proportion of the federal budget from 31.0 to 45.3 percent (Weaver, 1985:319). Some of the growth occurred as a result of expansive policy changes prior to 1974, but much of it occurred between 1973 and 1976 as a consequence of the inflation and recession that followed the oil price hike of 1973–74 (Weaver, 1985:312).

During the period since 1975 spending on federal entitlement programs has continued to grow, but the proportion of the federal budget devoted to them has stabilized in the 41 to 45 percent range. The continued growth of spending was a response to demographic changes, mainly an aging population, inflation, especially in health care costs, and sustained high (above 7 percent) unemployment. The stabilization of entitlement spending reflects changes in budgetary priorities and efforts to curb the growth of all federal domestic spending.

Governmental overload also involved regulatory programs. The economic regulation established in the late nineteenth and early twentieth centuries was complemented by more recent social regulation directed toward improving the quality of life by reducing risk, increasing equality, and minimizing pollution. Federal regulatory intrusions into the market, the workplace, the school, and the environment were extensive and restrictive of individual and corporate activity.

Ironically, the growth of federal domestic spending and the extension of federal regulation received their biggest impetus during the traditionally conservative administrations of Richard Nixon and Gerald Ford. Both attacked big government rhetorically and through proposed cuts in expenditures, but neither was successful in curtailing it. Nor were they able to control its perceived effects: inflation, slow economic growth, and rising unemployment.

Jimmy Carter won the presidency in 1976 primarily by campaigning as a Washington outsider who would set matters right in an overgrown and inefficient government tainted by scandal and immobilized by powerful interests. To the extent that policy entered the campaign, his promises were quite consistent with the New Deal public philosophy and the goals of the Democratic party's liberal wing, although he cloaked them in conservative rhetoric (Fishel, 1985:80). Among other things, he promised to seek the enactment of welfare reform, national health insurance, a comprehensive energy program, and a balanced federal budget. In his first two years he pursued a comprehensive liberal domestic policy agenda with limited success. He also maintained tight budgetary control that kept the goal of balance within reach. But stagflation persisted and domestic program expenditures continued to grow. Liberals, especially within the Democratic party, grew restless and criticized Carter for being unable to implement much of their agenda. Conservatives, within the party and outside it, attacked him for failing to balance the budget, curb the growth of spending, and for skimping on national defense.

Conservative criticism of Carter was led by Ronald Reagan and consisted of a broad-based attack that drew heavily on conservative economists such as Milton Friedman and Arthur Laffer. Their attack was less a critique of the incumbent administration than an assault on the New Deal public philosophy. The alternative conservative public philosophy stressed free market competition and individual freedom, called for replacement of Keynesian economics with monetarism, emphasized the supply of capital and labor rather than the demand for goods and services in macroeconomic policy, demanded limitation of the role of the federal government (except for defense, which required strengthening), and proposed a curtailment of the power of special interests, particularly labor.

Monetarism, led by Milton Friedman, gained support and credibility as the Nixon, Ford, and Carter administrations proved unable to control either inflation or unemployment and Keynesian economics fell into disrepute. Friedman and his disciples called for managing the economy by controlling the rate of growth in the money supply. Budgetary surpluses and deficits would no longer be used to stabilize the economy and to assist in achieving growth in economic output in the long run (Stein, 1984:224). Keynesian macroeconomics stressed the use of fiscal policy to control demand in the short run, while monetarism relied primarily on control of the growth of the money supply in the long run. Monetarists claimed that slow but steady growth in the money supply would bring inflation down to acceptable limits. This might, they acknowledged, produce a short-run increase in unemployment, but as soon as people realized that inflation was under control economic growth would resume and employment would rise. Governmental deficits and surpluses were unimportant in the long run and had only short-run significance, almost all of it political.

The monetarists' deemphasis of demand-oriented management of the economy opened the door for the development of a supply-side approach. Led by Arthur Laffer and the *Wall Street Journal*, supply-side economists argued that slow growth and unemployment were due to the diversion of resources to the public sector. The solution they proposed was simple, direct, and politically painless: reduce taxes. The resulting economic expansion, they claimed, would produce enough revenues, even at lower rates, to allow the budget to be balanced. Supply-side economics gained congressional champions in Representative Jack Kemp and Senator William Roth, who introduced legislation in 1977 calling for 10 percent across-the-board cuts in income tax rates in three successive years. Although the supply-side approach won few adherents among traditional conservative economists, it enhanced the political appeal of the conservative alternative.

The proposed conservative alternative to the New Deal public philosophy advocated a major reduction in the role of the federal government. The reduction would be accomplished by deregulation, privatization, limitation of entitlement program expenditures by curtailing their growth and preventing their extension, and either the outright elimination or transfer to state and local governments of several domestic spending programs. Deregulation and privatization would greatly increase reliance on market competition and encourage private investment. Extensive scaling back of nonentitlement domestic spending would reduce the federal deficit, increase reliance on voluntarism, and place responsibility for deciding what government should do closer to the people, where it properly belonged but whence it had been removed by the welfare state. The government's proper role, the conservative alternative held, was to aid in the creation of wealth by promoting economic growth, not to redistribute wealth through programs that inhibited growth.

Criticism of special interests focused upon organized labor, clientele of major benefit programs, and other groups that had managed to secure the enactment of legislation that increased federal intrusiveness. Business organizations were not criticized unless they sought special treatment in the form of subsidies or bailouts. Labor bore the brunt of the attack on special interests because of its close association with the Democratic party and its long-standing support for the development and expansion of the welfare state.

Finally, the conservative alternative advocated an extensive and protracted military buildup. Conservatives argued that previous administrations had failed to understand the nature of the threat that the Soviet Union and international communism posed to the security of the United States and the Western world. In the wake of the unpopular and unsuccessful Vietnam War, America's military strength had been allowed to decline to a dangerously weak level. Pursuit of liberal goals such as détente and arms reduction, coupled with military weakness, could only encourage Soviet expansion.

The alternative conservative public philosophy had its first major impact on public policy during the Carter administration. President Carter began his presidency by proposing to Congress the enactment of an extensive agenda that included a comprehensive national energy program; welfare reform; national health insurance; a comprehensive employment stimulus program that included public service employment, public works, and youth employment; increased aid to education, especially to college students; establishment of a consumer protection agency; expansion of federal protection for wilderness areas; regulation of strip mining; reform of labor law that strengthened organized labor's bargaining and organizing rights; and reorganization of the federal bureaucracy (Fishel, 1985:89–92). Significantly, Carter did not initially place a high priority on controlling inflation or reducing federal spending.

Carter's initial agenda was compatible with the established New Deal public philosophy. It contained all of the important unaccomplished liberal goals of the New Deal, the Fair Deal, and the Great Society. Carter's accomplishments were limited: establishment of new departments of Energy and Education; enactment of a compromise energy program and a strip mining bill; and substantial expansion of national parks and protected wilderness areas.

During Carter's third and fourth years in office he made selective revisions in his agenda in response to surging inflation, increased cold war pressures, and the criticism of conservatives touting their alternative public philosophy. He embraced deregulation of air transportation, motor transport, and oil and natural gas. He abandoned the traditional liberal approach to recession, economic stimulation, abolished the Pay Board and the Council on Wage and Price Stability, which were the last vestiges of Nixon's 1971–73 experiment with incomes policy, and deemphasized such other liberal objectives as national health insurance, labor reform, and a consumer protection agency.

Perhaps most important, Carter embraced monetarism with his appointment, in August 1979, of Paul Voelcker as chairman of the Federal Reserve Board. Shortly after his appointment, Voelcker announced a shift in the Fed's approach to monetary policy, from controlling interest rates to controlling the growth of the money supply. Carter's fiscal 1981 budget, submitted in January 1980, embraced traditional conservative austerity by proposing spending restraints, except for defense, and projected a balanced budget in 1982 while resisting the political popularity of a tax cut. The proposed increase in defense reflected Carter's disenchantment with the Soviet Union and the ascendancy of National Security Adviser Zbigniew Brzezinski over

Secretary of State Cyrus Vance as the principal influence on his national
security policy views.

By the time Carter entered his reelection campaign he had embraced economic conservatism—monetarism, deregulation, and fiscal
restraint—and backed away from much of the unfinished liberal
agenda.[3] However, his approach was so tentative that he failed to convince many people that he had a sense of direction. Moreover, he still
adhered to many of the tenets of the liberal public philosophy such as
egalitarianism. He wanted to curb the growth of the federal government without abandoning its major programs. From the perspective of
the chairman of Nixon's Council of Economic Advisers, Carter wanted
to avoid harming any important interest or group with the result that
his approach would be of little good to anyone (Stein, 1984:236).
According to Jeff Fishel, the Carter administration, by rejecting traditional liberal solutions to inflation and international conflict, had
"failed to provide a useful alternative, reverting instead to [the] time-
honored 'moderate' policies of fiscal and monetary balance" that are
"historically associated with 'sensible' Republicans and moderate Democrats" (1985: 115). Both Stein and Fishel conclude that Carter's solutions to the major problems confronting his administration lacked
integration within a "central strategic vision" (the phrase is Fishel's).

In 1980 Ronald Reagan convinced the electorate that he had such
a vision, and he demonstrated a capacity to subordinate the details of
policy to it. In his first presidential campaign Reagan attacked Carter's
indecisive leadership and blamed inflation, slow economic growth,
rising unemployment, and diminished international prestige on the
policies of the liberal welfare state. His rhetoric was thematic and
symbolic rather than specific, and it aimed to set forth the broad
dimensions of a new conservative public philosophy. Economic growth,
price stability, and full employment could be achieved only through
monetary restraint, reductions in personal and business income taxes
and domestic spending, and deregulation. Social problems would be
solved by a return to traditional family-oriented values. National security would be strengthened by building up the armed forces and by
realistic assessment of the Soviet Union's expansionist objectives.
Reagan did not propose to dismantle such key welfare state programs
as Social Security, unemployment compensation, and veterans' benefits.
For the most part he was vague, unspecific, and inconsistent in his

treatment of issues (Fishel, 1985: chap. 5). There were few if any position papers that outlined proposed policy solutions. Instead, a set speech that contained his basic themes, fleshed out by anecdotes about welfare cheating and fuzzy liberal thinking, carried Reagan's conservative message to a receptive electorate.

Perhaps the key element in Reagan's 1980 campaign strategy was the employment of supply-side economics in order to avoid traditional conservative calls for austerity and belt-tightening. Kemp-Roth-style tax cuts, coupled with elimination of waste, fraud, and abuse in the operation of the government, would enable the budget to be balanced and military strength restored. The only pain would be borne by undeserving recipients of government benefits. The contrast between Reagan's optimistic vision of America's future based on a conservative approach to government and public policy and the austere pessimism of Carter and the Democrats was striking. Reagan's campaign placed liberalism and the welfare state on the defensive. Cassandralike warnings, which had been the Republican stock in trade since the New Deal, came principally from the Democrats who appeared increasingly to be the party of opposition to change. By embracing supply-side economics, the Reaganauts abandoned the traditional conservative precept that there is no such thing as a free lunch and offered one to the affluent and much of the middle class. The Reaganauts discovered, as had the New Dealers, the political appeal of such an approach.

Once in office Reagan moved quickly to implement the key economic and national security features of the new conservative public philosophy. During his first year in office (1981) Reagan persuaded Congress to enact a sweeping cut in income taxes, especially to businesses and upper-income individuals, the most likely sources of new investment. The Reagan tax bill reduced the highest individual tax bracket rate to 50 percent and tied future rates, starting in 1985, to the consumer price index in order to prevent automatic increases or "bracket creep." Reagan accomplished the second component of his economic agenda, substantial cuts in nondefense program expenditures, through use of the reconciliation feature of the congressional budget process (Schick, 1981). Cuts amounting to $40 billion in constant dollars were implemented between 1981 and 1983 (Fishel, 1985:152). Programs with strong clientele support, such as Social Security and veterans' benefits, were spared the budgetary ax. Although the administration retained "social safety net" programs, the impact of its domestic spending reductions fell disproportionately on the poor and the near poor (Palmer and Sawhill, 1982, 1984). Lowi regards the Reagan administration's approach to public assistance as an attempt to identify its beneficiaries as undeserving. He contrasts it with the liberal approach that has sought to achieve distributive justice through unstigmatized rights (Lowi, 1984:42).

Reagan's first budget also contained funding for a major defense buildup, projected over five years from 1981 through 1986. Congress provided most of Reagan's request, increasing outlays from $156 billion in fiscal 1981 to $183 billion in 1982 and $209 billion in 1983 (Kaufman, 1983:42). A major change in federal domestic policies had been implemented through budgetary politics rather than the enactment of an extensive legislative program.

Immediately following his legislative triumphs Reagan still maintained that a balanced budget could be achieved by 1984 through the stimulative effects of the tax cut and through additional, but unspecified, reductions in nondefense spending. By late 1981 questions about the ability of Reagan's budget program to avoid large increases in the deficit over a sustained period of time became more widespread. At the same time the effects of tight monetary restraint pursued by the Fed since late 1970 became apparent; inflation was being brought to heel, but unemployment was rising sharply. This automatically activated countercyclical spending and further increased the deficit. However, President Reagan did not abandon his rhetorical commitment to a balanced budget and called upon Congress to pass and submit to the states a constitutional amendment to require one. Some Reagan administration officials and other exponents of the new public philosophy argued that large deficits would have the advantage, at least in the short run, of restraining congressional spending proclivities.

Deregulation constituted the third element of the Reagan administration's economic program. Reagan sought to expand deregulation, which had received major legislative support during the Carter administration, by appointing to key positions persons who were ideologically opposed to regulation. Shortly after taking office he created a cabinet Task Force on Regulatory Relief under the chairmanship of Vice President Bush and directed it to review major regulatory policies and proposals. He then established an Office of Information and Regulatory Affairs (OIRA) within OMB. OIRA's task was to apply cost-benefit analysis to proposed new regulations. Deregulation was to be obtained by relaxation and delay of enforcement and careful balancing of its economic and social costs against its prospective benefits.[4]

Beyond the economic policy changes and the defense buildup, the Reagan administration had limited success in implementing other conservative agenda items. The president gave strong public support to constitutional amendments to ban abortion and restore prayer to the public schools, and he proposed a New Federalism that would transfer major welfare programs to state governments. His proposal for federal income tax credits for parents of children enrolled in private schools received little public or congressional support. In spite of his expressed opposition to school busing and to affirmative action, nothing concrete was done. But Reagan left no doubt regarding his views and the position of the new conservative public philosophy with respect to a wide range of issues. What is most often overlooked is that Reagan's initiative and leadership have placed liberals on the defensive regarding issues such as abortion, busing, and school prayer.

With respect to the conduct of national security policy, the national interest has replaced human rights as the underlying objective. Toughness toward the Soviet Union and relentless opposition to communism and terrorism have been stressed in presidential and administration rhetoric. However, in spite of increased military strength it appears as if the Reagan administration's words have spoken louder than its actions. Use of military force has been limited in scope (Lebanon, Grenada, and Libya) and had mixed results. Nevertheless, the appearance of the United States "standing tall" after a decade of wimpishness has been incorporated into the conservative public philosophy.

Without question the major problem spawned by the Reagan administration's conservative solutions to the problems of the Keynesian welfare state has been and remains massive federal budget deficits. The deficits grew rapidly as a result of the recession of 1982, the tax cuts, and increased defense spending authorized in 1981. The latter created a large structural or permanent deficit as the increases in federal revenues promised by the supply-side advocates failed to materialize and sizable additional cuts in nondefense spending could not be obtained from Congress. The deficits have proved embarrassing to

Reagan because they contradict traditional conservative values of fiscal restraint.

The deficits have also brought political advantage to the Reagan administration. They served as the basis for a sustained recovery from the 1982 recession that remains in force at this writing. That recovery was a key factor in Reagan's 1984 reelection victory as voters concluded that his economic policies had worked quite well. The fact that Reagan had become an unwitting practitioner of Keynesian demand management on a grand scale was immaterial to him or to his supporters. The deficits also have given Reagan an effective short-run instrument for restraining the growth of nondefense spending, which he used to transform the domestic agenda.

To a considerable extent the success of Reagan's economic policies has produced a new politics of deficits (Peterson, 1985). The taming of inflation through monetary policy has undermined the traditional belief that large budget deficits cause inflation (Cameron, 1985:278). Insofar as the business cycle is the outcome of monetary policy, it is possible for politicians to ignore the short-run effects of deficits (Peterson, 1985:395). Politicians continue to make ritualistic denunciations of deficits, but few of them are willing to cut popular or strongly supported programs or to raise taxes to eliminate them.

It is only in the long run that deficits are now regarded as dangerous because eventually they reduce private investment by diverting capital into public sector spending. This slows the rate of growth in economic output and productivity (Stein, 1983:347). Paul Peterson argues that the new politics of deficits will continue until the next major recession, at which time even more massive increases in annual deficits and the public debt will lead to the general belief that "the cause of economic and political turmoil is the growing public debt" (1985:397).

It is too early to determine whether the conservative public philosophy established during the Reagan administration is a permanent feature of American politics. Theodore Lowi, citing the historic resiliency of liberalism, argues that Reagan's conservatism is but an interlude and that his only legacy will be the "lesson that we have nothing to fear from substantial innovation" (1984:49–56). Although Lowi does not believe the new conservatism provides satisfactory solutions to the problems of the policies based on the liberal public philosophy of the New Deal, he offers as a source of solutions only a small third-party movement. In contrast, Herbert Stein believes that a conservative public policy consensus has been established. That consensus seeks to restrain inflation rather than achieve full employment, to expand rather than redistribute wealth, and to place greater reliance on monetary than fiscal policy and on free markets over regulation and public enterprise (Stein, 1983:322).

The accomplishments of the Reagan administration attest to the political viability of the new conservative public philosophy and the policies based on it. The expansion of federal distributive programs has been brought under control, deregulation has been extended and markets made more competitive, the domestic policy agenda has been redefined in terms of conservative values, and the United States has strengthened its international standing. The durability of the new public philosophy and the conservative policies implemented pursuant to it will only be visible in the long run. It is apparent, however, that the rationalizing policies adopted as solutions to the problems of the welfare state, principally overload, have at least temporarily resulted in a new public philosophy and a greatly modified policy agenda. The proposition that policy produces its own politics has received additional support.

THE BRITISH CASE

The British welfare state originated during two reformist periods. The Liberal government of 1906–14 established old age pensions, unemployment insurance, and compulsory health insurance that provided sickness pay and limited medical services. The major remaining institutions and programs of the welfare state were primarily the handiwork of the Labour government of 1945–51. It established a system of family allowances and the National Health Service, nationalized several key industries, and embarked on a massive public housing program under which at least 40 percent of all dwellings were constructed by public authorities in every year from 1945 to 1969 (King, 1973:300).

The public philosophy that furnished the basis for the British welfare state was a social democratic consensus that combined Keynesian economics, Fabian socialism, and Tory pragmatism. At its core was a commitment to state action as a means of achieving a better life for all. State action included social welfare programs such as unemployment pay and social security benefits to alleviate the effects of unemployment and poverty, economic planning, and macroeconomic demand management through fiscal policy. A market-oriented economy coexisted with a substantial public sector. Decisions on the addition of social programs or the expansion of public enterprise were made on pragmatic rather than ideological grounds: the chief questions were how and when, and not whether to act (Heald, 1983:5). Wages and benefits for most workers, in the public as well as the private sectors, were determined through collective bargaining. Continued improvement of the quality of life would be made possible through economic growth resulting from government's management of the economy in accordance with Keynesian principles. For three decades after 1945 both Labour and Conservative governments worked, more or less successfully, within the framework of the social democratic consensus to "promote economic prosperity, provide generous welfare services, and increase the take-home pay of ordinary citizens" (Rose, 1986:18). Beer (1982) has described British politics during this period as "collectivist."

The social democratic consensus began to erode during the 1960s and 1970s owing to the inability of governments to control inflation and maintain full employment; economic growth slowed to the point where it could no longer sustain continued increases in the social benefit programs of the welfare state. The Conservative government of Prime Minister Edward Heath, elected in 1970, had pledged to rely on the free market to control wages and prices and keep government intervention in the economy to a minimum. It reduced taxes to stimulate investment and, as unemployment began to rise in 1971, it increased spending by more than 10 percent through 1973 (Ashford, 1981:112). The public sector current account surplus of £.7 billion in 1970 became a deficit of £1.6 billion by 1972. The Heath government also relaxed monetary policy so that the money supply increased by over 25 percent in 1972 and 1973. Employment rose rapidly in 1972, but so did inflation. The government's efforts to restrain wage increases buckled under union pressure that was highlighted by a national miners' strike in 1972. At that point the Heath government made a U-turn away from the neoliberal market-oriented policies that it had instituted in fulfillment of its 1970 election manifesto. It passed an Industry Act that authorized a three-stage incomes policy.[5] The government also reversed its opposition to intervention on behalf of failing industries when it provided subsidies to a nationalized shipbuilding firm and to Rolls Royce, the bankrupt aircraft engine manufacturer.

In October 1973, shortly before the first oil price shock, the government announced Phase III of its incomes policy. The miners' union refused to accept a settlement within the limits of Phase III and struck. The government called an election for February 1974 on the issue of its incomes policy and the strike. It lost narrowly.[6]

The new Labour government under Harold Wilson quickly settled with the miners, granting pay increases that averaged 2.5 times the Phase III limits and ended the incomes policy. It attempted to hold down wages through a voluntary "Social Contract" between the unions and the Labour party. In addition to restoration of free collective bargaining the Social Contract called for increases in pensions and in food and rent subsidies to be financed by redistributive income tax increases. The government kept its commitments under the Social Contract, but the unions, in the face of rampaging inflation that reached an annual rate of 24.2 percent in 1975 (Stewart, 1977:169, 262), sought and won large wage settlements.

In July 1975 the Wilson government announced a pay policy that limited weekly increases for a one-year period. The Wilson government's incomes policy was formally voluntary, but its acceptance by the Trade Unions Congress (TUC), in exchange for specific commitments to hold down prices and implement an industrial policy through a new National Enterprise Board, gave it statutory effect. The agreement between the government and the TUC was successfully renewed in 1976 and 1977, but it broke down in 1978 amid industrial unrest that led to large wage settlements.

The Labour government of 1974–79 also experienced difficulty in its efforts to limit the growth of spending. The commitments made to secure union restraint on wages, the effects of large settlements with public sector unions, and the overall impact of inflation pushed the deficit from £2.7 billion to £6.7 billion by the end of 1974 (Ashford, 1981:117). By July 1975 it was apparent that the Public Expenditure Survey Committee process for planning public spending at constant prices was unable to function effectively in an era of double-digit inflation. The Treasury announced that it would control spending by means of cash limits announced in advance and not subject to adjustment for inflation (indexing).

The Labour government was unable to restrain the growth of spending, and sterling suffered a series of crises in 1976. In order to restore stability to the pound, the government negotiated a loan from the International Monetary Fund in December 1976. In the Letter of Intent to the IMF, Chancellor of the Exchequer Denis Healy committed the government gradually to reduce public sector borrowing (by curbing spending) in order to limit monetary growth (Riddell, 1983:59). Earlier in 1976 Healy had begun to publish money supply targets (Keegan, 1984:92).

As the Labour government moved through its term, it became apparent that traditional Keynesian solutions to economic problems were increasingly ineffective. A change in both the popular mood and the intellectual climate occurred. Recipients of government benefits came under attack as undeserving "scroungers," and along with a growing governmental bureaucracy and powerful unions were blamed for Britain's economic decline (Heald, 1983:7). In the political community, politicians, journalists, academics, and civil servants embraced monetarism and adopted the view that Britain's problems stemmed from excessive diversion of resources to the public sector (King, 1985:478). Anthony King marks the end of Keynesian economic hegemony as occurring when Prime Minister James Callaghan told the 1976 Labour party conference that the Keynesian option "no longer exists," that increased public spending was economically harmful. However, his government did not follow through by implementing reductions in public spending. Nor did it offer an alternative to the social democratic consensus. However, it did adopt monetarism in 1976 when it signed an agreement to receive a loan from the IMF.

The conservative alternative to the postwar consensus was developed by Margaret Thatcher and her followers after she gained the leadership of the Conservative party in 1975. The alternative conservative public philosophy, often called Thatcherism, has two foundation stones, monetarism and an unswerving belief in the free market. Thatcherism's economic precepts are derived from Milton Friedman and Friedrich Hayek. Its principal theoretician has been Sir Keith Joseph, a close associate of Thatcher who, with her support, founded the Centre for Policy Studies and later served as education minister in her government. Joseph argued that since 1945 the Conservative party had compromised too much with socialism and acquiesced excessively in the collectivist policies of the Labour party (Riddell, 1983:25). This had led it to neglect the benefits of the free market. Joseph also maintained that Conservative support of egalitarian policies had undermined initiative and responsibility. What was required was a reassertion of the importance of the profit motive and the spirit of entrepreneurship.

In addition to reliance on monetarism, Thatcherism advocated fiscal discipline, privatization, and restraint of trade union power as necessary means to the control of inflation and the restoration of economic growth. Fiscal discipline required the reduction of public spending to keep borrowing under control. Excessive public sector borrowing was regarded as a major cause of inflation. The principal program areas targeted for cuts were nationalized industries, employment, housing subsidies, and transfer payments (Riddell, 1983:32). However, defense and law enforcement were to be increased. Privatization would strengthen markets and restore an entrepreneurial environment and incentives for investment (Wolfe, 1985). Closed shops should only be allowed after a secret ballot. Governmental involvement in pay settlements was in principle undesirable, which was one more reason for reducing the size of the public sector.

In contrast to the conservative public philosophy developed in the United States and implemented by the Reagan administration, Thatcherism rejected proposals to improve the supply side through broad tax cuts of the Kamp-Roth model. It did advocate selective reductions in personal income taxes to encourage investment, but not at the expense of raising the public sector borrowing requirement. Nor did it concern itself with such issues as abortion, pornography, and prayer in public schools. Although both the American and British conservative public philosophies have strong overtones of right-wing populism, the British variant is more exclusively economic in its orientation.

The Thatcher government took power in May 1979 committed to break sharply with the collectivist policies of its Labour and Conservative predecessors. The government set forth three primary economic objectives, based on its conservative public philosophy: reduction of inflation by controlling the growth of the money supply and restricting public sector borrowing; restoring investment incentives by reducing taxes on income; and limiting the growth of government spending so that it would be compatible with the objectives of reducing inflation and borrowing and enhancing economic growth (Pliatzky, 1982:176–77).

Monetarism has been the cornerstone of the Thatcher government's economic policies from the outset. However, it had difficulty meeting its targets for the rate of growth of the money supply (sterling M3) during its first four years in office. Moreover, its inability to limit the growth of expenditures has resulted in heavier public sector borrowing than planned. In 1979 the government found inflation running at a 10 percent annual rate and experienced further inflationary pressures as oil prices doubled late in the year. In its first budget the government reduced income taxes (the top marginal rate dropped from 83 to 60 percent and the basic rate from 33 to 30 percent). However, it had to increase the Value Added Tax (VAT) from 8 to 15 percent to balance the income tax cuts and to help compensate for an inflationary pay settlement reached with civil service unions that stemmed from a campaign promise. The VAT hike and the public sector pay settlement sharply increased inflation. In contrast to the Reagan administration, the Thatcher government refused to undermine its monetary policy by running a high deficit to finance the income tax cuts. Apparently that option was never considered.

In 1980 inflation soared past 20 percent, interest rates climbed sharply as a result of restrictive monetary policy, and unemployment began a sustained rise that has not yet abated. A deep recession that began in 1980, when economic growth was a negative 2.3 percent, continued until late 1982. The combination of inflation and recession frustrated efforts to cut spending, but the government benefited from North Sea oil revenues, thus reducing the need for additional public sector borrowing.

In March 1980 the government announced a Medium Term Financial Strategy (MTFS) for its macroeconomic policy. The MTFS extended the time frame for the principal monetary target, sterling M3, from one to four years. Sir Terry Burns, the Thatcher government's chief economic adviser, argued that an extended time frame was an important aspect to the government's monetary policy because it would insure sufficient stability for business planning (Burns, 1981:47). Burns also asserted that the MTFS would facilitate the coordination of monetary and fiscal policy, which itself was a central element in the MTFS. The government's principal objective was to control inflation. This would be accomplished through a progressive reduction in the rate of growth of the money supply, which would be achieved by reducing the Public Sector Borrowing Requirement (PSBR) and management of interest rates (OECD, 1984:9). Ideally, lower public expenditures and a smaller PSBR would lead to slower monetary growth with lower interest rates and much less inflation. Ultimately this would result in increased economic growth at full employment. As William Keegan observed, "the beauty of the MTFS was that it linked the government's principal political aims with its economic philosophy and offered light at the end of the tunnel if all went well" (Keegan, 1984:143).

In addition to the macroeconomic objectives of the MTFS, the Thatcher government pursued microeconomic policies designed to strengthen market forces. These efforts included extensive deregulation, ending of intervention in private sector collective bargaining, changes in tax policy designed to encourage investment, and a sweeping privatization program. Another major dimension of privatization was the sale of publicly owned council houses to their occupants. In addition to strengthening markets and reducing the role and size of government, privatization provided the additional advantage of replacing the "often ineffective political control of public sector unions with that of the market" (Wolfe, 1985:27).

The Thatcher government's antipathy toward labor unions was manifested in major changes in labor relations laws. The changes were designed to promote flexibility in labor markets. The effect of the changes was to weaken unions by making them legally liable for unlawful industrial action, including secondary boycotts, and to require the use of secret ballots to authorize strikes, elect executive union committees, and institute closed shops (OECD, 1986:30). Prospective strikes that union leaders supported against Austin-Rover in 1984 and British Rail in 1985 were avoided when members voted against them. A yearlong strike by the miners' union in 1984–85, for which the union leadership refused to request authorization in a secret ballot of the members, received limited support from other unions and the public and was opposed by the TUC. The new labor legislation and high levels of unemployment that accompanied and followed the recession of

1980–82 have resulted in a decline in industrial stoppages to the lowest level in fifty years (OECD, 1986:30).

The Thatcher government's efforts to reduce public expenditures were less successful as the public expenditure share of Gross Domestic Product (GDP) rose from 40.5 percent in 1978–79 to 43 percent in 1983–84 (Government's Expenditure Plans, 1984:9). This occurred as a result of deliberately increased spending on defense and law enforcement, agricultural program increases due to Common Market obligations, indexing of social security pensions and other entitlement programs, and countercyclical increases engendered by the recession (King, 1985:489). There were also expenditure overruns by local governmental authorities that the government was unable to prevent, and interest on public indebtedness climbed because of high interest rates. On the other hand, spending on housing was sharply reduced. Public sector borrowing has not been as high as might otherwise have been the case because of income from North Sea oil production, although the 1984–85 miners' strike is estimated to have added £2.75 billion to the PSBR (OECD, 1986:15).

The achievements of Thatcherism are substantial. Inflation has been brought to heel, the annual rate having dropped from 20 percent in 1980 to between 4.5 and 5 percent in 1986. The PSBR declined from 4.8 percent of GDP in 1978–79 to 3.1 percent in 1984–85 (OECD, 1986:9). Labor productivity rose by 13.5 percent during the same period (OECD, 1986:24). During 1981–85, and continuing into 1986, the longest sustained recovery from a recession since 1945 occurred, as GDP grew at an annual rate of 2.9 percent (OECD, 1986:35).

The principal negative outcome of Thatcherism has been the stabilization of unemployment at levels unknown since the Great Depression. For the past two years it has been at or above 13 percent (OECD, 1986:22). Part of the rise in unemployment stemmed from actions taken to "shake out" restrictive labor practices that contributed heavily to low economic productivity (Wilkinson, 1983). Another reason for high unemployment is continued inflexibility in the labor market. Workers who have lost their jobs either lack skills required by modern technology, or are unwilling to accept lower-paying employment in service industries or refuse to relocate to obtain work. A crucial issue is whether the benefits gained through low inflation, increased productivity, and more competitive markets are worth the costs of substantially greater structural unemployment (Heald, 1983:277).

Unquestionably, the Thatcher government's solutions to the problems of the Keynesian social democratic welfare state and its policies have changed Britain's political economy. The growth of government has peaked, the public sector has shrunk in size and importance, markets have replaced the state as the preferred instrument of resource allocation, competition has been strengthened internally and externally, and the power of labor has been greatly reduced. However, the basic structure of the welfare state remains intact: the National Health Service, social security and other entitlement programs, the educational system, and substantial residual state intervention in the economy. For the time being at least, a conservative public philosophy that is unabashedly committed to capitalism, nationalism, and Victorian values prevails. Its durability is problematic, however, given the high level of structural unemployment and accompanying personal hardship that have been its principal negative externalities. Anthony King warns that "in cities like Liverpool and Glasgow, demoralisation is almost total and violence lurks only a little distance below the surface" (1985:491).

In Britain as in the United States rationalizing policies adopted in response to governmental overload have, at least temporarily, altered the pattern of politics. The postwar social democratic consensus that produced over three decades of collectivist politics has been replaced by a conservative public philosophy, Thatcherism, that reduces substantially the role of the state and increases reliance on markets, and the policy agenda has been redefined with conservative issues predominating. In addition, there has been a major reduction in the political power of labor unions and of civil servants. The sweep of the changes in Britain exceeds that of those that have occurred in the United States under Reaganism, but there is substantial similarity between them. The main reasons for the greater extent of the changes in Britain than in the United States appear to lie in the greater amount of distress in the British economy and a higher degree of overload resulting from a more extensively developed welfare state. In both countries rationalizing policies have produced substantial new problems: high structural unemployment in Britain and a large and politically unmanageable budget deficit in the United States.

THE CANADIAN CASE

Unlike Britain and the United States, the Canadian welfare state did not have its origins in a period of reformist legislation. Public ownership, while much more extensive than in the United States, was extended gradually, starting with provincial telephone and electric utilities prior to World War I and moving to the Canadian National Railroad in 1919, broadcasting in the early 1930s, and air transport in 1937 (King, 1973:302). Similarly, social service programs were established incrementally, beginning with the development of educational systems by the provinces in the late nineteenth century and moving to old age pensions in 1927 and housing and unemployment compensation legislation during the 1930s.[7] Family allowances and expanded pension plans were adopted shortly after World War II, federally supported provincially administered medical insurance and service schemes developed in the period from 1947 to 1966, and a second round of federal social programs, including the Canada Pension Plan and assistance to higher education and manpower training, occurred during the 1960s (Doern and Phidd, 1983:233). Both Liberal and Conservative governments were involved in the development of the Canadian welfare state. For the most part that development took place without protracted ideological controversy. It was rather a series of pragmatic responses to economic and social problems and needs. Canada, unlike the United States, did not have a strong tradition of opposition to positive use of the state that had to be overcome.

Although Canada suffered economic decline and social privation during the Great Depression, it did not develop a reformist public philosophy equivalent to that provided by the New Deal in the United States (Doern and Phidd, 1983:231). Keynesian economics provided the basis of a Canadian public philosophy in the postwar period. It justified an economic stabilization role for the federal government through management of aggregate demand and an expanded program of state-supported social programs to protect individuals against the hazards of life in an industrial society. The Canadian public philosophy of the postwar era had a liberal foundation, but it had strong elements of socialism and traditional conservatism or Toryism that made it more hospitable to collectivism than the American public philosophy has ever been. Canada's postwar public philosophy stood between the social welfare democracy of Britain's collectivism and the organic liberalism of the New Deal.

Keynesianism provided the rationale for the Canadian public philosophy, but Canadian fiscal policy was not "fully Keynesian" (Doern and Phidd, 1983:232). Liberal governments also relied on tariff and tax policies to encourage foreign investment as a means of maintaining prosperity. The issue of how economic expansion would affect different segments of society was resolved by allowing the corporate sector substantial freedom to expand in exchange for support of government programs that enhanced individual economic security (Laxer, 1984:8). The first Trudeau government added a qualitative dimension to the public philosophy by emphasizing the reduction of regional economic disparities and the improvement of linguistic, cultural, and individual rights (Doern and Phidd, 1983:233). These objectives were to be accomplished by carefully establishing priorities and planning rationally to implement them.

During most of the Trudeau era (1968:84) Canada faced the problems of inflation, unemployment, and sporadic economic growth. As did the United States and Britain, it confronted such problems as big government and governmental overload that had emerged with the maturation of the welfare state. Public expenditures increased rapidly in the early 1970s, and the first oil price shock gave an indication that traditional fiscal measures to stabilize the economy were no longer adequate.

Following the July 1974 election in which the minority Trudeau government won a majority after its May anti-inflation budget was defeated in the House of Commons, an unsuccessful attempt was made to gain control over the growth of expenditures through planning. The Priorities Exercise that began in September 1974 ended a year later without clear resolution. According to Richard French, the Priorities Exercise failed primarily because it neglected to take account of inflation and unemployment (1980:80–84). It placed a list of sixteen abstract priorities ahead of the deteriorating condition of the economy. The exercise collapsed in October 1975 when the government announced a program of wage and price controls to be administered by an Anti-Inflation Board. The program remained in effect for three years and was moderately successful but lacked popular support.

The Trudeau government took two additional steps in 1975 that constituted a response to changed economic circumstances. It initiated indexing of income taxes to protect against bracket creep, and the Bank of Canada announced that it would set targets for growth of the money supply and deal with economic shocks by allowing greater flexibility in exchange rates (French, 1980:67). In 1977 the government adopted a limited industrial policy based on consultation with key economic sectors. The consultations dealt with public actions that could encourage economic development and help increase productivity. In November 1978 a new cabinet committee, the Board of Economic Development Ministers, supported by a new Ministry of State for Economic Development, was established to enhance industrial development. French describes the sectoral approach of Canadian industrial policy as an incrementalist compromise that maintained "a degree of movement . . . without the political pressures from threatened interests which the adoption of . . . 'bold alternatives' for an industrial strategy would inevitably create" (1980:129).

By late 1978 neoconservative themes became commonplace in Liberal statements. A 1976 discussion paper, The Way Ahead, stated the government's commitment to the market and "fundamental social goals" (French, 1980:69). The question was how to pursue social goals more efficiently. Other conservative themes that received attention from the Liberal government included the need for industrial expansion and expenditure restraint.[8] At the same time, however, the government initiated the Child Tax Credit and a program of investment tax credits for economically depressed regions.

The minority Conservative government of Prime Minister Joe Clark, elected in May 1979, was notable mainly for the brevity of its term in office and for the implementation of a new system of expenditure management. The Clark government fell in December 1979 when its first budget, which was strongly anti-inflationary, was defeated. The expenditure management system combined a five-year fiscal framework encompassing revenues and expenditures with a set of specific expenditure limits for policy sectors known as envelopes. The ten expenditure envelopes consisted of related departments and programs. Control over allocations to the expenditure envelopes was lodged in the Cabinet Committee on Priorities and Planning. Responsibility for making allocations within the ten envelopes resided in Planning and Priorities and four other cabinet committees (Campbell, 1983:196).

The envelope system, as it has come to be called, increased budgetary discipline by centralizing overall responsibility for allocations. This enabled the cabinet to indicate its priorities according to policy sectors and required new programs and programs seeking additional funding to compete within their particular envelope. The impact of envelope budgeting has been felt, however, "largely at the margin" (Van Loon, 1983:94). Normal political pressures, boundary disputes between envelopes, and emergency situations have resulted in special allocations and the creation of special envelopes that have weakened the effectiveness of the system, which has survived to this writing.

The Trudeau government that returned to power in February 1980 committed itself to a broad program of action that had both liberal and neoconservative elements. The major thrust of its program, however, was strongly nationalistic (as opposed to regional or provincial in orientation) and intended to enhance federal visibility and presence (Gillespie and Maslove, 1982:42–43). Whenever feasible, the government pursued its objectives by acting directly upon individuals, corporations, and institutions rather than through the provincial governments as had been traditional under the Canadian welfare state. The government's program was embodied in five major initiatives: patriation of the Constitution with an entrenched Charter of Rights; enactment of the National Energy Program (NEP); development of western Canada through establishment of the Western Development Fund; and renegotiation with provincial governments of funding arrangements for social programs. Macroeconomic policies emerged out of the context established by the five major initiatives.

Patriation of the Constitution with the Charter of Rights was intended to promote Canadian national unity and to bind Quebec firmly to Anglophone Canada. It also strengthened the federal government, and the Liberals sought to build party strength through it. It succeeded on the first and second counts, but not the third.

The NEP, announced in October 1980, was the second pillar of the Liberal government's nationalism/federal unity strategy. It was a comprehensive program through which the government pursued partisan political, fiscal, economic, and regional policy objectives. The key features of the NEP were Canadian determination of a national price for oil; diversion of resource revenue from the producing provinces to Ottawa; expansion of Petro-Canada, the state-owned oil company established in 1975; and a substantial increase in Canadian ownership in the industry (Doern, 1984:37). The NEP shifted incentives for exploration and development from the tax system to expenditure grants, thus strengthening the federal government's ability to direct exploration and development on the federally controlled Canada Lands in the Arctic and offshore and away from the provincially controlled Western sedimentary basin (Doern, 1984:34). The NEP also authorized revenues in the form of federal export taxes and petroleum surtaxes to help fund its provisions. Opposition to the NEP was strongest in Alberta, the principal oil-producing province, and in the United States.

The NEP sought to take advantage of the opportunities open to resource-based economies in international trade. It relied heavily on resource-related megaprojects and afforded opportunity for greater federal government intervention in the economy at the expense of the private sector and the producing provinces, and it promised to enrich the federal coffers at minimal cost to the government in terms of electoral support. Opposition in the lightly populated producing provinces was more than balanced by the benefits that flowed to the heavily populated consuming provinces.

The Western Development Fund of approximately C$2.0 billion to be spent between 1981–82 and 1985–86 was part of the Liberal government's strategy to strengthen the party in western Canada, a region in which it had ceased to be competitive since 1972. The fund concentrated almost entirely on improving the western transportation system. Its objective was to increase infrastructure investment with resultant benefits for economic development, but its impact has been minimal.

The renegotiation of federal-provincial fiscal arrangements grew out of the favorable revenue positions of the three westernmost provinces, which were running surpluses in the early 1980s, and the seven eastern provinces, which were incurring deficits. The federal government sought to reduce support for health and education programs so that it could redirect the funds into programs over which it exercised more control.

Beyond the Constitution and the NEP, the agenda of the Liberal government was both overly ambitious and unmanageable. There were political and economic difficulties. The political and ideological base was too narrow to support the five initiatives simultaneously and the nationalism/federal unity strategy could not overcome contradictions among them. The government's difficulty was especially acute with respect to the economic development initiative. As Doern put it: "how to foster *efficient* internationally competitive high growth industries, how to *stabilize* others, and how to do both while being *regionally* sensitive and suitably *nationalistic*" (Doern, 1983:13). Moreover, the Liberals were almost without support in the four western provinces that were contributing disproportionately to the costs of the Liberal policy initiatives and receiving few benefits.

Economic difficulties in the form of strong inflationary forces and rising unemployment frustrated the Liberal government's efforts to implement its energy, economic development, and social affairs priorities. It had approached macroeconomic policy by maintaining the use of monetary targets and continued use of the envelope system for expenditure control. The fiscal framework, which supposedly guides priority determination and expenditure control in the envelope system, was proving unreliable due to a combination of inflation, recession, high interest rates, and the unmanageability of the Liberals' agenda (Doern, 1983:14). The government's difficulties were made manifest in its budgets of November 1981 and June 1982.

The November 1981 budget, the government's second, stressed three somewhat contradictory themes, restraint, equity, and renewal. Restraint was necessary to reduce the deficit and control inflation. Equity would be achieved by closing tax loopholes and reducing income tax rates in the highest brackets. Presumably renewal of the economy and society would follow. The results were quite to the contrary. Expenditures rose as the recession deepened, inflation continued, and interest rates reached new highs. What additional revenues were produced were mainly redistributed to middle- and upper-income taxpayers. By most assessments the budget was a political and economic debacle (Doern and Phidd, 1983:252).

The June 1982 budget attempted to repair the damage that had resulted from the previous budget. It reaffirmed the commitment to monetary policy and budgetary restraint and rejected massive stimulation of the economy. Concentrating on inflation, it announced that it was holding increases in public sector wages to 6 percent in 1982–83 and 5 percent the following year. It also applied the "6-and-5" restraints to the indexing of federal income taxes and individual entitlement program benefits. The 6-and-5 approach appears to have reflected growing popular opposition to the bureaucracy and to the growth of government (Doern, 1983:14).

The Liberal government's economic difficulties eased as recovery from the recession began in early 1983 and continued through the remainder of its tenure. Inflation declined, interest rates dropped, and unemployment fell slowly from its peak of over 12 percent to near 10 percent. However, the recovery, which has continued to the present, did not end the government's political troubles. Two major economic problems remained unsolved: a large and growing federal deficit, which rose from 5.0 percent of GNP in 1982 to 6.3 percent in 1985 (OECD, 1985:18), and high unemployment. Canadians grew increasingly weary of Prime Minister Trudeau and the Liberals, in power since 1968 except for the brief interlude under the Clark government. The sense that change was likely and indeed desirable grew in 1983 when the Tories selected Brian Mulroney, a Quebec businessman with no prior parliamentary experience, as their new leader.

The Mulroney Tories did not, however, present a clear ideological alternative to the dominant liberal public philosophy. They maintained greater continuity with past Tory views on economic and social policy than either the Thatcherites in Britain or the Reaganauts in the United States. They did, however, stress greater reliance on the market and reaffirm their commitment to monetarism. They called for expenditure constraints, reduced regulation, some (but not too much) privatization, lower taxes, and less economic nationalism (Prince, 1983:45). They maintained that economic growth could come only through private investment and sought to stimulate it through tax policy. They pledged themselves to reduce the deficit, keep inflation under control, sustain healthy economic growth, and increase employment. In most respects their approach to economic policy resembled that of the Liberals. The principal differences in the Tory alternative were greater stress on market forces and the private sector and abandonment of economic nationalism.

In the area of social policy the Mulroney Tories remained what Michael Prince calls "reluctant but paternalistic collectivists" (1983:39). A major Tory proposal called for pension reform that emphasized greater reliance on the private sector, more individual responsibility, and increases in coverage, contributions, and governmental safeguards.

They also proposed to limit spending on a wide range of social programs: family allowances, unemployment compensation, higher education, medical services, and job creation.

The alternative to Liberal governments and the liberal public philosophy presented by the Mulroney Tories was distinctively different in several of its emphases. It resembled the conservative public philosophies developed by Thatcher and Reagan, but it also had strong overtones of the dominant liberal public philosophy. It was not a radical departure from the course of Canadian public policy since the 1930s nor did it promise a counterrevolution.[9] What it lacked to make it truly radical and counterrevolutionary was a strong, ideologically based rejection of both the party's recent past and the liberal public philosophy.

The Mulroney government came to power in a landslide in September 1984. (It won 211 of 282 House of Commons seats with the Liberals reduced to 39). Since taking power, the government has had to strike a balance between its promises to reduce federal spending and increase reliance on markets and pressures from economic, regional, and social groups to maintain programs of special interest to them. Its accomplishments after three years are both modest and mixed.

In its initial Economic and Fiscal Statement of November 1984 the Mulroney government proposed a strategy of deficit reduction and stimulation of the supply side. It moved quickly to downplay economic nationalism and reduce regulatory intrusiveness by repealing much of the NEP and transforming the Foreign Investment Review Agency (established by the Trudeau government in 1973) into Investment Canada, a promotional agency. It also relaxed transportation regulations. Privatization moves have featured the sale of DeHavilland, an aircraft manufacturer, to Boeing and plans to sell Canadian Arsenals, parts of Canada Development Corporation, and Teleglobe Canada. The approach to privatization has been pragmatic rather than ideological.

The Mulroney government continued monetary targeting with customary close attention to financial developments in the United States. Its fiscal policy has incorporated an initiative to reduce the deficit. In its first budget, in May 1985, decreases in economic development and energy expenditures were offset by increases in spending for social programs (Maslove, 1985:24–25). The combination of minor tax and budget changes that did little to reduce the deficit reflected the government's deep concern over the high rate of unemployment. In temporizing, the government passed up a major opportunity to reduce the deficit while placing the blame on its predecessor. The government's March 1986 budget attacked the deficit directly by proposing a C$5 billion reduction financed primarily through increased taxes. The budget appeared to be designed to shore up the Canadian dollar and paid little attention to its effects on investment, economic growth, and development.

The final major policy innovation of the Mulroney government has been its drive to open discussions with the United States leading to the establishment of free trade between the two countries. This is both a further step away from economic nationalism and a commitment to reliance on market forces to stimulate growth and insure long-run prosperity. The political consequences of this initiative, especially in central Canada, are problematic for the Tories. They may not be realized, however, as powerful protectionist forces in Washington, including a strong bipartisan majority on the Senate Finance Committee, are opposed to the idea.

The record of the Mulroney government to date does not provide convincing evidence that the Canadian policy agenda has been revolutionized or even profoundly altered. While there have been changes in emphasis, the government has yet to make its mark. Many of the policy changes associated with the resurgence of conservatism such as monetarism, fiscal restraint, and a concern over governmental overload occurred during the previous Liberal governments headed by Pierre Trudeau. Popular support for the Mulroney Tories had fallen sharply by the winter of 1986, and in 1985 the provincial Liberals gained control of the governments in Ontario and Quebec. Moreover, by mid-1987 the socialist NDP had passed the Conservatives and pulled even with the Liberals in the polls.

There are undoubtedly many reasons why the Canadian conservative resurgence was later in arriving and appears to be less well established than the British and U.S. counterparts. Three explanations come quickly to mind. First, the problems engendered by welfare state programs were not perceived as being as serious in Canada as in Britain and the United States. Canadians appear during the 1970s and early 1980s to have been more concerned with issues of national identity, Quebec separatism, and federal-provincial relations than with governmental overload. Second, it seems likely that Canadians recognize, consciously or not, that their economic well-being is substantially determined by events and conditions in the United States. Because Canada's ability to shape its economic destiny is limited, proposals for sweeping changes in economic policy are not embraced with ideological fervor. New policies that show signs of not living up to advance billing quickly lose support. Finally, the Canadian conservative resurgence has lacked forceful ideological leadership. Whatever else Brian Mulroney may be, he is not an ideologue seeking to change the role of government in Canadian life and to redefine the policy agenda.

Canada has adopted most of the rationalizing policies that the United States and Britain employed to cope with the overload problems of an expanding welfare state—temporary wage and price controls, monetarism, and expenditure restraint. However, the pattern of Canadian politics did not change as it did in the other two Anglo-American democracies. Neither the public philosophy, the agenda, nor the balance of political forces were appreciably altered. The Canadian case suggests that when economic problems are not the primary concern of an industrial democracy and rationalizing policies are not packaged ideologically, then the impact of those policies on political patterns is not readily apparent and marginal at most. Canada's continuing problems with budget deficits and structural unemployment suggest that those problems result primarily from factors other than the effects of rationalizing policies.

CONCLUSION

Beginning in the mid-1970s the three Anglo-American democracies sought solutions for the problems of inflation, slow economic growth, and governmental overload. Those solutions involved changes in macro and micro economic policies. The principal macroeconomic rationalizing policies were monetarism, fiscal restraint, and tax incentives to increase investment. The major microeconomic rationalizing policies were deregulation and privatization. The basic thrust of these policies was to solve major economic and social problems by reducing the role of government in the economy.

These efforts have had mixed results. The shift in macroeconomic policy, from primary emphasis on demand management to control of the money supply and increasing the supply of investment capital, has brought inflation under control, restored economic growth to moderate levels, and been accompanied by some increases in productivity. However, structural unemployment is very high in Britain (13 percent), high in Canada (10 percent), and at a higher level in the United States (7 percent) than would have been regarded as acceptable from 1945 to 1980.

The commitment to fiscal restraint, while rhetorically absolute, has been effective only in Britain. Both the American and Canadian deficits have continued to grow as governments in both countries have been unable or unwilling to make the politically difficult choices —cut popular spending programs and/or increase taxes—required to reduce them substantially. Large deficits appear to produce short-run political advantages to governments and to have few short-run economic disadvantages. It is only in the long run that deficits are regarded by some but not all economists and politicians as being potentially dangerous.

Microeconomic policy initiatives have led to substantial changes in economic infrastructures, resulting in increased roles for markets and a reduced role for the state. This transformation has been most extensive in Britain owing to a sweeping privatization program complemented by substantial deregulation, measures to reduce union power, government withdrawal from involvement in labor-management settlements, the sale of publicly owned housing, and reliance on the private sector to provide new housing stock. In the United States the commitment to enhanced market competition has been implemented primarily through deregulation and limited privatization. Canada has abandoned strong economic nationalism in favor of freer trade and encouragement to foreign investment. It has also engaged in limited privatization and deregulation. Problems resulting from such microeconomic policy initiatives are not yet apparent. The effects of rationalizing policies on political patterns in the three countries are mixed. Conservative governments have come to power with extensive electoral support, but their longevity has not been established. The Thatcher government won a decisive third election victory in June 1987. The Mulroney government's popular support has fallen below that of both opposition parties—the Liberals and the New Democrats—but much can happen before the next election. The Reagan administration's grip on power remains quite firm, but has been weakened by the Iran-Contra scandal.

More lasting than the current conservative governments perhaps has been the development of conservative alternatives to the liberal and social democratic public philosophies that have held sway since World War II. These have been most extensively developed in Britain and the United States where they were offered to the electorate as clear, ideologically based alternatives providing a sharp break with the past. The Canadian alternative is neither as sharply defined ideologically nor as clearly disdainful of the liberal welfare state. It is much too soon to determine whether any of the alternative conservative public philosophies have displaced their predecessors. At this time it appears more likely that this has happened in Britain or the United States than in Canada. The policy agendas in both of those countries have been substantially redefined to the point where the election of a Labour government or a Democratic administration seems highly unlikely to bring a return to the status quo ante Thatcher or Reagan. The economic and social role of government has been reduced substantially, more so in Britain than in the United States if only because it was greater to begin with, and restoration is not at issue. Opposition parties on the left are muted in their criticism of the market emphasis and focus their attacks on the government to appeals for greater compassion accompanied by promises to restore benefit cuts, distribute tax burdens more equitably, and administer the welfare state more efficiently.

Similar observations apply to Canada, but less emphatically. The Canadian conservative resurgence came later than the British and American and with less intensity. The alternative public philosophy is not as ideological and does not break as sharply with the past as do Thatcherism and Reaganism. Policy changes under the Mulroney government have been less sweeping than those made under Thatcher and Reagan. The emphases are similar—monetarism, free markets, and competition—although less emphatic.

The Canadian experience suggests another possibility: that the conservative resurgences in Britain and the United States are merely periods of adjustment in the established political regimes, albeit more intensely experienced than in Canada. The absence of any notable changes in the pluralistic pattern of politics in each country, with powerful organized interests still in a position to limit the scope of policy changes, supports this thesis.

Has then a new politics with a conservative regime and accompanying public philosophy been produced by rationalizing policies adopted in the three Anglo-American democracies? Not in the sense of radical transformation with political and economic upheavals. But at least in the United States and Britain there have been substantial changes in the form of modified political agendas, a reduced role for the state, and the development of a legitimate alternative to established liberal and social democratic public philosophies. This analysis does not provide complete confirmation of Lowi's thesis that policy determines politics, but at the least it has shown that policy can substantially affect the pattern of politics in a democratic society.

NOTES

1   Public philosophy is a broad term that acquired widespread recognition as the title of Lippmann's 1955 book in which he employed it to encompass natural law and the principles of bills of rights. It was for him "a body of positive principles and precepts which a good citizen cannot deny or ignore" (Lippmann, 1955:79). Lowi defined it as "any set of principles and criteria above and beyond the reach of government and statesmen by which the decisions of government are guided and justified" (1967:5). Beer later defined the public philosophy as "an outlook on public affairs which is accepted within a nation by a wide coalition and which serves to give definition to problems and direction to government policies dealing with them" (1979:5). Here the term will be used in the Lowi-Beer sense to refer to the dominant principles and values that guide policymakers in defining societal problems and developing solutions to them.

2   The reasons for this American exceptionalism are in dispute. Anthony King argues that the explanation lies in a broadly held belief that the state should play a limited role in society (King, 1973:422–423). Gary Klass rejects King's thesis that a Lockean consensus has limited the role of government in the United States. He maintains that ethnic, racial, religious, and regional conflicts have produced a disintegrative view of entitlement to social welfare services and a social service system that seeks to avoid such conflicts through limited and decentralized program structures (1985:427–450).

3   Carter's about-face on economic policy parallels the U-turn on monetary policy by the Labour government of James Callaghan in 1976. Both Callaghan and Carter were reacting to structural developments in the world economy, most importantly the increased price of oil.

4   The Reagan administration did not initially propose privatization as a means of enhancing economic competitiveness and reducing the role of government. Later it suggested the use of vouchers as a means of improving education. Most recently it

has called for the sale of Conrail, the public corporation created in the early 1970s to
take over the bankrupt Penn Central railroad system. Interestingly, it has not advocated sale of TVA or other major federal power facilities. The lack of emphasis on
privatization is more a reflection of the limited scale of public enterprise in the
United States than the absence of ideological opposition to it.

5 Phase III, which was administered by two new agencies, the Pay Board and the Price
Commission, called for limiting wage increases for a one-year period (Stewart,
1977:178).

6 Labour won 301 seats in the House of Commons, the Conservatives 297, and minor
parties 38. It formed a minority government. In the October 1974 election Labour
won a one-seat majority, with 319 seats as opposed to 277 for the Conservatives and
the remainder to minor parties.

7 The initial legislation, passed during the period 1930–35, was declared unconstitutional by the Judicial Committee of the Privy Council on the ground that under the
British North American Act it was beyond the power of the federal government (King,
1973:303). Later legislation (i.e., housing in 1938; unemployment compensation in
1940) remained in effect.

8 In August 1978, while most ministers were on vacation, Prime Minister Trudeau unilaterally ordered a C$2 billion cut in expenditures (Doern and Phidd, 1983: 249).

9 For an alternative perspective on the new Canadian conservatism, see James Laxer's
1984 report to the New Democratic party's Federal Caucus on Economic Policy. Laxer
describes the social contract offered by the "new conservatives" as harsh, mean, and
anchored in selfishness (Laxer, 1984:11).

REFERENCES

Ashford, Douglas E. 1981. *Policy and Politics in Britain: The Limits of Consensus.*
Philadelphia: Temple University Press.
Beer, Samuel H. 1979. "In Search of a New Public Philosophy." In Anthony King, ed.,
The New American Political System. Washington, D.C.: American Enterprise
Institute.
———. 1982. *Modern British Politics.* New York: W. W. Norton.
Birch, Anthony H. 1984. "Overload, Ungovernability and Delegitimation: The Theories
and the British Case." *British Journal of Political Science* 14: 135–60.
Brown, Lawrence D. 1983. *New Policies, New Politics: Government's Response to Gov-
ernment's Growth.* Washington, D.C.: Brookings Institution.
Burns, Terry. 1981. "Economic Policy and Prospects." *Public Money* 1: 45–52.
Cameron, David R. 1985. "Does Government Cause Inflation? Taxes, Spending, and
Deficits." In Leon N. Lindberg and Charles Maier, eds., *The Politics of Inflation and
Economic Stagnation.* Washington, D.C.: Brookings Institution.
Campbell, Colin. 1983. *Governments Under Stress.* Toronto: University of Toronto Press.
Doern, G. Bruce. 1983. "The Liberals and the Opposition: Ideas, Priorities and the
Imperatives of Governing Canada in the 1980s." In G. Bruce Doern, ed., *How Ottawa*

Spends 1983: The Liberals, the Opposition and Federal Priorities. Toronto: Lorimer.
————. 1984. "Energy Expenditures and the NEP: Controlling the Energy Leviathan." In Allan M. Maslove, ed., *How Ottawa Spends 1984: The New Agenda.* Toronto: Methuen.
————, and Richard W. Phidd. 1983. *Canadian Public Policy: Ideas, Structure, Process.* Toronto: Methuen.
Fishel, Jeff. 1985. *Presidents and Promises.* Washington, D.C.: Congressional Quarterly Press.
French, Richard D. 1980. *How Ottawa Decides: Planning and Industrial Policy-Making 1968–1980.* Toronto: Lorimer.
Gillespie, W. Irwin, and Allan M. Maslove. 1982. "Volatility and Visibility: The Federal Revenue and Expenditure Plan." In G. Bruce Doern, ed., *How Ottawa Spends Your Tax Dollars 1982: National Policy and Economic Development.* Toronto: Lorimer.
Government's Expenditure Plans. 1984. *The Government's Expenditure Plans 1984–85 to 1986–87.* London: Her Majesty's Stationery Office.
Heald, David. 1983. *Public Expenditure: Its Defence and Reform.* Oxford: Martin Robinson.
Huntington, Samuel P. 1975. "The Democratic Distemper." *The Public Interest* 41: 9–38.
Kaufman, William W. 1983. "The Defense Budget." In Joseph A. Pechman, ed., *Setting National Priorities: The 1984 Budget.* Washington, D.C.: Brookings Institution.
Keegan, William. 1984. *Mrs. Thatcher's Economic Experiment.* London: Allen Lane.
King, Anthony. 1973. "Ideas, Institutions and the Policies of Governments: A Comparative Analysis: Parts I and II." *British Journal of Political Science* 3: 291–313. "Part III." *BJPS* 3: 409–23.
————. 1975. "Overload: Problems of Governing in the 1970s." *Political Studies* 23: 284–96.
————. 1985. "Governmental Responses to Budget Scarcity: Great Britain." *Policy Studies Journal* 13: 476–95.
Klass, Gary M. 1985. "Explaining America and the Welfare State: An Alternative Theory." *British Journal of Political Science* 15: 427–50.
Laxer, James. 1984. "Taking Stock." *Canadian Forum,* January 7–16.
Lippmann, Walter. 1955. *The Public Philosophy.* Boston: Little, Brown. (References are to the 1956 Mentor edition. New York: New American Library.)
Lowi, Theodore J. 1967. "The Public Philosophy: Interest-Group Liberalism." *American Political Science Review* 61: 5–24.
————. 1969. *The End of Liberalism.* New York: W. W. Norton.
————. 1972. "Four Systems of Policy, Politics, and Choice." *Public Administration Review* 32: 298–310.
————. 1979. *The End of Liberalism,* 2nd ed. New York: W. W. Norton.
————. 1984. "Ronald Reagan—Revolutionary?" In Lester M. Salamon and Michael S. Lund, eds., *The Reagan Presidency and the Governing of America.* Washington, D.C.: Urban Institute Press.
Maslove, Allan M. 1985. "The Public Pursuit of Private Interests." In Allan M. Maslove, ed., *How Ottawa Spends 1985: Sharing the Pie.* Toronto: Methuen.

OECD, 1985. *OECD Economic Surveys 1984/1985 Canada*. Paris: OECD.

———. 1986. *Economic Surveys 1985/1986 United Kingdom*. Paris: OECD.

Olson, Mancur. 1982. *The Rise and Decline of Nations*. New Haven, Conn.: Yale University Press.

Palmer, John L., and Isabel V. Sawhill, eds. 1982. *The Reagan Experiment: An Examination of Economic and Social Policies Under the Reagan Administration*. Washington, D.C.: Urban Institute Press.

———, eds. 1984. *Reagan Record: An Assessment of America's Changing Domestic Priorities*. Cambridge, Mass.: Ballinger.

Peterson, Paul E. 1985. "The New Politics of Deficits." In John E. Chubb and Paul E. Peterson, eds., *The New Direction in American Politics*. Washington, D.C.: Brookings Institution.

Pliatzky, Leo. 1982. *Getting and Spending*. Oxford: Basil Blackwell.

Pollard, Sidney. 1982. *The Wasting of the British Economy: British Economic Policy 1945 to the Present*. New York: St. Martin's Press.

Prince, Michael J. 1983. "The Tories and the NDP: Alternative Governments or Ad Hoc Advocates?" In G. Bruce Doern, ed., *How Ottawa Spends 1983: The Liberals, the Opposition and Federal Priorities*. Toronto: Lorimer.

Riddell, Peter. 1983. *The Thatcher Government*. Oxford: Martin Robinson.

Rose, Richard. 1985. "The Programme Approach to the Growth of Government." *British Journal of Political Science* 15: 1–26.

———. 1986. *Politics in England: Persistence and Change*, 4th ed. Boston: Little, Brown.

Schambra, William A. 1982. "The Roots of the American Public Philosophy." *The Public Interest* 67: 36–48.

Schattschneider, E. E. 1935. *Politics, Pressures, and the Tariff*. Englewood Cliffs, N.J.: Prentice-Hall.

Stein, Herbert. 1984. *Presidential Economics*. New York: Simon and Schuster.

Stewart, Michael. 1977. *The Jekyll and Hyde Years: Politics and Economic Policy Since 1964*. London: J. M. Dent.

Thurow, Lester C. 1981. *The Zero-Sum Society*. New York: Penguin Books.

Van Loon, Richard J. 1983. "Ottawa's Expenditure Process: Four Systems in Search of Co-ordination." In G. Bruce Doern, ed., *How Ottawa Spends 1983: The Liberals, the Opposition, and Federal Priorities*. Toronto: Lorimer.

———, and Michael S. Whittington. 1981. *The Canadian Political System: Environment, Structure, and Process*, 3rd ed. Toronto: McGraw-Hill Ryerson.

Weaver, R. Kent. 1985. "Controlling Entitlements." In John E. Cubb and Paul E. Peterson, eds., *The New Direction in American Politics*. Washington, D.C.: Brookings Institution.

Wildavsky, Aaron. 1979. *Speaking Truth to Power: The Art and Craft of Policy Analysis*. Boston: Little, Brown.

Wolfe, Joel D. 1985. "Privatization and the Reshaping of Pluralist Democracy: The British Case." Paper presented at the annual meeting of the American Political Science Association, New Orleans.

5. Gulliver and the Lilliputians: Conservatism, Foreign Policy, and Alliance Relations

WILLIAM JAMES BOOTH

INTRODUCTION

The chapter that follows is principally concerned with the status of Alliance relations in a context that would have appeared uniquely favorable to increased Western solidarity in key foreign policy matters —that context being the presence of conservative governments in major Alliance partners, including the Anglo-American nations. This essay is not concerned with the impact of foreign policy issues on the electoral fortunes of the Anglo-American conservative parties. Foreign policy is largely an elite concern in these countries, and it had no role in the 1984 Conservative victory in Canada and little or no influence upon the coming to power of Prime Minister Thatcher in 1979 (though the Falklands War was important in Mrs. Thatcher's reelection). A more fruitful line of inquiry, then, is to explore the seemingly counterintuitive outcome alluded to above, that ideological affinities of these conservative governments failed to yield substantially increased cooperation in key foreign policy areas.

Among the many areas of foreign and trade policy that might have been selected for such a study, the issue of Alliance cohesion stands out in its singular importance. That importance rests on the Alliance's ability to secure its smaller members against threats to their independence and, on the other side, its ability to provide a consultative vehicle for America's leading role within the Western democratic com-

I would like to thank Ole Holsti and Peter Meekison for their valuable comments on the original version of this essay.

munity. Threats to the Alliance have come from without and within. The USSR has long sought to supplant the Atlantic Alliance with a continental European collective security arrangement, a development that would give the Soviets greater scope in the direct or, more likely, indirect employment of their military preponderance on the continent.

Tensions within the Alliance have, however, posed a greater challenge to its solidity than Soviet blandishments or saber rattling. Such tensions are not new (consider the 1956 Suez Crisis and the Euro-American conflict over the October 1973 Middle East war). What is characteristic of the recent period (roughly 1979–85) is the sustained nature of the tension as well as the fact that responsible political leaders and commentators on both sides of the Atlantic have openly called into question the value of the Alliance.

The argument of this essay is that whatever the common ideological ground of the Anglo-American governments may be, consensus in the foreign policy sphere remains elusive. Indeed, the presence in office of conservative governments has, in some important respects to be analyzed below, exacerbated rather than relieved strains within the Alliance. This perhaps unexpected development (see Prime Minister Thatcher's February 1981 speech quoted on p. 148) has its origins in the relations of dependency (especially in security matters) and the desire for independence and equality that form the core of the smaller powers' approach to the Alliance and, on the other side, in the superpower's understanding of the nature of its leading role (e.g., consultative or unilateral) and of what constitutes good faith among its partners.

This, in short, is the dilemma of Gulliver and the Lilliputians, the "Man-Mountain" and the little people among whom he must live. Readers of Swift's tale will recall the manner in which Captain Lemuel Gulliver extinguished the blaze in the Lilliputian Queen's apartment. This well-intentioned act clearly mortified Gulliver's little hosts and left them bitter; their bitterness must in turn have seemed to Gulliver to be nothing more than wretched ingratitude. However, in his voyage to Brobdingnag, Gulliver has the opportunity to experience the mortification of being a small man among giants. In Brobdingnag, Gulliver also learns how he must have been perceived by his Lilliputian hosts—how every fault, each wart, of the giants is magnified in the eyes of the little people and, moreover, how even the innocent actions of the Brobdingnagians can be menacing to their smaller visitor. It is regrettable that states do not have Gulliver's good fortune in being able to see themselves at one moment as a giant among the small and the next moment as powerless among giants. Such a change in perspective might enhance the large power's understanding of its smaller friends, who must necessarily worry over their independence and indeed existence in a world inhabited by two giants. It might also moderate the great power's suspicion of wretched ingratitude among its allies. As for the small and middle powers, it might teach them to moderate their criticisms of the giant's every flaw and instruct them in the difficulty of walking gently among so many fragile objects. The author in his study has this good fortune: in thought, he can conceive of Gulliver and his view of the world and of the Lilliputians, their fears and desires. The essay that follows is just such an experiment.

BACKGROUND

In order to properly appreciate the intra-alliance crisis of the 1980s it is necessary to sketch, with broad strokes, the recent origins of the foreign policy agendas of the Anglo-American partners, of Gulliver and the Lilliputians. This is necessary precisely because the conservative nationalism of the Reagan administration, on the one side, and the desire for both independence and cooperation with the United States that characterizes the policies of the conservative governments of the United Kingdom and Canada are fully intelligible only against the background of the earlier evolution of their respective foreign policies.

Gulliver in the 1970s: A Sketch

U.S. foreign policy in the first half of the 1970s was marked by domestic criticism of foreign entanglements, especially military ones, an emphasis on the role of regional powers as a substitute for direct U.S. involvement, and the attempt to construct détente, i.e., reciprocal U.S./USSR moderation, as a shield to cover this strategic retreat from the international stage. This period, however, witnessed the growth of Soviet military power, the Soviet achievement of nuclear parity with the United States (and the codification of that parity in SALT I), increased Soviet activism in the Third World, and, lastly, a major rift in the Alliance in the midst of the U.S.-proclaimed Year of Europe (1973).

The resulting perceptions, not least among Americans themselves, of U.S. weaknesses and of European crassness were the legacies of this period. For some, the "realization" of the modesty of U.S. power was salutary, the recognition of limits of influence; for others, it was largely self-incurred and thus avoidable. The Carter administration (January 1977–January 1981) revealed the consequences of this weakness and set the stage for the ascendancy of a new conservative foreign policy agenda in the United States.

The Carter administration came to power having in its own mind learned the limits of American power and calling for a restructuring of U.S. foreign policy. Its key theme was that U.S. preoccupation with East/West relations had distorted foreign policy and had put the United States on the side of those forces resistant to change rather than, as its own history and political culture would have indicated, on the side of progress. Carter remained committed, of course, to the foundation of U.S./Soviet relations as set down in the Nixon-Ford years: détente and the SALT process. However, he was also committed to reducing the "confrontational aspects" of U.S. foreign policy, to emphasizing North/South issues, and to promoting human rights worldwide (Gray and Barlow, 1985:59; Tucker, 1980:462–63).

This doctrine Robert Tucker has aptly entitled the "foreign policy of maturity." Essentially, it may be viewed as a variant of the post-Vietnam Nixon-Kissinger view that growing Soviet power and declining U.S. domestic support for defense and foreign military involvements had reduced American influence and dictated a retreat from the international stage. Starting from the premise of the decline of U.S. influence, it sought a remedy not so much in providing the USSR with inducements to good behavior (though certainly that idea—the heart of détente—was not dropped) or in a refurbishing of U.S. power, but in the notion that in a less hierarchical and more interdependent world order U.S. influence could be reconstituted on the basis of the promotion of progress and peaceful change (see Tucker, 1980:463–65).

The optimism of this approach, and the ongoing vulnerability of the United States, were revealed by events in short order. In East/West relations the USSR became still more assertive: it shifted the European nuclear equation in its favor (1977 deployment of SS-20 missiles); it became directly involved in the 1978 conflict between Ethiopia and Somalia and in assisting Muscovite loyalists in their 1978 coup in

South Yemen; in December 1979 the USSR invaded Afghanistan, thus bringing to a close the decade of détente in a manner similar to the way in which it had begun, the 1968 invasion of Czechoslovakia.

In regional crises Carter fared hardly better. The failure of his attempts to guide post-Somoza Nicaragua toward a moderate future was but a small defeat in comparison with the 1979 events in Iran. The Khomeini revolution showed the dangers inherent in the policy of using local powers as a surrogate for direct American involvement; measured against the Soviet response to developments in Afghanistan, Carter's uncertain and ragged answer to the crisis of the shah's final months and of the November 1979 Iranian seizure of American hostages highlighted U.S. weaknesses (Tucker, 1980:481). The coda of the concluding year of the decade was a fitting recapitulation of the themes of declining U.S. influence both in regional and superpower affairs.

From the American perspective the lessons of the Carter presidency, or rather those of the 1970s, were twofold. (1) In East/West relations and in regional events the United States had been seriously weakened, in part by the growth of Soviet power and its willingness to use it, and in part by self-inflicted weaknesses, e.g., cuts in defense spending and the cultivation of a foreign policy of "maturity." Détente was thus seen as a failure. (2) The behavior of the Allies was, at best, only grudgingly cooperative and often seemed plainly hostile to U.S. interests, e.g., the Year of Europe, the October 1973 war, the "neutron bomb" controversy of 1977–78, the 1978 NATO call for 3 percent increases in defense spending, the question of an Allied response to the invasion of Afghanistan, and the 1980 EEC Venice Declaration on the Middle East.

The developments of a decade, highlighted and magnified by the often inept Carter management of foreign policy and by developments in the external environment, produced what Daniel Yankelovich called a "watershed" in American politics (Yankelovich and Kaagan, 1981: 696). Polls in 1980 indicated an unusually high level of American public concern (42 percent) with foreign policy (Yankelovich and Kaagan, 1981:701). A majority of Americans believed that the USSR thought it had superiority over the United States, and some 53 percent of those polled stated that the United States was weaker than the Soviet Union. A still larger majority held that U.S. handling of the Iranian hostage crisis had diminished American prestige abroad. The new assertiveness of the American public was shown in the major growth in support for defense spending (74 percent after Afghanistan), in increased support for a peacetime draft, and in the 77 percent of those polled after Reagan's election victory who said that his principal concern should be to see to increasing U.S. prestige in the world (Yankelovich and Kaagan, 1981:708).

Gulliver was once again ready to behave in a manner consistent with his stature. For some, this change, this watershed in America, promised a strengthened Alliance (Tucker, 1980:484); for others (Sommer, 1980:628), it posed difficult questions since this reawakened giant would now have to deal with Allies grown more united, self-confident, and economically powerful, Allies no longer willing to accept without hesitation U.S. guidance in foreign or economic policy matters.

Lilliputians in the 1970s: A Sketch

The postwar foreign policy of both British and Canadian Conservatives came to center on relations with the United States and the problem of maintaining independence in the light of American preponderance. The British option was to emphasize relations with Europe; the Canadian response was to promote multilateral institutions and, with the Diefenbaker Conservatives, to seek a strengthening of ties with Britain, Europe, and Asia as a countervailing strategy against Liberal continentalism. In both countries the desire to be good allies (bipartisan support in Britain and Canada for the creation of NATO; the close connection in Britain of its independent nuclear force to NATO and the United States; in Canada, NORAD), especially in East/West relations, had to be brought into balance with the wish to remain independent.

From the point of view of the smaller and middle powers in the Alliance the 1970s represented a period of maturation, of the fruition of policy decisions taken in the preceding decades. Specifically, it was a period that saw the Heath Conservative government leading Britain into the European Community and increasingly sharing in European attitudes toward relations with the United States. Those relations reflected, in turn, the relative decline of U.S. power, the achievement of USSR/U.S. strategic parity, the centrality of détente in Europe, and the growing confidence and cohesiveness of European foreign policy.

By no means did this amount to a rejection of the United States; rather, it was the right of a self-confident Britain and Europe to shape policies in their own interests while, simultaneously, remaining good allies. Thus, this period saw a sharpening of European reaction to perceived U.S. unilateralism and a demand to be consulted in matters of importance to it.

For Canada the 1970s were a period in which it became fully apparent that the principal question was independence and that a moral role on the international stage, the "helpful fixer" function of Pearsonian diplomacy, was not an answer to that question. How could Canada hope to retain sovereignty, domestic or in foreign policy, if, in every aspect of her national life, American influence was growing? The early Trudeau answer was the "Third Option" in foreign policy and an element of "statism" in domestic economic development. As in the case of Britain, Canada in the postwar world was trying to discover her proper place. For Britain the problem was a downward readjustment of its former status coupled with measures to preserve independence. For Canada it was to find its own voice in world affairs and to secure its sovereignty in a situation (geographic, economic, military, and cultural) that magnified the threat of subordination.

Such was the situation at the beginning of the 1980s: an assertive America, an independent and more cohesive Europe, Britain firmly entrenched in Europe but interested in rejuvenating the special relationship with the United States, and lastly, Canada, nationalistic and witnessing the final stage call of sixteen years of Trudeau Liberal government—in short, a fairly explosive mixture.

GULLIVER AND THE LILLIPUTIANS: THE 1980S

Gulliver's Viewpoint

The November 1980 election victory of Ronald Reagan brought to power an administration more prepared to take a hard line with the Soviets and less tolerant of the compromising behavior of U.S. allies. Within the new administration, Secretary of State Alexander Haig set out the "four pillars" of U.S. foreign policy, which included the reinvigoration of the Alliance (see Osgood, 1982:473). Yet in the administration, and among American conservatives, there were voices arguing that if the Europeans were blindly committed to social welfare at home and regional détente in foreign affairs, the United States should "go it alone." Thus, for example, one conservative commentator, Irving Kristol, wrote an article entitled "Does NATO Exist?" in which he asserted that this question would, in the 1980s, be asked by many Americans. Essentially, Kristol's argument was that NATO had already been tested and had been found wanting. Eurocentric in foreign policy, social democratic in domestic policy, Europe was well on the way to Finlandization. Consequently, U.S. policy, increasingly nationalistic in tone, would of necessity become unilateralist (see Kristol, 1979:45, 47, 48, 52–53). The message for Europe, Kristol concluded, was *il faut choisir*. Inside the administration similar voices could be heard. For example, Richard Allen, the president's national security adviser, expressed distress at the "mood of Europe," especially the growth in pacifist sentiment and the conviction that arms control negotiations could be a substitute for military strength.

The idea that the resolve of the allies was in doubt, that the United States would act unilaterally if the Europeans failed to show solidarity, was first put to the test in the debate over what response to make to Soviet pressure on Poland in the Solidarity period and subsequently to the imposition of martial law in Poland (December 1981).

European responses to developments in Poland fell far short of U.S. expectations. While NATO foreign ministers condemned martial law (January 11, 1982), their "moderation" in answer to U.S. calls for tough sanctions on Poland and the USSR offended America. When the United States decided on December 29, 1981, to embargo U.S.-made parts for the Euro-Siberian Yamal natural gas pipeline, the West German government's response was to say that it would not prevent German firms from ignoring the embargo. The French, a little more than one month after martial law, signed a twenty-five-year agreement to purchase Soviet natural gas and one month later announced a loan of $140 million to the USSR to purchase French equipment for the pipeline. The British were somewhat firmer, but there was no question of preventing their firms from participating in the Yamal project.

American reaction was harsh. There was agreement that Europe would have to be pushed, particularly on the pipeline issue. Haig urged diplomatic pressure, Secretary of Defense Caspar Weinberger argued for more forceful measures (Knight, 1983:521–22). Conservative commentators in the United States called European actions "pitiful" and condemned those who were more afraid of U.S. sanctions than of events in Poland. Perhaps it was time, Walter Laquer (1982) wrote, to "think the unthinkable" in relation to the Alliance, i.e., to consider its dissolution.

At first, under the influence of "Atlanticists" in the administration such as Haig, the diplomatic route was chosen. At the June 1982 Versailles Summit President Reagan pressured the Europeans into adopting firmer measures on economic relations with the East bloc. The result was an agreement to exercise "commercial prudence" in trade with the East, an agreement that, in the Reagan administration's view, meant no further credit for the Yamal pipeline. President Mitterrand promptly corrected that misapprehension, reducing the Versailles agreement to a vague and weak statement of intent. Outraged, the Reagan administration on June 18, 1982, expanded its December 1981 embargo to include not simply U.S. firms but foreign companies producing items under U.S. licenses for the pipeline project.

Major firms in Britain, France, West Germany, and Italy were the targets of the new U.S. embargo. European reaction was quick and negative. The foreign ministers of the EEC called the move an extraterritorial application of U.S. law. Margaret Thatcher denounced the embargo and warned that British companies would be compelled to obey British, not American, law. The French foreign minister, Claude Cheysson, spoke of a progressive divorce between the United States and its European allies and West German Chancellor Helmut Schmidt said that the U.S. action affected not only the interests but the sovereignty of European nations.

The severity of the American action, the "turning of U.S. fury" on every major ally including such steadfast ones as Great Britain, was evidence of the depth of U.S. resentment over European behavior. What the United States saw as the crassest European preference for its own interests, especially trade, above the needs of the Alliance no doubt confirmed in the minds of the American critics the suspicions that had arisen in 1973 and during the Iranian and Afghanistan episodes: that Europe wanted U.S. protection, nuclear and conventional, but was unwilling to act forcefully when circumstances required.

One major consequence of this transatlantic alienation *a deux* was that "Atlanticists" in the United States were in retreat and globalistnationalists in the ascendancy (see Joffe, 1983:570; Cohen, 1982–83: 336; Knight, 1983:523). Responsible American political leaders, such as Senator Sam Nunn, and commentators such as Elliot Cohen, called for a fresh look at the structure of the Alliance. European timidity, particularly in the Polish sanctions dispute, called forth American unilateralism, which in turn reinforced European anxieties about U.S. behavior. In sum, while the U.S. embargo was finally lifted, while the demonstrators all but disappeared from the streets of Europe, and, lastly, while the Pershing IIs and GLCMs were indeed deployed, a conservative constituency had been established in the United States that called into question the foundation of the Alliance and sought to shift the focus of U.S. foreign policy toward its unilateral-global responsibilities and away from the timid and carping European allies.

If the view across the Atlantic was bleak for the Americans, the northern vista was hardly more appealing. Committed to free trade and free enterprise, the Reagan administration confronted a newly elected Trudeau government dedicated to toughening and expanding the economic nationalism of the 1970s and, in international affairs, increasingly critical of the United States.

On the economic front Trudeau examined ways to strengthen the Foreign Investment Review Agency (FIRA), and there were suggestions that FIRA's powers would be extended from monitoring new foreign investment to covering the ongoing activities of foreign subsidiaries in Canada (Drouin and Malmgren, 1981–82:402). More irritating for the United States than FIRA was the October 1980 decision to launch the National Energy Program (NEP). The NEP had as its target 50 percent Canadian ownership in the energy sector. The NEP's instruments were many, but central among them were tax and exploration incentives favoring Canadian firms (especially Petro-Canada) over their U.S. competitors, and a "back-in" scheme whereby the federal government would be able to acquire 25 percent of *existing* leases without compensation (see Clarkson, 1985:24; Drouin and Malmgren, 1981–82:400–401). The scheme was seen by some Canadian conservatives not only as unnecessary economic nationalism but as amounting to the beginning of the nationalization of the energy sector in Canada (see Walker, 1981:27–29).

If there were concerns in some quarters in Canada, American reaction was unambiguously hostile. The Reagan administration sent a sharp series of notes to the Canadian government objecting to the measures under the "national treatment" clause of GATT and intimating that retaliation would follow should the policies remain in place. By mid-1982 U.S. pressure had proved largely effective in moderating some of the more objectionable provisions of the NEP (Bromke and Nossal, 1983–84:348; Clarkson, 1985:334).

The dominant foreign policy issue of the last Trudeau year was East/West relations and, in particular, the Reagan approach to those relations. Polls at the time indicated that following the Soviet shooting down of the KAL aircraft (with 10 Canadians aboard) and the 1983 "hot autumn" of INF deployments in Europe, a substantial number of Canadians identified international affairs as their top priority (Gwyn and Gwyn, 1984:20). Some 57 percent believed that the danger of war had increased, and 21 percent thought that the United States was a greater danger to peace than the USSR (see Bromke and Nossal, 1983–84:341, 346). Trudeau himself was plainly worried by the Reagan stance and voiced his opinion that the concerns of Canadians in this regard were justified.

The result of these reflections was the Trudeau Peace Initiative, launched officially in October 1983. The unspoken target of this attack on what Trudeau termed "megaphone" diplomacy in East/West relations was the United States. Trudeau's political and arms control proposals, which were presented to the Commonwealth heads of government, the West European allies, and the United States as well as to the governments of Czechoslovakia, the GDR, Romania, and ultimately the USSR itself, were innocuous. However, coming in the midst of the INF deployment crisis and during a period when the USSR was trying to generate an atmosphere of crisis in order to influence Western publics, the initiative savored of unilateralism and the breaking of Alliance solidarity.

American reaction to Trudeau's foreign policy moves was quiet in comparison to the response to FIRA and the NEP. In part this was due to the fact, which Trudeau himself had observed in the early 1970s, that the mistakes of a small power are relatively inconsequential in comparison to those of the superpowers. Such U.S. reaction as there was consisted in bland wishes of "God's speed" and, from one senior administration official, the statement that Trudeau's behavior resembled that of an erratic, drug-crazed leftist. The Initiative itself, however, was wildly popular at home (85 percent support), though in an attitude that speaks volumes of the nature of Canadian foreign policy, an almost equally large percentage (65 percent) thought the Initiative would not be effective.

The Lilliputians' Viewpoint

In Europe many welcomed the renewed confidence of an assertive America (Schmidt, 1981:745). The shifting foreign policy sands of the Carter years had not been a comforting sight, for it left the Alliance all but leaderless. In Britain the recently elected Conservative government of Margaret Thatcher seemed to be virtually the twin of the Reagan administration. In her December 1979 address to the Foreign Policy Association in New York, Mrs. Thatcher called for a stronger Alliance and identified the military threat posed to the West by the USSR (Thatcher, 1980:14–15). A little over a year later Prime Minister Thatcher expressed her confidence that the special relationship between Britain and the United States would be enhanced by the conservative ideas she shared with President Reagan. And, in a statement going considerably further than her conservative predecessor, Edward Heath, would have allowed, she asserted that "if we are safe today, it is because of America; if we are to remain safe tomorrow it is because of America" (New York Times, February 17, 1981:3).

There were, however, reasons to doubt that sanguine assessment. An assertive America, the leader of which during the election campaign had denounced SALT II, suggested that military strength rather than arms control and détente was the best guarantee of Western security, and some of whose advisers and sympathetic commentators had called into question the worth of the Alliance, could hardly be reassuring to governments for which détente and arms control had been the centerpiece of a decade's foreign policy. Leadership, coupled with consultation, was indeed desirable; American unilateralism, particularly of the sort that threatened détente in Europe, was menacing.

The unilateralism of the 1982 U.S. sanctions was offensive to the Europeans for the reasons just discussed. Yet for Britain (and West Germany and Italy) it awakened yet other fears: if the United States was prepared to take action affecting its allies without prior consultation, how credible were assurances that the INF host governments would have any say in the use of the nuclear weapons deployed on their soil (see *Economist*, March 10, 1984:31ff.)?

For the British Conservatives this question of prior consultation was to be raised yet again, much to the embarrassment of a government that had prided itself on cultivating its special relationship with the Reagan administration. The October 25, 1983, U.S. invasion of Grenada, a Commonwealth nation independent only since 1974 and with the queen's representative, Sir Paul Scoon, resident on the island, was a shock to Britain as, in a more modest way, it also was to Canada. The invasion was denounced by the Labour party and by virtually the whole of Europe; the Thatcher government, which had not been fully apprised of American plans, was left red-faced in the ensuing Commons debates (see *Economist*, October 29, 1983:57–58). Thatcher reportedly was livid and swore that Anglo-American relations could never be the same again (*Economist*, March 10, 1984:34).

From the Canadian point of view, or at least that of the Liberal government from 1980–84, U.S. pressure against FIRA and the NEP was a major assault on a national economic development policy that had its origins in deep-rooted Canadian fears for her economic, political, and cultural autonomy. That this pressure (combined, in the case of the NEP, with provincial objections) succeeded in rolling back some of the more contentious facets of these policies was testimony to the continuing vulnerability of the Canadian economy. The independence that Canada could not achieve in economic matters was, however, possible in international affairs. Hence, Canadian criticism of U.S. Central American policies, of the invasion of Grenada, and, in more general terms, of the "megaphone" Reagan approach to East/West relations satisfied a desire for independence denied Canada in other areas. It was that anomalous combination of dependency and a politically satisfying but largely ineffectual posturing on the international stage that characterized the last Trudeau government and, indeed, has been typical of much Canadian foreign policy. The Conservative government of Prime Minister Brian Mulroney was to break, though not completely, with that approach.

THE 1980S: A LAST LOOK, PLUS ÇA CHANGE...

On June 9, 1983, Margaret Thatcher's Conservatives easily won reelection, an outcome that in 1981 would, in light of her low popularity, have seemed unlikely. The 1982 British victory in the Falklands War (with substantial U.S. assistance) was of considerable importance in this upswing of Thatcher's popularity (*Economist*, May 21, 1983:26), though the prime minister did not (and did not have to) make the war an explicit theme in her campaign. Given the typically low level of British public attention devoted to international affairs (other than relations with Europe), the prominence of defense and foreign policy questions in the 1983 campaign was unusual (see Fotheringham, 1983:84; *Economist*, May 21, 1983:9). As was just mentioned, this resulted in part from the Falklands War but also from the fact that the Labour party was being led by a convinced unilateral disarmer, Michael Foot, whose party had pledged to implement a non-nuclear defense policy (i.e., to scrap Britain's independent nuclear forces) within the life of the next Parliament, to reduce defense spending, and to reconsider Britain's role in Europe. Polls suggested that these policies were radically out of line with British public opinion that supported Britain's nuclear forces and was receptive to higher defense spending and even to the possibility of British participation in "out of area" military operations (see *Economist*, May 28, 1983:35; Fotheringham, 1983: 92–93, 96–98).

However, while Thatcher's reelection victory, coming as it did after the crises of the early 1980s, might have seemed to be an encouraging development for the Alliance, her success does not appear to have rested on her good relations with the Reagan administration. If Britons are strongly in favor of NATO and of their own status as a nuclear power, only a small minority of them admired President Reagan and few (6 percent) believed that Britain's future lies with the United States (25 percent chose the Commonwealth, 27 percent Europe—see *Economist*, June 12, 1982:58). The tension in British politics over military involvement with the United States (e.g., cruise missile deployment) was clearly displayed in the massive popular rejection of Prime Minister Thatcher's cooperation with the United States in the latter's April 1986 raid on Libya. This courageous, but potentially costly, support was attacked not only by Labour but by some prominent Tories, including Edward Heath—a reminder that there are some in the Conservative party (to say nothing of the opposition parties) who share Enoch Powell's view that Thatcher's policies threatened to Finlandize Britain not in relation to the USSR but to the United States.

Less than a year and a half after Prime Minister Thatcher's reelection, Brian Mulroney and his Conservatives scored a landslide victory over the Liberals (now led by John Turner) in the September 4, 1984, Canadian election. While part of the Conservative campaign focused on the need to be a good ally in NATO (increased defense spending) and a good neighbor to the United States, the Tories were not running against a Liberal party guided by the militant nationalism of the early 1980s. Indeed, Turner, the Liberal leader and briefly prime minister after Trudeau's resignation, stated that his foreign policy would center on doing business "as it used to be" with the United States (see Clarkson, 1985:352–53).

The explicit pro-American views of the new Conservative government were clearly a shift away from the Conservative policies of the last major Tory government, that of John Diefenbaker. Times had changed. The Third Option and trade diversification had failed, and the nationalist measures of the last Trudeau government had served only to provoke the Americans, a dangerous development given protectionist pressures in Congress. An improvement in the tone of relations with the United States was deemed vital as, on a more substantive level, was the dismantling of the instruments of Trudeau economic nationalism, FIRA and the NEP. The Mulroney government has also initiated free trade negotiations with the United States, again a departure from earlier Conservative approaches.

Yet, on another level, the familiar strains of Canadian foreign policy, internationalism in world affairs and nationalism vis-à-vis the United States, are still to be heard in the Mulroney government. The internationalist character of Mulroney foreign policy took the traditional two forms: (1) Canada's contribution to the grand issues of world politics, particularly East/West relations and (2) dedication to multilateral institutions. The prime minister himself, less than one month after his election, signaled this continuity of policy. In his speech at St. Francis Xavier University, Mulroney stated that his "most cherished ambition" was to reduce the threat of war and "embrace the promise of peace." The foreign policy Green Paper, *Competitiveness and Security,* identified peace as a "transcendent" objective of Canadian foreign policy (see Clark, 1985: Foreword and 14). The pursuit of peace was couched in explicit disavowals of neutrality and an equally explicit avowal of Alliance solidarity (Clark, 1985:13).

In the second facet of internationalism, the emphasis on multilateral institutions, the Conservative government has continued the strong Canadian support for the UN system, a policy that distinguishes it from the governments of the United States and Britain, which have been critical of the UN in general and UNESCO in particular. In short, multilateralism for the Mulroney government served the same purpose that it had for previous governments—an expression of a certain idealism and as the best forum in which small and middle powers can have their voices heard (see Clark, 1985:15, 41).

Consistent with the Mulroney government's intention, announced in its first Throne Speech, to restore a "spirit of good will" and "true partnership" to relations between Canada and the United States, the tone of Canadian nationalism has been moderated. It nevertheless remains a principal theme in the new government's policies. Thus, while the Green Paper states (Clark, 1985:6–7) that it is the government's intention to establish a constructive and civil relationship with the United States, it also emphasizes that "we are at once North American and not American" (Clark, 1985:1). Indeed, the Conservative government has portrayed its better relations with the United States as a policy of mature nationalism compared to the politics of fear and weakness that were the source of FIRA and the NEP (see SSEA's September 19, 1985, speech to the Canadian Club). The government has also argued that enhanced trade with the United States is a means to preserve the distinctiveness of Canadian social programs and culture and to preserve Canadian sovereignty in the Arctic (see SSEA's speech to the Waterloo Chamber of Commerce, October 10, 1985). Closer economic relations with America are thus seen not as a threat to independence, but as its guarantee.

Prime Minister Mulroney's government has stated that closer relations with the United States do not mean that Washington will dictate foreign policy to Canada. And it has made an effort to show that that is, in fact, the case. Thus, to cite a few instances, the SSEA in a statement to the House (September 10, 1985) said that the sovereignty question had concerned the Conservative government since it came to power. He then listed a variety of areas in which Canada had made its own decisions in foreign policy, e.g., Central America (Canada refused to participate in the embargo on Nicaragua), South Africa (sanctions), and in asserting its sovereignty in the Arctic (Canadian observers were put aboard an American ship, the *Polar Sea*, as it navigated the Canadian Arctic). In the previously cited speech to the Canadian Club, the SSEA presented much the same list but added Canada's decision to remain in UNESCO and its refusal to accept an American offer to participate in the Strategic Defense Initiative (SDI).

On the whole, however, the Mulroney government has brought about a reorientation in Canadian foreign policy away from the militant nationalism of the previous decades toward a more mature appreciation of the fact that, for better or worse, close relations with the United States, particularly of the economic sort, are and are likely to remain a dominant feature of Canadian life. Side by side with that coming to terms with the fundamental character of Canada's varied interactions with the United States is a foreign policy in many respects traditional. Since the end of World War II Canada has felt the need to express its independence and vision of the world on the international stage. Lacking the economic and military instruments of a great power, this expression often appears to be moralistic in the worst sense, i.e., posturing for its own sake, and not action that can hope to alter the conditions addressed by these actions. Nevertheless, Canadian foreign policy, including substantial elements of the Conservative government's policies, serves to affirm a distinct political identity. This is also the reason that even a government as dedicated as Prime Minister Mulroney's is to the building of good relations with the United States will seek to differentiate itself from American positions, and why it will resist encroachments on Canadian sovereignty as vigorously as earlier Canadian governments. Those encroachments, e.g., the *Polar Sea* voyage and the extraterritorial application of U.S. law to firms operating in Canada, are an offense to a country that has good reason to worry over its independence, not because its neighbor is menacing, but because that neighbor is Gulliver and even its small moves can have a serious impact upon its smaller friend.

And, finally, to complete our concluding note on the 1980s, in November 1984 President Reagan was elected to a second term in office. To what extent foreign policy played a role in this victory is a matter still debated, but some commentators have argued that the more moderate tone of the president's second term comments on relations with the USSR as well as his meeting with then Foreign Minister Gromyko and the later Geneva Summit were at least in part the result of broad American popular support for greater efforts toward arms control with the Soviet Union (see Hoffman, 1985:631, 634; Yankelovich and Doble, 1984). This shift of emphasis toward negotiation was presumably welcomed by the Europeans, particularly after the fearful atmosphere of crisis leading up to the INF deployments. On the other hand, the President's Strategic Defense Initiative, first alluded to by Reagan in March 1983 but increasingly prominent in 1984, was an ambiguous development from the European perspective.

American critiques of European difficulties in meeting NATO's 3 percent defense spending increases have also continued. Indeed, Senators Sam Nunn and Ted Stevens proposed legislation that would reduce U.S. troop commitments in proportion to the allies' failure to meet that target. Their amendment was defeated but won the votes of over forty senators. On the positive side, NATO voted a substantial sum, close to $8 billion, for the expansion of its military infrastructure. However, with the growing emphasis on conventional strategy (Shultz, 1985:210 ff.) to defeat possible Soviet aggression in Europe, demands for increased allied defense spending are not likely to abate in the near future.

What effect these and the other events of the 1970s and 1980s discussed previously will have on divisions between "Atlanticists" and "unilateralists" is difficult to predict. While Secretary of State George Shultz has spoken and written of the importance of Europe for America (Shultz, 1985), Secretary of Defense Weinberger has recently written an article on "U.S. Defense Strategy" (Weinberger, 1986) in which Europe is not mentioned at all, and the "allies" are referred to only once. That carefully worded reference can hardly be reassuring to Europeans. It states that American combat forces are only to be committed for "*vital* interests" and then adds: "our interests include our Allies' vital interests" (Weinberger, 1986:686). Read closely, what this passage suggests is that the allies' vital interests are America's interests but *not* its vital interests; hence, no U.S. combat forces would be committed to the task of preserving the Europeans' vital interests. Thus, while the years 1984–86 have been relatively tranquil ones in intra-Alliance relations, they have not been without disputes that mirror those of the first years of the decade, e.g., European charges of unilateralism and militarism in U.S. policy and American counteraccusations of European weakness and crass self-interest. That these disputes have not been more severe is attributable in large measure to the fact that they have involved gray "out-of-area" issues, principally responses to terrorism originating in the Middle East, rather than being centered on U.S./USSR tensions in the European theater. There is no evidence to suggest that the sources of these different perceptions, those of the United States and of her allies, have been removed or, that given the occasion, that this disenchantment à deux will not produce consequences still more severe than those of the past several years. That prospect must be a source of optimism for the Soviet leadership whose own campaigns this decade failed to yield the divisions that intra-Alliance tensions themselves brought about.

CONCLUSION

The origins of the crisis and tensions of the 1980s, including those between the United States, Britain, and Canada, are to be found less in the ideologies of the makers of foreign policy than in the relationship between the large power and its smaller allies, between Gulliver and the Lilliputians. The presence of conservative governments in these three countries has, in some measure, helped to moderate the severity of the tensions that underlie their relations; in other ways it has exacerbated those same tensions. From the perspective of the smaller powers, the wellspring of Alliance crises is an asymmetry of military and, to a lesser extent, economic dependence and the imperative of independence in domestic and foreign affairs. From the standpoint of the superpower, dependency and independence are not the principal concerns. Quite the contrary. From its perspective the major power judges its allies on the basis of loyalty and resolve, particularly in instances where the superpowers can be seen as testing each other (e.g., Afghanistan, Poland, INF deployment) but also in secondary problem areas such as Middle East policy or the formulation of a response to terrorism. Irving Kristol's phrase, cited above, "il faut choisir," nicely sums up the superpower's benchmark for judging its allies. "Are they with us in East/West relations, on terrorism, or on a peace settlement in the

Middle East?" Many American commentators, and not a few administration officials, have since the 1970s answered that question negatively or have observed the grudging and foot-dragging manner in
which the allies have behaved.

For the small and middle powers the issue of "*il faut choisir*" is
wrongly, and dangerously, put. They *have chosen*: the status of NATO is
hardly a question in Europe (see Szabo, 1985:269) and Canada. The
Soviet Union holds virtually no ideological appeal for them, and economic relations with the USSR and its empire, though greater than
U.S. trade with Eastern Europe, are nevertheless small in comparison
with their trade among themselves and with America. Soviet military
power in Europe is massive, but its use in the nuclear age and with the
U.S. presence on the continent seems to be such a "cosmic roll of the
dice" that its political consequences are not seen as great.

While Canada and Europe have indeed made their choice, they do
not accept the notion that their adherence to this basic choice is to be
measured by their unswerving loyalty to the varied foreign policies of
successive U.S. administrations. Canada and Britain, in the postwar
world, have made fundamental decisions about their future, decisions
that shape the policies of conservative, liberal, and (at least formerly)
social democratic governments alike. Canada's commitment to international institutions, multilateral diplomacy, and independence in
foreign policy, consistent with Alliance obligations, is an enduring
feature (with a few episodic lapses) of her international behavior. The
Mulroney government believes that those features of Canadian policy
are compatible with closer relations with the United States. There is
no indication, however, that Canada would be prepared to sacrifice her
fragile independence for the sake of better relations.

If the basic problem of Canadian political life has been independence, that of Great Britain has been to find an appropriate world role
for herself in the radically altered post-World War II international environment. In essence, Britain's basic choice has been for independence,
for Europe and NATO, and, for the most part, for a close relationship
with the United States. Under various Conservative governments different elements of this mix have been highlighted. If Heath's vision
was cast primarily toward the continent, Thatcher's has been rather
more directed toward Reagan's America. That, however, has not prevented the Thatcher government from opting for Europe (and Britain)

against the United States, particularly in instances where her sovereignty and influence were directly challenged by American actions, e.g., the 1982 Soviet pipeline embargo and the Grenada invasion.

In short, Canada, Britain, and Europe have sought to find their own domestic and foreign policy voices within a Western Alliance containing a superpower. That superpower is both their protection (hence European fears of American isolationism, the 1977 Schmidt speech, and concerns over the impact of SDI) and a threat to their independence (thus, for example, European and Canadian worries over U.S. unilateralism and extraterritorial application of American law). This apparently contradictory array of concerns is written in the nature of the relationship between Gulliver and the Lilliputians. The institutions of the Alliance are important for the smaller powers as a vehicle for moderating their dependence through consultation. Their freedom of action in areas not touched by the basic commitment to the Alliance is a key element in the assertion of their independence. The idea that their basic commitment will be tested across a broad range of U.S. demands for solidarity is a threat to that independence and holds before them the specter of Finlandization in a form more vivid than the Soviet Union could impose, given the military and economic interdependence of the West.

From the U.S. standpoint the rise of conservatism in the 1980s was, in part, a response to the perceived weakness of America in the 1970s. The issue for Americans was strength (as weakness or dependence in relations with the United States was for the Europeans; see Hassner, 1982:477), especially in relations with the USSR. In such a seemingly clear-cut struggle the dictum *il faut choisir* allowed precious little room for concern with independent allied positions. Objections, differences, demands for consultation appeared, at best, as petty quibbling, at worst, as the beginning of self-Finlandization. If the allies refused to choose America, America would go it alone. Such an attitude, increasingly fashionable in some U.S. conservative circles in the late 1970s and 1980s, contributed to the gravity of the crises discussed earlier and continues to pose a threat to the Alliance.

For better or worse, Gulliver and the Lilliputians share the same city, that still rare and fragile city of freedom. The accommodations required by such an arrangement demand *courage civile* from statesmen and others who value freedom and therefore fear the consequences of a collapse of the Alliance. For the Americans such *courage civile* would suggest that the United States ought to opt for consultation rather than unilateralism, that it should allow its allies a healthy margin of independence without the exercise of that independence being interpreted as weakness or anti-Americanism, and, finally, that it must be recognized that the Manichaean criterion, *il faut choisir*, is much more likely to weaken the West in the face of its opponents than to strengthen it.

For the smaller powers that *courage civile* would indicate that (as Prime Ministers Mulroney and Thatcher have already attempted) leaders ought to educate their publics in the idea that independence and close cooperation with the United States are not incompatible policies, that however great Gulliver's flaws may appear to Lilliputians they dwindle in comparison to the alternatives, that, in short, the Alliance, for all its faults, serves them better than other arrangements. They should also understand that however many their complaints may be against the United States, frivolous displays of independence coupled with an apparent unwillingness to share the costs (political and financial) of preserving freedom threaten only to alienate Gulliver, a loss that would most certainly be *à deux*.

REFERENCES

Aron, Raymond. 1983. "Ideology in Search of a Policy." *Foreign Affairs* 60 (America and the World 1982): 503–24.
Art, Robert J. 1982. "Fixing Atlantic Bridges." *Foreign Policy* (Spring): 67–85.
Bertram, Christoph. 1981–82. "The Implications of Theater Nuclear Weapons in Europe." *Foreign Affairs* 60 (Winter): 305–26.
———. 1982. "Political Implications of the Theater Nuclear Balance." In Barry M. Blechman, ed., *Rethinking the U.S. Strategic Posture: A Report from the Aspen Consortium on Arms Control and Security Issues.* Cambridge, Mass.: Ballinger, pp. 101–28.
———. 1984. "Europe and America in 1983." *Foreign Affairs* 62 (America and the World 1983): 616–31.
Bloemer, Klaus. 1983. "Freedom for Europe, East and West." *Foreign Policy* (Spring): 23–38.
Bromke, Adam, and Kim Richard Nossal. 1983–84. "Tensions in Canada's Foreign Policy." *Foreign Affairs* 62 (Winter): 335–53.
Bundy, McGeorge, George F. Kennan, Robert S. McNamara, and Gerard Smith. 1982. "Nuclear Weapons and the Atlantic Alliance." *Foreign Affairs* 60 (Spring): 753–68.
Chace, James. 1973. "The Concert of Europe." *Foreign Affairs* 52 (October): 96–108.

Clark, Joe (The Right Honourable, Secretary of State for External Affairs). 1985. *Competitiveness and Security: Directions for Canada's International Relations*. Ottawa: Minister of Supply and Services Canada.

Clarkson, Stephen. 1985. *Canada and the Reagan Challenge: Crisis and Adjustment, 1981–85*. Toronto: Lorimer.

Cohen, Eliot A. 1982–83. "The Long-Term Crisis of the Alliance." *Foreign Affairs* 61 (Winter): 325–43.

Creighton, Donald. 1976. *The Forked Road: Canada, 1939–1957*. Toronto: McClelland and Stewart.

Dewitt, David B., and John J. Kirton. 1983. *Canada as a Principal Power: A Study in Foreign Policy and International Relations*. New York: John Wiley and Sons.

Dickey, John Sloan. 1972. "Canada Independent." *Foreign Affairs* 50 (July): 684–97.

Drouin, Marie-Josée, and Harold B. Malmgren. 1981–82. "Canada, the United States and the World Economy." *Foreign Affairs* 60 (Winter): 393–413.

Eayrs, James. 1980. *In Defense of Canada: Growing Up Allied*. Toronto: University of Toronto Press.

Edmunds, Martin. 1984. "British Foreign Policy." *Current History* 83 (April): 157–59.

Fontaine, Andre. 1981. "Transatlantic Doubts and Dreams." *Foreign Affairs* 59 (America and the World 1980): 578–93.

Fotheringham, Peter. 1983. "Great Britain: Generational Continuity." In Stephen F. Szabo, ed., *The Successor Generation: International Perspectives of Postwar Europeans*. Boston: Butterworth.

Goldsborough, James Oliver. 1982. *Rebel Europe: How America Can Live with a Changing Continent*. New York: Macmillan.

Gowing, Margaret. 1981. "Britain, America and the Bomb." In David Dilks, ed., *Retreat from Power: Studies in Britain's Foreign Policy of the Twentieth Century*, vol. 2: *After 1939*. London: Macmillan, pp. 120–37.

Gray, Colin S., and Jeffrey G. Barlow. 1985. "Inexcusable Restraint: The Decline of American Military Power in the 1970's." *International Security* 10 (Fall): 27–69.

Grunwald, Henry. 1984–85. "Foreign Policy Under Reagan II." *Foreign Affairs* 63 (Winter): 219–39.

Gwyn, Richard, and Sandra Gwyn. 1984. "The Politics of Peace." *Saturday Night* (May): 19–32.

Hassner, Pierre. 1982. "Plus c'est la même chose, plus ça change: Reflexions sur les nouvelles dimensions de la crise atlantique." *Etudes Internationales* 13, no. 3 (September): 473–96.

Hoffman, Stanley. 1981–82. "NATO and Nuclear Weapons: Reason and Unreason." *Foreign Affairs* 60 (Winter): 327–46.

———. 1985. "The U.S. and Western Europe: Wait and Worry." *Foreign Affairs* 63 (America and the World 1984): 631–52.

Holmes, John W. 1982. *The Shaping of Peace: Canada and the Search for World Order, 1943–1957*. Toronto: University of Toronto Press.

Huntington, Samuel P., ed. 1982. *The Strategic Imperative: New Policies for American Security*. Cambridge, Mass.: Ballinger.

Hyland, William G. 1982. "The USSR and Nuclear War." In Barry M. Blechman, ed.,

Rethinking the U.S. Strategic Posture: A Report from the Aspen Consortium on Arms Control and Security Issues. Cambridge, Mass.: Ballinger, pp. 41–76.

Ignatieff, George. 1981. "NATO, Nuclear Weapons and Canada's Interests." *International Perspectives* (November–December): 14–18.

Joffe, Josef. 1980. "European-American Relations: The Enduring Crisis." *Foreign Affairs* 59 (Spring): 835–51.

———. 1983. "Europe and America: The Politics of Resentment (cont'd)." *Foreign Affairs* 61 (America and the World 1982): 569–90.

Karber, Phillip A. 1983. "To Lose an Arms Race: The Competition in Conventional Forces Deployed in Central Europe, 1965–1980." In Uwe Nehrlich, ed., *Soviet Power and Western Negotiating Policies*, vol. 1: *Military Power in the Competition Over Europe.* Cambridge, Mass.: Ballinger, pp. 31–88.

Kissinger, Henry. 1979. *The White House Years.* Boston: Little, Brown.

———. 1982. *Years of Upheaval.* Boston: Little, Brown.

Knight, Andrew. 1983. "Ronald Reagan's Watershed Year?" *Foreign Affairs* 61 (America and the World 1982): 511–40.

Kristol, Irving. 1979. "Does NATO Exist?" *Washington Quarterly* 2 (Autumn): 45–53.

Laqueur, Walter. 1980a. "Defeatist France: The Heritage of Vichy." *Harper's* (June): 14–16.

———. 1980b. "Euro-Neutralism." *Commentary* (June): 21–27.

———. 1981. "Hollanditis: A New Stage in European Neutralism." *Commentary* (August): 19–26.

———. 1982. "Poland and the Crisis of the Alliance." *Wall Street Journal*, January 4.

———. 1984. "U.S.-Soviet Relations." *Foreign Affairs* 62 (America and the World 1983): 561–86.

Lellouche, Pierre. 1981. "Europe and Her Defense." *Foreign Affairs* 59 (Spring): 813–34.

Leyton-Brown, David. 1985. "The Mulroney Gamble." *International Perspectives* (September–October): 27–30.

Luttwak, Edward N. 1983. *The Grand Strategy of the Soviet Union.* New York: St. Martin's Press.

Lyon, Peyton V., and Bruce Thordarson. 1975. "Professor Pearson: A Sketch." In Michael G. Fry, ed., *"Freedom and Change": Essays in Honour of Lester B. Pearson.* Toronto: McClelland and Stewart, pp. 1–8.

Martin, James J. 1983. "How the Soviet Union Came to Gain Escalation Dominance: Trends and Asymmetries in the Theater Nuclear Balance." In Uwe Nehrlich, ed., *Soviet Power and Western Negotiating Policies*, vol. 1: *Military Power in the Competition Over Europe.* Cambridge, Mass.: Ballinger, pp. 89–122.

Montbrial, Thierry de. 1986. "The European Dimension." *Foreign Affairs* 64 (America and the World 1985): 499–514.

Osgood, Robert E. 1982. "The Revitalization of Containment." *Foreign Affairs* 60 (America and the World 1981): 465–502.

Pearson, Geoffrey. 1985. "Trudeau Peace Initiative Reflections." *International Perspectives* (March–April): 3–6.

Pearson, Lester B. 1949. "Canada and the North Atlantic Alliance." *Foreign Affairs* 27 (April): 369–78.

Peele, Gillian. 1980. "The Changed Character of British Foreign and Security Policy." *International Security* 4 (Spring): 185–98.

Poccock, David H., and Grant W. Manuge. 1985. "The Mulroney Doctrine." *International Perspectives* (January–February): 5–7.

Porter, Bernard. 1983. *Britain, Europe and the World 1850–1982: Delusions of Grandeur*. Boston: George Allen and Unwin.

Pym, Francis. 1982–83. "British Foreign Policy: Constraints and Opportunities." *International Affairs* (London) 59 (Winter): 1–6.

Record, Jeffrey. 1982. "Should America Pay for Europe's Security?" *Washington Quarterly* 5 (Winter): 19–23.

Richards, Peter G. 1973. "Parliament and the Parties." In Robert Boardman and A. J. R. Groom, eds., *The Management of Britain's External Relations*. London: Macmillan, pp. 245–62.

Rogers, Bernard W. 1982. "The Atlantic Alliance: Prescriptions for a Difficult Decade." *Foreign Affairs* 60 (Summer): 1145–56.

Rohrlich, Paul E. 1985. "Canada and Star Wars." *International Perspectives* (May–June): 17–20.

Rosenfeld, Stephen S. 1983. "Testing the Hard Line." *Foreign Affairs* 61 (America and the World 1982): 489–510.

Schmidt, Helmut. 1981. "A Policy of Reliable Partnership." *Foreign Affairs* 59 (Spring): 743–55.

Schwartz, David N. 1983a. "A Historical Perspective." In John D. Steinbruner and Leon V. Sigal, eds., *Alliance Security: NATO and the No-First-Use Question*. Washington, D.C.: Brookings Institution, pp. 5–21.

———. 1983b. *NATO's Nuclear Dilemmas*. Washington, D.C.: Brookings Institution.

Sharp, Mitchell. 1970. *Foreign Policy for Canadians*, vols. 1–6. Published by authority of the Honourable Mitchell Sharp, Secretary of State for External Affairs. Ottawa: Information Canada.

Shultz, George P. 1985. "New Realities and New Ways of Thinking." *Foreign Affairs* 63 (Spring): 705–21.

Sigal, Leon V. 1984. *Nuclear Forces in Europe: Enduring Dilemmas, Present Prospects*. Washington, D.C.: Brookings Institution.

Sommer, Theo. 1980. "Europe and the American Connection." *Foreign Affairs* 58 (America and the World 1979): 622–36.

Spiers, Edward. 1981. "The British Nuclear Deterrent: Problems and Possibilities." In David Dilks, ed., *Retreat from Power: Studies in Britain's Foreign Policy of the Twentieth Century*, vol. 2: *After 1939*. London: Macmillan, pp. 152–69.

Stacey, C. P. 1981. *Canada and the Age of Conflict: A History of Canadian External Policies*, vol. 2: *1921–1948, The MacKenzie King Era*. Toronto: University of Toronto Press.

Szabo, Stephen F. 1985. "European Opinion After the Missiles." *Survival* 27 (November–December): 265–73.

Talbott, Strobe. 1980. *Endgame: The Inside Story of Salt II*. New York: Harper Colophon Books.

Thatcher, Margaret. 1980. "Foreign Policy: The West in the World Today." *Atlantic Community Quarterly* 18 (Spring): 12–19.

Thordarson, Bruce. 1972. *Trudeau and Foreign Policy: A Study in Decision-Making.* Toronto: Oxford University Press.

Tucker, Robert W. 1980. "America in Decline: The Foreign Policy of Maturity." *Foreign Affairs* 58 (America and the World 1979): 449–84.

Ulam, Adam B. 1983. *Dangerous Relations: The Soviet Union in World Politics, 1970–1982.* New York: Oxford University Press.

Walker, Michael A. 1981. "The National Energy Program: An Overview of Its Impact and Objectives." In G. C. Watkins and M. A. Walker, eds., *Reaction: The National Energy Program.* Vancouver: Fraser Institute.

Weinberger, Caspar W. 1986. "U.S. Defense Strategy." *Foreign Affairs* 64 (Spring): 675–97.

Wolfe, Alan. 1984. "After Deployment: The Emergence of a New Europe." *World Policy Journal* (Spring): 549–74.

Yankelovich, Daniel, and Larry Kaagan. 1981. "Assertive America." *Foreign Affairs* 59 (America and the World 1980): 696–713.

Yankelovich, Daniel, and John Doble. 1984. "The Public Mood: Nuclear Weapons and the U.S.S.R." *Foreign Affairs* 63 (Fall): 33–46.

Z. 1974. "The Year of Europe." *Foreign Affairs* 52 (January): 237–48.

6. Conservatism and the Courts in the United States and Canada

F. L. MORTON

INTRODUCTION

The recent electoral successes of conservative political parties in the United States and Canada have had different impacts on the political role of the courts in these two nations. The political role of federal judges and especially of the Supreme Court has become highly partisan in the United States. Following the 1980 presidential election, conservatives have used a variety of "court curbing" methods to arrest or reverse the development of Supreme Court decisions. The most successful has been President Reagan's use of the appointment power to create a more conservative federal judiciary. This attempt to remold the ideological disposition of the federal judiciary has itself become the source of acrimonious political and academic debate.

The relationship between conservatives and the judiciary in Canada stands in sharp contrast with recent American experience. During the 1984 federal election campaign there was simply no mention of judicial appointments or "court curbing." Indeed, the latter concept is foreign to Canadian political experience.[1] Judicial interpretation of the Canadian Charter of Rights, which took effect in 1982, has not yet provoked any partisan conflict. Yet there are some early indications that this might change. Beginning in the same summer that the Progressive Conservatives swept to power, the Supreme Court of Canada embarked on a string of activist, libertarian Charter decisions.[2] As preoccupation with national unity and constitutional reform fades, "American-style" issues such as censorship of pornography, sexual equality, abortion, and education policy have emerged as potential new areas of political conflict. If Canadian Supreme Court judges accept the invitation to act as an agency of law reform, the Charter of Rights may serve as a catalyst for re-creating a northern version of the "social issues" that have contributed to the reshaping of the American political landscape in recent years.

AMERICAN CONSERVATIVES AND THE COURTS

During the summer of 1986 President Reagan chose then Associate Justice William Rehnquist to replace the retiring Chief Justice Warren Burger and elevated Antonin Scalia (whom he had earlier appointed to the Washington, D.C., Circuit Court of Appeals) to fill the new opening. While the Scalia nomination was approved with little controversy, a small band of Senate liberals, led by Edward Kennedy, tried to block President Reagan's nominee for chief justice. Rehnquist's critics used four days of televised hearings to publicize obscure events from his past that they hoped would tarnish his reputation and discredit his nomination.[3]

While some of the charges gave cause for concern, the real reason for the opposition of American liberals to the Rehnquist nomination was not so obscure. In the fifteen years since Richard Nixon has appointed him, William Rehnquist had established himself as the most conservative member of the Burger Court. On every constitutional issue that divides liberals and conservatives,[4] Rehnquist has taken the conservative position. As Senator Kennedy himself declared in a candid moment, Rehnquist was "too extreme on race, too extreme on women's rights, too extreme on freedom of speech, too extreme on separation of church and state, too extreme to be Chief Justice."

Despite the opposition, Rehnquist was eventually recommended by the Judiciary Committee and confirmed (despite a record-breaking thirty-three negative votes) by the Senate. He is now the sixteenth chief justice of the United States. The personal antagonism and ideological bitterness displayed at the Rehnquist nomination hearings are indicative of the increased politicization of the American Supreme Court. Moreover, the Rehnquist-Scalia hearings were simply the most recent and most public skirmish in an ongoing partisan struggle to control the "meaning" of constitutional law by controlling the appointment of federal judges.

The Reagan administration's attempt to remold the ideological orientation of the federal judiciary actually represents the second wave of conservative reaction against the liberal activism of the Warren Court. In his 1968 presidential campaign Richard Nixon intentionally exploited the unpopularity of some of the Warren Court decisions and promised to appoint as judges "strict constructionists who saw their duty as interpreting law and not making law" (Murphy and Pritchett, 1979:124). Nixon subsequently had the opportunity to appoint four new justices to the Supreme Court, including a new chief justice, Warren Burger, and William Rehnquist. Liberal critics argued that the Nixon appointees amounted to an attack on the political autonomy of the Court (Simon, 1973; Levy, 1974). For Nixon and his conservative supporters his appointments served to redress the balance upset by an overly partisan Warren Court.

The Supreme Court and judicial appointments reemerged as an important issue in the 1980 presidential elections. The Reagan wing of the Republican party was not satisfied with the performance of the Nixon appointees. Affirmative action, court-ordered busing, and the exclusionary rule had all been upheld. Worse still, it was the Burger Court's 1973 decision in *Roe v. Wade* that had overturned forty-seven state laws and created in effect a national "abortion on demand" policy. The "counterrevolution" that conservatives had hoped for in the "Nixon Court" had failed to materialize (Blasi, 1983).

After Reagan's victory in the 1980 Republican primaries his conservative supporters redrafted the Republican party platform. The new platform called for the appointment of judges who believe in "the decentralization of the federal government and efforts to return decision-making power to states and local elected officials." It also supported the appointment of judges "who respect the traditional family values and the sanctity of innocent human life." This not-so-covert criticism of the Court's *Roe v. Wade* decision was countered by the Democratic party platform, which explicitly supported "the right of women to choose whether and when to have a child" and denounced any attempt to abridge this "right" through constitutional amendment. And, finally, the Republicans dropped their support for the Equal

Rights Amendment (ERA) for the first time since it had been proposed. The reason given was not opposition to equality of the sexes, but that the practical meaning of sexual equality could better be developed by legislators than by judges.

The sweeping Republican electoral victories in the 1980 general elections led to more direct attempts at "court curbing." Not only did Reagan capture the White House, but the Republicans gained control of the Senate for the first time since 1954. In the first six months of the Ninety-Seventh Congress, twenty-seven bills were introduced to restrict or remove Supreme Court or lower federal court jurisdiction to hear cases dealing with abortion, school prayer, and busing to achieve racial integration in public schools. In effect these bills proposed to return decisionmaking authority for these issues to state and local authorities. While several of these bills were adopted in the Senate, none was passed by the House, in part because Peter Rodino, Democratic chairman of the House Judiciary Committee, refused to report them out of his committee.

Conservative discontent with Supreme Court decisions has been voiced from the White House as well as the Hill. At the end of the Supreme Court's 1984–85 term Ronald Reagan's old friend and new attorney general, Edwin Meese, took the unprecedented step of publicly criticizing the Supreme Court for some of its "inaccurate" and "incoherent" interpretations of the Constitution. In a speech to the American Bar Association in July 1985 Meese declared that the justices had abandoned their "intended role . . . as the 'faithful guardians of the Constitution' . . . [by] departing from the literal provisions of the Constitution." Because of this error the Court's decisions were "more policy choices than articulations of constitutional principle." This was inadequate, Meese continued, since "a Constitution that is viewed as only what the judges say it is, is no longer a constitution in the true sense." The solution, Meese concluded, should be a "jurisprudence of original intention," an approach "that would not be tainted by ideological predilection" of the judges, and thus consistent with democratic principles (Meese, 1985).

This public attack on the Court by the highest law enforcement officer of the nation provoked an equally vituperative reply from liberal members of the Court. In a public address at Georgetown University, Justice William Brennan labeled Meese's call for judicial fidelity to "the intention of the Framers" a "little more than arrogance cloaked as humility" and "facile historicism." Not only is it often impossible to "gauge accurately the intent of the Framers," said Brennan, but to restrict claims of right to the values of 1789 would be to ignore "social progress" and simply enshrine a conservative presumption against any novel types of constitutional claims. "The ultimate question," Brennan emphasized, "must be what the words of the text mean in our time" (Brennan, 1985).

This same controversy has been pursued with the same zeal in legal academia. An especially telling example was Ronald Dworkin's article (1984) attacking federal judge Robert Bork for his decision in a "homosexual rights" case. Dworkin, professor of law at both Harvard and Oxford, is a leading member of the liberal activist or "noninterpretivist" school of constitutional law. Bork is one of three nationally prominent "conservative" law professors that Reagan has appointed to federal appeals courts (Scalia was another) and at the time was thought to be Reagan's first choice to fill the next vacancy on the Supreme Court.[5] In his decision in *Dronenberg v. Zech* (1984) Bork not only rejected the proposition that consensual homosexual activity is protected by a constitutional "right to privacy," but questioned the very existence of the "right to privacy" doctrine. Since the implied "right to privacy" was the legal foundation for the Supreme Court's 1973 abortion decision, Bork's opinion was viewed with alarm and outrage among homosexual rights groups, feminists, and civil libertarians.[6]

Dworkin ridiculed Bork's view that judges "must stick close to the text and history [of the Constitution] and their fair implications," which was essentially the approach advocated by Attorney General Meese, by calling it a "jurisprudence of fiat not argument" that is "sadly consistent with the Republican platform, which calls for the appointment of judges . . . with the proper, that is to say right-wing, views about 'traditional family values and the sanctity of innocent human life.'" Dworkin concluded with the suggestion that Bork's decision was motivated by sycophancy to the Reagan administration and predicted a dire future for the Supreme Court: "If justices with that view of their work colonize the Supreme Court, earning their places through decisions like Bork's, the Court will no longer be what our traditions celebrate, a forum of principle where unpopular minorities can argue for liberty on grounds of right. It will become the Moral

Majority's clubhouse, where the prejudices of the day are called constitutional law."

Conservative dissatisfaction with activist judges has not been confined to the federal courts. Conservatives waged a successful campaign to unseat the presiding Chief Justice of the Supreme Court of California, Rose Bird. Under California law all appeal court judges must submit to a "confirmation election" every twelve years. Nineteen eighty-six was Bird's year for confirmation, and conservatives, upset with her voting record on capital punishment, mounted an all-out campaign against her confirmation.

Chief Justice Bird's "offense" was her leading role in the California Supreme Court's campaign against capital punishment. The California court first struck down the state's capital punishment law in 1972. Twice the California legislature reenacted an amended law, and twice again it was struck down. A third capital punishment law was enacted in 1977 (over the veto of then governor Jerry Brown, who also appointed Bird) and was finally upheld by the court, with Bird dissenting. Still, there have been no executions since the 1977 amendments. The court upheld only three of fifty-five convictions in capital punishment cases, and Chief Justice Bird was the only judge to vote to overturn the death penalty in all fifty-five cases. Her "reward" was to become the first California appellate judge ever to lose a confirmation vote.

The events reviewed above provide anecdotal evidence of an increasingly bitter partisan conflict over the proper role of judges in American politics. The existence of this trend is also supported by more systematic studies of Reagan's judicial appointees and their decisions. Supported by the Republican-controlled Senate, the Reagan administration has used the president's appointment power to reshape the political face of the federal judiciary. Given the tenure-for-life status of American judges, this may well prove to be the most enduring achievement of the Reagan presidency.

Reagan's dramatic reorientation of the political composition of the Supreme Court has been widely publicized.[7] The Rehnquist and Scalia appointments complement Reagan's earlier appointment of Justice Sandra Day O'Connor, creating a unified, articulate, and energetic voting bloc for conservative constitutional doctrines. The O'Connor appointment was a political coup of the first order. By appointing the first woman ever to serve on the Supreme Court, Reagan successfully deflected feminist criticisms that his administration was hostile to "women's issues" (Press, 1981). At the same time he appointed a justice whose conservative track record has been second only to Rehnquist's since her appointment in 1981 (Greenhouse, 1982).

Rehnquist and O'Connor gain an important new ally in Antonin Scalia. While probably no more conservative than Warren Burger, Scalia is considered to be a stronger intellect and a much more forceful voice for conservative positions. Rehnquist's elevation to chief justice will also enhance his influence within the Court. Even his critics concede that his personal charm and shrewd intellect will make Rehnquist a more forceful leader than the retiring chief.

A final indication of conservative dominance on the Supreme Court is the "age factor." The three most conservative members of the new Court—Rehnquist, O'Connor, and Scalia—are sixty-one, fifty-six, and fifty, respectively. The three most liberal members of the Court —Brennan, Marshall, and Blackmun—are eighty, seventy-seven, and seventy-seven, respectively. The difference between the average age of these two voting blocs is more than twenty years. As a result, conservative constitutional perspectives will be well represented on the Court for at least the next fifteen years. Liberal constitutional doctrines —such as the "right to privacy"—may be without a dependable voice in less than four years, unless there are new liberal appointments. This could happen only if a Democrat wins the presidency in 1988.

The impact of Reagan's appointments on the remainder of the federal judiciary has received less publicity but may well be more important. During his first term Reagan appointed 160 federal judges. By the end of his second term, given normal retirement rates, it is estimated that Reagan will have appointed more than half of all lower federal judges, a record equaled by only two other modern presidents —Roosevelt and Eisenhower (Goldman, 1985:314).

Not only will Reagan have appointed more federal judges than any president in American history, but it also appears that he is succeeding in appointing judges who share his political conservatism. Goldman's (1985) study of the demographic and attribute profiles of Reagan's first-term judicial appointments found that they differ from other presidents in important ways. At the district court level 97 percent of his appointees have been from his own political party, a higher percentage than for any president since Woodrow Wilson. At the appeal court level he is the first president since Warren Harding not to appoint a single member from the other party. Reagan has also appointed a higher percentage of Catholics to the district courts than any Republican president, and even more than Johnson and Carter (Goldman, 1985:323). This trend probably reflects the importance of the Catholic vote in the Reagan coalition and the administration's conservative views on the social issues. Reagan's choice of Antonin Scalia, the first Italian-American ever appointed to the Supreme Court, and a devout Roman Catholic and father of nine, is likely to further consolidate Republican inroads into what was once a solidly Democratic voting bloc.

In the spirit of affirmative action the Carter administration appointed unprecedented numbers of women and minorities to federal judgeships (Goldman, 1981). This trend has been abruptly reversed. Reagan has appointed fewer black judges to the federal district courts than any president since Eisenhower, who appointed none. Reagan's appeal court appointees have included only three female and minority judges (out of thirty-one), while Carter appointed twenty-three (out of fifty-six). The Reagan administration's explanation for the small percentage of minority appointments is its inability to find candidates who "share the President's philosophy" (Goldman, 1985:322).

Concern with the right judicial philosophy also explains the unusually high percentage of Reagan appointees who have prior judicial experience. The existence of a prior judicial track record has allowed the Reagan administration to be more certain that a candidate has the right judicial philosophy (Goldman, 1985:323). The concern with judicial philosophy also explains one final anomaly in the Reagan appeal court appointees—five of thirty-one were law professors, the highest percentage (16.1 percent) of any recent president. Like Scalia and Bork, all were "well known as conservative thinkers and advocates of judicial self-restraint." It was hoped that they would provide conservative intellectual leadership on their respective judicial circuits as well as serving as a pool of candidates for Reagan's next Supreme Court appointments (Goldman, 1985:325–26). The Scalia appointment represented the first fruit of this strategy.

In stressing ideological and policy considerations Reagan is acting more like a Democratic president and departing from past Republican practice of choosing judges based on legal expertise (Murphy and

Pritchett, 1976:154). To maximize its goals in the field of judicial appointments, the Reagan administration has centralized the recruitment process in the White House to a far greater extent than did any of its predecessors. Recruitment processes that in past administrations had been more "informal and fluid" have been institutionalized in a new "Presidential Selection Committee" that bridges the White House and the Justice Department, but is tilted toward the former. This committee, Goldman concludes, "has resulted in the most consistent ideological or policy-orientation screening of judicial candidates since the first term of Franklin Roosevelt" (Goldman, 1985:315).

Appointment by the president is no guarantee that he will be pleased by the results. American history is strewn with examples of presidents who came to regret their judicial appointments. Most pertinent to the present controversy was Eisenhower's appointment of Earl Warren, which he later lamented as "the biggest damn fool mistake I ever made" (Murphy and Pritchett, 1979:155). Several recent studies of the actual decisions of Reagan-appointed judges, however, suggest that he has avoided this pitfall.

A qualitative study of over seven hundred decisions by Reagan appointees concluded that they were indeed exercising the kind of judicial self-restraint that the Republican platform had promised (Stern, 1984). Of the sixty-two judges evaluated, thirty-one were found to "exercise restraint in all of their significant cases without exception"; sixteen exercised restraint in "nearly all of their significant cases"; while nine did so in less than half (Stern, 1984:5). (Six published no opinions.) Jon Gottschall's (1986) more quantitative study of the same decisions disclosed a number of conservative trends. In non-unanimous cases in which both Carter- and Reagan-appointed judges were involved, the Carter appointees voted for the "liberal outcome" in 95 percent of the cases, while the Reagan appointees did so in only 5 percent. Even when compared with the Nixon-Ford appointees, the Reagan appointees' ideological profiles tended to be slightly more conservative.

Constitutional law is made from the top down, but administered from the bottom up. The precedent-setting influence of the Supreme Court's decisions in landmark cases is obvious. But these number less than 150 a year, while lower federal court decisions number in the thousands. The quantity of federal litigation is so great and the time of the Supreme Court so limited that the lower federal courts operate with substantial autonomy and independence (Howard, 1973). To consolidate a national political realignment in the federal judiciary a president must substantially alter the composition of both the tip and base of the federal judicial "pyramid." Reagan may well be the first president since Franklin Roosevelt to do so.

Conclusion

The liberal-conservative struggle for control of the federal judiciary manifests itself at two levels. At a theoretical level there is a conflict over the proper approach to constitutional interpretation—the interpretivist-noninterpretivist debate. At a more immediate or practical level there is a struggle over federal judicial appointments, especially to the Supreme Court. These two dimensions of the conflict are linked by the fact that each side wants to appoint judges with the "right" constitutional philosophy. Stated more bluntly, both sides are attempting to control the meaning of constitutional law by controlling the appointment of judges.

Victory in this struggle will go to the side that controls the process of judicial appointments and exercises the power of appointment in a partisan manner. The future political role of the Supreme Court is thus directly linked to such practical matters as whether the Republicans can sustain their control of the White House and the Senate. If another ideologically conservative Republican is elected president in 1988, there is a real probability that there will be a Supreme Court that facilitates rather than impedes the conservative policy agenda. Just as Roosevelt used his judicial appointments to consolidate the political realignment of 1932, American conservatives will be able to consolidate the political realignment (or dealignment) that has occurred since 1968. When one recalls that the Roosevelt Court simply abandoned entire areas of prior constitutional precedent and policy, the significance of a Reagan Court becomes apparent.

Winning the war over judicial appointments, however, will not entail a parallel victory at the level of jurisprudence. Conservatives are correct in their critique of noninterpretivism as radically unprincipled and antidemocratic. But the liberals are equally correct in their critique of interpretivism as usually impossible and often undesirable. Strict judicial fidelity to original understanding of constitutional text may have made good sense in the era of John Marshall. Indeed, it may still be the only way to reconcile the practice of judicial review with democracy. In contemporary practice, however, it is no longer a realistic option. That original meaning has become either too dim, too archaic, or too controverted to serve as a consistent guide to contemporary constitutional practice.

This does not mean that we might not see a new conservative jurisprudence that presents itself as faithful to the original meaning of constitutional text. It is unlikely, however, that such a jurisprudence would be any closer to the Constitution, or any more deductive, than the liberal, noninterpretivist jurisprudence that conservatives now criticize. A new conservative jurisprudence would not necessarily lack internal consistency or legal predictability. It would clearly be more deferential to state legislatures and Congress and less interventionist in its remedies. But its coherence would come not from legalistic fidelity to original understanding, but from a conservative ideological consensus. In effect, "fidelity to original understanding" would be transformed from a legal method that minimizes judicial discretion to a rhetorical technique that conceals it.

Liberals are disturbed by this prospect, but their charges of judicial duplicity and abdication are otiose. The same charges could just as easily be leveled at the Roosevelt Court after 1937. The Court and the Constitution do not exist separately and apart from the rest of American politics. Sooner or later they must follow sustained shifts in public opinion, as expressed in political realignments in presidential and congressional elections (Dahl, 1957). If the tradition of constitutionalism is to be preserved, some judicial sleight of hand is required to smooth over the rupture with the preceding (but now discredited) regime. In the 1930s this function was filled by the concept of a "living constitution." In the 1980s the jurisprudence of "fidelity to original understanding" may serve a similar purpose.

CONSERVATISM AND THE COURTS IN CANADA

No modern federal minister of justice has ever launched a Meese-like attack on the decisions of the Supreme Court of Canada. One who did would almost certainly be attacked in question period for interfering with the judicial process. One would search in vain for an article with such a vituperative tone as Dworkin's attack on Judge Bork. As for the

American practice of electing judges, Canadians regard it as a dangerous corruption of the common law tradition of judicial independence.
In Canada federal judges are not even allowed to vote, much less run
for office. The spectacle of the chief justice of the most populous state
in the union being voted out of office because of the political unpopularity of her decisions would confirm Canadians' skepticism about
this American practice.

If anything, Canada is moving in the opposite direction as far as
federal judicial appointments are concerned. While patronage considerations have always been an important factor in judicial appointments in Canada, political ideology has not (Russell, 1969; Bouthillier, 1971, 1972, 1978; Klein, 1975). The Reagan administration's
institutionalization of an ideological screening process for prospective
judicial appointments, as reported by Goldman, is foreign, if not repug-
nant, to Canadian legal tradition. Currently there is a reform movement to insulate judicial appointments from partisan political considerations. The Canadian Bar Association (1985) has recently endorsed
two major reports calling for independent judicial nominating councils and is currently lobbying the Mulroney government to introduce
the proposed reforms.

The explanation for this contrast is relatively simple. There was
no equivalent to the Warren Court in recent Canadian experience and
thus no conservative reaction to the liberal policy impact of judicial
activism. Unlike in the U.S. presidential elections of 1968, 1980, and
1984, the courts and judicial appointments were nonissues in the
election that brought Mulroney and the Progressive Conservatives to
power in 1984.[8]

Judicial politics in Canada for the past two decades has been almost
the reverse of the American counterpart. At the height of the American Supreme Court's reformist intervention in various aspects of American politics and policy, the Supreme Court of Canada was minimizing
the political impact of Canada's new (1960) Bill of Rights through a
series of restrictive interpretations (Tarnopolsky, 1975).

Although the American Court struck down restrictive state abortion laws (Roe v. Wade, 1973), the Canadian Court declined a similar
opportunity (Morgentaler v. R., 1976). While the American Court was
fashioning an entirely new area of "sex discrimination" jurisprudence
(Craig v. Boren, 1976; Morton, 1984), the Canadian Court refused to

strike down gender-based legislation that had a negative impact on female litigants (*A.-G. Canada v. Lavell and Bedard*, 1973; *Bliss v. A.-G. Canada*, 1978). In the area of pornography the American Court made it practically impossible for states to enforce their censorship laws (*Memoirs v. Massachusetts*, 1966). In Canada the Supreme Court routinely upheld the powers of provincial censorship boards (*Nova Scotia Board of Censors v. McNeil*, 1978). The American Court gave the traditional "right to counsel" important new meaning by extending it far into the pretrial stages (*Miranda v. Arizona*, 1966). The Canadian Court refused to do so (*Regina v. Wray*, 1971). The American Court further expanded the rights of criminal defendants when it ruled that evidence gathered in violation of the Constitution must be excluded from the trial (*Mapp v. Ohio*, 1961). A decade later the Canadian Supreme Court refused to adopt such an "exclusionary rule" (*Hogan v. The Queen*, 1974).

Dissatisfaction with the 1960 Bill of Rights' alleged ineffectiveness was a major factor leading to the adoption of the new and much broader Canadian Charter of Rights in 1982 (Romanow, Whyte, and Leeson, 1984: chap. 5). The adoption of the Charter created strong expectations that the Supreme Court of Canada should abandon the practice of judicial self-restraint associated with the 1960 Bill of Rights and forge a more activist and more libertarian jurisprudence. Ironically, the implicit model for such a jurisprudence was the American example of the Warren Court. To the extent that the Supreme Court of Canada does develop an activist libertarian Charter jurisprudence, the likelihood of similarities to American experience increases.

Similarities

While there may be nothing intrinsically liberal about judicial review of constitutionally entrenched rights, the political genesis of the Canadian Charter strongly suggested that it would have a liberal policy impact, at least in its early years. From its inception the Charter was strongly supported by civil libertarians, feminists, and other "human rights" groups (Knopff and Morton, 1986). Having influenced its drafting, members and supporters of these same liberal groups have dominated professional and scholarly discussion of Charter issues and have been vocal in advocating broad interpretations of Charter provisions (Flanagan, 1986). These same groups have also been active in planning and bringing Charter litigation to advance their policy objectives (Morton, 1987a).

The Canadian Supreme Court has absorbed much of the substance and style of this new Charter-inspired environment. In its decisions to date the Court has explicitly rejected the self-restraint and narrow interpretation characteristic of its earlier Bill of Rights jurisprudence. It has ruled in favor of Charter litigants in nine of fourteen cases. The Court has nullified all or parts of six statutes and has adopted an American-style "exclusionary rule" to overturn lower court convictions in several criminal cases (Russell, 1985; Morton, 1987b).

In certain cases the Canadian Supreme Court has actually gone further than its American counterpart. Where the American Supreme Court has upheld Sunday closing laws by emphasizing their contemporary secular (i.e., common day of rest) purpose, the Canadian Supreme Court struck down a similar law by stressing its original purpose (The Queen v. Big M Drug Mart, Ltd., 1985). In another case a coalition of "peace groups" challenged the federal government's decision to allow the United States to test the cruise missile in western Canada. In the United States legal challenges to foreign and defense policy decisions are automatically dismissed because they are said to raise "political questions" and are thus nonjusticiable. The Canadian Court refused to accept a "political questions" doctrine and proceeded to hear the case on its merits. It eventually rejected the Charter challenge but left open the possibility that the government could be called upon to defend the legality of its foreign policy decisions before the Court (Operation Dismantle v. The Queen, 1985).

On the critical issue of how to interpret the meaning of constitutional rights, the issue that has so divided American judges and commentators, the Canadian Court has blithely adopted a radical version of the noninterpretivist method. Historical records of legislative intent have been characterized as being "inherently unreliable," and judicial fidelity to "original understanding" as "freezing" the meaning of the Charter, rendering it incapable of "growth, development and adjustment to changing social needs" (British Columbia Motor Vehicle Reference, 1985). If the Court adheres to this approach, it will be able to read an unlimited "new meaning" into the Charter in coming years.

The Charter has also mobilized various interest groups to turn to the courts to pursue their policy objectives. The most publicized was the unsuccessful challenge by "Operation Dismantle," a coalition of disarmament groups, to the testing of U.S. cruise missiles in Canada. More successful was a conservative group's challenge to provisions of the Canadian Election Act that prohibited independent expenditures by "political action committees" on behalf of candidates for Parliament (*National Citizens' Coalition, Inc. v. A.-G. Canada*, 1984). Both sides of the abortion controversy have resorted to Charter litigation in attempts to change existing policy, thus far without success (Collins, 1985). Canadian feminists have published a sophisticated study that draws heavily on American interest group experience and details resources and tactics for achieving policy change through "systematic litigation strategies" (Atcheson, Eberts, and Symes, 1984). In 1985 the feminists announced the implementation of a key element of that strategy—a single, nationwide legal action fund to support the systematic litigation of strategic "test cases." Finally, the federal government has itself contributed to interest group use of Charter litigation by creating a C\$9 million "court Challenges Program" to assist litigation raising claims under the equality and language rights provisions of the Charter (Morton, 1986).

Prior to 1982 interest group use of litigation as a political tactic was rare. The dramatic increase in such political behavior indicates that the Charter is having an impact not just on judicial behavior but on the Canadian political system as a whole. Only a decade ago a leading Canadian historian could describe interest group use of litigation as a political tactic "illegitimate" and un-Canadian (McNaught, 1975:138). The Charter appears to have changed this perception, and thereby the practice of politics in Canada.

Even prior to the Charter the Supreme Court had been moving toward a greater policymaking role. Until the 1970s the Court's institutional and procedural characteristics closely conformed to the "adjudication of disputes" model of judicial decisionmaking (Weiler, 1968). Until appeals to the Judicial Committee of the Privy Council were abolished in 1949, the Supreme Court was not even the nation's final court of appeal. A reform of equal significance was the abolition of almost all "appeals by right" in 1975. This has allowed the Court to control its own docket and to hear only cases raising issues of sufficient "national importance" (Laskin, 1975:474). Prior to this reform, almost three-quarters of the Court's cases were "appeals as of right." Subsequently, this figure has dropped to less than one-quarter (Bushnell, 1982:497). An important consequence has been a dramatic increase in the number of public law cases decided by the Court, a trend that has become even more pronounced since the adoption of the Charter (Morton, 1985).

Other innovations in the way the Court conducts its business also indicate a more politically conscious court. The Court recently abandoned the practice of absolute adherence to *stare decisis* and has shown a new willingness to overrule earlier decisions (Morton, 1985). The Court has also relaxed the criteria necessary to attain "standing," which -in turn has facilitated easier access to the courts for interest groups. A related development has been the Court's new interest in receiving "extrinsic evidence" or "social" facts through the medium of factums akin to the "Brandeis brief" (Morton, 1984a: chap. 7). Collectively, these procedural changes suggest that the Supreme Court has moved from the British model of judicial behavior and toward a more American, and therefore more policymaking, role. The adoption of the Charter of Rights in 1982 has further reinforced this trend.

This is not to suggest that the Supreme Court of Canada has picked up where the Warren Court left off. Compared to American experience, the political impact of the Charter seems quite modest. However, it has begun to change important aspects of Canadian politics. During the 1960s and 1970s Canadian politics were dominated by a single issue—the national unity crisis. The resulting political agenda, as shaped by Prime Minister Trudeau and the Liberal party, was dominated by the issues of federal-provincial relations, constitutional reform, and language rights. This preoccupation with national unity issues partially immunized Canadian politics from the ideological influences of other liberal democracies.[9] This was especially true of the new "politics of rights" and the accompanying social issues controversies that were brewing in the United States during this same time (Scheingold, 1974).

The politics of national unity culminated in the Constitution Act of 1982. As Gibbins has noted elsewhere in this volume, the new Constitution and the subsequent Mulroney landslide have suddenly changed the landscape of Canadian politics. The old issues of national unity and constitutional reform have disappeared, at least for the time being. In their place Mulroney has shaped a new national agenda dominated by economic issues such as national debt, the deficit, and free trade. Closer economic integration with the United States, Gibbins notes, may bring not just more American products into Canada but American political controversies as well.

It is suggested here that a new "politics of rights" has already been imported and is fast becoming part of Canada's political agenda for the 1980s. Canadian civil libertarians, human rights groups, and feminists have successfully used both the Charter and existing antidiscrimination laws (Flanagan, 1985) to bring a number of new issues to the center of national and provincial politics. Scarcely a day passes that there is not a prominent newspaper article on issues such as "equal pay for work of equal value," the abolition of mandatory retirement, or a recent court decision striking down a censorship law or freeing an imprisoned criminal because his rights were violated.

Recent American experience demonstrates how these kinds of issues can divide an electorate along conservative-liberal lines. While they have not yet done so in Canada, the potential clearly exists (Gibbins, Knopff, and Morton, 1985). The strong libertarian bias of the Supreme Court's early Charter decisions suggests that this trend may already be developing. If it continues, the American spectacle of a politicized judiciary may not long remain alien to Canadian experience.

An event at the 1986 annual meeting of the Canadian Bar Association may indicate the course of future events. On a panel discussing judicial appointments, Roy Romanow, the former attorney-general of Saskatchewan and a key architect of the Charter of Rights, called for American-style confirmation hearings for Supreme Court nominees. In the future, he said, political ideology would determine how Canadian judges decided such Charter issues as abortion and pornography. It was inevitable, Romanow predicted, that "prime ministers will campaign on a promise to appoint liberal or conservative judges." Copanelist David Matas quickly denounced Romanow's recommendation as "an attack on the independence of the judiciary" (CBC, The National, September 1986). No doubt Canadian judicial tradition and a majority of the audience were on Matas's side. Time, however, may be on Romanow's side.

NOTES

1   An important exception to this generalization was the "judicial nationalists" of the
     1930s, who organized the movement to abolish appeals to the Judicial Committee
     of the Privy Council. Cairns (1972), Russell (1975), and Snell and Vaughan (1985)
     all emphasize that the desire to remove the JCPC as Canada's final court of appeal
     was politically motivated. The judicial nationalists all hoped that the Supreme
     Court of Canada, once free of the superintendence of the JCPC, would develop a
     more centralist or pro-Ottawa jurisprudence of federalism.
2   I agree with and am following Pye's distinctions made elsewhere in this volume. The
     liberal-conservative dichotomy denotes the determination of cases on their merits or
     outcomes. The activist-restraint dichotomy refers to those procedural issues that
     determine whether a court will even consider matters on their merits (i.e., granting
     leave to appeal or certiorari, and the issues of standing, mootness, and ripeness); and
     whether a court will use broad remedial orders to rectify or compensate for violations
     of constitutional rights.
3   Rehnquist's sins consisted of alleged harassment of minority voters at polling places
     as a Republican official in Arizona in the 1950s; the presence of restrictive racial
     covenants in the deeds of homes he bought in 1961 and 1974; and his advice to the
     Nixon administration on how to deal with antiwar protestors during the 1960s. These
     and other *allegedly* damaging incidents were recounted for the committee and the
     millions watching on television.
4   Affirmative action, abortion, sex discrimination, court-ordered busing, voluntary
     school prayer, state assistance to parochial schools, censorship of pornography, capi-
     tal punishment, and the exclusionary rule.
5   Robert Bork, formerly a professor of law at Yale University; Antonin Scalia and
     Richard Posner, both former professors at the University of Chicago Law School.
6   To appreciate the political dimensions—and thus the bitterness—of Dworkin's attack
     on Bork, it is necessary to know something about the "right to privacy." The "right to
     privacy" is arguably the most politically controversial right in contemporary consti-
     tutional jurisprudence. Not found in the actual wording of the constitution, the
     "right to privacy" was first articulated by Justice Douglas in 1964 as being implicit in
     certain of the enumerated rights. Such judicial invention of rights not explicitly
     found in the language or original understanding of the Constitution is precisely the
     kind of jurisprudence that Attorney General Meese was attacking. A short nine years
     later, this judicially created right to privacy served as the basis for the Court's contro-
     versial abortion decision, in which it invalidated the antiabortion statutes of forty-
     eight states and in effect legislated an abortion-on-demand policy for the United
     States. In short, the "right to privacy" is one of those constitutional doctrines that
     liberals love and conservatives detest. For a federal appeals court judge to publicly
     question the legitimacy of the right to privacy was an outrage to liberals. Enter Ronald
     Dworkin.
7   The Rehnquist appointment was the cover story for both *Time* ("Reagan's Mr. Right")
     and *Newsweek* ("Reagan's Law") on June 30, 1986.
8   I am excluding the flurry of judicial patronage appointments made by the Liberal

government of John Turner in June 1984. The Tories successfully exploited the negative public reaction to these appointments during the campaign. These appointments were all based on prior political service in, or for support of, the federal Liberal party or the departing prime minister and had none of the ideological overtones that characterize the controversy over Reagan's judicial appointments.

9 Lipset (1985: chap. 5) discusses the development of the "new politics" in post-industrial Western democracies during the 1960s and 1970s. He points out that an "oppositionist intelligentsia" has emerged as "the most dynamic agent of change, taking over the role assigned by Marxism for the proletariat." The "new politics" agenda is characterized by such issues as women's and gay liberation, environmental issues, and antinuclear and peace issues. Canada is not included in Lipset's comparative analysis. The reason is because the "new politics" issues in Canada were preempted by the politics of national unity during this period. With the adoption of the Constitution Act in 1982, this is no longer the case. Note also that constitutional litigation became a preferred tactic of the practitioners of the "new politics" in the United States. The Charter now offers a similar opportunity in Canada.

REFERENCES

Atcheson, M. Elizabeth, Mary Eberts, and Beth Symes. 1984. *Women and Legal Action: Precedents, Resources and Strategies for the Future*. Ottawa: Canadian Advisory Council on the Status of Women.

Blasi, Vincent. 1983. *The Burger Court: The Counter-Revolution That Wasn't*. New Haven, Conn.: Yale University Press.

Bouthillier, Guy. 1971. "Matériaux pour une analyse politique des juges de la Cour d'appel." *La Revue Juridique Themis* 6: 563.

———. 1972. "Note sur la carrière politique des juges de la Cour supérieure." *La Revue Juridique Themis* 7.

———. 1978. "Profil du juge de la Cour des sessions de la paix." *Revue du Barreau* 38: 178.

Brennan, William J., Jr. 1985. "The Constitution of the United States: Contemporary Ratification." Paper presented at the Text and Teaching Symposium, Georgetown University, Washington, D.C., October 12.

Bushnell, S. I. 1982. "Leave to Appeal Applications to the Supreme Court of Canada: A Matter of Public Importance." *Supreme Court Law Review* 3: 479–558.

Cairns, Alan. 1971. "The Judicial Committee and Its Critics." *Canadian Journal of Political Science* 4: 301–45.

Canadian Bar Association. 1985. "The Appointment of Judges in Canada."

Collins, Anne. 1985. *The Big Evasion: Abortion—The Issue That Won't Go Away*. Toronto: Lester and Orpen Dennys.

Dahl, Robert A. 1957. "Decision-Making in a Democracy: The Supreme Court as a National Policy-Maker." *Journal of Public Law* 6: 279–95.

Dworkin, Ronald. 1984. "Reagan's Justice." *New York Review of Books* 31 (November 15), no. 8: 27–31.

Flanagan, Thomas. 1985. "Policy-Making by Exegesis: The Abolition of 'Mandatory Retirement.'" *Canadian Public Policy* 11: 40.

———. 1986. Review of Anne F. Bayefsky and Mary Eberts, eds., *Equality Rights and the Canadian Charter of Rights and Freedoms*. In *Canadian Journal of Law and Society* 1: 174–76.

Fowler, W. Gary. 1984. "Judicial Selection Under Reagan and Carter: Comparison of Their Initial Recommendation Procedures." *Judicature* 67: 6.

Gibbins, Roger, Rainer Knopff, and F. L. Morton. 1985. "Canadian Federalism and the 1984 Elections." *Publius* 15: 153–69.

Goldman, Sheldon. 1981. "Carter's Judicial Appointees: A Lasting Legacy." *Judicature* 64: 355.

———. 1985. "Reaganizing the Judiciary: The First-Term Appointments." *Judicature* 68: 313.

Gottschall, Jon. 1986. "Reagan's Appointments to the U.S. Courts of Appeals: The Continuation of a Judicial Revolution." Forthcoming in *Judicature*.

Greenhouse, Linda. 1982. "Justice Sandra Day O'Connor on the Supreme Court." *New York Times*, June 4.

Klein, William. 1975. "Judicial Recruitment in Manitoba, Ontario, and Quebec, 1905–1970." Unpublished Ph.D. dissertation, University of Toronto.

Knopff, Rainer, and F. L. Morton. 1986. "Nation-Building and the Canadian Charter of Rights and Freedoms." In Alan Cairns and Cynthia Williams, eds., *Constitutionalism, Citizenship, and Society in Canada*. Toronto: University of Toronto Press.

Ladd, Carl Everett. 1985. "As the Realignment Turns: A Drama in Many Acts." *Public Opinion* 4: 1–6.

Laskin, Bora. 1975. "The Role and Functions of Final Appellate Courts: The Supreme Court of Canada." *Canadian Bar Review* 53: 469–81.

Levy, Leonard. 1974. *Against the Law: The Nixon Court and Criminal Justice*. New York: Harper & Row.

Lipset, Seymour Martin. 1985. *Consensus and Conflict: Essays in Political Sociology*. New Brunswick, N.J.: Transaction Books.

McClellan, James. 1984. "Advertisement to Our Readers." *Benchmark* 1, nos. 4 and 5.

McNaught, Kenneth. 1975. "Political Trials and the Canadian Political Tradition." In M. L. Friedland, ed., *Courts and Trials: A Multidisciplinary Approach*. Toronto: University of Toronto Press.

Meese, Edwin, III. 1985. Address to the American Bar Association, Washington, D.C., July 9.

Morton, F. L. 1984a. *Law, Politics, and the Judicial Process in Canada*. Calgary: University of Calgary Press.

———. 1984b. "A Case Study of Judicial Policy-Making: The Supreme Court's Promotion of Sexual Equality, 1971–1981." *Polity* 18: 3, 467–83.

———. 1985. "The Changing Role of the Supreme Court of Canada: From Adjudicator Toward Policy-Maker." Paper submitted at the Research Committee on Comparative Judicial Studies, Thirteenth World Congress of the International Political Science Association, Paris, July 15–19.

————. 1987a. "The Political Impact of the Charter of Rights." *Canadian Journal of Political Science* 20: 31–56.

————. 1987b. "Charting the Charter, 1982–1985: A Statistical Analysis." Forthcoming in the *Canadian Human Rights Yearbook 1986.*

Murphy, Walter, and C. Herman Pritchett. 1979. *Courts, Judges, and Politics: An Introduction to the Judicial Process.* New York: Random House.

Press, Aric. 1981. "A Woman for the Court." *Newsweek,* July 20.

Romanow, Roy, John Whyte, and Howard Leeson. 1984. *Canada Notwithstanding: The Making of the Constitution 1976–1982.* Toronto: Carswell-Methuen.

Russell, Peter H. 1969. *The Supreme Court of Canada as a Bilingual and Bicultural Institution.* Ottawa: Queen's Printer.

————. 1975. "Judicial Power in Canada's Political Culture." In M. L. Friedland, ed., *Courts and Trials: A Multidisciplinary Approach.* Toronto: University of Toronto Press, pp. 75–88.

————. 1985. "The First Three Years in Charterland." *Canadian Public Administration* 28: 367–96.

Scheingold, Stuart A. 1974. *The Politics of Rights: Lawyers, Public Policy, and Political Change.* New Haven, Conn.: Yale University Press.

Simon, J. F. 1973. *In His Own Image: The Supreme Court in Richard Nixon's America.* New York: McKay.

Snell, James G., and Frederick Vaughan. 1985. *The Supreme Court of Canada: History of the Institution.* Toronto: University of Toronto Press.

Stern, Craig. 1984. "Judging the Judges: The First Two Years of the Reagan Bench." *Benchmark* 1, nos. 4 and 5: 1–118.

Tarnopolsky, W. S. 1975. "The Supreme Court and the Canadian Bill of Rights." *Canadian Bar Review* 53: 649–74.

Weiler, Paul. 1968. "Two Models of Judicial Decision-Making." *Canadian Bar Review* 46: 406–71.

AMERICAN LEGAL REFERENCES

Craig v. Boren, 429 U.S. 190 (1976).

Dronenberg v. Zech et al., U.S. Court of Appeals, DC Circuit, decided August 17, 1984.

Mapp v. Ohio, 367 U.S. 643 (1961).

Memoirs v. Massachusetts, 383 U.S. 413 (1966).

Miranda v. Arizona, 384 U.S. 436 (1966).

Roe v. Wade, 410 U.S. 113 (1973).

CANADIAN LEGAL REFERENCES

A.-G. Canada v. Lavell and Bedard, [1973] 38 D.L.R. (3d) 481.

Bliss v. A.-G. Canada, [1979] 1 S.C.R. 183.

Hogan v. The Queen, [1974] 48 D.L.R. (3d) 427.

Morgentaler v. R., [1976] 1 S.C.R. 616.
National Citizens' Coalition Inc. v. A.-G. Canada, [1985] WWR 436.
Nova Scotia Board of Censors v. McNeil, [1978] 2 S.C.R. 662.
Operation Dismantle v. The Queen, [1985] 1 S.C.R. 441.
The Queen v. Big M Drug Mart [1985], 18 D.L.R. (4th) 321.
Reference re British Columbia Motor Vehicle Act. [1985] 2 S.C.R. 486.
Regina v. Wray, [1971] S.C.R. 272.

7. Conservatism and the Courts: A Comparative Analysis of Canada and the United States

A. KENNETH PYE

INTRODUCTION

The number of opinions and judgments rendered by courts and the variety of approaches reflected in decisions of different courts make it infeasible to comment generally upon attitudes of courts. Even limiting inquiry to the two supreme courts is too broad. The Supreme Court of Canada is a court of last resort in a wide range of cases over which the Supreme Court of the United States would have no jurisdiction.[1] Questions of statutory interpretation and common law issues presented to either court frequently do not provide good examples for comparison.

Constitutional decisions involving basic rights provide a broad, but discrete, area where the behavior of the two supreme courts can be compared, and this chapter will be limited to this focus, with special emphasis upon the field of criminal procedure. Such an approach is particularly appropriate at this time when the Supreme Court of Canada is wrestling with the difficult task of drawing a map of "Charterland" (Russell, 1985:367).

OF LIBERALISM, ACTIVISM, AND CONSERVATISM IN COURTS

The problem of assessing courts in terms of their liberalism or conservatism differs from that of assessing legislatures. Substantively, it is possible to evaluate much of legislative (or executive) behavior on a continuum ranging from extreme Tory to Marxist. Even in the center of such a continuum it may be possible to form prudential judgments concerning relative conservatism in terms of the balance that has been struck between governmental power and individual liberties; the progressive or regressive nature of tax policies; analyzing the impact of monetary policy on different economic classes in a society; the sensitivity displayed toward various forms of discrimination or programs to alleviate past discrimination; or the beneficiaries of social, political, and economic policy and which segments of society pay for them. It is conceded that such an analysis is not free from difficulty, particularly in a federal system where some states and provinces may reflect directions contrary to those of the central government.

Evaluation of court behavior involves more complex factors. Of course, analysis of some court decisions may involve the same or similar value judgments as legislative or executive decisionmaking, overtly or covertly. Despite disclaimers of judicial lawmaking, court decisions such as those striking down or permitting governmental practices that result in racial discrimination or permit or prohibit affirmative action, or those permitting or prohibiting government intrusions into the privacy of the individual, may sometimes be appropriately evaluated in much the same way as evaluations of legislative judgments on similar issues (see Cardozo, 1921).

There are differences, however. Most supreme courts would at least pay lip service to the concept that their roles are primarily to (a) interpret the law or (b) strike down legislation where governmental powers are exceeded. Even an "activist" court may sustain a policy that it thinks unwise, or overturn one that it thinks wise, because of self-restraint imposed by its concept of its appropriate role in a democratic society.

Both the Supreme Court of the United States and the Supreme Court of Canada obviously have some latitude in determining when a legislature or an executive has exceeded its powers or when an individual's rights have been invaded. How broadly each perceives its role is a significant measure of the degree of its activism. When either should act, or refrain from acting, deferring to the executive or legislative branches, has spawned considerable controversy and a variety of constitutional theories (see Tribe, 1985; Ely, 1980; Bickel, 1969; Cox, 1976; Miller, 1985; Horowitz, 1977). Not infrequently an "activist" court is perceived as "liberal" and a "nonactivist court" is considered "conservative."

Sometimes labels are applied on the basis of how a court approaches the task of constitutional interpretation or application. A "strict constructionist" approach looking to the "original intent" of the framers as reflected from the text, context, and/or history of a provision[2] may be viewed as conservative. A "living instrument" approach that treats the language as a broad statement of principle intended to mean different things at different times and in different contexts may be considered "liberal," particularly if neutrality in interpretation is disdained. The oft-urged and rarely accepted concept of neutrality in constitutional adjudication should not properly be denominated liberal or conservative (Wechsler, 1959; Christie, 1975). This is especially true when constitutional issues are viewed as "fundamental choices of principle, not . . . instrumental calculations of utility or . . . pseudoscientific calibrations of social cost against social benefit" (Tribe, 1985:viii, note 4; Oakes, 1985:862–63). Positions of relative neutrality that would limit a court's role to protecting the representative character of the political process, except in extreme cases where absence of political representation or accountability has deprived a group of equal distribution of benefits and burdens, would be more conservative than the second position, although more liberal than the first (Ely, 1980:87; Oakes, 1985:864).

A supreme court in Canada or the United States also inevitably becomes an arbiter of federalism. Each must determine whether governmental powers reside in the central government or the states or provinces. Determinations on such a limited basis may, nevertheless, appear progressive or reactionary in political terms, depending upon the result that occurs. A court that strikes down legislation of a progressive state or province because it has legislated in the exclusive domain of a reactionary or conservative central government may appear to be rendering a conservative decision. A court that sustains such power may appear to be rendering a liberal decision.

Equally important are factual situations where courts reach "liberal" or "conservative" results by declining to decide cases presented to them. A supreme court that refuses to consider a lower court decision, for whatever reason, is permitting a result to stand that in political terms may be viewed as liberal or conservative, although such a characterization may be quite inappropriate in strictly legal terms.

The inconsistent use of criteria for review permits covert liberalism or conservatism by a court that might not be characterized as such on its substantive decisions. Willingness to disregard procedural objections and proceed to the merits may be the hallmark of a court that is activist without regard to whether its decisions on the merits are conservative or liberal.

There are several techniques by which either supreme court can preclude judicial review of a legislative pronouncement or decisions of a lower court. A decision to preclude any judicial intervention means that a legislature can call the shot. A decision to decline to review what a lower court has decided permits lower courts to do so.

An American court may consider only a case or controversy (U.S. Constitution art. III, 2). The judicial power of the federal courts is limited to the right to determine actual controversies arising between adverse litigants instituted in courts of competent jurisdiction. The Canadian Supreme Court can render advisory opinions and does so regularly. Indeed, one-quarter of cases involving constitutional issues decided by the Supreme Court of Canada have had their origins in constitutional reference (Strayer, 1983:271).

The American Supreme Court has traditionally declined to consider "political questions." During the last twenty-five years it has narrowed the scope of the doctrine but clearly will decline to render opinions in some cases that the Canadian Supreme Court would decide. The Supreme Court of Canada has commented that the American "political question" doctrine is predicated upon the concept of separation of powers that is inapplicable in the Canadian context. One wonders why the doctrine is inapplicable when the Court can invalidate a statute enacted by Parliament and Parliament can reenact the law notwithstanding the Court's action.

Both American and Canadian courts require that a plaintiff have standing, but the meaning of "standing" is quite different (Blake, 1984). In American cases a plaintiff is required to assert only his own rights, whereas Canadian cases permit a plaintiff to litigate issues that are not personal when the issue is of broad public importance (Pickard, 1986).

Either court may decline to take a case because it is not ripe, i.e., it has not yet reached the level where it is thought appropriate for judicial intervention (Macklem and Gertner, 1984). And either court may decline to take a case because it is moot, i.e., the real issue between the parties has already been decided, although the Canadian courts have "seemingly not concerned themselves unduly with the need for an actual and continuing dispute" so long as the issue is precise (Strayer, 1983:191–92). Again, the Supreme Court of the United States may decline to consider cases that the Supreme Court of Canada may deem appropriate for judicial resolution.

Absence of a unitary judicial system within the United States provides another example where American federal courts sometimes decline to consider issues on the merits. If state courts are in general unsympathetic with "liberal" interpretations of the Constitution by the Supreme Court, availability of access to the lower federal courts may be essential to a realistic implementation of federal constitutional rights. Absence of access to federal district courts means that the only manner in which a litigant may achieve a federal court determination of whether his federal right has been violated is on review by the Supreme Court of the United States, which can hear only a few cases annually. The Supreme Court has limited access to the federal courts through the writ of habeas corpus during recent years (Rosenberg, 1986). In fairness, however, it should be noted that the Court has considered a wide range of constitutional claims in cases that arose in federal habeas corpus proceedings without mentioning the landmark, *Stone v. Powell*, 428 U.S. 465 (1976) (LaFave and Isreal, 1984, sec. 27-3). Moreover, the Court has not reversed the holding in *Fay v. Moia* 372 U.S. 391 (1963) that a federal court has the power to consider federal constitutional questions despite state default (Seidman, 1980:465–67). Simultaneously, it has been increasingly reluctant to permit federal injunctive relief against state governmental authority alleged to have violated a federal constitutional right.

Finally, a supreme court may, through its process of discretionary review, greatly affect the impact of the legal system without ever deciding a case on the merits. The Supreme Court of the United States annually will be requested to review over 4,200 cases. Only about 180 of these cases can be determined on the merits (Hellman, 1985:948). The choice of when to grant or deny certiorari may be as important indicia of whether a court is conservative or liberal as any analysis of its decisions on the merits (Griswald, 1985:831; Songer, 1979:185).

Questions of procedure and remedy also affect the calculus of whether a court is "conservative" or "liberal." A court that has a broad doctrine of "harmless error"[3] may be prepared to render a liberal substantive opinion on the meaning of a right, yet it can simultaneously affirm a conviction because violation of the right was deemed to be "harmless." If one looks only at its decision on the merits, it may appear liberal. The result may be viewed differently if one looks at the impact upon the defendant who raised the question or the probable impact upon future defendants. A court that uses a broad concept of "fruit of the poison tree"[4] enforces a right to its fullest extent. Application of a narrower doctrine permits a court to interpret a right broadly with knowledge that its impact will be much more modest in practice.

A "conservative" or "liberal" view of a court's remedial powers may be as significant as a "conservative" or "liberal" view of the meaning of a right. Thus, decisions of American federal courts to exercise equity jurisdiction over school districts and prisons when constitutional rights were found to have been violated may have been as "liberal" as the decisions that determined that rights had been violated. Recent judicial decisions concerning the scope of the "exclusionary rule" may have narrowed the protection provided by the Fourth Amendment as much as if the Supreme Court had interpreted the Fourth itself more narrowly.

One way of assessing conservatism or liberalism of the two supreme courts would be simply to concentrate on these kinds of procedural issues. Courts that are expansive in their concept of jurisdiction, that open their doors to litigants, and that are prepared to provide creative remedies would be regarded as liberal. Courts that have a narrow concept of cases that they should review, tight requirements for standing, ripeness, and mootness, and a narrow concept of the remedial relief that is appropriate would be regarded as conservative.

But efforts to characterize judicial behavior as liberal or conservative also must deal with the problem that a court may appear to be acting "liberally" from one perspective and "conservatively" from another. Application of a "conservative-liberal" litmus test may yield a different conclusion depending upon whether the focal point of inquiry is whether the court is willing to reach the merits of a controversy as distinguished from how it decides cases it has considered on the merits. A court that may be "liberal," if assessed from the point of

view of the degree of judicial activism reflected by it, i.e., its willingness to decide issues that arguably invade the province of a coordinate
branch of government, may be adjudged "conservative" when it decides
on the merits the case over which jurisdiction has been asserted. The
American Supreme Court in the 1930s arguably utilized an "activist"
concept of substantive due process to assert extraordinarily broad judicial review of legislative judgments on economic measures. But having assumed the right to determine which legislation violated substantive due process, it then produced extremely conservative results by
limiting legislative powers.[5] It may be more accurate to refer to a court's
willingness to consider matters on the merits in terms of their
"activism" and reserve the "liberal-conservative" dichotomy to their
determinations on the merits.

An additional problem is posed by the reality that courts respond
differently to different issues. A court may be "conservative" on some
issues and "liberal" on others. To take an example from the Burger
Court: whatever its attitude on other issues of criminal procedure, it
has been consistent in striking down claims of racial exclusion in the
criminal process. *Vasquez v. Hillery* 106 S.Ct. 617 (1986) and *Batson v.
Kentucky* 54 L.W. 4425 (1986) preclude the use of peremptory challenges by a prosecutor to strike blacks from a jury. Likewise, despite
little sympathy for the *Miranda* rule, the Court has refused to permit
silence after *Miranda* warnings to be admitted as evidence of a defendant's sanity. It also has held that admission of the testimony of a
government psychiatrist on the issue of sanction based on examination of a defendant without a warning and in absence of his counsel
violated the Fifth and Sixth Amendments. Disposition of such cases,
shifting alliances among justices on individual cases, and the complexity of the tasks facing the court (see Amsterdam, 1974:349) necessarily result in at least apparent inconsistencies in approach that make
classification as conservative or liberal difficult. Thus, a leading critic
of the U.S. Supreme Court's search and seizure decisions (Kasimar,
1984:557; Kasimar, 1983:565; Kasimar, 1980) has viewed the Burger
Court criminal procedure decisions with some ambivalence (Kasimar,
1983a:62). Either supreme court may also use its procedural arsenal to
mask what it is doing. Issues of motive frequently confuse analysis. A
refusal of a court to be "activist" may be because of belief that its
appropriate constitutional role in society dictates such restraint; or it

may be because of a desire to achieve more conservative or liberal results and an appreciation that judicial restraint is an effective manner of achieving such an end. These and other problems make it exceedingly difficult to assess a court from the point of view of its relative conservatism.

THE AMERICAN EXPERIENCE

Despite the complexity of the required analysis it is possible to make some general observations concerning the relative conservatism or liberalism of our courts in the 1980s. The Burger Court, as it is familiarly known, has a track record of a decade and a half. The Canadian Supreme Court has had a much shorter period within which to interpret the Charter.

At the outset it is important to appreciate that the Warren Court did not end on one day, and the Burger Court begin on the next. The Burger Court developed over time, with the appointments of Justices Blackmun, Powell, and Rehnquist in the early 1970s and Justice O'Connor more recently. Likewise, the "Burger Court" is not a unitary concept. Over time, attitudes and alliances among justices change. In more recent years, for instance, its opinions have been arguably more conservative than during the 1970s.

Opinions differ about its relative conservatism. Dean Paul Bender (1984:635) has concluded that the Burger Court movement toward conservatism has been quite significant, while Mark Tushnet (1984: 1257) has asserted that the Burger Court has accomplished no counterrevolution because the Warren Court achieved no revolution. One of the most thoughtful collections of commentaries upon the Court has concluded that the major landmark decisions of the Warren Court have remained in place; in some areas the court has adopted a strongly activist posture; but, in general, its work can be characterized more as "rootless activism" neither primarily conservative nor liberal in perspective (Blasi, 1983; cf. Nichol, 1984:315).

A strong case can be made for the proposition that while the Court has sometimes been activist, particularly in a few substantive areas, its decisions are in general conservative, particularly in areas of procedure. In the field of criminal procedure it has, on balance, been arguably conservative in procedure and substance.

The Court has not backtracked significantly in areas such as school desegregation, "one-man, one-vote," and right to counsel. Recent cases requiring court appointment of a psychiatrist to assist an indigent defendant follow the same tradition, as do those limiting the right of the police to renew questioning after a suspect has requested counsel. Once the right to counsel has attached, the Court has permitted no policy interference unless the right is waived. It is less clear that its continued adherence to the principles of these cases can be categorized as "liberal." Adherence to precedent is a hallmark of judicial conservatism. In addition, there are limits to the degree to which any court could have retreated in these areas.

The record of the Burger Court is clearly "activist" and "liberal" in other cases. Its willingness to determine the limits of power of coordinate branches is an example. Perhaps most significant are its decisions striking down state abortion laws and limiting capital punishment, where the textual foundation and evidence of historical consensus was weak, if not nonexistent. Its gender decisions and creation of a right of action against federal officers for violation of a constitutional right also charted new horizons (see Dellinger, 1972:1532).

The Court has not shied away from breaching the "wall of separation between church and state," but arguably without consistency, allowing inclusion of a crèche in a municipal Nativity scene and permitting the opening of legislative sessions with a prayer, while striking down statutes authorizing public funds to provide part of the compensation of teachers in religious schools and declaring unconstitutional one law permitting students to devote a moment to silence or prayer in a public schoolroom.

It has extended First Amendment freedom of speech protection to commercial speech, but denied it the full breadth of the traditional protection; permitted the government to exclude legal defense organizations from government-sponsored charitable giving programs aimed at government employees; denied the press exemption from the copyright laws that would have permitted them to report unpublished expressions of public officials; permitted extension of the law of libel; and permitted the use of zoning laws to restrain adult movie theaters to certain areas. The Court's concern with protection of property rights may explain much of its approach in civil liberties cases (see Van Alstyne, 1980:66).

Less obvious has been the Court's use of procedural devices to avoid decisions on the merits. One technique has been to interpret a statute in a way that precludes judicial review of administrative action.

The "standing" cases provide more common examples. Although the Court has erected a complex conceptual framework, its doctrine, on occasion, appears to have been used inconsistently (Tribe, 1980: 118–20). Examples of selective use of standing arguably to achieve desired substantive results are cases such as *City of Los Angeles* v. *Lyons* 461 U.S. 95 (1983) where the Court denied a victim of a police chokehold the right to seek injunctive relief against the City of Los Angeles, and *Duke Power Co.* v. *Carolina Environmental Study Group, Inc.*, 438 U.S. 59 (1978), in which the Court chose to find standing to contest a statute that limited liability of nuclear energy producers in the event of disaster. Likewise, court opposition to the breadth of the exclusionary rule was well served by a decision significantly limiting those who can assert to claim for a Fourth Amendment violation.

Commentators differ upon whether the Court's standing decisions have been motivated by political expediency. Some assert that the decisions provide "scant support" for such a conclusion, arguing that the Burger Court decisions reflect a principled reliance upon federalism and separation of powers instead of an earlier emphasis upon whether questions were presented in an adversary context in a form historically viewed as capable of resolution through the judicial process (Floyd, 1985). On balance, the analysis of Professor Gene R. Nichol (1984) that the Court has been engaged in a "covert counter-revolution" limiting review in areas of greatest concern to the Warren Court, those insuring equality and adherence to the individual rights of the citizen, seems more descriptive (Nichol, 1980, 1982, 1983). The areas in which the Court has found standing frequently have been those that are more difficult to analyze on a liberal-conservative spectrum.

CRIMINAL PROCEDURE: SEARCH AND SEIZURE

Limits of governmental power and rights of individual privacy inevitably come into conflict in search and seizure cases. They pose an excellent vehicle for viewing the Court's relative liberalism and conservatism, and determining how substantive and procedural decisions can complement each other in moving toward a desired result.

The Burger Court inherited a body of law interpreting the Fourth Amendment, which held that a search could not intrude into an individual's reasonable expectation of privacy except when justified by a valid warrant or in a limited number of other specific situations, generally predicated upon exigency. A warrant could be issued only upon probable cause, and it was necessary to establish both the informer's reliability and how he was in a position to know the information that he had provided when probable cause was based on information provided by a third person. An unreasonable search, i.e., one not based on a warrant or falling within a limited number of exceptions, had significant effect. Evidence directly obtained as a result of a violation, or derivative evidence, was inadmissible unless the chain of causality was so attenuated that the taint of the primary illegality had been dissipated. This exclusionary rule applied in state and federal cases and was enforced by federal district courts by issuing writs of habeas corpus as well as on direct review by the Supreme Court.

Over the past fifteen years, protections accorded to a citizen by the Fourth Amendment have been significantly eroded. The landmark cases of *Katz v. United States* 389 U.S. 347 (1967) and *Mapp v. Ohio* 367 U.S. 643 (1961) have not been overruled, but they have been effectively undermined.

The concept of "reasonable expectation of privacy" continues to be the standard for determining whether a Fourth Amendment interest has been invaded by a search, but the case law has greatly narrowed its meaning. Neither use of a pen register to determine numbers dialed on a telephone, seizure of private bank records, nor use of an informer wired for sound who enters a suspect's house involves invasion of a reasonable expectation of privacy in the eyes of the current Court. Nor does entry onto fenced land in violation of state law to search for marijuana, engaging in aerial observation of a backyard in order to discover evidence not visible at ground level, search of a prisoner's cell, or tracking of a beeper device on a highway or in a public warehouse. Furthermore, the Court has determined that there is not reasonable expectation of privacy in any business establishment that is pervasively regulated, such as a gun dealership or a mine. Use of a dog to determine whether contraband is present likewise raises no serious constitutional issue.

Probable cause is still required for governmental intrusion where there is a reasonable expectation of privacy, but the standard has been weakened. The "two-pronged test" requiring inquiry into an informant's veracity or reliability and the basis for his knowledge has been abandoned in favor of a "nontechnical," "commonsense" approach that looks at the issue of whether there is a "substantial basis" for concluding that probable cause existed, considering all the circumstances.

Several members of the Court have sought abandonment of the traditional rule that a warrant should be required in any except a limited number of circumstances, preferring to focus on the broader issue of the "reasonableness of a search,"[6] regulating failure to obtain a warrant to the status of only one factor in the determination of reasonableness. Thus far the Court has rejected this approach, but perimeters of exceptions to the warrant requirement have been expanded significantly. Thus a search of an arrestee incident to a custodial arrest has been authorized when there is no danger of destruction of evidence and no reasonable suspicion that a person arrested is armed. The scope of such arrests has been extended to include the passenger compartment of a car, including those areas not within immediate control of the arrestee. The traditional doctrine permitting a vehicle search when there is probable cause to believe that an object subject to seizure is within a car has been extended to permit a search conducted significantly after the car has been stopped and the driver arrested, and has been applied to motor vans and to containers within cars. Police have been granted wide authority to impound motor vehicles and to inventory their contents. "Consent" searches have been authorized when the person allegedly consenting has not been informed that he has right to object and where a third party jointly using premises has "consented."

Rules of standing have been tightened significantly to preclude litigation of Fourth Amendment claims by persons who would have been permitted to litigate such issues previously. Today a person will be heard to complain of a Fourth Amendment violation only when he is able to assert that his personal "reasonable expectation of privacy" has been invaded. The prohibition against admission of derivative evidence from a Fourth Amendment violation has been diluted to permit admission of evidence where it would have been otherwise discoverable in the normal course of the police investigation.

The exclusionary rule has also been subjected to significant limitation. Evidence will no longer be excluded even though it was obtained as a result of an admittedly unlawful search where a police officer reasonably relied on a warrant in its seizure. This restriction on the exclusionary rule not only limits the holding of *Mapp v. Ohio*, but also the protection first accorded defendants in federal courts seventy-two years ago in *Weeks v. United States* 232 U.S. 383 (1914).

Access to federal review has also suffered. A federal district court cannot consider a claim for a Fourth Amendment violation in a state criminal procedure proceeding if the defendant received a full and fair hearing on the issue in a state court or if he was provided an opportunity to have a Fourth Amendment claim heard and did not avail himself of a chance in a state court.

Not all Fourth Amendment cases have been decided in favor of the government, but the number decided in favor of defendants has been small. An arrest warrant is necessary before police may enter a house to arrest a suspect in the absence of an emergency. A search warrant is required before police may enter the house of a third party to arrest a suspect. Police may not use deadly force while attempting to arrest a person who does not constitute a danger to them or to others. A principal must have reasonable grounds to believe that a law or school rule has been violated before he may search a student's handbag. A court may not order surgery to remove a bullet where an operation will be lengthy and involve a significant risk to the patient. There are a few other cases where a defendant has prevailed, but it is impossible to review the recent cases without concluding that there has been a major movement toward conservatism in the law of search and seizure between 1971 and 1986.[7]

Additional examples could be given from other areas of criminal procedure, particularly in application of the *Miranda* rule. For example, the Court has created an exception for "public safety" situations even when the officer does not claim that he was worried about his safety. Definition of what constitutes a custodial interrogation has been narrowed significantly, evidence clearly obtained in violation of the rule has been admitted for the purpose of impeachment, and police have been permitted to return to a suspect after he has initially asserted his desire to remain silent, inform him of his rights again, and elicit a waiver. Cases where a defendant has requested counsel, and cases where the right to counsel under the Sixth Amendment has attached, however, reflect a more consistent support for Warren Court approaches.

While there is room for disagreement, my own analysis suggests that the present Court can properly be appraised as basically conservative, though more covertly than overtly, granted that it has been "activist" or "liberal" in some areas.

THE CANADIAN EXPERIENCE

The Canadian Supreme Court presents a different picture. The contrast is most striking in the Charter cases. The new Charter predictably expanded the number of constitutional cases heard and the scope of questions presented to the Court (Hovivs and Martin, 1983). The Court, although experienced with issues of division of governmental power, was now faced with the clash of governmental power and individual rights. The new focus under the Charter could involve invalidation of majoritarian outcomes absolutely rather than allocation of the power of decision either to the provinces or the central government (Fairley, 1985). Whether the Supreme Court of Canada would adopt an approach radically different than that which it had traditionally demonstrated in civil rights matters was unclear. Embedding the doctrine of written constitutional restraint on the will of the majority into the jurisprudence of the nation, insisting upon the legitimacy of unfettered judicial review to determine whether a law or governmental action was unconstitutional, and recognizing the importance of implementation of whatever rights were found to exist could themselves have been significant developments in Canadian constitutional jurisprudence during the early days of the Charter. There was reason to suspect that judges who had been interpreting the Canadian Bill of Rights for almost a quarter of a century might be affected by a tradition of judicial restraint deep in the jurisprudence of the nation (Pye, 1985; cf. Friedland, 1983). While some hoped that the Court would approach the Charter with more enthusiasm than had been evidenced in decisions interpreting the Bill of Rights, there was reason for concern that the Court might view the Charter as a political compromise effected by the party in power rather than a legitimate expression of a national consensus (Pye, 1982). Such reservations proved unduly conservative.

In retrospect there was reason for prediction of a more activist posture by the Court. Until recently the Supreme Court had no control over its docket, and its decisions were subject to judicial review by the Privy Council (Morton, 1985). Explicit provision in the Constitution (Part I, s.33[1]) that the Charter was the supreme law of the land conferred upon the Court a status it had not previously enjoyed. Even restrictions upon the potential impact of its decisions implicit in Section 33 could not change the reality that the Court was granted power by written instrument, which the Supreme Court of the United States had proclaimed in *Marbury v. Madison*. Under such circumstances it is not surprising that the Court would seize the opportunity to solidify its newly achieved stature. Even a tradition of strict construction and conservative interpretation of individual rights was unlikely, at least in the short run, to prevail over the institutional imperative to promote the Court's power in a way that would assure it a status equal to those of the constitutional courts in other great democracies.

The Court took its first opportunity to interpret the Charter to assert a broad authority of judicial review and in doing so relied upon those early American cases in which the power of judicial review was first asserted by the Supreme Court of the United States. In subsequent cases the Court has been more than willing to assume a role at least equal to that ever asserted by the Supreme Court of the United States. There can, for instance, be few more activist or liberal positions than those reflected in decisions that assert the right of a court to determine the validity of cabinet decisions that intimately affect foreign affairs and national security; hear cases by plaintiffs not directly affected by litigation because broad public issues are involved; grant standing to assert Charter rights by aliens not yet in the country; assert the right to interpret provisions "purposively," reserving for itself the right to determine what is meant by the term; assume the right to ignore the clear parliamentary history of a provision in determining its meaning; and proclaim authority to strike down legislation because substantively it does not measure up to the Court's standards of "fundamental justice." The Court has thus far rarely accepted thoughtful advice that there may be good reason to permit basic issues to be canvassed by lower courts, have more than one case serve as a testing ground for the impact and implications of various choices of interpretation, and avoid interpreting the Charter when a decision can rest upon another ground (Whyte, 1984). A brief survey of the cases during the last two years is illustrative.

In *Law Society of Upper Canada* v. *Skapinker* (1984) 9 D.L.R. 4th 161 the Court found that Section 6(2) of the Charter had not been violated when a citizen of South Africa was refused entrance into the Law Society of Upper Canada because he was not a citizen of the Commonwealth. The case, however, has greater import than merely interpreting Section 6(2). In the first place the Court could have declined to hear the case on the ground of mootness or other procedural grounds if it had chosen to do so (Macklem and Gertner, 1984).

Second, Mr. Justice Estey used the case to assert the nature of the Charter—"It is a part of the Constitution of the nation"—and the power of the Court to interpret it flexibly. According to the learned justice, the Constitution Act of 1982 presented "a new dimension, a new yardstick of reconciliation between the individual and the community and their respective rights, a dimension which, like the balance of the Constitution, remains to be interpreted and applied by the court."

The Court's second case, *Attorney General of Quebec* v. *Quebec Association of Protestant School Boards et al.*, was a per curiam decision affirming a judgment of the Quebec Superior Court holding that Bill 101 of the Quebec legislature violated Section 23. The language of the statute was flatly inconsistent with Section 23; the intent of Section 23 was to outlaw legislation such as Bill 101; Bill 101 was passed after Section 23. Few cases are likely to be as clear.

Hunter et al. v. *Southam, Inc.* (1984) 11 D.L.R. 4th 641 involved the first interpretation of Section 8 of the Charter (see Connelley, 1985; Rosenberg, 1985). Pursuant to the Combines Investigation Act, the director of Investigations and Research of the Combines Investigation Branch authorized investigating officers to enter and examine documents and other things at Southam's business premises in Edmonton and "elsewhere in Canada." The authorization was certified by a member of the Restrictive Trade Practices Commission as was required by the act. The act authorized entry into premises when the director believed that there may be evidence relevant to the matters being inquired into and seizure of evidence disclosed by such a search. Pursuant to the authorization, officers entered the premises of Southam in Edmonton and indicated that they wished to search everywhere except the newsroom.

The Supreme Court, speaking through Chief Justice Dickson, delivered a far-reaching judgment, determining (1) the interests that are protected by Section 8; (2) the standard that should be applied for justifying government intrusion when there is a protected interest; (3) who should make the decision whether such justification exists; (4) when such a decision should be made; (5) and special issues that might require a different kind of analysis.

The Court chose to discuss the interests that are protected from unreasonable intrusion by Section 8 as the starting point of its inquiry despite the fact that a search had clearly taken place in *Southam*. Chief Justice Dickson warned that the "terms of the Fourth Amendment are not identical to those of s.8, and American decisions can be transplanted to the Canadian context only with the greatest caution," but then chose to rely upon the standard of "reasonable expectation of privacy" enunciated in the American case of *Katz v. the United States* to determine the nature of the interests protected by Section 8.

Katz was a case involving warrantless electronic surveillance of a conversation from a telephone booth. The U.S. Supreme Court enunciated the concept that each citizen has a reasonable expectation of privacy. Any intrusion by the government required justification under the Fourth Amendment. The thrust of the *Katz* standard was that protection from unreasonable searches and seizures would not be limited to concepts of property or trespass, and that language as well as tangible objects were protected. Chief Justice Dickson suggested in *Hunter* that Section 8 may even go further. At the least, Section 8 means that everyone has a right to reasonable expectation of privacy and an assessment must be made whether a citizen's interest in being left alone must give way to the government's interest in intruding upon privacy in each particular situation.

The Court proceeded to address the issues of upon what basis such an assessment should be made, by whom, and when. It found little assistance in the language of Section 8 and adopted what it called a "purposive" approach, indicating that such issues must be based on the purpose of the section in the context of the Charter as a whole when the text did not yield an answer.

Such an approach, when applied to Section 8, resulted in the conclusion that, where feasible, an assessment must be made before the search because the purpose of Section 8 is to protect individuals from unjustified intrusions, not simply declare that rights have been invaded after an intrusion has taken place. The Court noted that prior authorization is usually in the form of a warrant and again relied on *Katz* for the proposition that a warrantless search is prima facie invalid, recognizing that there may be occasions where prior authorization is infeasible.

Necessarily, the Court was required to face the issue that prior authorization existed in *Southam*. Again relying on its "purposive" approach, the Court determined that since the purpose of the prior authorization is to assure that an individual's right will not be invaded except when the interest of the state is demonstrably superior, the person assessing such evidence must act in an "entirely neutral and impartial manner." In the judgment of the Court a decision by the director of Investigations and certification by the member of the RTPC did not meet the requirement because each was acting in an investigatory rather than a judicial manner.

The Court could have ended the case at this point. However, it did not hesitate to proceed further and reach issues not required for decision. The Court held that the Combines Act was inadequate even if the member of the RTPC had acted in a judicial manner and even if the member of the RTPC was authorized to determine the reasonableness of the director's belief, because the statute authorized a search on the basis that evidence "*may*" be discovered. Only where there is a basis that a crime has *probably* been committed and evidence *probably* will be found can an impartial magistrate grant authority to search. It expressly refused to avoid the constitutional issue by narrowly considering the statute in a manner that would save it from constitutional attack.

The Court recognized that its approach might require modification in state security matters or where a search threatened bodily integrity. It left open the issue of whether a search could ever be unreasonable under Section 8 and still justified under the "reasonable limits" provision of Section 1.

Four points deserve mention. Initially, the observer is struck by the breadth of the decision. The Court chose to promulgate a code of search and seizure procedure in a manner similar to the Warren Court's promulgation of a code of interrogation procedure in *Miranda*.

It is not clear what is meant by a "purposive" approach to interpretation. Certainly the purposes of a Constitution should be considered in determining its meaning. Depending upon the definition given to "purposive," however, a court may engage in extraordinarily broad or narrow construction. It is the arbiter of the meaning of "purposive."

Southam does not suggest the potential problems that may result from ignoring the Court's own admonition of the danger of adopting a standard incorporated from the jurisprudence of another nation. *Katz* is cited for the standard of "reasonable expectation of privacy." But none of the Burger Court cases considered earlier narrow what is meant by that phrase or are even mentioned in the judgment. By adopting the American standard, is the Court also intending to adopt the American interpretation of that standard? If so, the protection afforded Canadians by *Hunter* may be less than is generally assumed.

In adopting the standard the court ignored a significant difference between the American Fourth Amendment and Section 8 of the Charter. The American Fourth Amendment also has a warrant clause, i.e., not only do the "people have a right to be secure against unreasonable searches and seizures," but "no warrants shall issue but upon probable cause." There is still a major debate raging within the American Supreme Court about whether the determination of reasonableness in the first clause should be made on the basis of appraisal of "the totality of the circumstances" in which failure to obtain a warrant is only one factor, or whether the warrant clause requires a decision that no search will be reasonable in the absence of a warrant except in a limited number of cases traditionally based on exigency. *Katz* clearly accepted the notion that a search without a warrant was prima facie unreasonable. Why this should necessarily be true in a case governed by Section 8, which contains no warrant clause, is less than self-evident.

The defendant in *The Queen v. Therens* (1985) 18 D.L.R. 4th 655 was involved in a motor vehicle accident. An officer demanded that the driver accompany him to a police station and submit to a breathalyzer test. The Supreme Court of Canada determined that the driver had been "detained" within the meaning of Section 10(b) of the Charter and had been denied his right to obtain an instruct counsel and to be informed of these rights assured by that provision. Mr. Justice LeDain indicated that there was no reason to presume that the framers of the Charter intended that the words used in it should be given the meaning that had been given to them by judicial decisions at the time the Charter was enacted, again asserting the need to interpret the Charter in a "purposive" manner.

Equally important, however, was the decision by the Court that such conduct, although consistent with traditional practice in Saskatchewan and prior Supreme Court precedent, constituted such a flagrant violation of the Charter as to bring the "administration of justice into disrepute," thereby maintaining exclusion under Section 24(2). The interpretation that a clear violation of the Charter, regardless of the good faith of the officer, required exclusion is in striking contrast to pre-Charter cases. Implicit in the majority's decision is the conclusion that subjective or objective good faith on the part of the police officer does not prevent a violation from being "flagrant."

The theory behind Section 24(2), of course, is not the same as that of the American exclusionary rule, which is at present predicated upon deterrence, and *Therens* did not involve police action authorized by a warrant. Nevertheless, the difference in attitude toward the question of good faith as reflected in recent American cases, which have narrowed the protection provided by the Fourth Amendment, and that evident in *Therens* is striking.

The degree to which the Court is prepared to entertain cases which it might avoid adjudicating is reflected in *Singh* v. *Minister of Employment and Immigration et al.* (1985) 17 D.L.R. 4th 422, in which the Court granted aliens outside Canada who were seeking to enter Canada the right to adjudicate whether the procedural scheme established in the Immigration Act was consistent with the requirements articulated in Section 7 of the Charter (see Lee, 1985). American precedents that provide constitutional protection to aliens within the country, but deny such protection to those seeking entry, were rejected. Equally significant may be Madame Justice Wilson's rejection of any distinction between rights and privileges as unacceptable in an interpretation of the Charter. Justice Wilson was speaking of substantive limitations. In this sense the doctrine has long been dead in American law (Van Alstyne, 1968).

Whether Canadian jurists will approach the "right-privilege" distinction in the same way in a procedural context remains to be seen. Under the Burger Court the doctrine has reemerged in the procedural due process area of American constitutional law under the guise of "entitlement" theory (see Smolla, 1982; Van Alstyne, 1977).

In *The Queen v. Big M Drug Mart, Ltd.* (1985) 18 D.L.R. 4th 321 the Court presaged the possibility of a broad interpretation of freedom of conscience and religion under Section 2(a) of the Charter (Macklem, 1984) when it vacated an injunction restraining a defendant from operating a business on Sunday in violation of a statute that was patently enacted for religious purposes, holding that the section was not limited to persons who could prove a genuinely held religious belief. The Court used the case also to expound upon its remedial powers under the Charter, holding that where legislation was challenged as being unconstitutional, recourse to remedies authorized in Section 24(1) was unnecessary because a successful challenge would result in the legislation being of no force and effect pursuant to Section 52 of the Constitution Act.

In *Operation Dismantle, Inc. et al. v. Canada et al.* (1985) D.L.R. (4th) 481 the Supreme Court of Canada held that a cabinet decision relating to matters of national defense and external affairs, which resulted from exercise of the royal prerogative and common law authority of the Crown, was subject to review under the Charter because the decision was "within the authority of Parliament" within the meaning of Section 32(1) of the Charter. The action challenged a decision by the cabinet to permit testing of the cruise missile over Canada by the United States.

The Court interpreted Section 52 of the Charter to apply not only to statutes, regulations, and the common law, but all acts taken pursuant to powers granted by law. On the facts of the case before it, the Court held that the decision to allow testing of the missile did not violate the right of life, liberty, and security of the person protected by Section 7 because no causal relationship between testing the missile and threat of nuclear war was reasonably stated in the claim. But the Court made it clear that cabinet decisions relating to matters of national defense or external affairs were not exempt from review if a claim stated a reasonable cause of action for violation or threatened violation of a right guaranteed by the Charter. The approach to "political questions" adopted by the Supreme Court of the United States was again rejected by all justices, and Madame Justice Wilson attacked the theory of such judicial self-restraint in a lengthy judgment.

In *Manitoba Language Rights Reference* (1985) 19 D.L.R. 4th 1 the

Supreme Court held that it could consider unwritten postulates that form the very foundation of the Constitution of Canada, including principles of federalism and the rule of law in the process of constitutional adjudication. While American courts would undoubtedly do so, they would be much more likely to attempt to relate their approach to the text of the Constitution.

The Queen v. Dubois (1985) D.L.R. 4th—, 62 N.R. 50 (1985) produced a remarkable result from an American viewpoint, although arguably justified from a literal reading of the Charter. The accused was convicted of murder. A new trial was ordered because of error in the trial judge's charge to the jury. Evidence voluntarily given by the accused at the first trial was introduced by the Crown at the second trial. The Court held that admission of the evidence denied the defendant his protection against self-incrimination assured under Section 13 of the Charter. The Court read the privilege against self-incrimination in 11(c) in conjunction with 11(d) to indicate that there was a close relationship between the right to be presumed innocent and the right not to be compelled to be a witness in any proceedings against that person with respect to that offense. The Court proceeded to read Section 13 in the context of 11(c) and (d) and concluded that it must exclude the challenged testimony to protect individuals from being indirectly compelled to incriminate themselves, to "insure that the Crown will not be able to do indirectly that which Section 11(c) prohibits." To hold otherwise, in the opinion of the Court, would also permit an indirect violation of the right of the accused to be presumed innocent and remain silent until proven guilty by the prosecution. However, in this particular case, the accused was not "compelled" to be a witness in his first or second trial; his voluntary testimony at his first trial was admitted to his second. Why the presumption of innocence is involved is unclear to this observer. At an earlier time I predicted the possibility of such an interpretation of Section 13, not because of any relationship to 11(c) or 11(d), but because of the drafting of Section 13 that neither speaks of compulsion nor requires any prior invocation of the right against self-incrimination and the legislative history of the proposal (Pye, 1982:235). The result would clearly be different in American law unless the accused testified in the first trial in order to counter unlawfully obtained evidence that had been admitted against him and his testimony was then admitted at a second trial after reversal of his first conviction (*Harrison* v. *United States* 392 U.S. 219 [1968]).

Perhaps the most important decision to date is *Reference Re Section 942 of the Motor Vehicle Act* (B.C.) (D.L.R. 14th)—, 63 N.R. 266. The British Columbia Motor Vehicle Act provided that a person who drove while his license was suspended was guilty of an offense punishable by fine and imprisonment without proof that he knew of the suspension. The Supreme Court of Canada held that a conviction of a citizen of an absolute liability offense punishable by a penalty of imprisonment constitutes a deprivation of liberty other than in accordance with the principles of fundamental justice, and thus violated Section 7 of the Charter.

The Court declined to go so far as to hold that all absolute liability offenses per se violate Section 7. Its judgment was limited to cases in which an absolute liability offense was combined with a penalty of imprisonment. It also indicated that Section 1 could save a statute otherwise invalid under Section 7, but only in cases arising out of exceptional conditions such as national disaster, outbreak of war, and epidemics.

The theory of the Court was that Section 7 should not be interpreted more narrowly than the rights in Section 8-14. In short, it should read as if the phrase "and without limiting the generality of the foregoing" was inserted at the end of Section 7, before Section 8-14.

The distinction between substantive and procedural due process developed in the American precedents was viewed as irrelevant: "It imports into the Canadian context American concepts, terminology and jurisprudence, all of which are inextricably linked to problems concerning the nature and legitimacy of adjudication under the U.S. Constitution. That Constitution, it must be remembered, has no s.52, nor has it the internal checks and balances of section 1 and 33. . . ."

It also declined to accept the unambiguous evidence of the intention of the Trudeau government that introduced the measure. The Court paid lip service to the use of extrinsic aids to determine meaning, but held that such aids were entitled to "minimal weight." Thus, the comment of Mr. Justice Strayer, then assistant deputy minister, Public Law, that Section 7 did not cover "substantive due process," that "fundamental justice" was intended to connote "procedural due process," and that the provision was not designed to permit courts to apply principles of substantive due process to the right to life was considered unpersuasive. Statements of the deputy minister and minister of justice to like effect were also disregarded.

The Court dismissed the significance of the testimony on the grounds that the Charter is not the product of a few individual public servants and that to accept what they intended would be to assume a matter impossible of proof—the intention of legislative bodies that adopted the Charter. It also expressed concern that acceptance of contemporaneous intention would mean that the values embodied in the Charter would in effect become "frozen in time to the moment of adoption with little or no possibility of growth, development and adjustment to changing societal needs." Weiler (1984:62) has argued that searching for the framer's intent leads into a blind alley, in part because of "the virtually insoluble questions of whose intentions are to count, or what the notion of collective intent means." Granted that this observation may be true when applied to some issues, it is difficult to see how it is applicable when the record is unambiguous, at least among those who expressed a view.

The case is fascinating. Assumption of power by a court to determine that the substantive decisions of a legislature are impermissible is a declaration that the judiciary is prepared to invalidate the public will in the most controversial issues facing society. Presumably the Supreme Court of Canada now presumes to determine whether abortion can be prohibited or whether capital punishment can be reinstituted. The newly discovered power will become even more formidable if the Court defines "security" in Section 7 broadly. Even the Supreme Court of the United States has refrained from asserting such power except in a few celebrated cases. Indeed, the B.C. Motor Vehicle Act case may constitute a worrisome answer to Professor Walter Berns's (1983:99) thoughtful query four years ago: "The question of interest to Canada is whether, with the new Charter of Rights, we can expect Canadian judges to follow the examples of their American brethren and seize powers properly belonging to other branches of government."

Second, the Court's treatment of the intention of the framers seems somewhat cavalier. It was not confronted with a case in which evidence of the intent of the government was ambiguous. The minister of justice made the intent completely clear in opposing a proposal that "due process" be used instead of "principles of fundamental justice" in testimony not referred to by the Court.[8] There is no reason to believe that the Parliament in Ottawa had a different intent than that manifested by the drafters, or that the Parliament in Westminster considered the matter at all. The case in substance says that within two years of adoption the Court can substitute its view of what a provision of the Charter means for an opposite interpretation clearly intended by the framers. One wonders if, when it was enacted, anyone thought that the Charter denied a province the power to enact an absolute liability statute with a limited imprisonment provision.

A third interesting point is the Court's treatment of the possible effect of Section 1. Its criterion for when Section 1 can permit what Section 7 would otherwise prohibit presumably is limited to Section 7 cases. Certainly in *Dubois* it suggested that a much less stringent principle might be applied to the application of Section 1 to Section 13.

The Court appears to have adopted that it will first look to see if a right has been violated and then apply Section 1 to determine whether the violation can be justified, rather than using Section 1 as a fundamental principle to be used in the interpretation of the rights that follow (see Bender, 1983; Greschner, 1985; Gibson, 1985). It will be interesting to see how this approach will be applied to some of the rights contained in the Charter. It boggles the imagination to speculate how a person can be subjected to a cruel and unusual punishment that is demonstrably justified in a free and democratic society.

In a sense, the judgment is extremely conservative in that non-elected judges, one of the most elitist groups in any society, can determine the validity of the most difficult choices of the elected representatives of the people. The decision is both liberal and activist from another perspective. It is extraordinarily activist for judges to assume that they have been entrusted with such a role by a constitution, or that they can substitute their judgment concerning meaning for the only meaning suggested at the time of adoption. It is liberal in that it broadens the protection of citizens from majoritarian decisions by legislatures that limit their liberty.

One additional case deserves mention. Under the Narcotic Control Act (Can. Stat. C-35, s.10(3) (1960-61)) a person found in the unlawful possession of narcotics is presumed to have the substance for the purpose of sale. The act places the burden to rebut this presumption upon the suspect. In *The Queen v. Oakes* (1986) D.L.R. 4th—, 65 N.R. 87 the Court found that the provision transferring the burden of persuasion to the accused violated his presumption of innocence guaranteed by Section 11(d) of the Charter. It is difficult to understand how it could have decided otherwise.

CONCLUSION

My analysis leads to the conclusion that the Supreme Court of Canada during the last two years has been both activist and liberal in its interpretation of the Charter, while the Supreme Court of the United States has been more conservative in dealing with similar issues in recent years. If I am correct, the obvious question is why such a difference in approaches should have taken place.

In the first place the periods of comparison may be arbitrary. It may be more appropriate to compare the Supreme Court of Canada between 1984 and 1986 with the Supreme Court of the United States during the first two decades of the nineteenth century. Power to declare majoritarian decisions of legislatures invalid is heady; the urge to assert institutional power is almost irresistible. It may be more appropriate to look at the Supreme Court of the United States under Chief Justice Marshall and compare it with the Supreme Court of Canada under Chief Justice Dickson than to look at contemporary comparisons.

In the second place the gap between the constitutional protection of civil liberties in the United States and that in Canada was quite striking fifteen years ago. The high water mark of the Warren Court virtually coincided with the low water mark in interpretation of the Canadian Bill of Rights from the viewpoint of a civil libertarian (Tarnopolsky, 1975). In some areas the Supreme Court of Canada continues to sustain police powers in circumstances where the Supreme Court of the United States would find police action unconstitutional, for example, random stops of cars where there is no reasonable suspicion that the person stopped has committed an offense. Even as late as 1984 the Supreme Court of Canada could interpret the Charter quite liberally for some time and the overall result would not produce a balance between the state and the individual significantly more "liberal" than that prevailing south of the border.

In the third place the Court was faced with fairly clear language in some cases in which room for interpretation was relatively small. The Charter is a twentieth-century document and is much more specific in many instances than is the Bill of Rights. Interpretations of Section 19(b) in *Therens* and Section 13 in *DuBois* can as easily be defended on the grounds that they are literal interpretations of the language of the Charter as on the basis that they reflect a liberal or activist approach to it.

The question of whether Canada has really been moving toward conservatism during recent years and whether the election of the conservative government reflects a rejection of the Liberal party more than it reflects an adoption of the principles of conservatism poses another issue, dealt with elsewhere in the volume. There is good reason for concluding that the United States has moved toward conservatism politically, and it is not the first time in American history that the Supreme Court of the United States has been mindful of the ballot box. Perhaps even more significantly, President Nixon and President Reagan have been avowedly strict constructionists and have attempted to place justices on the Court who adhered to their philosophy (Levy, 1974).

Finally, it has been argued persuasively that the Burger Court decisions are the inevitable by-product of the diffusion of the New Deal consensus previously implemented by the Warren Court (Shapiro, 1983). In the 1970s the United States entered a period of rising expectations arguably beyond the capacity of any economy or democratic society to fulfill. Inability to do so contributed to the breakdowns of historic alliances. For instance, much of the reason for the extraordinary changes in criminal procedure of the 1960s had its origin in the civil rights movement (see Pye, 1982; Caplin, 1985). As the movement toward civil rights slowed down, in part because of an increased disenchantment with concepts such as affirmative action by a white majority, and fear of crime in the streets increased, concern for expanding the rights of defendants became weaker. As states assumed their responsibility for enforcing rights, agreement about the need for federal intervention decreased. These public attitudes find expression in court decisions as well as in legislatures.

Simultaneously, in Canada there appears to have developed a broader consensus of the importance of the Charter and the necessity of implementing it than some would have predicted when it was enacted. The fact that the Charter as it emerged in 1981 was significantly different from the document that was proposed in 1980 does not seem to have precluded acceptance of the 1981 version as the legitimate expression of the will of the people. It may be significant that with the exception of the rejection of the Charter by Quebec at the outset, only one province, on one occasion, has seen fit to exercise its powers under Section 33, and it has done so to deal with a difficult political situation (Morton, 1985; Lyon, 1984). The euphoria that has accompanied repatriation, broad support from both parties, general disenchantment with the narrow interpretation of the Canadian Bill of Rights, and an understandable desire of the Supreme Court to establish its status as the supreme arbiter between the individual and the state may best explain the differences.

NOTES

1   Most civil and criminal law in the United States is state law, the meaning of which is determined ultimately by a state supreme court. The Supreme Court of the United States usually becomes involved in the determination of contract or tort law only to the degree that such an issue may arise under a federal statute or in the narrow areas governed by the federal common law. In addition, there is no American counterpart of the Canadian doctrine of "convention" as a basis for constitutional decision. It should be recognized, also, that much American constitutional law is "state constitutional law" determined by state courts. See Collins, 1985.

2   One distinguished commentator (Bobbitt, 1982) has analyzed constitutional approaches as textual, structural, historical, doctrinal, precedential, or ethical.

3   I.e., a finding that a constitutional error did not contribute to a jury verdict because of overwhelming evidence of guilt. It was most recently applied in United States v. Mechanik 106 S.Ct. 938 (1986); United States v. Lane 106 S.Ct. 725 L.W. 41 (1986); Delaware v. Van Arsdall 106 S.Ct. 1431 (1986); and has been strongly criticized by Goldberg, 1980.

4   I.e., any evidence derived from a violation of the Constitution should be excluded from evidence unless it is so attenuated as to dissipate the taint. Wong Sun v. United States 371 U.S. 471 (1963).

5   The technique was, of course, abandoned in economic matters in favor of a more restrictive approach in United States v. Caroline Prods. Co. 304 U.S. 144, 152 n.4 (1938).

6   Mr. Justice Rehnquist has been a principal exponent of the approach, at one time accepted by the Court in United States v. Rabinowitz 339 U.S. 76 (1950). The approach sometimes seems to control, as in New Jersey v. T.L.O. 105 S.Ct. 733 (1985).

7   See, e.g., Chadwick v. United States 433 U.S. 1 (1977) (denying police authority to search a suitcase seized on a public street). The Court has continued to protect the

home. *Payton* v. *New York* 445 U.S. 73 (1980); *United States* v. *Karo* 468 U.S. 705 (1984); but see *United States* v. *White* 401 U.S. 745 (1971). It has on occasion also been solicitous where entrusting unfettered discretion to police could result in discriminatory action. See *Brown* v. *Texas* 443 U.S. 47 (1979); *Delaware* v. *Prouse* 440 U.S. 648 (1979); *Almeida-Sanchez* v. *United States* 411 U.W. 266 (1973). On balance, in numbers and in significance, cases favoring the government have predominated. See Heck, 1985; Gilligan, 1977; McMillan, 1979; Yackle, 1978.

8   The statement of Mr. Chretien, *38 Spec. Joint Comm. of the Senate and of the House of Commons on the Constitution of Canada Minutes of Proceedings and Evidence of the Special Joint Committee of the Senate and of the House of Commons on the Constitution of Canada*, 2d Parl., 1st Sess. 41 (1980). I have elsewhere attempted to summarize the legislative history of Section 7 (Pye, 1982:223–24). A useful collection of "Documents Relating to the Constitution Act, 1982" has been published in 30 *McGill L.J.* 645 (1985); see also Elliott, 1982.

REFERENCES

Amsterdam, Anthony G. 1974. "Perspective on the Fourth Amendment." *Minnesota Law Review* 58: 349.
Bender, Paul. 1983. "Justifications for Limiting Constitutionally Guaranteed Rights and Freedoms: Some Remarks About the Proper Role of Section One of the Canadian Charter." *Manitoba Law Journal* 13: 669.
———. 1984. "Book Review." *Michigan Law Review* 82: 645.
Berns, Walter. 1983. "The Legislative Protections of Rights." In William Russell McKercher, ed., *The U.S. Bill of Rights and the Canadian Charter of Rights and Freedoms*. Toronto: Ontario Economic Council, pp. 94–99.
Bickel, A. M. 1986. *The Least Dangerous Branch*. Indianapolis: Bobbs-Merrill.
Blake, Sara. 1984. "Standing to Litigate Constitutional Rights and Freedoms in Canada and the United States." *Ottawa Law Review* 66.
Blasi, V., ed. 1983. *The Burger Court: The Counter-Revolution That Wasn't*. New Haven, Conn.: Yale University Press.
Bobbitt, P. 1982. *Constitutional Fate: Theory of the Constitution*. New York: Oxford University Press.
Caplin, Gerald M. 1985. "Questioning Miranda." *Vanderbilt Law Review* 38: 1417, 1473.
Cardozo, B. N. 1921. *The Nature of the Judicial Process*. New Haven, Conn.: Yale University Press.
Chretien, Jean. Minister of Justice, Testimony.
Christie, George C. 1975. "A Model of Judicial Review of Legislation." *Southern California Law Review* 48: 1306.
Collins, Ronald K. L. 1985. "Foreword: Reliance on State Constitutions Beyond the New Federalism." *University of Puget Sound Law Review* 8: v, i.
Connelley, Peter. 1985. "The Fourth Amendment and Section 8 of the Canadian Charter of Rights and Freedoms: What Has Been Done? What Is to Be Done?" *Criminal Law Quarterly* 27: 182.

Cox, A. 1976. *The Role of the Supreme Court in American Government.* New York: Oxford University Press.

Dellinger, Walter A. 1972. "Of Rights and Remedies: The Constitution as a Sword." *Harvard Law Review* 85: 1532.

Elliott, Robin. 1982. "Interpreting the Charter—Use of the Earlier Versions as an Aid." *University of British Columbia Law Review* 17: 11.

Ely, J. H. 1980. *Democracy and Distrust.* Cambridge, Mass.: Harvard University Press.

Fairley, H. Scott. 1985. "Developments in Constitutional Law: The 1983–84 Term." *Supreme Court Review* 7: 63.

Floyd, C. Douglas. 1985. "The Justiciability Decision of the Burger Court." *North Dakota Law Review* 60: 862.

Friedland, Martin L. 1983. "Criminal Justice and the Charter." *Manitoba Law Journal* 13: 549–51.

Gibson, Dale. 1985. "Reasonable Limits Under the Canadian Charter of Rights and Freedoms." *Manitoba Law Journal* 15: 27.

Gilligan, Francis A. 1977. "Continuing Evisceration of [the] Fourth Amendment." *San Diego Law Review* 14: 823.

Goldberg, Steven H. 1980. "Harmless Error: Constitutional Sneak Thief." *Journal of Criminal Law and Criminology* 71: 421.

Greschner, Donna. 1985. "Two Approaches for Section One of the Charter." *Saskatchewan Law Review* 49: 336.

Griswold, Erwin N. 1985. "Foreword, The Burger Court and American Institutions." *North Dakota Law Review* 60: 827, 831.

Heck, Edward V. 1985. "Searching for the Elusive Balance Between State Power and Individual Liberty: The Burger Court and the Fourth Amendment." *Capital University Law Review* 15: 1.

Hellman, Arthur D. 1985. "Case Selection in the Burger Court." *North Dakota Law Review* 60: 947–48.

Horowitz, D. L. 1977. *The Courts and Social Policy.* Washington, D.C.: Brookings Institution.

Hovius, Berend, and Robert Martin. 1983. "The Canadian Charter of Rights and Freedoms in the Supreme Court of Canada." *Canadian Bar Review* 61: 354.

Kamisar, Y. 1980. *Police Interrogation and Confessions: Essay in Law and Policy.* Ann Arbor: University of Michigan Press.

———. 1983a. "The Warren Court (Was It Really So Defense-Minded?)" and "Policy Investigatory Practices." In V. Blasi, ed., *The Burger Court: The Counter-Revolution That Wasn't.* New Haven, Conn.: Yale University Press.

———. 1983b. "Does (Did) (Should) the Exclusionary Rule Rest on a 'Principled Basis' Rather Than an 'Empirical Proposition'?" *Creighton Law Review* 16: 565.

———. 1984. "Gates, 'Probable Cause,' 'Good Faith,' and Beyond." *Iowa Law Review* 69: 557.

Lee, Tanya. 1985. "Section 7 of the Charter: An Overview." *University of Toronto Faculty Law Review* 43: 1.

Levy, L. 1974. *Against the Law: The Nixon Court and Criminal Justice.* New York: Harper & Row.

Lyon, Noel. 1984. "The Charter as a Mandate for New Ways of Thinking About Law." *Queen's Law Journal* 9: 241.

Macklem, Patrick. 1984. "Freedom of Conscience and Religion in Canada." *University of Toronto Faculty Law Review* 42: 50.

———, and Eric Gertner. 1984. "Re Skapinker and the Mootness Doctrine." *Supreme Court Review* 6: 369–76.

McMillan, Theodore. 1979. "Is There Anything Left of the Fourth Amendment?" *St. Louis University Law Journal* 24: 1.

Miller, A. S. 1985. *Politics, Democracy and the Supreme Court.* Westport, Conn.: Greenwood Press.

Morton, F. L. 1985. "The Changing Role of the Supreme Court of Canada: From Adjudication Toward Policy Maker." Unpublished paper, Thirteenth World Congress of the International Political Science Association, Paris.

Nichol, Gene R. 1980. "Causation as a Standing Requirement: The Unprincipled Use of Judicial Restraint." *Kentucky Law Journal* 69: 185.

———. 1982. "Backing Into the Future: The Burger Court and the Federal Forum." *University of Kansas Law Review* 30: 341.

———. 1983. "Standing on the Constitution: The Supreme Court and Valley Forge." *North Carolina Law Review* 61: 798.

———. 1984. "Book Review." *Harvard Law Review* 98: 315.

Oakes, James L. 1985. "Book Review." *Harvard Law Review* 99: 862–63.

Pickard, Michael. 1986. "Why Joseph Borowski Has Standing." *University of Toronto Law Journal* 36: 19.

Pye, A. Kenneth. 1982a. "The Rights of Persons Accused of Crime Under the Canadian Constitution: A Comparative Perspective." *Law and Contemporary Problems* 45: 221.

———. 1982b. "The Warren Court and Criminal Procedure." *Police Practices and the Law* 49.

———. 1985. "An American Perspective and the Charter of Rights." In *Proceedings of the International Symposium of the Role of the Legal Profession in the Twenty-First Century.* Vancouver: Law Society of British Columbia.

Rosenberg, Marc. 1985. "Unreasonable Search and Seizure: Hunter vs. Southam, Inc." *University of British Columbia Law Review* 19: 271–95.

Rosenberg, Yale L. 1986. "Constructing Federal Habeas Corpus: From Great Writ to Exceptional Remedy." *Hastings Constitutional Law Quarterly* 12: 597.

Russell, Peter H. 1985. "The First Three Years of Charterland." *Canadian Public Administration*: 367–96.

Seidman, Louis Michael. 1980. "Factual Guilt and the Burger Court: An Examination of Continuity and Change in Criminal Procedures." *Columbia Law Review* 80: 436, 465–67.

Shapiro, Martin. 1983. "Fathers and Sons: The Court, the Commentators, and the Search for Values." In V. Blasi, ed., *The Burger Court: The Counter-Revolution That Wasn't.* New Haven, Conn.: Yale University Press.

Smolla, Rodney A. 1982. "The Reemergence of the Right-Privilege Distinction in Constitutional Law: The Price of Protesting Too Much." *Stanford Law Review*: 69.

Songer, Donald. 1979. "Concern for Policy Output as a Cure for Supreme Court Decisions on Certiorari." *The Journal of Politics* 41: 1185.

Strayer, B. L. 1983. *The Canadian Constitution and the Courts.* Scarborough, Ont.: Butterworth.

Tarnopolsky, W. S. 1966. *The Canadian Bill of Rights*, 2nd ed. Toronto: Carswell.

Tribe, L. H. 1980. *Constitutional Choices.* Cambridge, Mass.: Harvard University Press.

———. 1985. *Constitutional Choices.* Cambridge, Mass.: Harvard University Press.

Tushnet, Mark. 1984. "Book Review." *University of Pennsylvania Law Review* 132: 1257.

Van Alstyne, William. 1968. "The Demise of the Right-Privilege Distinction in Constitutional Law." *Harvard Law Review* 81: 1439.

———. 1977. "Cracks in 'The New Property': Adjudicative Due Process in the Administrative State." *Cornell Law Review* 62: 445.

———. 1980. "The Recrudescence of Property Rights as the Foremost Principle of Civil Liberties." *Law and Contemporary Problems* 66: 66–82.

Wechsler, Herbert. 1959. "Towards Neutral Principles in Constitutional Law." *Harvard Law Review* 73: 1.

Weiler, Paul C. 1984. "Rights and Judges in a Democracy: A New Canadian Version." *Michigan Journal of Law Reform* 18: 62.

Whyte, John D. 1984. "Developments in Constitutional Law: The 1982–83 Term." *Supreme Court Review* 6: 49–52.

Yackle, Larry W. 1978. "The Burger Court and the Fourth Amendment." *University of Kansas Law Review* 26: 335.

8. New Wine in Old Bottles: Thatcher's Conservative Economic Policy

JAMES E. ALT

In 1983 the Thatcher government became the first British government in a quarter century to be reelected after a full term in office. The American press quickly sensed the implications. "Thatcher's Victory May Offer Lessons for '84 US Election" headlined the *Wall Street Journal.* The key supposedly was Thatcherism, a package of fiscal and monetary austerity with tight restraint on government spending and borrowing intended to curb inflation and reduce interest rates, thereby overcoming the electoral burden of an unemployment rate that had more than doubled during Thatcher's first term. A more balanced view is that Thatcher's electoral success owed most to two events, the formation of the Social Democrats and the Falklands War, and little to economic outcomes (Schier and Vig, 1984). Nevertheless, at least in right-wing circles the belief persisted that Thatcherism exemplified a political strategy that others, particularly in the United States, could follow.

Is Thatcherism a resurgence of conservatism? How distinctive is it? We construct an answer in three main steps. First, we look at several meanings of conservatism to see which have been important themes in British Conservatism, and what should be expected of a conservative economic policy. Then we describe what the Thatcher government did, what happened, and why, in order to assess the outcomes for which they are responsible. Finally, we consider those pol-

The support of the National Science Foundation under grant SES 8512037 is gratefully acknowledged.

icy changes that experience leads us to expect whenever the Conservative party has held office. Combining these allows us to say which aspects of Thatcher's policies are conservative, and which of these are familiar or novel in the context of the British Conservative tradition.

Theory suggests that party competition has two sorts of economic effects. One sort, corresponding to economists' ideas of activities carried out in different ways by different parties to maximize social welfare, predicts effects on aggregate quantities like the supply of money, economic growth, or inflation. The other, the political scientists' model of policy as party competition, predicts effects on the distribution of wealth or welfare among individuals and groups, largely targeted through taxing and spending policies. We will consider both aggregate and distributional effects.

However, many factors are beyond the control of politicians, whatever they may promise and aspire to achieve. Such factors as world trade, institutional limitations, and past commitments are impossible —or at least too expensive—to alter at will. They are constraints on decisions and actions. Constraints establish margins on which politicians can act, and the observable effects of party competition are therefore marginal. This does not mean that party competition is irrelevant or that its effects are unobservable. It simply means that more care must be taken to specify the constraints ex ante.

We will look for changes in a variety of policy indicators closely linked to taxation and public expenditure, the nuts and bolts of economic policies. Observed changes include an increase in the burden of taxes borne by corporations rather than households, increases in defense spending over welfare spending, and a reduction in public investment relative to consumption. Some of these effects are familiar aspects of Conservative politics. Some are unfamiliar, but nevertheless conservative. Some are neither, and reflect the effect of constraints rather than decisions. Indeed, the largest departure of the Thatcher years, the persisting high level of unemployment, does not appear to be an obvious consequence of any domestic policy changes. It results rather from the collision of persisting, traditional British practice with changes in international markets in which exchange rates are determined. We show how the novel features of these markets (the new wine) interacted with the familiar constraints of British political ideas and institutions (the old bottles) to produce the present British situation.

A CONSERVATIVE ECONOMIC POLICY

Does Thatcherism represent a resurgence of conservatism in British economic policy? This depends on three things. One is whether there is a typical "conservative" economic policy. A second is whether British Conservative economic policies have been typically conservative. Finally, there is the question whether Thatcher's policies have been either typically conservative or Conservative. As we shall see, conservative policies can be many things, and Conservative policies have been several of them. Therefore, Thatcher's policies can easily combine aspects novel in Britain but familiar in other conservative contexts with elements familiar in Britain but absent elsewhere.[1]

Varieties of Conservative Economic Ideas

The idea of a conservative economic policy evokes many different, possibly contradictory themes. We will ignore several possibilities such as attempts to associate conservatism with consensual goals like prosperity. All politicians seek these associations. We will ask instead what is characteristically conservative about the means proposed to achieve them. Similarly, we shall assume that organizational themes like populism and corporatism describe ideas and organizations of conservatives and nonconservatives alike, and describe emphases that make one a conservative populist, or a populist conservative. Even leaving these aside, there are enough themes in conservatism to provide conflicting guidance for any politician raising the banner.

First, and most familiar, is the conservative value of *stability*: conservatives conserve, they do not change or innovate. Thatcher said, however, one might *actively* attempt to *stabilize* something, for instance prices, in an effort to control inflation. Alternately, one might stabilize expectations by resisting change, governing instead in a pragmatic, flexible, and adaptive fashion, rationalizing and consolidating (rather than reversing) changes initiated by others. Thus, even a concern for stability permits two potentially contradictory lines of policy such that one could claim to be doing one or the other at almost any time.

Second, conservative economic policy generally is *nonegalitarian*. Variations on this theme include claims that conservative policies favor the better-off, or business or capital rather than workers. Recently, under mass suffrage, overt attempts to redistribute to the better-off are infrequent. However nonegalitarian redistributive actions may be cloaked in the apparent passivity of restoring market forces, leaving markets to preserve or magnify initial disparities in endowments. Moreover, conservative interventions frequently are justified as likely to foster common national interests rather than sectoral advantages. Such a case is argued for inegalitarian policies designed to increase investment: the long-run gains in jobs and economic activity are claimed to benefit all.

Nevertheless, in spite of this latter conservative "statism," conservative economic policies ordinarily would be viewed as *antipublic*, though the reasons for this vary. One the one hand, some argue that states should not promote a particular conception of the good. Only public order is seen as a good by all, and thus is appropriately provided by states. Others argue that public enterprise is inefficient. Still others hold that a large public sector either becomes an end in itself, stifles work incentives through reducing self-reliance, or disproportionately rewards some organized groups. Finally, some even claim that the benefits from public goods are less likely to be secured through time. This attenuation of property rights makes a high discount rate on public activities appropriate (Brennan and Buchanan, 1986).

British Conservative Policies

Of course, few policies are simultaneously stabilizing, nonegalitarian, and antipublic. Thus those who would pursue conservative policies frequently must compromise among these broader ends. For instance, the desire to win elections repeatedly led Conservatives to put flexibility before nonegalitarianism and maintain popular social reforms instituted by others. Major segments of Conservative opinion consistently eschewed neoliberal, promarket noninterventionism. These were the "one-nation" Tories, whose intellectual roots lay in organic conceptions of society and a concern for stability, order, and authority. Within British history, imperialism and international adventurism, the construction of a strong navy and defense system, and tariffs were their policies.

Ever since World War II both sides of the neoliberal-Tory debate have been present in Conservative policies. Conservative governments accepted the managed economy and commitment to full employment, the welfare state, most nationalization of industry, and regional industrial support policies. On the other hand, some acts of denationalization, decontrol and the end of rationing, commercial television, and the abolition of resale price maintenance, all display a promarket emphasis on restoring competition (Leach, 1983). Obviously, as successor to all this pragmatism and policy diversity, Thatcherism will represent a resurgence of some kind of conservatism: what kind will be a matter of emphasis and degree.

Thatcherism

There are plenty of journalistic treatments of Thatcherism that stress its moral underpinnings in themes of thrift, self-reliance, competition, and patriotism. The first two are familiar ethical colorants for efficiency arguments against public assistance of various sorts. Thus, economically, Thatcherism is usually described as "market monetarism" (Riddell, 1983). What is novel is that the government no longer takes the responsibility for high employment as a goal of policy. As we shall see in a moment, this is more than exaggerated blame-shifting. Indeed, it makes a decisive break with the "Keynesian" economic policy consensus of the postwar years. Apparently the public accepts the new stance. At the end of the Heath government in 1974, few believed that inflation was the fault of the government, or that government activity could reduce it (Alt, 1979). By 1983 much the same was true of unemployment (Riddell, 1983).

The basic ideas of the new approach were monetarist in a narrow sense, that money was the proximate cause of inflation. The ideas started among academics and fringe politicians in the 1960s, gained ground among journalists in the early 1970s, and found public expression in speeches and pamphlets by Sir Keith Joseph after the Conservatives' 1974 defeat. Joseph's ideas were formalized in the work of the Centre for Policy Studies and embraced by Margaret Thatcher, who became leader of the Conservative party in a coup owing more to dissatisfaction with Heath after his electoral defeat than warmth for Thatcher's central economic ideas. This rapid spread of a new economic doctrine in the mid-1970s helps to explain why some of Thatcher's policies are unprecedented among Conservative policies but nevertheless display little discontinuity with those of her immediate predecessors.

For convenience, consider the specific intentions that Thatcher brought to office circa 1979 in three separate areas of policy. First, with respect to *growth and distribution of income*, inflation, which was seen as producing uncertainty harmful to investment, became the central target of policy. Economic growth was relegated to a long-run outcome of political reform and high employment dropped completely. Also, taxation was to be switched from personal incomes to spending (and subsequently oil profits) and reduced if possible. Typical supply-side arguments about disincentive effects were introduced to support the necessity of switching taxation from high marginal income tax rates to broad indirect consumption and excise taxes. Second, with regard to *monetary and fiscal policy*, money growth targets were explicitly tied to medium-term targets for public borrowing. Controls over bank lending and foreign exchange were to be eliminated where possible to support market determination of interest rates and the value of sterling. Public expenditures were to be cut to reduce public sector borrowing, promote efficiency, and avoid the need for high taxes. The stabilization role of government economic policy was to be reduced and deemphasized. Finally, in the area of *labor market and industrial policy*, legal reforms would reduce the frequency of strikes and eliminate wage pressure as a source of inflation. Industrial intervention (i.e., bailing out failing firms, loan guarantees, incentive policies) was to be reduced, and some publicly owned enterprises were to be sold ("privatized").

This represents a major departure from the postwar consensus. Predominantly, the conduct of economic policy by both parties from 1948 or so to 1973 had both a demand side and a supply side. Keynes's macroeconomics was the principle for managing the demand side, punctuated by episodes of explicit controls on the growth of incomes. The supply side had less formal theory behind it but was based initially on nationalization and rationing and later on regional aid, industrial bailouts, and tripartite consultation among government, business, and unions. All agreed to accept the constraint (so to speak) of a decentralized labor market with no central control over shop floor or local union activities and an internationally oriented, decontrolled financial sector.

Clearly, Thatcher's aim was to replace these macro, demand-centered strategies with micro, supply-oriented regimes (Hall, 1986). Removal of controls on movements of foreign capital, privatization, deregulation of the domestic securities market, all bespeak a desire to create new institutions promoting competition, the importance of market sentiment, and the efficiency of private enterprise. The question, however, is not just how (c/C)onservative is what Thatcher did, but how fundamental were the changes.

THATCHER'S ECONOMIC POLICIES

Unions, Labor Market, and Industrial Policy

Thatcherism includes a series of legal reforms affecting the position of unions. Many of the reforms had been Conservative party policy for some time. Measures to date include among other things a legal ban on secondary picketing, removal of union immunity to sequestration of funds by courts to pay fines imposed for violations of industrial relations law, and the mandating of periodic secret ballots to reaffirm closed shops, elect leaders, and retain political affiliation of unions to the Labour party. In a more general way union leaders are no longer consulted, even ritualistically, over economic policy, and active union cooperation is not sought in policy implementation. This lack of a policy role, added to union unpopularity stemming from strikes in the winter of 1978–79, has weakened the political position of the unions.

Other aspects of labor market policy include the creation and extension of job training and temporary employment schemes. While spending in this area was cut in the early years of the Thatcher government, persisting unemployment has led to the enhancement of Community Enterprise and Youth Training programs. These programs have been accompanied by incentives to firms to obtain financial and technical assistance for technological innovation, as well as some official intervention to encourage contracts with British rather than foreign firms in high technology.

Monetary and Fiscal Policy

Central to the fight against inflation was the Medium Term Financial Strategy (MTFS),[2] unveiled in the March 1980 budget. The MTFS consisted of a four-year target path for the growth of the broad measure of change in the money supply ΔM3, with supporting levels of the Public Sector Borrowing Requirement (PSBR). Its innovation is not the announcement of explicit monetary targets, which began under Labour Chancellor Healey in 1976 as part of the IMF agreement, but the restriction of targets to narrow goals like money and borrowing and the *absence* of explicitly stated goals for prices and output. ΔM3 was deliberately chosen as the target in order to put downward pressure on PSBR (Fforde, 1983). Its connection with PSBR derives from two monetary accounting identities that, for a given interest rate, make ΔM3 a function of PSBR.[3] While more recently the government has diversified somewhat the monetary indicators that are monitored, the basic principles of the MTFS—planning projections for monetary policy with a public sector borrowing target—remain unaltered.

Tax Composition

The first Thatcher budget in June 1979 changed *tax composition*. The basic rate of income tax was reduced by 3 percentage points to 30 percent, and the top marginal rate was reduced from 83 to 60 percent. However, this did not reduce total revenues, since the rate of value-added tax (VAT) was increased to 15 percent, eliminating the formerly high rate on luxuries. Similar arguments about benefits to investment and growth were used to support the Thatcher tax changes and the American 1981 Tax Act. The March 1981 budget added another link in Thatcher's fiscal strategy with the extension of "cash limits" for government consumption and planning, introduced by Healey after 1975.[4] While early budgets witnessed disproportionate increases in excises and a freeze (1981) on personal allowances, from 1982 on allowances were increased by more than inflation, and excise tax rates rose with inflation. Most recently corporate taxes have been cut and employers' national insurance charges reduced.

Privatization

Another element in the new fiscal strategy is *privatization*. Although introduced into the 1979 Conservative Manifesto almost as an afterthought, sales of publicly held assets from 1979–80 through 1984–85 totaled nearly £5 billion, a substantial part of the cumulative reduction in public sector deficit achieved by the Thatcher government.[5] Moreover, the increase in asset sales has been accompanied by aggressive pursuit of efficiency through reorganization and rationalization in public corporations. Capital spending cutbacks and labor force reductions in steel, coal, railways, airlines, and other state enterprises have cumulatively reduced public corporation employment by a quarter of a million jobs, accompanying the 400,000 jobs sold back to the private sector.

Social Security and Social Policy

There are three basic aspects to Thatcher's social policy. First, the privatization of housing has been as aggressive as that of state enterprise. However, at the same time the privatization of health care, much advertised and widely discussed, even at cabinet levels, has gone practically nowhere. Encouragement of the contracting out of services resulted in perhaps 10 percent of laundering being turned over to private enterprise; even less contracting out was achieved in catering and cleaning. National Health Service expenditures continue to rise, and the reported increase of nine hundred private hospital beds between 1975 and 1980 (Klein, 1984) hardly compensated for the loss of 96,000 NHS beds between 1963 and 1978 (Fuchs, 1986). Finally, reduction of personal transfer payments has had significant real effects only in the area of unemployment compensation, where the earnings-related supplement was abolished, the indexing link to earnings and prices was depreciated, and benefits were subjected to tax.

AGGREGATE EFFECTS

Those are the Thatcher actions. Obviously they look conservative. The package is evidently promarket, particularly in the aspect of privatization of industry, rather than stabilizing or even predominantly antiegalitarian. In its retention of planning (though around intermediate monetary targets rather than output) it has been pragmatically Conservative. Our next question is what has happened, and whether it is a consequence of these actions. Only when the outcomes are tied to actions can we assess what kind of resurgence, if any, Thatcherism represents.

The principal success of the Thatcher regime is that the British inflation rate was reduced, from the 10 percent annual rate they inherited to about 4.5 percent since 1983. The latter is at about the OECD average and represents the first time British relative inflation has been that low since 1972.[6] However, there is no sign of further relative improvement. British unit labor costs increased by 4.4 percent in the year ending with the first quarter of 1984, while both Japanese and American unit labor costs fell by similar amounts. Moreover, the reduction in inflation has been achieved at great cost in terms of lost output and particularly unemployment. There was virtually no growth in real British GDP between 1979 and 1983. Since then there has been a total growth of about 5 percent in real terms. This places the average per annum growth rate under Thatcher at about 1 percent per annum, half the growth rate obtaining under her postwar predecessors.

While inflation was halved, unemployment more than doubled. This unemployment as well as past inflation are both persistently worse than OECD averages (Buiter and Miller, 1983).[7] Corresponding to the increased unemployment is a precipitous (nearly 30 percent) decline in manufacturing employment since 1978. The loss of over 1.5 million jobs in manufacturing equals the increase in unemployment in the same period (Chrystal, 1984). The duration and acceleration of this decline after 1978 are unprecedented in the recent history of business cycles in Britain. It is matched by a depression in manufacturing investment of extraordinary severity, with no significant upturn until 1984 from the 40 percent decline at which investment bottomed out in 1982–83 (NIER, 1984).

Indeed, the distinctive feature of the political economy of Thatcher's Britain is its high and persisting level of unemployment. This unemployment is part of a major structural change in the British labor force. Nearly all the extra unemployed since 1979 come at the expense of manufacturing. The proportion in private sector manufacturing is now two-thirds the proportion similarly employed in Germany (OECD, 1983), more typical of countries with large fishing or agricultural sectors.

So as a first conclusion there are major changes in macroeconomic aggregates under Thatcher, declines in output, investment, and inflation, and an increase in unemployment. The differences do not normally arise between parties in Britain in the case of investment and output; the changes under Thatcher are far larger and more durable than those estimated for earlier administrations in unemployment and inflation. Moreover, even after controlling for the effects of institutional differences and prevailing world economic conditions, both the change in British unemployment and inflation are unusually large in comparison with the recent experience of other Western industrial democracies.[8] Nevertheless, the question remains, by what actions were these changes brought about?

Labor Market

The Thatcher government hoped to restore competition in labor markets and balance in collective bargaining by reducing the power of unions and if possible the extent of unionization in the work force. Since 1979 employment has fallen by 8 percent and union membership by 15 percent. However, the rapid increase in unemployment explains much of the decrease in union membership. The decline in union density—the proportion unionized of those still in employment —is much smaller. As union power was used to secure pay and conditions for those remaining in employment rather than organizing the unemployed (Glyn and Shaw, 1981), those out of work let their union memberships lapse for economic reasons.

Although these shifts reflect the major changes in the labor force under Thatcher, neither probably is a direct result of labor market policies.[9] The collapse of manufacturing investment and employment has had major effects on the composition of the British labor force. Very importantly, these changes in employment have not resulted in changes in relative pay. Those in private sector manufacturing gained rapidly relative to others in 1975–79 (while the public corporations and general government tended to fall behind) and have held on to most of these gains since then. Strike volume appears to be increasing again after a few quiet years, and some highly visible secondary actions (for example, railwaymen refusing to carry coal to steel plants in support of the miners' strike) have been undertaken in spite of government and management opposition. The symbolic exclusion of unions from policy may merely have reinforced existing tendencies for unions to be most active and effective at the shop floor level (Crouch, 1981).

Interest Rates and Money

It is difficult to show that monetary control under Thatcher was consistently tight. The target range for $\Delta M3$ has centered near 10 percent annual growth since 1979. Actual $\Delta M3$ was never below that target range until 1984, and for the first two years of the Thatcher administration was well above it. The narrower money supply measure, $\Delta M1$, falls sharply in Thatcher's first year but then rises to over 10 percent annual growth after the abolition of banking controls. Nor is it clear that Thatcher's policies were significantly tighter than Healey's in the era immediately before. $\Delta M3$, the announced target, is generally looser under Thatcher. $\Delta M1$ is generally tighter than before, especially compared to the peak rates of money growth in 1977–78.[10] While estimates vary, there is little evidence of a significant contraction in money growth coinciding with the beginning of Thatcher's term (Whiteley, 1985). Money growth appears to have slowed enough under Thatcher to account for reduced inflation, but there are no changes large, sudden, or tight enough to explain the decline in output and rise in unemployment in this period. Econometrically tested models of money and output produce estimates that are insufficient to explain the level of unemployment (Darby and Lothian, 1983).

Regardless of money supply figures, one might regard Thatcher's monetary policy as tight if it resulted in interest rates that were high by international standards, especially after allowing for differences in inflation rates between countries. However, relative interest rates suggest that British policy was typical of other industrial countries. British relative real interest rates (nominal money market rates minus expected inflation, based on recent experience) were predominantly negative under Healey (it paid to borrow, vis-à-vis inflation) until near the end of Labour's term, and then were first negative but increasingly positive under Thatcher, so there is some evidence of increased tightness after 1979. Nevertheless, real rates in Britain even after recent increases are not high by international standards. British nominal interest rates are not significantly higher under Thatcher than Healey (Chrystal, 1984). They are always toward the high end of the range of rates offered by Britain's competitors (recall Britain's high relative inflation) but not exceptionally high, and if anything are lower under Thatcher than before.

Assuming that tight money was Thatcher's goal, why the apparent weakness in monetary control? Basically, ΔM3 never did respond as expected to changes in interest rates, whose uncertain effects on bank lending and domestic credit expansion prevented the expected clear response of ΔM3 to PSBR changes.[11] Moreover, monetary policy was made not only with the domestic ΔM3 target in mind, but frequently also with regard to international concerns. For instance, even with ΔM3 well over target in 1980–81, interest rates were lowered in an attempt to decrease the attractiveness of sterling and reduce the exchange rate. Finally and most important, PSBR targets were uniformly missed, interfering with reducing ΔM3 targets.

Fiscal Policy and Deficits

Missing PSBR targets seems all the more remarkable in view of the contributions of major new revenue sources in oil royalties and public asset sales. Indeed, as figure 8.1 shows, oil royalties approached 3 percent of GDP in the early 1980s, more than trebling the effect of the 1979 reduction in income taxation. Nevertheless, the MTFS has a history of missed targets. The March 1980 budget forecast PSBR as a percentage of GDP for the next four fiscal years of the Thatcher government. The forecasts, beginning with fiscal 1980–81, were 3.8, 3.0, 2.3, and 1.5 percent, respectively, for a cumulative borrowing through 1983–84 of 10.6 percent of GDP. The final PSBR outturns for those years were, respectively, 5.6, 3.4, 3.4, and 2.5 percent of GDP, for a total of 14.9 percent of GDP. The final borrowing requirement reveals overshooting by 40 percent, and by 50 percent in three of the four years. Finally, Whiteley (1985) also concludes that the PSBR under Thatcher did not deviate significantly from a time path predictable from the experience of earlier administrations.

Figure 8.1 shows why the overshooting occurred. Both consumption and transfer payments increased sharply under the Thatcher government. In neither case does the Thatcher experience appear to diverge from longer-term trends. The greatest overshooting of expenditures was in precisely those areas hardest hit by recession: unemployment compensation and support for industry. We return to this below. The

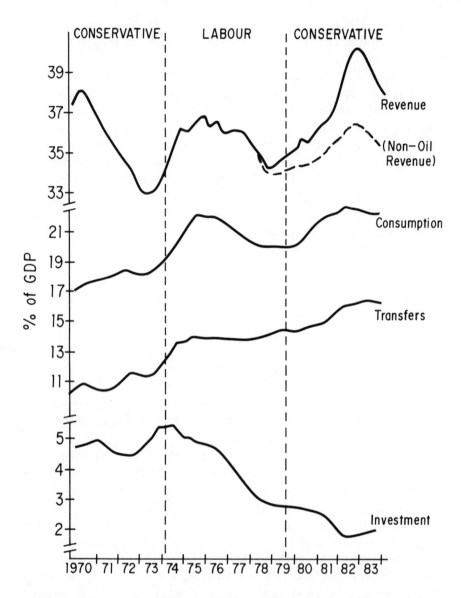

Figure 8.1. Shares of GDP Going to Government Revenues and Expenditures, Britain, 1970–83.

£10 billion collected in oil revenues between 1979–80 and 1984–85 just more than offsets the estimated final cost from the extra 2 million unemployed in that period. Some increases are compensated by reductions in public investment, but figure 8.1 also shows these to be smaller than those achieved by their Labour predecessors.

Vitally, however, PSBR targets could be missed but policy still be tight if world recession produced high unemployment and a fiscal deficit despite the government's wishes. Measures of fiscal "stance" that separate the effects of discretionary policy from automatic effects of boom and recession are required to estimate party differences accurately. In Britain "high" or "full employment" estimates of fiscal stance under conditions of full capacity usage are published by the National Institute. Their figures (not shown) for annual changes in the "weighted cyclically adjusted deficit," adjusted both for the "automatic" effects of the business cycle (the deviation of growth of GDP from trend) and varying short-term impacts on demand of different sources of revenue (see Blackaby, 1978; Savage, 1982), indicate that fiscal policy has been contractionary (that is, the deficit has been reduced) each year since 1968. The only exceptions are the "Barber boom" years from 1971–73, and the three fiscal years containing or immediately preceding elections, 1974–75, 1978–79, and 1982–83. However, allowing for the recent business cycle effects and choices of revenue composition, there is little difference between parties. Under Labour the weighted deficit changed by −0.51 percent per annum, compared to −0.63 percent per annum under Thatcher's Conservatives. Indeed, if 1974–75 is omitted (a year of electioneering subsidies under a minority government), the subsequent decline under Labour in the adjusted financial deficit from 1975–79 was just over 1 percent of GDP per annum, more severely contractionary than under Thatcher.[12] In fact, the cumulative increase in adjusted surplus since 1975 is about as large as the cumulative increase in deficit from 1970–75. So if unemployment is a function of domestic fiscal stance, it is a case of tight fiscal policy in a monetarist era from 1976, or more generally in an era of fiscal distress since the 1967 devaluation, rather than Thatcherism.

Expenditures and Revenues

However, the adjusted deficit could mask systematic differences between parties and administrations in the extent or composition of revenues and expenditures. The postwar consensus involved demand management coupled with weak indicative planning (ignoring incomes policies for the moment) to direct the economy. The result, as Alt and Chrystal (1983) show, was that major categories of expenditures were planned relative to expected long-run growth in national income (permanent income) with variations at the margin due to economic conditions (stabilization policy). In the context of this basic model of aggregate revenues and expenditures, interparty differences or a conservative resurgence could mean several different things. Perhaps the postwar consensus also involved larger target shares of national income in the public sector under Labour than Conservative administrations, or increases in public expenditures under Labour preserved under subsequent pragmatic conservative governments. There could be more stabilization, or more stabilization of particular targets, like prices, for instance. And in each case one can see whether Thatcher departs from previous practice, and whether previous or present practice involves regular differences between competing political parties.

Our approach is to estimate a version of the permanent income model for the public sector (see Alt and Chrystal, 1983, Table 10.1, for examples) and then systematically search it for evidence of party differences in policy. This is done as follows. Central government revenues, three categories of expenditure (consumption, transfers, and capital investment), and the current financial deficit were regressed on four sets of independent variables that reflect aspects of the postwar consensus. The independent variables include (1) indicators of *planning*, a lagged dependent variable and an instrument for national income; (2) potential targets for *stabilization*, such as unemployment, the balance of payments, and the inflation rate; (3) a variety of seasonal variables to pick up systematic quarter-to-quarter differences unrelated to the other concerns under analysis; and finally (4) *party differences*, a series of dummy variables representing each successive administration, from the Conservatives (up to 1964), Labour (1964–70), Conservatives again (1970–73), Labour again (1974–79), and finally the Thatcher government from 1979 on. Expenditure categories include government consumption, transfers to individuals, and investment (capital spending in roads, buildings, and equipment, not in public corporations).

The regressions are run separately for three time periods, 1955–73

Table 8.1.   Regression Results and Forecasts for British Expenditures
and Revenues.

| | Public sector category | | | | |
	Consumption	Transfers	Investment	Revenues	Deficit
Planning					
1955–73	PI	PI	PI	CI	CI
1955–79	PI	PI	PI	CI	CI
1955–83	PI	PI	PI	CI	No
Stabilization					
1955–73	BP	U*	NGI	BP	BP
1955–79	I	U*	NGI, I	—	U, BP
1955–83	I	U*	NGI, I	I	U, BP
Party differences					
1955–73	No	Yes	Yes	Maybe	No
1955–79	No	Yes	No	No	No
1955–83	No	No	No	No	No
Forecast					
1955–73	+ 5%	−15%	−67%	=	=
1955–79	+10%	− 8%	−45%	+5%	=

Note: This table summarizes results from replications of the modified permanent income model for government revenues, expenditures, and deficits discussed in Alt and Chrystal (1983). Planning is represented by reasonable, significant, correct-sign estimates for an instrument for national income and a lagged dependent variable; results may represent permanent income (PI), current income (CI—no lagged term), or no planning effect at all. Stabilization is indicated by significant estimates for the targets Unemployment (U), Inflation (I), and Balance of Payments (BP), as well as private investment (NGI) in one case. Automatic effects are starred; wrong sign cases are italicized. Party differences by administration (dummy variables) either yield significant effects of the right sign (Yes) or not. Forecasts are expressed as the average difference between observed values under Thatcher and those forecast out from the estimation period, with the lagged dependent variable replaced in the forecast by the lagged endogenous forecast.

(most evidently the period of the "postwar consensus"), 1955 to mid-1979 (which includes the Healey years and the coming of monetarism), and 1955–83. The parameter estimates from the longest regression can be compared to those from the earlier period to identify and characterize changes occurring under Thatcher. More important, parameter estimates from regressions for the earlier period will be used to generate forecasts for the Thatcher period, in which the outturns can be compared to the results "as if nothing had changed." They compare what happened under Thatcher with what would have happened under unchanged relationships from the period of postwar consensus.[13]

The results, summarized in table 8.1, are as follows. The permanent income hypothesis is sustained for all three categories of expenditure, which appear to continue to be planned around some target share of long-run expected national income. It turns out that the target share (not shown) under Thatcher is lower than at the end of the Healey period in all three cases, though it is still higher than at the end of the previous Conservative administration. Planning is still the dominant relationship between national income and expenditure, with no evidence of an end of the effects of forecasting in real terms, and no obvious effects of the introduction or reintroduction of cash limits on the long-run proportionality of expenditure with respect to income. Stabilization policy is most evident in the case of transfers. However, there the stabilizer is automatic in that transfers include an entitlement payment to the unemployed. So total payments increase automatically when unemployment increases. The coefficient linking unemployment to transfer payments falls steadily as the estimation period is extended through time, indicating erosion of the real value of benefits to the unemployed. Inflation appears as a distortion in the longer-run equations, owing to the price surges in the 1970s and 1980s. Public investment offsets nongovernmental investment and is affected by inflation.[14] Revenues and thus the deficit respond to contemporaneous income only, and thus represent the short-run concerns of financing expenditure rather than independent planning targets. The deficit appears to vary in response to unemployment levels, as Keynesian policy prescriptions indicate it should.

Most important, regular party differences do not appear since the end of the Heath administration. This might be a consequence of the first OPEC shock, unprecedented inflation, higher deficits, or monetarism. However, the post-1973 era is definitely different from before. Until 1973 planning and stabilization policy were evident throughout the expenditure accounts, and regular party differences (rise under Labour, fall under Conservatives) were observed in transfers and investment, and possibly even in total central government revenues. Revenues fell significantly (relative to national income) under Heath, but there is no regular pattern of alternation between parties.

The forecast picture is varied. Government consumption at the end of 1983 is 10 percent above the expectation generated from the standpoint of statistical relationships through the end of 1973. Transfer payments end below the forecast by a similar amount, though they forecast well until the 1982 budget. Investment alone is far lower than expected, and lower still than expected after its fall in the late 1970s. This reduction in public capital parallels the sale of assets in nationalized industries. Revenues and deficits remain at levels typical of those in earlier periods, allowing of course for the effects of changes in economic conditions.

Thus, we concluded what is distinctive in the Thatcher administration is a sharp rise in unemployment, a sharp fall in investment and output, and initial increases in money supply and inflation, with the results that real rates of interest have increased. The fall in output and employment may "explain" the subsequent fall in inflation and money growth, but the rise in real interest rates comes too late to explain the falls in investment and output, which occur simultaneously with the great increase in unemployment. Fiscal policy as a whole continues tight, but, allowing for the effects of changes in unemployment and the like, it is the composition of the public sector aggregates, though not the sheer scale of the public sector, that is what Thatcher has altered. Government consumes more and invests less, but within this sharp move toward the present over the future, the aggregate scale of public spending is about what would have been predicted from models based on data ending in the early 1970s.

DISTRIBUTIONAL CHANGES

The fact that one term of Thatcherism has not resulted in major changes in the aggregate scale of British public expenditure does not mean that there could not be large distributional changes beneath the surface. Distribution relates ultimately to the allocation of benefits among individuals or groups. We shall examine changes in taxation to see whether there are novel conservative features in the distribution of burdens across different classes of taxes, or in the incidence of these taxes on different individuals or groups. We will also consider tradeoffs in allocating expenditures across programs and over time.

Inegalitarian Conservatism: Individuals and Groups

Group conflict and the tax code. What tax policy might one expect of conservatives? If they conserve, they might merely preserve tax codes altered by others. If conservatism means antipublic attitudes, one would expect the total tax burden to drop. If it means antiredistribution, we expect the emphasis to be away from (progressive) income tax onto expenditures and other taxes, or more generally away from direct onto indirect taxes. If conservatives are proenterprise (investment), we expect taxes on capital as well as income to decline. Other expectations are contingent on assumptions about the nature of politics. If politics is assumed to be dominated by group conflict, and if conservatives are anticorporatists, one might expect to see the tax burden shifted onto business from individuals. If political action is motivated by vote-seeking, there should be pre- or postelection shifts that affect masses. If tax policy is essentially a tool for indicative planning, one should expect longer-term changes that may not produce numbers of converts as much as aggregate adjustments in the economy.

But conservative tax policies also encounter tradeoffs. For instance, one may seek to foster enterprise, but do you do it through individual or corporate incentives? If you reduce individual burdens, you have to find the foregone revenues elsewhere, which generally means taking more from corporations given that all taxes are paid either by business or households.[15] Antistatist or anticorporatist bias would lead you to expect less attention to desires of organized interests and thus to see the usual business advantage in political conflict reduced. But if enterprise is what you seek, businesses are organized and will resist strongly if their burdens are raised. Thus, the result in tax politics is often stasis, with the highly symbolic quality of changes at margin.[16]

Tax yields depend on rates and bases. These in turn may be affected by economic growth and inflation, party control of government, and proximity of elections. Karran (1984) finds little evidence of regular partisan effects on taxation. Income and excise tax yields are basically determined by the effects of economic growth on the tax base. Inflation squeezes company profits, reducing company tax yields (see, however,

Morrissey and Sandmo, 1986). Only the rates of value-added tax reflect significant party differences.

Nevertheless, there is some further evidence of partisan changes in tax policy, which illuminates the continuity and changes of Thatcher's economic policies with those of earlier Conservative administrations. For simplicity of interpretation, we can summarize changes in several categories of taxation by using indices. Figure 8.2 shows the ratio of direct (income plus capital plus national insurance) taxes to indirect (expenditure plus excises and others) taxes since 1955. There is an overall rise in direct taxation, led by income tax and company taxes in early 1960s, an upward surge in the relative contribution of direct taxation from 1970 to the end of 1975, and a steep decline over the next five years, ultimately settling at the ratio of the 1960s again. Nor is there more evidence of regular partisan alternation in the underlying individual tax components. Both income and expenditure tax yields fall under Heath and subsequently rise again, national insurance yields trend upward throughout the period, and revenues from

Figure 8.2. Ratio of Direct to Indirect Taxes, Britain, 1955–83. *Note:* Numerator of ratio is sum of taxes on income, capital, and national insurance contributions. Denominator is sum of taxes on expenditures and other taxes. *Source:* CSO.

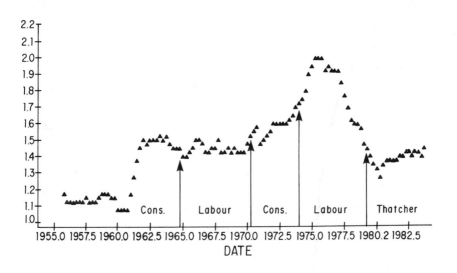

other sources rise steeply after 1975, as oil royalties become a significant revenue source. Only taxation of capital rises sharply under Labour both times, though it declines again rapidly in the second Labour administration. Nevertheless, there is no clear evidence of the sort of partisan promise-keeping that would be consistent with regular changes in unemployment and inflation (other than on capital taxes).

However, a clear pattern emerges if real yields from direct taxes borne by persons (households) rather than businesses are isolated. For each of the first four postwar partisan transitions, figure 8.3 compares the early-term behavior of personal direct taxes with an expectation based on recent performance under the previous incumbents. Thus, for example, in 1951–52, when the Conservatives return under Churchill, the early-term trend of personal direct taxes is below its expected trend based on 1950–51. Similarly, the upward trend in personal direct taxes under Labour after 1964 is above what would have been predicted from the last few years of the Conservative government. After 1970 the trend is initially down, and after 1973, initially up again, as one might expect. Oddly, considering the centrality of promised tax reductions in 1979, the Thatcher incumbency is the first in

Figure 8.3. Direct Taxes on Households, Britain, 1950–83. Note: Chart shows real (constant price) burden of direct (see note to figure 8.5) taxes borne by households, with early-term direction under new incumbents. Source: OECD.

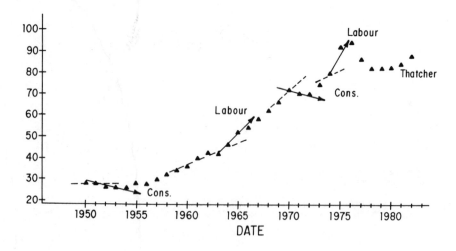

thirty years not to show the expected effect. The reduced burden of personal direct taxation in Healey's last few years was so substantial that the Thatcher administration can at most be said not to have changed things.[17] Even though allowances were increased and rates cut under Thatcher, it appears that yields did not fall, partly at least because of increased national insurance contributions.

The battle over tax burdens is fought not only between individual supporters of different political parties occupying different socioeconomic locations, but also between and among various organized groups and individuals. Foremost among organized groups seeking relief from taxation is business. "Favors to business" measures yet another aspect of conservatism: the success of business in shifting tax burdens onto individuals indicates whether corporatism or populism was the dominant strain of conservatism in economic policy. In terms of expected party differences, one would expect business to do better (higher profits, lower incidence of taxation) under "normal" conservatives than left-wing administrations, though whether business does better under populist conservatism or corporatist leftism is indeterminate.

Figure 8.4 shows that the changes in direct taxation have fallen predominantly on individuals. In real terms corporate income tax receipts have been effectively constant since the early 1950s, while real tax receipts from household income have more than tripled. The marginal differences observed in personal taxation have been matched by slight partisan effects on corporate income taxation. Real corporate income tax receipts fall steadily from 1952 to 1964, rise steadily to 1970, fall again slightly to 1973, rise again in 1974–75, but then drop sharply (due to the fall in profits post-OPEC) for a couple of years and rise steadily thereafter. Thatcher's novel contribution is to alter slightly the distribution of taxation from individuals toward corporations.

This trend is even more clear in the shares of national insurance contributions, also shown in figure 8.4. Employers' and employees' contributions had been equal until 1964. Labour then raised employers' contributions relative to employees' contributions, and did so again in 1974. Recall that Thatcher's early interventions included both reductions in employers' contributions and increases in individuals'. Thus explicit assistance to business is especially large under Thatcher. Given that national insurance contributions are small relative to income tax receipts, the overall share of business in taxation is substantially below

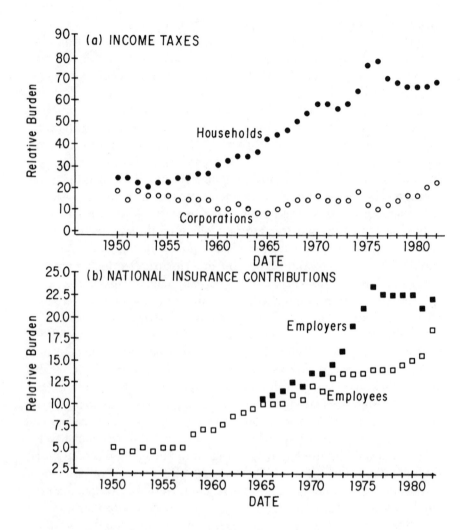

Figure 8.4. Tax Burdens on Households and Corporations, Britain, 1950–83.
Note: Chart shows real (constant price) burden of taxes by class of payer.
Source: OECD.

where it was in the early 1950s, and about back to where it was in 1964, before a decade of interparty competition over relative burdens.

Distribution of Income. Even so, organized business as a whole has not done badly under Thatcher. Indeed, under the corporatist conservatism of Heath's incomes policies the allowable rate of profit was used to convert wage increases into permissible price increases. That is, what firms were allowed to charge for a product was calculated from their costs plus an allowed markup. Under Healey's chancellorship between 1974 and 1979 the real rates of growth in the trading profits of companies and the average earnings for the whole economy were about equal (3.8 vs. 3.6 percent, respectively). However, since 1979 under Thatcher profits have grown at three times the rate earnings have grown (6.0 vs. 1.9 percent). This is probably the first time in two decades that business has done that well relative to households.

Within personal incomes the distribution of income also has moved in an inegalitarian direction.[18] Table 8.2 contrasts the effects on the distribution of income achieved in the first three years of Thatcher's first term (more recent figures are not available) with the Reagan first term. The changes in both countries are inegalitarian, but they are sharper and more concentrated at the top in Britain. The Reagan record is what one might expect, with rapid growth in real personal disposable incomes among the top 20 percent of households, and a contraction in the lowest 20 percent. Table 8.2b shows that the changes in household *shares* of disposable income have been modest. Importantly, American aggregate growth in real incomes in the Reagan years prevented an even sharper decline in the real incomes of the poor. For example, the income share of the lowest quintile falls from 6.8 to 6.1 percent, a decline of 11 percent. Only the aggregate real 3.5 percent growth in incomes holds their loss to the 7.6 percent decline in actual income.

Table 8.2 shows that incomes in the top 20 percent have also grown in Britain, though by less than in the United States, but that outside this top group incomes have been declining. Some of this is because aggregate incomes have shrunk, but table 8.2b, summarized in table 8.2c, shows just how marked the concentration of benefits has been. The increase in the share of the top group is 2.4 percentage points from an original share of just under 40 percent. This is a change of about 6 percent in only three years, very rapid by the usual snail-paced standard of changes in income distribution. Most remarkable, as table 8.2c shows, this change has nothing to do with changes in tax allowances and rates, since the changes in shares of disposable income

Table 8.2.   Real Personal Disposable Income Under Reagan and Thatcher.

(a) Change in average household real personal disposable income by quintile under:

	Reagan 1980–84	Thatcher 1978–79-1981–82
Top 20%	+8.7	+4.7
Next 20%	+3.4	−4.3
Middle 20%	+0.9	−6.4
Next 20%	−0.7	−1.1
Lowest 20%	−7.6	−9.7
The "Pie"	+3.5	−1.1

(b) Household share of real personal disposable incomes under Reagan and Thatcher by quintile

	Reagan		Thatcher			
	Posttax		Posttax		Pretax	
	1980	1984	1978–79	1981–82	1978–79	1981–82
Top 20%	37.0	38.9	39.7	42.0	42.6	45.0
Next 20%	24.5	24.5	24.8	24.0	24.7	23.9
Middle 20%	18.5	18.1	17.0	16.1	16.5	15.6
Next 20%	13.2	12.5	11.5	11.5	10.3	10.2
Lowest 20%	6.8	6.1	7.0	6.4	5.9	5.5

(c) Percentage changes in household share of personal disposable income under Thatcher

	Posttax	Pretax
Top 20%	+2.3	+2.4
Next 20%	−0.8	−0.8
Middle 20%	−0.9	−0.9
Next 20%	0.0	−0.1
Lowest 20%	−0.6	−0.4

Note: Source for the American data is the Urban Institute, The Reagan Record, and for Britain the Central Statistical Office.

are identical whether pretax or posttax incomes are considered. If all income groups but the top have declining real disposable incomes, and if this was not a consequence of tax changes, then these changes are probably consequences of increased unemployment, which has little effect on those in the top income group, but otherwise reduces incomes largely across the board. Indeed, Hall (1986) provides evidence that changes in the distribution of income were caused by unemployment, though he presents the results in terms of the concentration of unemployed at the bottom of the income distribution, rather than their absence at the top.

Antipublic Conservatism: Distribution Across Programs and Time

The basic ideas of antistate conservatism are that public activity should be restricted to the basic "public good" provisions of national defense and law and order and that public power is too insecure to permit the state to be used for long-run infrastructure type programs. Thus, even if the parties do not differ significantly in the total amount of public spending, one would expect conservatives to spend relatively more on law and order and defense and less on welfare. Similarly, if one expects a higher discount rate on public activities under conservatives, they will choose public consumption over public investment at the margin.

If conservatives take distinctive positions on the "guns-welfare" tradeoff, we would expect oscillations in spending between different partisan incumbencies on such basic components of public expenditure as defense and the National Health Service. By now few readers will expect to observe large oscillations, but some may nevertheless be surprised by the smoothness. Figure 8.5 plots the ratio of defense to NHS spending among current government consumption expenditures (the two jointly comprise a quarter of central government consumption). Basically, the ratio declines steadily from the end of the Korean War to 1975, when it reaches unity (equal shares), and stays more or less at unity from then on. The usual marginal sort of party differences are there: the rate of decline is faster from 1964–70 than before, the decline ceases from 1970–74, and then accelerates again in 1974 and 1975. The trend is slightly up after 1979, and has probably continued so through 1985. So in this respect a difference between nonconservative and conservative parties is continued, but again it exists only on a fine margin.

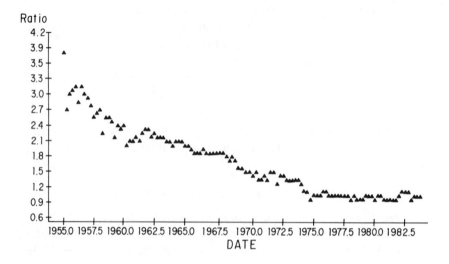

Figure 8.5. Spending on Defense and the National Health Service, Britain, 1955–83. *Note:* Chart shows ratio of central government consumption expenditures on defense and national health.
Source: CSO.

Indeed, there are not many other policy areas in which such interparty differences could be found. Table 8.3 reports annual real rates of growth in different expenditure programs under five British administrations. It shows that only defense, law and order, and (maybe) "culture" (education, science, arts, and libraries) are subject to regular partisan alteration. The Conservatives spend slightly more in each area. Nor has Thatcher departed from other established patterns of party conflict. Apart from agriculture such interparty differences either never existed (transport, health, social security), had broken down earlier (industry, energy, and employment, cut sharply under Healey), or were the opposite of what might have been expected (housing). There are as many startling departures from Thatcher's early plans (agriculture, employment, social security) as departures from earlier practice (housing). Indeed, in the latter case, the Thatcher cuts decisively reverse earlier Conservative policies even more clearly than earlier Labour policies. Nevertheless, the most important observation here is the extent to which the composition and overall level of govern-

Table 8.3. British Expenditures Growth by Program, 1957–85.

Average annual percentage real growth

Program	1957–64	1964–70	1970–73	1974–79	Plan 5 years from 1980	1979–80 1984–85
Defense	0.3	−1.3	2.8	0.3	2.5	4.2
Overseas aid	7.7	−0.8	14.7	7.6	−3.1	−4.1
Agriculture	−3.0	−1.8	−0.7	−16.4	−1.2	6.7
Industry, employment, energy	4.9	9.0	3.3	−7.9	−9.9	3.3
Transport	6.0	5.8	3.9	−4.1	−2.6	−0.9
Housing	5.3	2.6	11.7	−4.2	−12.3	−14.6
Law and order	9.5	6.0	7.6	2.1	2.0	5.2
Education, science, libraries	7.2	5.8	6.9	0.0	−2.1	0.4
Health	4.6	4.9	5.3	1.7	0.9	2.7
Social security	6.5	5.7	3.6	4.4	0.7	5.1
Total	4.2	4.2	5.0	0.4	−1.0	1.4

Sources: Klein (1976), Hall (1986), Whiteley (1985), Expenditure White Papers 1979, 1980, 1985 (Cmnd. 7439, 7841, 9428).

ment spending under Thatcher appear to continue earlier practices with the obvious exception of housing.

The same is true of the composition of expenditure with respect to time. If conservatives carried out Buchanan's advice and operated with a higher discount rate on public projects, one would expect the investment share of public expenditure to fall under conservative administrations.[19] Given the privatization campaign in public corporations, one might expect a mirroring of such activities in the sphere of general public investment. Indeed, under Thatcher public investment plunges and is now a far smaller share of GDP than at any time since World War II. Nevertheless, whether this public investment is taken as a proportion of public consumption or compared with private investment, the picture is the same. Public investment falls slowly relative to private investment under the first postwar Conservative administration, rises under Labour, and falls again under the next Conservative administration, at least initially in each case. But since 1974 public investment has fallen steadily, and has fallen little faster under Thatcher than under her Labour predecessors. The sacrifice of the future implicit in this jettisoning of public investment looks more like a response to fiscal pressure (growing deficits) than ideology. Under the pressure to cut back, the future is the first to go.

THE REST OF THE STORY:
INTERNATIONAL EFFECTS

The basic tenets of Thatcherism, we have argued, are monetary control to reduce excess demand and contraction of state activity to promote entrepreneurship. Thatcherism, however, is more than a set of mechanical principles applied to the instruments of economic policy. It includes both an underlying philosophy about the values of competitiveness and private sector efficiency and an old-fashioned liberal political philosophy of individualism. However, in these respects its consequences are not altogether novel. For example, the fiscal and monetary policy strategies of the Thatcher government rely heavily on "market sentiment," rather like the "National Plan" of twenty years ago. Moreover, while the big change under Thatcher may well be the market philosophy and the move toward market-determined prices, it is by no means clear that the philosophical changes have been accompanied by the requisite structural reforms. People may no longer believe in nationalization of industry, but the part that has been privatized is a fraction of the public sector. Supporting reforms in labor market policy, housing, and capital markets have not yet been shown to be sufficient to alter the nature of the British economy (Batchelor, 1983). Even if these changes offered hope for the long run, the real costs of adjustment probably outweigh the benefits at any reasonable discount rate. Thus, while Thatcher may have communicated a new philosophy and convinced many to accept its tenets, such acceptance is capricious and in the absence of obvious payoffs may disappear with changes in intellectual fashion.

Nevertheless, Thatcherism has consequences in tax and expenditure composition. Some of the changes are familiar conservative aspects of interparty competition, like the shifts in expenditure priorities toward defense and law and order. Some are conservative but decisive reversals of earlier Conservative policies, like the trends in profits and housing expenditures. In some cases, like changes in personal tax burdens, the expected familiar conservative shift could not be found. And in some respects, like the overall scale of the government sector (nationalized industry apart), there was little change to be observed.

However, none of these changes are clear and large enough to explain the increase in unemployment. The biggest changes, like privatization, are probably economically neutral (though convenient deficit-reducers). Increased unemployment rather than tax policy appears to explain the major coincident changes in income distribution. Fiscal and monetary policy do not generally show consistent party differences, though low interest rates, especially in 1977–78, and loose fiscal policy in 1972–75 probably had real stimulative effects. Otherwise, two decades of persistently tight fiscal policy eliminated any absorption of the unemployed into public sector employment. Even so, none of these changes explains the fall in investment, decline in manufacturing employment, and persistence and scale of British unemployment.

External Factors

The missing elements in all this discussion are external: the dramatic loss of trade competitiveness in Britain over the last decade (mostly before 1981) and the world recession. Two factors preeminently explain this loss of competitiveness and its effects on employment, particularly in manufacturing: a change in resources (the discovery and exploitation of North Sea oil and subsequent oil-based speculation in sterling) and a change in institutions (the growth of Eurocurrency markets and the switch to a system of floating exchange rates). I will only sketch the argument here. It is developed fully in a separate study (Alt, 1987).

Oil was discovered in the British sector of the North Sea in the 1960s, and the first British North Sea oil came ashore in June 1975. Competitiveness was lost through the impact of oil on currency valuations in international exchange markets. The petro-pound has been more of a journalistic preoccupation, but a recent study (Alt, 1987) shows that at least half the massive surge in the real exchange value of the pound is due to oil-based speculation. From its low point in 1976 to its peak in early 1981, the increase in the real exchange rate is 63 percent. Contrary to those who believed that a $1.50 pound meant that the competitiveness problem was solved and overvaluation a thing of the past, restoration of the early 1950s position would require a $1 pound. A further fall to 70–75 cents would be required to provide a competitive advantage equal to the disadvantage under which Britain has labored for the last eight years.

This competitive decline reduces manufacturing employment as the change in relative prices shifts spending away from British goods and encourages British manufacturers to economize on labor. Alternately, it makes imports into Britain cheaper and drives workers in import-competing industries out of jobs. Indeed, import-competing industries are where most of the jobs in recent years appear to have been lost. In either case the fall in British manufacturing employment increases unemployment.[20] Model simulations based on estimates in Alt (1987) attribute an increase of 3.6 percentage points in British unemployment to declining world demand (recession) and 2.1 percent to declining competitiveness. The total is 5.7 percentage points out of an increase of 7.8, over two-thirds of the total.

New Wine, Old Bottles

Should all this be seen as inevitable rather than the result of political choice? What is the role of Thatcherism in all this? Alternately, if Labour had won the 1979 election, what would now be different? My answer is, probably not too much. Oil presented novel problems of structural adjustment as well as exchange rate speculation. These adjustment problems can be understood in the context of models of what economists call the "Dutch disease," a description of the way in which an injection of wealth creates strains between sectors exposed to world trade and those sheltered from it.[21] The British failure to adjust or indeed to find a credible opposition policy reflects a mix of structural, institutional, and intellectual constraints far older than Thatcherism, whose ideological inclinations made only a modest difference.

Economic theory and policy analysis show that the way to combat the effects of speculation and Dutch disease is through some mix of exchange rate pegging and employment subsidy aimed at redistributing employment from uncompetitive, exposed industries to sheltered industries. Neither was done in Britain. While more was spent on employment subsidy, it was done on a piecemeal basis unrelated to promoting opportunity in the context of competitive advantage (see Hall, 1986). The reason for this is found in several familiar old bottles or constraints of British policy: the power and independence of international finance, inappropriately "large country" assumptions about exchange rate policy, lack of sectoral disaggregation in economic models, and decentralized political organization.

First, a financial sector heavily involved in international bank transactions, with a balance sheet unaffected by the fate of exporting industries, would strongly prefer floating, since price uncertainty maximizes arbitrage profit possibilities. Britain's financial system is far and away the most international in Europe: the share of bank liabilities with some international character is higher in Britain by at least a factor of three than in any other major European banking system. The separation of British industry and finance is well-known, and those attributes that normally militate against financial power over industry are all largely absent. Indeed, the Bank of England has a long-standing preference for floating. Thatcher did not invent any of this, though Dutch disease strains enormously reduced the power of manufacturing interests vis-à-vis finance within the CBI, and thus more generally the representation of those interests in Conservative circles.

Second, the environment of the international financial sector is now largely an offshore interbank market transferring Eurocurrencies. These markets are very fast-growing, averaging 30 percent per annum from 1964 to 1981, meaning they multiplied eighty-fold in the period. Eurocurrency deposits in London exceeded the British money supply as early as 1969. Now two days' turnover on the international wholesale currency market equals the British money supply. In such circumstances it is foolish to design policy around the assumption that Britain can affect its own exchange rate in any significant way. But Thatcher was certainly not the first to make this mistake, and in fact she probably made it less than most.

Third, major British economic models are aggregate in orientation. They are designed to explain and forecast quantities measured over the whole economy. The model used by the Treasury is typical. Central relationships relate to consumption and investment. Much attention has been paid to modeling the financial sector to incorporate monetary effects on prices. Following the consumption orientation, imports are heavily disaggregated by product (to pick up relative price effects), but there is only one equation for exported manufactures, even though (before oil) they composed over three-fourths of visible exports (Holden, Peel, and Thompson, 1982). There is no basis here for modeling or planning the intersectoral supply-side effects of differential employment subsidies to industries. Although Treasury spokesmen in 1977 mentioned manufacturing jobs that would be lost if the pound appreciated (Hall, 1982:579), sectoral analysis has never been central in the British policy debate.

It is hard to say what would be different if Labour had won in 1979. In its first public document (*The Challenge of North Sea Oil*, HMSO, 1977), the Callaghan government gave priority to industrial investment and restoring industrial competitiveness, while warning against using oil revenues to raise living standards and expand public services. The Thatcher government used oil revenues instead to finance general tax cuts, hoping to stimulate spending, investment, and economic growth outside the oil sector. The oil has produced a £10 billion gain in revenues in the period from 1979 to 1983, though about 80 percent has been offset by the costs of extra unemployment.

There is no reason to think that Labour would have been less ready to spend the oil revenues on unemployment compensation, and inclined instead to subsidize selectively. This is because neither the modeling apparatus for planning nor the centralized union-management structures for bargaining and enforcement are available in Britain, as they are in Norway. Union cooperation is essential in order to attack the unemployment consequent on lost competitiveness in Britain. Union real wage maintenance is not irrational or the cause of unemployment (as the chancellor argued in his 1985 budget speech). Those in manufacturing would have to take a 30–40 percent cut in compensation to equalize the effect of international market-induced changes in competitiveness, with no guarantees about the conduct of other unions or any basis on which to rely on future parties being restored. Whether there really was a basis for reciprocity between those in the tradable goods and nontradables sector anyway is doubtful. In that sense the Dutch disease came at the worst time possible, for any probability of government-union cooperation was disappearing with the collapse of the Social Contract.

In the absence of such "corporatist" remedies, however, those blaming the unemployment on Thatcherism recommend alternative policies involving fiscal stimulation and exchange rate intervention. For instance, the 1982 TUC economic review suggested reflation. Two other noteworthy alternatives are based on simulations in economic models. Desai's (1983) review of policy alternatives suggests that even a very large positive fiscal shock has relatively small positive employment effects, unless it is accompanied by some international measures like a deliberate depreciation of the pound or import controls. Hall and Atkinson (1983:188–92) suggest a sustained six-year strategy that triples real public investment relative to 1980 levels. This, coupled with an 8 percent devaluation in 1981, gets unemployment down to 2.3 million (the world level) by 1986. Very large fiscal shocks have little effect on unemployment that results from market-induced lack of competitiveness and the Dutch disease. Moreover, the fiscal shocks have no impact unless accompanied by devaluation. However, when a country is too small to influence its exchange rate, stimulating a model at a lower exchange rate is more like wishing away the competitiveness problem than saying how it can be made to go away.

Thus, the Dutch disease also presents some short-term policy conflicts for left-wing parties. There appears to be no obvious way for conventional demand management-type policies to square with party incentives in dealing with the Dutch disease. For example, the alternative strategies of devaluation and import controls simulated by Desai (1983), while they offer something over a 10 percent reduction in the present level of unemployment, do so largely by expanding profits to stimulate investment and growth, and for a given level of output will actually reduce the real wage rate. The Dutch disease squeezes profitability, which fiscal remedies reverse. The best that Labour's Alternative Economic Strategy planners could offer was that the cure for the recession required "sacrifices by workers" to ensure profitability for investment in future growth. In such circumstances it was easy for the Thatcher government to dismiss stimulation as inflationary, deflect much of the blame for unemployment from itself, and continue to split the left-wing vote. While many may originally have thought the problem of oil-induced competitiveness transitory, it appears that the Conservative party will get a decade, or more, of competitive advantage out of it.

NOTES

1   In many countries the conservative party is a coalition of separate organizations representing agrarian, clerical, and petit bourgeois interests, so that conservative party politics is a matter of finding appropriate compromises among those groups' conflicting interests.

2   Two other monetary measures were the abolition of foreign exchange controls in late 1979 and the abolition of the "corset," or Supplementary Deposits Scheme, in June 1980. The corset, in effect since 1973, was a quantitative ceiling on lending and competition for deposits. It enabled the Bank of England to call for excess non-interest-bearing deposits from commercial banks if interest-bearing deposits were too large. Some form of exchange controls had been continuously in effect since at least the 1960s. Their abolition opened up the Eurodollar market to domestic investors, resulting in inflows of funds previously directed away from London.

3   The dependence of M3 on the PSBR was achieved by manipulation of two banking system identities (Buiter and Miller, 1983):

$$= \Delta M3/\text{DCE} + \text{NEF} - \text{BNL} \quad (1)$$
$$= \text{DCE}/\text{PSBR} + \text{IBL} - \text{PNS} \quad (2)$$

where DCE is domestic credit expansion, NEF is net external flows, BNL is the change in banks nondeposit liabilities, IBL is the increase in bank lending, and PNS the public sector debit sold to the private nonbank sector. In (1), next external flows were to be taken care of by a floating exchange rate and nondeposit liabilities by bank equity financing, making DCE the real target. In (2), in which DCE is determined, an increase in interest rates should reduce IBL and increase PNS, but the signs of these terms in (2) make these effects complementary (i.e., both negative). Thus, at any given interest rate in this accounting, ΔM3 depends directly on the remaining term, PSBR. Hence, control of M3 required control of PSBR.

4   Cash limits squeeze public spending by having the budget guarantee a cash amount and not a real volume of services. With a cash limit, any increase in public sector pay must be set against a reduction in public sector employment; an increase in employment must be set against a reduction in pay. Making the trade-off explicit is expected to reduce expansionary pressures. There were other policy changes. Dividend controls and exchange controls were abolished during the early months of the Thatcher administration. While the 1980 and 1981 budgets increased excise duties and petroleum revenues, the 1982 budget provided extra income tax relief. Indeed, the further tax cuts in the spring of 1983 were subsequently retracted in July and November through spending cuts and tax adjustments, with accelerated sales of assets (notably BP). Nevertheless, even then the estimate of PSBR for 1984 had to be revised upward by 25 percent, from £8 billion to £10 billion.

5   Public asset sales reduce PSBR as a matter of accounting, while as a matter of economics they have no negative short-term effects on aggregate demand.

6   The inflation rate Thatcher inherited had itself been reduced from that which the Heath administration had left behind in 1974. The Thatcher reduction would have come more quickly if early changes in tax policy that increased retail prices had

been avoided. Honoring of pay comparability awards from a commission established by the previous government passed these price increases through to wage increases, and inflation in 1980 stood at 20 percent before the general reduction began to work through.

7 Since 1980 the British economy appears to have slid down and to the right along a short-term Phillips curve, as it did in 1971–72 and 1975–78. This implies that unemployment was above the "natural" rate in these periods, and thus that the natural rate must have risen in 1973–74 and 1979, now standing above 6 percent. The timing of increases in the natural rate suggests that crisis increases in oil prices were an input shock causing a structural change leading to a rise in the underlying equilibrium level of employment.

8 There is a close relationship between British unemployment and the "world rate," with transitory deviations near the formation of governments. These transitory deviations reflect new administrations' promise-keeping. World demand expands and contracts demand for countries' traded goods, increasing and decreasing employment. Estimates from such a model hold up well for Britain 1947–83 and many other countries from 1960–83, at least provided that parties actually promised economic policies before the government formed and secured the parliamentary majorities with which to implement policies initially. Final estimates for Britain of normal political effects would have raised unemployment by 1.5 percentage points after 1979. Full adjustment to the world recession of 1979–81 would independently add at least a further percentage point. Given the extent of openness of the British economy, this degree of response to world trends would not be unusual (Alt, 1985a). So stable political-economic models of British postwar unemployment would explain at least half its increase after 1979. Even so, this leaves a further 2–4 percentage points of unemployment (.5–1 million unemployed) unexplained, as well as the failure of British unemployment to respond when the world rate begins to drop after 1982.

In a country with an open economy, domestic inflation is also likely to be heavily influenced by the American inflation rate. As Alt and Chrystal (1983, figure 3.1) show, the connection between countries' inflation rates under fixed currency exchange rates is very close. Under floating exchange rates there is more scope for variations in inflation rates from country to country. If right-wing governments stabilize prices, that is, are more likely to promise to reduce inflation, periods of right government in two-party systems should show lower inflation rates relative to recent American inflation. Empirically, this is probably true, at least in the few countries that have had at least three years under each of the major partisan blocs since the first OPEC shock of 1973. Partisan differences in broad coalition countries (Belgium, Denmark, Italy) are either absent or of unexpected direction, with inflation lower under left-wing governments. However, in the countries with two-party majoritarian systems, differences in inflation rates appear relative to imported American inflation. For instance, in Australia inflation is on average about 1.5 percentage points higher (for any level of recent American inflation) under Labor governments, a magnitude of difference echoed in several other countries (France,

Ireland, Sweden). In Britain the difference is at least five times as large. So if the reduction in inflation (like the increase in unemployment) is due to Thatcher's policies, it is unprecedentedly large, at least by international standards.

9   The biggest question of performance is whether the changes in the labor market brought about by the Thatcher government have contributed to greater efficiency. Much was made in 1980–81 of the rapid increase in labor productivity, as output per man-hour increased, sometimes at annual rates over 10 percent. Corrected for utilization of capacity, productivity appears to have increased by 3 percent in 1980, 8 percent in 1981, but only by 1.5 percent in 1982. Thus it appears that the "productivity boom" was a transitory phenomenon stemming from labor-shedding during the rapid rise in unemployment in 1980–81 and not a longer-term structural change in British industry. The biggest change in the labor market has been the increase in unemployment, and once again most other changes are reflections of this.

10   This growth was caused by massive capital inflows following the Labour government's fruitless attempt to stop the sterling exchange rate rise in late 1977. See Hall, 1982: chap. 7.

11   Since current PSBR contains a great deal of interest charges, an increase in nominal rates could have had PSBR effects offsetting those expected on interbank lending and debt sales to the nonbank sector. Moreover, it is not clear that the exchange rate was sufficiently flexible in this regard to "clear" net external flows in any meaningful way.

12   This allowed 1982–83 to be only the third year since the Barber boom in which adjusted fiscal policy was expansionary. These all contained general elections 1974–75, 1978–79, and 1982–83, testifying to the importance of the convention that allows prime ministers to call general elections in good times. A number of sources show further fiscal tightness under Thatcher. Extra tightness will appear in any "high employment" concept that (1) treats government debt as being serviced at real rather than nominal rates or (2) adjusts for unemployment rather than output or (3) ignores the low impact of oil revenues and privatization on aggregate demand.

13   The forecasts are generated by feeding in observed values of national income and the other independent variables at each quarter, adding the lagged forecast value rather than the observed lagged dependent variable.

14   This is a complex issue and is examined in a separate study (Freeman and Alt, 1986).

15   In a sense all taxes are borne ultimately by individuals. It is just a convenience to think of households and corporations, but it captures two scenarios of political conflict.

16   The other problem is adjustment. Put a tax on some activity and you raise its price. Raise its price and, at the margin, you deter someone from undertaking that activity. Deter someone and, at the margin, the revenue yield of that tax is reduced, or at least not increased in proportion to the increase in the tax rate. The uncertain relationship between the incentive effects of changes in rates and the ultimate revenue changes makes analysis difficult, but still worth attempting.

17   Of course, the increase in VAT puts up the real burden of indirect taxes on persons, which is why the direct/indirect ratio appears to fall initially. There is a suggestion of a relationship between party changes and the ratio of direct to indirect taxes if one looks closely at the first years of each incumbency. In these years direct taxes are up twice (1965, 1974) under Labour, and down twice (1970–71, 1979–80) under the Conservatives. These effects are very short-lived and are dwarfed by subsequent adjustments.

18   Rose (1980: figure 7.6) shows that parties have marginal effects on distribution of income, as one would expect. Income distribution heads off in a more egalitarian direction under Labour, a more inegalitarian direction under Conservatives. Morrissey and Sandmo (1986) confirm this by examining effects of the tax code on different income groups, showing that the best-off have traditionally become less well-off in disposable income under Labour. Their series ends in the mid-1970s, as does Rose's. Recent changes in data-keeping bedevil extension of some earlier series.

19   The question of a distinctive conservative attitude to the future (in the public sector) is complex, and developed in a separate study. The complexity arises because the stance to the future is a function simultaneously of both preference for investment (deferred satisfaction) over consumption and of taxing over borrowing.

20   The magnitude of changes (upward for number of unemployed, to downward for those employed in manufacturing) was about equal from 1979 to 1983, about 1.5 million in each case. Of course, this does not prove that there were no second-order effects of transfers of employment between manufacturing and other sectors.

21   Dutch disease effects arise in any two-sector model with an exposed and sheltered sector, excepting those with a full set of new classical assumptions (Eastwood and Venables, 1982). However, the scale of effects depends on a variety of assumptions about full employment, labor elasticities, indexation or other rigidities, and so on.

REFERENCES

Alt, J. 1979. *The Politics of Economic Decline.* Cambridge: Cambridge University Press.
———. 1985a. "Political Parties, World Demand, and Unemployment: Domestic and International Sources of Economic Activity." *American Political Science Review* 79: 1016–40.
———. 1985b. "Party Strategies, World Demand, and Unemployment in Britain and the United States, 1947–83." *Political Behavior* 7: 7–33.
———. 1987. "Crude Politics: Oil and the Political Economy of Unemployment in Britain and Norway, 1970–85." *British Journal of Political Science.* Forthcoming.
———, and Chrystal, K. A. 1983. *Political Economics.* Berkeley: University of California Press.
Atkinson, F, S. Brooks, and S. Hall. 1983. *Oil and the British Economy.* London: Croom Helm.
Blackaby, F, ed. 1978. *British Economic Policy 1960–74.* Cambridge: Cambridge University Press.

Brittan, S. 1984. "The Politics and Economics of Privatisation." *Political Quarterly* 55: 109–28.

Buiter, W., and M. Miller. 1981. "The Thatcher Experiment: The First Two Years." *Brookings Papers on Economic Activity* 2: 315–79.

———. 1983. "Changing the Rules: Economic Consequences of the Thatcher Regime." *Brookings Papers on Economic Activity* 2: 305–79.

Chrystal, K. A. 1984. "Dutch Disease or Monetarist Medicine?: The British Economy under Mrs. Thatcher." *Federal Reserve Bank of St. Louis Review* 66, no. 5: 27–37.

Crouch, C. 1983. "The Peculiar Relationship: The Party and the Unions." In D. Kavanagh, ed., *The Politics of the Labour Party*. London: Allen and Unwin.

Darby, M., and J. Lothian. 1983. "Measuring and Analyzing the Cyclically Adjusted Budget." In Federal Reserve Bank of Boston, *The Economics of Large Government Deficits*. Boston: Federal Reserve Bank.

Desai, M. 1983. "Economic Alternatives for Labour 1984–9." In J. Griffith, ed., *Socialism in a Cold Climate*. London: Unwin.

Eastwood, R., and A. Venables. 1982. "The Macroeconomic Implications of a Resource Discovery in an Open Economy." *Economic Journal* 92: 285–99.

The Economist. 1984. "When the Oil Runs Out." June 9: 67–70.

Fforde, John. 1983. "Setting Monetary Objectives." *Bank of England Quarterly Bulletin* 23, no. 2: 200–208.

Forsyth, P., and J. Kay. 1980. "The Economic Implications of North Sea Oil Revenues." *Fiscal Studies* 1, no. 3: 1–28.

Foster, N., S. Henry, and C. Trinder. 1984. "Public and Private Sector Pay: A Partly Disaggregated Study." *National Institute Economic Review* 107: 63–73.

Fuchs, B. 1986. "British and American Health Policy in a Period of Resource Limits." Mimeographed.

Glynn, S., and S. Shaw. 1981. "Wage Bargaining and Unemployment." *Political Quarterly* 52: 115–26.

Hall, P. 1982. "The Political Dimensions of Economic Management." Ph.D. dissertation, Harvard University.

———. 1986. *Governing the Economy*. Oxford: Oxford University Press.

Hamilton, A. 1978. *North Sea Impact*. London: IIER.

Holden, K., D. Peel, and J. Thompson. 1982. *Modelling the UK Economy*. Oxford: Martin Robertson.

Karran, T. 1984. "The Determinants of Taxation in Britain." Strathclyde Studies in Public Policy 141.

Klein, R. 1976. "The Politics of Public Expenditure: American Theory and British Practice." *British Journal of Political Science* 6: 401–32.

———. 1984. "The Politics of Ideology vs. the Reality of Politics." *Health and Society* 62: 82–109.

Leach, R. 1983. "Thatcherism, Liberalism, and Tory Collectivism." *Politics* 3: 9–14.

McKinnon, R. 1979. *Money in International Exchange*. New York: Oxford University Press.

Morrissey, O., and S. Sandmo. 1986. "Tax Policy by Party." Paper presented to the Western Political Science Association.

National Institute Economic Review. 1984. "The Home Economy." February: 5–27.

OECD. 1984. *Revenue Statistics 1965–83*. Paris: OECD.

Riddell, P. 1983. *The Thatcher Government*. London: Martin Robertson.

Rose, R. 1980. *Do Parties Make a Difference?* Chatham, N.J.: Chatham House.

Savage, D. 1982. "Fiscal Policy, 1974/5–1980/1: Description and Measurement." *National Institute Economic Review* 99: 85–95.

Schier, S., and N. Vig. 1984. "Economic Performance and Mass Support: The Thatcher and Reagan Regimes." Mimeographed.

Whiteley, P. 1985. "Evaluating Thatcher's Monetarist Experiment." Paper presented to the American Political Science Association.

9. Mrs. Thatcher's Crusade: Conservatism in Britain, 1972–1986

IVOR CREWE AND DONALD D. SEARING

To most observers of contemporary British politics Thatcherism is a radical departure from the Keynesian postwar consensus and, at the same time, from the mainstream of British Conservatism (Bulpitt, 1986:19). Moreover, Thatcherites have been remarkably successful in implementing dramatic changes in Britain's economic and social policies. Yet, contrary to popular impressions, there has been no renaissance of the Right, no resurgence of conservatism in Britain. As we shall show, there has been no increase in the Conservative vote, nor in Conservative partisanship, nor in Conservative party membership. Nevertheless, something peculiar has happened that needs to be explained. Between 1974 and 1983 the Conservative party moved sharply to the right without any apparent electoral incentive to do so; and, more peculiar still, it did not lose support among the electorate for having made this move. We propose to argue that the party was pushed to the right by the ideological convictions and determination of a surprisingly small number of Conservative leaders. And we shall speculate that the party did not lose support in the electorate because British voters placed value on the quality of leadership as well as (perhaps more than) on most particular policy initiatives. Four interrelated questions structure our study: (1) What are the organizational origins and ideological principles of Thatcherism? (2) How Thatcherite were Conservative politicians on the eve of her election to the leadership of the party in February 1975? (3) How Thatcherite was the public at the general elections of 1979 and 1983? and, (4) Under Thatcher, how Thatcherite has the British public become?

THATCHERISM IN THE CONSERVATIVE PARTY:
DATA AND MEASUREMENT

A great deal of data are required to examine these questions. For this section the primary data set consists of survey responses collected during 1972 and 1973, two years before the leadership election, from British Members of Parliament, candidates, and electorate. Members of Parliament ($N = 521$) were interviewed by means of tape-recorded discussions. They also filled in printed forms and returned a mail-back questionnaire. A response rate of 83 percent applies to backbenchers, members of the government and opposition spokesmen alike. At the same time a sample of candidates was constructed of 107 individuals (response rate 90 percent) who stood and came closest to winning in the 1970 general election but who had never themselves been MPs.

Two distinct types of attitude measures are involved. Specific views about institutions and about economic and social policies are assessed by Likert-type scales offering four responses. Political ideals such as "community" or "free enterprise" are measured by a technique derived from the work of Milton Rokeach, which requests respondents to rank-order items from an inventory of political values (Searing, 1978; Rokeach, 1968, 1973, 1979). In the first part of this chapter we shall treat political values as the core of ideology and define Thatcherism and other varieties of British Conservatism in these terms. Then, Thatcherite values will be linked with Thatcherite policy beliefs, with the operant ideological dimensions that will provide the focus for examining the views of the electorate.

The rank-order instrument we employed is based on the assumption that individuals generally give certain values precedence over others, and that these hierarchies can be roughly reconstructed on a values form. The instrument asks respondents to examine four lists of values separately and to write the number one alongside the ideal that is personally most important to them, two alongside the next most important value, and so on. The items were familiar to the respondents because they were drawn from an inventory of political ideals assembled from parliamentary debates, political memoirs, journalistic commentaries, and academic attempts at synthesis and had been reviewed through pretests with former members of Parliament. Nonetheless, it should be emphasized that value hierarchies, particularly those of many Conservatives, are certainly not inflexible and may not be well-crystallized. In fact, the exercise compels respondents to represent their political values with more structure than usually characterizes their thinking about such matters.

THE ORIGINS OF THATCHERISM

Mrs. Thatcher drew a preliminary sketch of Thatcherism in a speech to her party's annual conference at Blackpool in 1968, two years before she was appointed a minister in the Heath government, and seven years before the election that made her party leader. This talk expressed skepticism about the welfare state and its tendency to undermine middle-class values such as hard work, self-discipline, and personal responsibility (reprinted in Wapshott and Brock, 1983:276–87). People should not, she argued, expect the government to solve their problems. She also expressed skepticism about a system of higher education whose main achievement seemed to be to teach people to criticize and question everything. And she spoke particularly strongly against the idea of a government running a prices-and-incomes policy. The way to control prices, she said, was through competition, not governmental action. The element most obviously missing from this Blackpool lecture is what will be discussed below as "statecraft." In fact, it sounded so much like old-fashioned laissez faire that she felt obliged to claim apologetically that it was not.

After the Conservative party was defeated in October 1974, the second time that year, Thatcher and Keith Joseph, who had been loyal members of the Heath government, began to publicly criticize the directions it had taken (Wapshott and Brock, 1983:108ff). Joseph developed and delivered a series of public lectures to critically examine the postwar consensus on the mixed economy and welfare state. His major conclusion was that since the war the Conservative party had steadily moved toward the center, but the center had constantly been pulled toward the left.

The party was at this time preparing to ditch its leader, Edward Heath. Backbenchers approved the overall direction in which the party was being led but were deeply worried that it had now lost four of the last five general elections and that in canvassing for the last two they found Heath's public image to be an electoral liability (Wapshott and

Brock, 1983:108–14). They didn't much like the private reality either. Many Conservative MPs who voted for Mrs. Thatcher as leader in February 1975 did so to get rid of Mr. Heath and had no idea that she was about to hatch a new ideology and behind it march the party off to the right (Wapshott and Brock, 1983:106–41). Thus, it was not for Thatcherism that she was elected Leader of the Conservative party. In fact, it is widely accepted that she became leader more by a "succession of accidents"—the withdrawal of Sir Keith Joseph from the race and the bungled campaign by William Whitelaw—than by design. Thatcherism emerged as an ideological force only after the leadership election in 1975. We shall compare Thatcherite policy positions with those favored by the electorate between 1974 and 1983. But first it is necessary to clarify exactly what Thatcherism is.

THATCHERISM DEFINED

Mrs. Thatcher does not stand for ambiguity either in her own arguments or in those of her opponents. She despises waffling and spends a great deal of energy making her extreme positions perfectly clear. These positions revolve around three principal ideals: discipline, free enterprise, and statecraft.

Discipline, obedience to the rules, is probably the value that Mrs. Thatcher has held the longest. It is associated with self-discipline and the Victorian virtues of hard work, thrift, and deferred gratification. The Thatcherite interpretation of discipline places strong emphasis on law and order. This is reflected by support for bringing back capital punishment and by proposals to increase the severity of sentences handed down in the court system. Discipline also embraces the notion of self-reliance, of a respect for self-help and individual enterprise that disdains the creation of social service benefits for anyone except the really poor. Mrs. Thatcher talks about these middle-class values without apologizing for them and complains that they are not more generally implanted in all social classes, in British society as a whole (Norton and Aughey, 1981:79–89).

Discipline is the handmaiden of free enterprise, which has been described as Mrs. Thatcher's central aim (Utley, 1978). Thatcherites believe that by giving a new prominence to free enterprise, by rolling back the state from involvement in the economy, they can reverse

Britain's economic decline. This is the doctrine to which they have worked to convert first the Conservative party and then the electorate. Along with Sir Keith Joseph, Mrs. Thatcher has tried hard to state the case for capitalism in a way that might appeal to English tastes for freedom and tradition. Wealth, she argues, is created by competition, risk-taking, and efficient marketing. The perspective of the small capitalist is, in reality, a perspective suitable for the entire economy (Norton and Aughey, 1981:79–89).

Thatcherite free enterprise attempts to create financial stability and reduce inflation by curbing the growth of the money supply and by reducing government borrowing and public expenditure. In addition, attempts are made to expand the economy by using tax cuts and trade union reform to remove barriers to profitability. Monetarism has played a major part in the package because it reduces the role of the government in the economy and at the same time promises to control inflation and to unshackle capitalism (Norton and Aughey, 1981:79–89). During the first Thatcher government, 1979–1983, some changes were introduced in targets and techniques, but the continuity in the central free-enterprise strategy was plain (Burch, 1983).

Statecraft is the ideal of strong central government. It was the last of the three major principles to be put in place. Authoritative leadership is an essential Tory doctrine that demands that leaders be given wide discretion and is based on the conviction that some people are best suited to lead and others to follow (Beer, 1965:92–94). This doctrine is what Thatcherism offered other Conservatives. The government would pursue free enterprise, but not laissez faire. It would pull out of the economy but strengthen its control in other areas (Beattie, 1979:283–85; Bulpitt, 1986:21–26). Statecraft is about strong government led by strong leaders who have the ability and judgment to choose policies that inspire followers and produce results.

According to Bulpitt's (1986:34–39) reading of the first Thatcher government, statecraft was its dominant concern, dominant even over free enterprise and certainly over discipline. This was because by 1979 the Thatcherites saw as their chief problem the restoration of the autonomy of the center, the restoration after the "winter of discontent" of a strong central government that would be capable of governing. And by 1983 when privatization became the chief and most publicized government policy, it is noteworthy that the practice of selling off state-owned industries was justified as much in terms of statecraft (strengthening the government by getting it out of areas it couldn't control satisfactorily and by weakening the grip of the unions on the Treasury) as in terms of free enterprise.

Discipline, free enterprise, and statecraft. This is the tripod of Thatcherism. Where does it fit in the pantheon of Conservative values? Where did it fit in the ideologies of the sorts of Conservative politicians who chose Mrs. Thatcher as their leader in February 1975?

Areas of Consensus

Although it is widely acknowledged that the Conservative party has been a "broad church," it is equally widely believed that "divisions have generally been of less significance than views held in common" (Norton and Aughey, 1981:56). Conservatives like to claim that the party has long been highly consensual, that there are few rigid factions, few sharply crystallized differences in outlook, and much agreement about bedrock Conservative beliefs.

However, table 9.1 suggests that much less consensus exists among Conservative politicians than might be anticipated on the basis of the party's image and political propaganda. Table 9.1 reports on the percentage of Conservative politicians who ranked the named values either at the top (1, 2, or 3) or at the bottom (7, 8, 9) of their lists, in other words the proportion of Conservative politicians who are in broad agreement that a given political ideal is either very important or very unimportant. The crucial point about this table is that it includes every value that attracted such agreement at the level of 60 percent or higher.

It is striking that there are only three values (freedom, economic equality, and socialism) out of a total of thirty-six where eight out of ten Conservative politicians agreed in ranking them as either very important or very unimportant. If elite consensus defines what the party stands for and what it opposes, the party's stand in table 9.1 includes items we would expect to see, but it does not include very much. It does not have much to do with Thatcherism, but then it does not have much to do with any other particular variety of Conservatism either. Conservative politicians are most certain about what they oppose—100 percent place socialism at the bottom of their lists.

To add to the picture of what the party stands for beyond the

Table 9.1.   The Scope of the Party's Consensus: Values Supported
or Rejected by Most Conservative Politicians.

Political value	Percentage ranking 1, 2, or 3	Percentage ranking 7, 8, or 9
Freedom	87	01
Public order	60	10
Compassion	61	12
Duty	63	06
Caution	07	78
Economic equality	02	88
Socialism	00	100

N = 319.

vague ideal of freedom, it is necessary to drop down to a consensus
criterion of 60 percent. Here three more values enter table 9.1 on the
positive side (including public order, which is associated with the
Thatcherite package) and one on the negative side. In fact, dropping
the criterion further to 50 percent would add only another five values,
all positive. That would make a grand total of only twelve out of the
thirty-six political ideals where even half the Conservative politicians
agreed in placing them near the top or the bottom of the party's tree.
This may be enough to permit joint collective action in a "broad-
church" or "catch-all" party, but it doesn't constitute an impressive
degree of consensus behind Thatcherism or any other variety of
Conservatism.

    These first few steps in the investigation indicate that there may
be many different ways of thinking Conservatively. But are there so
many different ways of thinking Conservatively that the party's ideological blanket turns out to be a patchwork quilt of idiosyncratic views,
or, are there some general patterns, characteristic varieties of Conservatism among the party's higher circles?

An Exploratory Investigation

We turn now to search for the components of a mosaic that may recover
for us the patterns of conservatism before Thatcher. For this purpose
an exploratory factor analysis was applied to all thirty-six values. If
there are distinct ideological communities dotting the landscape, the

factor analysis should give us at least a rough indication of their presence and a rough impression of their character. The results of several such factor analyses indicate very little consensus about the political ideals of Conservatism across the party as a whole. Nor is there much sign of a party composed of a multiplicity of sharply defined ideological subcommunities. However, the analysis of all Conservative politicians did generate a first factor that placed concern with economic interests in opposition to community. Moreover, an inspection of the correlation matrix for this first factor showed even more clearly that the strongest correlations by far in the data (aside from items measuring much the same thing) were negative relationships between the values of community on the one side and the values of economy on the other. Community and economy have long been the respective concerns of Toryism and Whiggery, the two outlooks that Norton and Aughey (1981: chap. 2) have suggested (correctly, we believe) are the touchstones of ideological thought in the twentieth-century Conservative party.

By drawing our attention to the differences between Toryism and Whiggery, the exploratory factor analysis has begun our reconstruction of the Conservative ideological landscape. This picture needs to be developed by dividing each side, Tories and Whigs, into their principal subtypes. Rather than using the value-ranking data to generate the types, we shall use them to check on the verisimilitude of the types we have generated. We believe there are two types of Tories, "Progressive" and "Traditional," and two types of Whigs, "Liberal" and "Corporate." These, it should be noted, represent heuristic constructions of ways of thinking conservatively rather than actual reconstructions of the views of four self-contained groups of Conservative politicians. In the empirical world we would expect to see considerable overlap among the subtypes, for, as Norton and Aughey (1981:63) put it, "Every good Conservative . . . is a little bit of a Tory and a little bit of a Whig."

Progressive Tory thought seeks to promote a sense of community by having the state serve as a balancing force in society, a balancing force that seeks to maintain social harmony and to see that the people are protected and comfortable (Behrens, 1980:13). These paternalistic roots of Progressive Toryism help explain why its support for the welfare state is so closely connected with its conception of community

and why its strong emphasis on compassion complements disposi-
tions associated with social hierarchy. The natural acceptance of hierarchical distinctions in a system of integrated social strata is what
best distinguishes many Progressive Tories from the Social Democrats
whose new party they never crossed over to join (Norton and Aughey,
1981:66–79).

Progressive Tories also value the idea of social progress, effective
social reform. They do not see themselves simply as defenders of
bourgeois interests and prefer "the middle way" as a desirable compromise between reactionary revolutionary prescriptions (Behrens,
1980:14). Social progress, rationalism, and social planning appeal to
Progressive Tories because such Tories are determined that their party
should be literate, up-to-date, well-informed, and facing forward rather
than backward. They propose to adapt Conservative principles to the
modern world (Norton and Aughey, 1981:75–79). To prosper in this
modern world, Progressive Tories argue, the Conservative party must
pursue a pragmatic, empirical approach. They avoid chaining themselves to particular policy stands—if it works, they keep it; if it doesn't,
they are prepared to try something else, including attractive ideas
being pursued by other parties (Norton and Aughey, 1981:75–79).

Traditional Toryism, by contrast, tends to be more patriotic, devoted
to Old England and to think of the Conservatives as the "national
party." At times such Tories feel they live in an alien world and are
pessimistic about modernity (Norton and Aughey, 1981:66–75). They
realize that change is inevitable, but they do not expect to like it very
much. And they look suspiciously at Progressive Tories who wax
so enthusiastic about continuous social improvement. In the same
vein Traditional Tories are cynical about the social planning to which
they feel the Progressive Tories have become addicted. It comes as no
surprise that Traditional Tories have been very ambivalent about capitalism. Capitalism has made important contributions to material well-
being, but it has also shredded the fabric of traditional British society
and contributed to the deterioration of the quality of life (Norton and
Aughey, 1981:66–75). If Traditional Tories must have an economic
policy, then they would prefer less of it to more of it and lean toward
free enterprise over state capitalism.

There is much that Traditional Tories dislike, but there is much
that they like too. Their rock-bottom political values are strong govern-

ment, strong leadership, and an authority that inspires confidence and trust in people and strength at the center of the political system and the party (Gilmour, 1971:88).

Liberal and Corporate Whiggery share a dominant interest in preserving the system of private property. They differ over the most effective means for doing so (Norton and Aughey, 1981:68). Liberal Whigs prefer the free-enterprise approach of small business. Corporate Whigs prefer, by contrast, the managerial roles for government that are associated with large-scale capitalism.

Although free enterprise was connected with the poverty of the interwar period and looked electorally dangerous, *Liberal Whigs* refused to give up on it. According to Liberal Whiggery, it is competition, not governmental planning, that creates real wealth. This taste for crisp efficiency is often accompanied by a Victorian morality, the complement to Liberal Whiggery's Victorian political economy. Thus, Liberal Whigs wish to reestablish the predominance of middle-class values such as thrift, hard work, and discipline in society, and self-discipline and self-reliance in society's members. Self-reliance is a virtue because it encourages people to take risks, like the small entrepreneur, and to accept the consequences (Norton and Aughey, 1981:81–84).

Liberal Whigs also believe that there has been a decline of morality in contemporary society, a decline that they attribute to the meddling of a wet collectivism both in the socialist party and in the progressive wing of their own tribe. They don't have much use for caution, gradualism, or an empirical approach (Norton and Aughey, 1981:80–89). They don't have much use for compromise either because they believe that compromise nearly always ends by giving away the shop. Liberal Whigs tend to be politicians of principle who only very reluctantly make concessions to their political enemies.

Corporate Whigs, by contrast, are collectivists who believe that government should work with industry to promote large-scale capitalism. This should be done through indirect fiscal intervention to stimulate demand, reflating the economy as necessary and adjusting public expenditure. Government should be prepared to act to reduce unemployment, guide the location of new industries, and even experiment with nationalization and public works. Corporate Whigs, unlike their Liberal relatives, are quite sympathetic to many of the values of Progressive Tories. They appreciate, for instance, the ideals of community and compassion. But Corporate Whigs are not just compassionate politicians; they are compassionate capitalists. It was a Corporate Whig, Edward Heath, who as Conservative prime minister denounced a spectacularly successful property developer who was neglecting his obligations to the community as "the unacceptable face of capitalism." The acceptable face of capitalism is the essence of Corporate Whiggery (Norton and Aughey, 1981:83).

Rationalism, a rigorously reasoned approach to planning, is also highly regarded by these technocratically oriented Conservatives. Corporate Whigs hope to create a stable economic environment, a dependable world of the sort conducive to large capital's long-range planning. Corporate Whigs are prepared to get involved not only in industrial planning, but in industrial relations as well. Both sides of industry must join the team in order to achieve a satisfactory economic performance.

The description of these four types covers the Conservative spectrum. But we still have not yet located Thatcherism with satisfactory precision. The Thatcherite combination of free enterprise and discipline is squarely in the Liberal Whig tradition. What is missing is the third pillar, statecraft; and perhaps it is missing because we are dealing with Weberian "ideal types" that were foreshadowed long before Thatcherism arose. We now turn to a confirmatory factor analysis that will help assess the verisimilitude of our four ideal types and that may, from its foundations in the empirical world of the early seventies, reveal clearer signs of Thatcherism.

A CONFIRMATORY FACTOR ANALYSIS

We have argued that the most convincing approach to understanding postwar Conservative thought is to follow up the distinction between Tories and Whigs by drawing a further division within each camp. Thus, Tory thinking has been partitioned into Progressive and Traditional outlooks, and Whig thinking into Liberal and Corporate perspectives. We now have a hypothesized structure that a confirmatory factor analysis can put to the test. Such an analysis can suggest the extent to which our four-cell typology corresponds to the realities of Conservative thinking on the eve of Thatcherism.

Four Types Recovered

Tories are said to value community more than the creation of wealth, and Whigs are said to value the creation of wealth more than community. The ranking instrument is ideally suited to model these comparative evaluations. Thus, for purposes of our analysis, we shall count as Tories all those who ranked community above property, and as Whigs all those who ranked property above community. This step produces 149 respondents classified as predominantly Tories and ninety-seven as predominantly Whigs, a proportion in line with general impressions of the rough distribution of such views in the party at the time.

Next, a confirmatory factor analysis was performed for each of the two groups separately to assess the verisimilitude of our classification schemes and, also, to attempt to recover a sharper picture than emerged for the party as a whole in the exploratory factor analysis. To reduce the large number of value items and to suppress "noise" in this procedure, several values were combined into additive indices and several others were removed altogether. Thus, on the basis of connotations and correlations, the following items were combined into additive indices: strong government + strong leadership = statecraft; self-discipline + self-reliance = autonomy; authority + discipline = authority; empirical approach + gradualism = empirical; and, property + capitalism = capitalism. The following values were dropped from the analysis because they were either too Labour, that is to say too focused on distinctions in the Labour party, or too skewed, or both: economic equality, freedom, socialism, privacy, unity, social equality, duty, fellowship, meritocracy, participatory democracy, loyalty, cooperation, and security. After these steps, eighteen vetted items remained with which to assess the argument that, beyond our basic division into Tories and Whigs, which has already been secured by some empirical support, the chief distinction among Tories is Progressive versus Traditional, and among Whigs, Liberal versus Corporate. At the same time we hope to spot Thatcherism within the landscape.

This confirmatory factor analysis is not seeking to uncover dimensions beneath a wide field of values, but rather (a) to assess our claims about the main factor that structures Tory thinking on the one side and Whig thinking on the other, and (b) to assess our interpretation of the values that are relatively most important within each of the four sub-

Table 9.2.   Types of Whigs. Factor Analysis of Conservative Values:
First Principal Component.*

Political values	Correlation with first principal component	
Authority	−0.72	Liberal
Statecraft	−0.53	Whiggery
Free enterprise	−0.45	
Deference	−0.32	
Patriotism	−0.31	
Efficiency	−0.19	
Autonomy	−0.17	
Public order	−0.16	
Social hierarchy	0.15	Corporate
Empirical	0.19	Whiggery
Social progress	0.25	
Intelligence	0.26	
Caution	0.37	
Rationalism	0.42	
Compassion	0.46	
Capitalism	0.46	
Community	0.51	
Social planning	0.55	

*Eigen value = 2.77.
$N = 97$.

types. The strategy concentrates attention on the first principal component, the component that best depicts linear relationships among the items.

Table 9.2 reports the first factor emerging from the analysis of the Whigs. This factor has an eigen value of 2.77 and explains 15.4 percent of the variance. It is substantially stronger than the second component, which tends to look a good deal like the third, and so on. In short, the eigen values and percentage of variance explained drop off more precipitously from the first to the second factor than they do thereafter. Hence, the first principal component can be interpreted as the best single summary of the linear relationships in the data. And this component clearly represents the division between Liberal and Corporate Whiggery.

Liberal positions cluster at the negative pole where free enterprise and authority (discipline + authority) are found alongside statecraft. The Corporate ideals at the positive pole are led by social planning and, as projected in the ideal type, mix together values such as capitalism and compassion, rationalism and community. Although there is certainly ambiguity about the interpretation of some of these values, and uncertainty about the proper relative locations of others, there are no values with respectable loadings in the Liberal list that were projected for the Corporate side, or vice versa. At the same time it must be emphasized that the structure even among these values is relatively weak.[1]

Table 9.3 summarizes the first principal component for the Tories. It has an eigen value of 3.05 and explains 17.3 percent of the variance.

Table 9.3.   Types of Tories. Factor Analysis of Conservative Values: First Principal Component.*

Political values	Correlation with first principal component	
Compassion	0.62	Progressive
Social hierarchy	0.48	Toryism
Empirical	0.46	
Social progress	0.46	
Caution	0.44	
Community	0.43	
Intelligence	0.31	
Rationalism	0.31	
Social planning	0.30	
Efficiency	0.04	Traditional
Capitalism	0.00	Toryism
Autonomy	−0.16	
Free enterprise	−0.25	
Deference	−0.26	
Public order	−0.44	
Patriotism	−0.50	
Statecraft	−0.53	
Authority	−0.69	

*Eigen value = 3.05.
N = 149.

Again, the component displays acceptable strength; and again it supports handsomely the theoretical expectations.[2] At the positive end are the key values that have been associated with Progressive Toryism: compassion, social hierarchy, empirical approach, and community. And at the negative end are clustered the values of Traditional Toryism, notably, patriotism, statecraft (strong government + strong leadership), and, as the anchor, the value of authority before which Lord Amery once said nearly anything else would, if necessary, be cast overboard. Again, none of the values with respectable loadings in the hands of Traditional Toryism obviously belongs to Progressive Toryism, or vice versa.

The present analysis was applied to Conservative Members of Parliament and candidates together. This has the advantage of producing a large N and of broadening the elite net to capture some opinion outside Westminster. Members of Parliament were also analyzed separately. The results were much the same: the eigen values and percentage of variance explained were slightly higher for the Whigs and slightly lower for the Tories. Moreover, the correlations between the value items and the first principal component were virtually identical. This reinforces results reported elsewhere that suggest Conservative MPs and candidates have quite similar value profiles (Searing, 1978).

Overlaps and Alliances

One of the most striking features of tables 9.2 and 9.3 is that authority (authority + discipline) anchors the perspectives of both Traditional Toryism and Liberal Whiggery. To some extent this is due to the choice of components from which the authority index has been constructed, albeit they are strongly intercorrelated (Gamma = .50). The position of statecraft (strong government + strong leadership) in second place in both is more intriguing still. In fact, its incorporation into Liberal Whiggery in this empirical type, in contrast to its absence from the ideal type, presents the third pillar of Thatcherism we have been seeking. Now we have together: discipline (authority) + free enterprise + statecraft. The obvious differences in the results for Traditional Toryism and Liberal Whiggery/Thatcherism is that the Liberals place, as would be expected, much greater weight on free enterprise, less emphasis on patriotism, and much less on public order.

In the same vein the Corporate Whigs share with the Progressive Tories an interest in community and compassion. The obvious, and predicted, difference here is that, as Whigs, they care much more about capitalism: and as Corporate Whigs they care even more about social planning, a value that expresses their determination to use government to guide the economy. Actually, the correlation between the Whig results in table 9.2 and the Tory results in table 9.3 is quite high $(V = .755)$, reflecting an overarching pattern that works across both major groups while accommodating ideologically important differences of emphasis within each.

It is not so surprising to see a melding of Corporate Whiggery with Progressive Toryism, for this is the direction in which the Heath government and the Heathmen drove the party: through careful social planning they would make a success of capitalism in Britain. This alliance had since the 1950s dominated the party's ruling circles. With Heath, the tilt moved further toward Whiggery than it had been under Macmillan, but definitely toward Corporate Whiggery, for Heath and his associates regarded the morality of Liberal Whigs as old-fashioned, mean-spirited, and likely to lose the party essential working-class votes (Wapshott and Brock, 1983:109).

Soil for Thatcherism

What is much more remarkable is the Thatcherite association in table 9.2 between the authority (discipline) and free enterprise of Liberal Whiggery and the deeply rooted statecraft (strong government + strong leadership) of Traditional Toryism. This seems remarkable because of the natural tension that exists between these two subtypes, between the country party that loves best its nostalgic England, and the business-oriented politicians who are devoted to efficiency and smart shopping precincts. The bridge across the cleavage appears in our picture where the Liberal Whigs reach out for the statecraft of the Traditional Tories and grasp it nearly as firmly as it is held by its older defenders. Mrs. Thatcher and her followers were soon working hard to resuscitate Liberal Whiggery by convincing such circles in the party that free enterprise was nothing to be ashamed of and, above all, by locking on to the symbols of statecraft to produce a package with much better prospects for widespread legitimacy in the party than Liberal Whiggery might otherwise have been able to achieve. Although she made the most of the connection between free enterprise and statecraft, she did not forge the link. It was there already.

THATCHERISM COMPLETED: VALUES
AND POLICY

A Thatcherism Index has been created to reconstruct linkages between policy beliefs and political values. This is a simple additive index based on the three items, strong government, free enterprise, and discipline, that our reading of the ideology suggests constitute its core. These items are satisfactorily intercorrelated with one another with Gammas ranging from .38 to .52. The scale was constructed and then divided into four sections. Results for the first and fourth of these sections, Low and High, are reported in tables 9.4 and 9.5. The policy items appearing in these tables are based on Likert-type scales, salience rankings, and coding of transcribed discussions.

Tables 9.4 and 9.5 flesh out Thatcherism by helping us identify Thatcherite policy views, views linked to Thatcherite political values. Believing in free enterprise, for example, Thatcherism naturally wishes to reduce the size of the state sector of the economy. To the surprise of many commentators, it has in government been doing just that, particularly since 1983. Thus, the connection between the Thatcherism index and the denationalization campaign is apparent in table 9.4 where item 1 proposes that profitable sectors of nationalized industries should be denationalized.

Thatcherism's monetarism has led it to accept levels of unemployment that have not been seen since the interwar years. This is believed necessary to prepare the way for future growth in a reinvigorated economy. Thatcherism depreciates, therefore, the problem of employment, and perhaps also depreciates it because many Thatcherites suspect that a considerable proportion of the unemployed are simply workshy. Items 2–5 in table 9.4 were coded from tape-recorded conversations about unemployment. And it can be seen that the higher a Conservative politician's score on the Thatcherism index, the less likely he is to believe that unemployment is a critical problem or to be aware of the humiliation and suffering it can cause. He is also less likely to offer up state intervention as a solution.

Table 9.4.   Thatcherism in Policy: Attitudes Toward the Economy
and Corporatism by Thatcherism Index.*

Items	Thatcherism Index Low (%)	High (%)	(N)	Gamma	Significance
Denationalization and unemployment					
1. Denationalize nationalized industries	47	84	(208)	.31	.0001
2. Unemployment is a critical problem	56	26	(236)	.29	.0001
3. Unemployment—the statistics exaggerate	17	38	(235)	.29	.003
4. Unemployment causes humiliation and suffering	37	14	(235)	.31	.002
5. Unemployment—solutions require direct or indirect state intervention	97	71	(137)	.49	.002
Corporatism and consultation					
6. Trade unions don't have right to consultation	43	58	(211)	.19	.04
7. Business doesn't have right to consultation	41	57	(212)	.28	.003
8. Business viewed more favorably than trade unions	63	80	(232)	.21	.02
9. Unfavorable view of trade union leaders	46	79	(230)	.28	.002
10. Trade unions always put sectional interest before the public interest	37	61	(197)	.18	.04
11. Compromise with adversaries is dangerous	24	39	(212)	.27	.001

*Thatcherism Index = Strong Government + Free Enterprise + Discipline.
Note: Questionnaire items for entries in this table are presented in appendix A.

The commitment to statecraft, to strong government, and to strong leadership has led Thatcherites to increase control over local government, the National Health Service, universities, and other large organizations and has led to conflict with alternative centers of power, particularly the trade unions. Items 6–11 in table 9.4 show the seeds of the future policies that would weaken functional representation, a doctrine said to be on the verge of attaining constitutional status during the Wilson and Heath years. The higher the score on the Thatcherism Index, the less likely the respondent is to believe that trade unions have an automatic right to be consulted about the making of policies that affect their interests. Thatcherites, consistent with their convictions, and despite the fact that they regard business favorably, apply the same principle to business as well. These items are derived from transcriptions of responses that further suggested that trade unions were peculiarly blind to the public interest and that compromise with such adversaries is dangerous "because it normally leads to the betrayal of one's own side."

A substantial portion of the electorate, Thatcherites tend to believe, is attracted to the Conservative party despite unemployment and other problems because they value leadership. Twenty-five percent or more of the electorate, they say in table 9.5's item 12, still feels some political deference toward leaders from political families, public schools, and Oxford and Cambridge. As Liberal Whigs, however, Thatcherites are not so keen on the class system, for it interferes with efficiency and looks like an albatross that socialists would like to hang about their neck (Norton and Aughey, 1981:83). The higher the score for Thatcherism, therefore, the less likely respondents are to perceive the electorate as thinking of itself as belonging to particular social classes (table 9.5, item 13), another measure derived from the taped conversations.

Thatcherism's Victorian morality, which is injected into our index through the discipline value, draws decisive conclusions about obscenity, social welfare, and law and order. It would like to see government decrease the first two and increase the third. Thus, Thatcherism is ready to step into the constitutionally questionable area of prior censorship (item 14). And, on a scale of comparative concern for housing, violent crime, education, strikes, and unemployment, Conservative politicians who score high on the Thatcherism index find that housing issues are not very central to their everyday interests. The welfare

Table 9.5.   Thatcherism in Policy: Attitudes About Society and Order by Thatcherism Index.*

Items	Thatcherism Index Low (%)	High (%)	(N)	Gamma	Significance
Deference and class awareness					
12. Proportion of electorate deferential—25% or more	40	67	(201)	.17	.05
13. Proportion of electorate aware of social class—25% or more	69	52	(205)	.21	.03
Obscenity					
14. Government prohibit sale of obscene magazines	26	51	(209)	.22	.01
Social welfare					
15. Housing as a political issue —very concerned	64	29	(218)	.34	.0003
16. Restrict social service benefits to the really poor	41	55	(208)	.22	.02
Law and order					
17. Death penalty should be reintroduced	29	75	(208)	.47	.0000
18. Harsher sentences for violent crimes	27	50	(212)	.28	.001
19. Violent crime as a political issue—very concerned	23	57	(218)	.33	.001
20. Strikes as a political issue —very concerned	26	61	(217)	.35	.0003

*Thatcherism Index = Strong Government + Free Enterprise + Discipline.
Note: Questionnaire items for entries in this table are presented in appendix A.

state is too large, not too small; and if any changes are to be made, they ought to be made in the direction of seeing that social service benefits are provided only to the really poor rather than to all low wage earners (item 16).

Overall, the strongest correlations between Thatcherite values and policy preferences are found with law and order issues, items 17–20 in table 9.5. Thatcherism takes discipline seriously. Mrs. Thatcher has been a prominent public advocate of reintroducing the death penalty for the murder of police officers (item 17), as well as seeing that criminals convicted of violent crimes are given longer prison sentences and fewer paroles (item 18). Thatcherites are very concerned with violent crime as a political issue and also with strikes, which they have tended to add to their law and order agenda (items 19 and 20).

The chairman of the Conservative party during the early sixties, Ian Macleod, used to find it necessary to remind supporters in the country that "One road for us is clearly marked 'No Thoroughfare' —the road back. That way lies defeat." And yet Mrs. Thatcher won. She won the leadership election, and she won the general elections of 1979 and 1983. She won the leadership election because Conservative MPs in 1975 cared more about leadership, and particularly about removing Mr. Heath, than they did about values and policy. Thus, for the leadership election it didn't matter that only a small minority of politicians were sympathetic to her views. What about the general elections and the Conservative electorate?

THATCHERISM IN THE ELECTORATE

The previous section has described the changing ideological landscape in the Conservative party. This section examines whether the electorate has undergone a parallel ideological change. Prima facie grounds for believing it has changed are provided by the Conservative party's two successive election victories in 1979 and 1983. Both broke long-standing electoral records. The first was won on the largest swing of the vote recorded at an election since 1945. The second produced the largest majority in votes and seats secured by one major party over the other since 1935, on the basis of the biggest swing ever won by a government seeking reelection.

Not surprisingly, these triumphs have been accompanied by impressionistic assertions of a "new Conservative mood" in the electorate which parallels that in the Conservative party. There are references to the collapse of the social democratic consensus, a turning of the tide against collectivism, a fresh spirit of realism at the workplace, and a resurgence of patriotism. The intellectual ferment on the new right and quiescence of the new left is also commented upon. These impressions are given some plausibility by the pedagogic impulse of Thatcherism itself. A marked feature among its strongest advocates is the sense of mission to educate the electorate about "realities," especially economic ones. Indeed, one of the few positive roles that Thatcherites give to the state is that of changing public expectations and values. Mrs. Thatcher's own behavior is important in this respect. Not since Gladstone has a prime minister held so many personal political convictions and sought to use her office to persuade the electorate of their truth.

The Electoral Evidence

Mrs. Thatcher regards herself as tutor to the nation. Has the nation been a good pupil? The purely electoral evidence is, in fact, ambiguous. On the one hand, Mrs. Thatcher's handsome parliamentary majority is deceptive: as our introduction stresses, there has been no electoral surge toward the Conservatives under her leadership. In 1979 the Conservative share of the vote, although up from 35.8 percent to 43.9 percent, was well below that obtained at their earlier postwar election victories. When the Conservatives took office in 1970 under Edward Heath their vote was 46.4 percent, and in their successive victories of 1951, 1955, and 1959 it averaged 49.0 percent. In 1983 the Conservative share of the vote *fell* by 1.5 percent to 42.4 percent, its share of the electorate by 2.5 percent to 30.8 percent. In this sense the new conservatism of Mrs. Thatcher has received a far from overwhelming mandate; instead it has benefited from the twin bonus of a majoritarian electoral system and an Opposition vote evenly split between two parties.

These historically unimpressive electoral figures are matched by similar trends for other aspects of partisan support. The Conservative party has been almost as subject as the Labour party to a long-term partisan dealignment. Party membership has steadily declined from about 2.8 million in 1953 to 1.2 million in the early 1980s (Leonard, 1975:2–3; Pinto-Duschinsky, 1984:331). Changes in the level and strength of self-declared identification with the Conservative party also cast doubt on the idea of a Conservative renaissance. The proportion of Conservative identifiers in the electorate in 1983 (39 percent) was barely different from 1979 (38 percent), or 1970 (40 percent), when the Conservatives won under Edward Heath, or 1964 (38 percent) when it lost under Sir Alex Douglas-Home. Moreover, Conservative partisanship has weakened since the 1960s. In the three elections of 1964, 1966, and 1970 about half of all Conservative identifiers described themselves as "very strong" identifiers; in 1983 the proportion was down to a quarter (26 percent), which was less than in the party's disastrous 1974 elections. Thatcherism may have put backbone into Conservatism but not, it would appear, into its rank-and-file supporters.

It appears, too, that Mrs. Thatcher has not succeeded in creating a new Conservative generation that might form the foundation for further electoral advance in future elections. The recovery in the Conservative vote has not been accompanied by a strengthening of Conservative partisanship among young cohorts of electors. The mean partisan strength (scoring 3 for "very strong," 2 for "fairly strong," and 1 for "not very strong") of Conservative identifiers among 18–33 year olds at successive elections has fallen at each election since 1966 (see table 9.6). This trend is even more pronounced among 18–25 year olds, i.e., *new* cohorts of electors, whose Conservative partisanship continued to weaken in 1979 and 1983 during the period of Mrs. Thatcher's party leadership. Moreover, the more combative and confident Conservatism of recent years has not accelerated the usual process of partisan consolidation; if anything, the reverse. In 1964–70, when Edward Heath led the Conservative party, partisanship among its younger identifiers strengthened further and faster than among comparable cohorts in the period 1974–1983 under Mrs. Thatcher's leadership. On this evidence, at least, Thatcherism has not tapped a hitherto hidden conservatism among postwar generations.

Table 9.6.   Average Intensity of Partisan Strength, 1964–83.

Election year	Aged 18–25	Aged 18–33
1964	2.10	2.12
1966	2.26	2.27
1970	1.97	2.05
1974*	1.85	1.87
1979	1.78	1.82
1983	1.71	1.80

*Average of February 1974 and October 1974 elections.

The Ideological Evidence

It would be premature, however, to dismiss the claim that the electorate has become Thatcherite on the electoral evidence set out above; for
the 1983 result can be interpreted differently. In 1983 the Conservatives
faced a more serious third-party challenge—in terms of finance, pro-
fessionalism, leadership, media coverage, and recent electoral success
—than at any election since the 1920s. Their 42.4 percent vote in
1983 was less than their 43.9 percent in 1979, but it was obtained in a
three-party rather than two-and-a-bit party contest, and in that sense
was perhaps the more impressive achievement. More significantly, the
Conservatives were reelected despite presiding over the worst recession since the 1930s. According to the "misery index"—the combination of the unemployment and inflation rates—the British economy
was in a sorrier state at the end of the Conservative government than at
the beginning. In almost every other Western democracy a rising misery index has taken its electoral toll (Lipset, 1983).[3] Yet in Britain the
Conservatives were returned with a larger majority. One plausible explanation is that the Conservatives overcame the electoral damage of their
record by achieving a favorable ideological change in the electorate.

"Ideological change" is shorthand for a variety of scenarios. We
distinguish between three, each of which might explain the Conservative party's electoral survival. Each is depicted in terms of the shifting
position of the electorate, and partisan subgroups, on a left-right or
liberal-authoritarian spectrum between 1974, 1979, and 1983. For
the purposes of analysis the electorate is divided into five groups
—committed Conservatives, uncommitted Conservatives, Liberals (in
1983, Alliance supporters), uncommitted Labour supporters, and committed Labour supporters.

The first scenario is called "The Great Moving Right Show" after
the influential article of that title in *Marxism Today* (Hall, 1979; Hall
and Martin, 1983:19–39). Its author, Stuart Hall, argued (already in
1978) that Mrs. Thatcher and Sir Keith Joseph were succeeding in
their crusade to convert the British electorate to a new conservatism.
The forces of the Right created a new, national, cross-class conservatism out of existing but hitherto unconnected discontents and popular
beliefs. This pushed free market doctrines of competitive capitalism
and anti-collectivism together with "authoritarian populism." The lat-

ter is an umbrella term for "law and order," immigration restrictions, "standards" in family and school, and patriotism—and their implied interconnections—and is close to two of the core components we have identified in Thatcherism, discipline and statecraft. To weld these elements together into a "new historic bloc between dominant and dominated," Conservative ideologists made skillful use of the domestic idiom, linking the national economy to the household budget and the sound household budget to traditional family morality and vir-

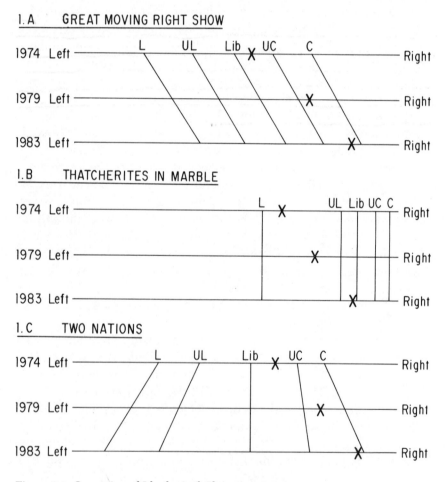

Figure 9.1. Scenarios of Ideological Change.

tues. The result was a new "reactionary common sense" in which both party and electorate abandoned the postwar social democratic consensus and moved sharply to the right along a broad policy front. This is conveyed in figure 9.1A.

The second scenario is called "Thatcherites in Marble" after Disraeli's remark that he "saw the working class Tory in the British proletariat as the sculptor sees the angel in a rough lump of marble." Unlike the previous scenario, it assumes that a large majority of the electorate held Thatcherite views before the Conservative party did. This view was expressed in 1978 by a Thatcherite MP, Rhodes Boyson: "There is a very large centre group in Britain making up possibly 80 to 90 percent of my fellow countrymen and women who have firm views on law and order, morality, personal initiative and responsibility, educational standards, discipline and national pride. The Conservatives lose elections only when they lose contact with this central group . . ." (Prologue to Centre Forward). According to this scenario, Mrs. Thatcher's service to her party has been to move it closer to the electorate rather than vice versa. Unlike her predecessors, she recognized that the electoral middle ground was not the same as the ideological center ground, but to its right. This scenario is conveyed in figure 9.1B.

The third scenario is called "Two Nations," another term borrowed from Disraeli. It is predicated on the familiar partisan-mobilization assumptions of the Michigan School of electoral studies. The Conservative party's ideological shift, it is argued, mobilized its own supporters. Loyal Conservatives moved rightward because their party did, not vice versa. The remainder of the electorate, the non-Conservative "Nation," stayed put or moved leftward, thus making for an ideological polarization in the electorate. In other words, a *partial* mobilization behind Thatcherite ideas has enabled the Conservative party to survive electorally. This proposition is depicted in figure 9.1C.

Data

Ideally we would like to have available a time series of multiple indicators, going back to at least 1974, for each of the values and issues identified as distinctive to Mrs. Thatcher's brand of Conservatism. Unfortunately, we must make do with less. We rely mainly on the British Election Study cross-sectional samples for October 1974 ($N = 2{,}365$), 1979 ($N = 1{,}893$), and 1983 ($N = 3{,}955$). Frustratingly few policy issue questions have been replicated in the British Election Studies even over the short period from October 1974 to 1983. They have therefore been supplemented by the BBC/Gallup election-day surveys for 1979 ($N = 2,435$) and 1983 ($N = 4,141$) and by Gallup opinion poll data. It must be acknowledged from the outset that ideal trend data are simply not available for some distinctively Thatcherite values. Nonetheless, the data are wide enough in scope to produce a consistent picture of ideological change, or its absence, in the electorate.

Method of Analysis

We examined ideological change in the British electorate by plotting its "position," and that of partisan subgroups, in 1974 (where the data were available), 1979, and 1983 for a series of issues, or groups of issues, that illuminated the distinctive features of Thatcherism. The position on a line representing the spectrum of views on an issue was simply the average (mean) of a scatter of positions of the individuals composing the group; the degree of scatter would, of course, vary across issues and between groups. The five groups depicted in figure 9.1 are defined by the standard three-category party identification question:

(1) *Committed Conservatives*: very strong + fairly strong Conservative identifiers;
(2) *Uncommitted Conservatives*: not very strong Conservative identifiers;
(3) *Liberals*: all Liberal identifiers in 1974 and 1979; all Liberal, SDP, and Alliance identifiers in 1983;
(4) *Uncommitted Labour*: not very strong Labour identifiers;
(5) *Committed Labour*: very strong + fairly strong Labour identifiers.

We differentiate between the committed and uncommitted in this way because of extensive evidence from past election studies that very/fairly strong identifiers are more readily mobilized than not very strong identifiers to "follow the party line" when it changes (Alt, Crewe, and Sarlvik, 1976: 273–90). In the Two Nations scenario, therefore, we would expect committed Conservatives to move further than uncommitted Conservatives; whereas in the Great Moving Right Show, which represents a cultural change throughout the country, we would expect all groups to shift to the right, and the uncommitted more so than the committed.

We shall proceed by exploring public attitudes on those issues that are most closely related to the distinctively Thatcherite values of free enterprise, strong government, and discipline. We begin with three components of economic Thatcherism: its stands on denationalization, unemployment, and the cost of the welfare state. We then turn to an issue that straddles economic and political Thatcherism: trade union power. Finally, we shall examine some of the components of social Thatcherism known as "authoritarian populism." (The data reporting the positions of the several subgroups are available to interested readers upon request to the authors.)

Nationalization Vs. Privatization

In Britain the ideological battle between socialism and capitalism is fought most fiercely over the issue of nationalization. No issue has more sharply divided the two parties in Parliament, or the electorate. But it is also the touchstone of true faith and thus the cause of divisions *within* both parties. Thatcherite Conservatives are not content, unlike conventional Conservatives, merely to maintain the frontier between the private and public sectors. The parliamentary data from the early 1970s show that their precursors were particularly likely to advocate a positive policy of privatization (see table 9.4). Mrs. Thatcher's governments have engaged in a massive sale of British industry that compares in its scale only with the nationalization program of the postwar Labour government. This has been justified as a means of reducing public expenditure, and thus taxes, but also as a means of creating a "people's capitalism" in which share ownership is more widely spread.

Table 9.7 suggests that the Great Moving Right Show accurately describes the electorate's shift in attitudes toward nationalization. From 1964 to 1974 public attitudes were evenly balanced between further nationalization and privatization, with the plurality in favor of the status quo. But between October 1974 and 1979 the proportion supporting further nationalization halved from 32 percent to 17 percent and the proportion in favor of privatization doubled from 22 percent to 40 percent. In 1983 the distribution of opinion was similar, although, for the first time, supporters of privatization outnumbered supporters of the status quo. This pattern of change applied to all partisan groups, but it is notable that Labour supporters, especially the uncommitted, shifted most sharply to the right.

It might be objected, of course, that it was not the electorate but the political situation that changed between 1974 and 1979. In that period the Labour government bought a majority shareholding in British Leyland, established the British National Oil Corporation, and took large sections of the aerospace and shipbuilding industries into public ownership. Thus an elector who favored the status quo in 1974 and privatization in 1983 might not have changed his personal position at all. There is no certain way of knowing how much of the 1974–79 change in attitudes can be explained in this way. But a comparison with the period 1964–66 is instructive. Then the Labour government renationalized the steel industry in a fiercer blaze of controversy, but public attitudes did not change. This tentatively implies that much of the 1974–79 change represents a real shift of conviction. Moreover, the consolidation of this change between 1979 and 1983

Table 9.7.   Attitudes to Nationalization, 1964–83 (in percentages).

Question: "Which of these statements comes closest to what you yourself feel should be done?"

A lot more industries should be nationalized.
Only a few more industries should be nationalized.
No more industries should be nationalized, but the industries that are nationalized now should stay nationalized.
Some of the industries that are nationalized now should be denationalized.

The first two answers are combined into the single category "further nationalization" in the table below.

Percentage supporting	1964	1966	1970*	1974**	1979	1983
Further nationalization	28	29	22	30	17	18
No change	51	49	45	47	43	40
Denationalization	21	22	33	24	40	42

*The 1970 wave of the 1963–70 panel sample.
**February 1974 and October 1974 elections combined.

occurred despite the government's significant program of privatization and its promises of much more—British Leyland, British Telecom, British Gas, British Air, and the Water Boards—to come. If respondents held an unchanging view of the right boundary line between the private and public sectors, they would have reverted at least to their October 1974 position. That they did not suggests that, on this matter at least, Thatcherism produced a significant change in public attitudes.

Job Creation

The maintenance of the mixed economy was only one part of the postwar consensus on which the moderate wings of both major parties were agreed. Another element was the commitment to full employment as the overriding government priority in economic policy. In its depreciation of the problem of unemployment (see table 9.4) Thatcherism broke with this consensus, claiming that it was neither desirable nor practical for governments to strive to maintain full employment in all circumstances. The first priority was to beat inflation (which had risen above 25 percent in 1975); only then would "genuine" jobs be created. Moreover, the private sector was a more efficient generator of long-term employment than the government.

Public opinion on this issue presents a contrast with that on nationalization (see table 9.8). In 1979 there was public acceptance of the new government's priorities and strategy. In mid-1980 a modest majority (52 percent to 42 percent) thought the government should give more attention to curbing inflation than reducing unemployment. But by the May 1983 election there was a dramatic reversal (22 percent to 69 percent), which has since proceeded further. This is hardly surprising, as it corresponds with the steady fall in the inflation rate and the sharp rise in unemployment levels over the same period. But it shows that the public's priorities are a response to immediate problems and have not been shaped by the government's strategic thinking. Similarly, in 1979 the electorate concurred with the Conservative view that jobs should be created "by allowing companies to keep more of their profits" rather than the Labour view that "it was up to Government to use tax money to create jobs." But by 1983 all sections of the electorate, including committed Conservatives, had shifted leftward on the issue. To say that the Conservative government's position had been decisively rejected would be an exaggeration, as the electorate

Table 9.8.   Thatcherism's Economic Priorities: Curbing Inflation vs. Reducing Unemployment.

Question: "Which do you think the government should give greater attention to—trying to curb inflation or trying to reduce unemployment?"

Month/ year	Curb inflation	Reduce unemployment	Don't know	
10/76	54	36	10	
				—(May 1979 election)
6/80	52	42	7	
11/80	30	62	8	
1/82	23	70	8	
11/82	21	73	6	
5/83	22	69	9	(June 1983 election)
7/84	18	75	7	
6/85	14	78	8	
8/85	16	77	7	

Source: Gallup Political Index.

still placed itself marginally to the right-of-center. But, equally, the 1983 election result cannot be interpreted as a mandate for Thatcherism's renunciation of responsibility for employment levels.

The Welfare State

The Conservative party is ambivalent and divided about the welfare state. The data on Conservative MPs and candidates revealed that limiting "social service benefits only to the really poor" distinguished potential Thatcherites from others, although not as strongly as many other policies (see table 9.4). Under Mrs. Thatcher, the Conservative party has attempted to combine electoral advantage with lower welfare expenditures by directing reforms to the less popular sectors of the welfare state. Before the 1979 election the party promised a drive against the welfare scrounger, a folk devil who allowed the party to play simultaneously on themes of self-reliance, law-abidingness, hard work, and economic sabotage. Since the election, the Thatcher governments have reduced the eligibility for, and real value of, the unpopular unemployment and supplementary benefits and constantly reiterated the trade-off between taxation and welfare spending.

Once again, however, the evidence does not suggest that the electorate has adopted a Thatcherite position on these issues. For example, in 1974, 1979, and 1983 the public was asked whether welfare benefits "nowadays have gone too far." This question, like others in the "gone too far" format, is slanted to provoke a conservative response. In October 1974 partisan groups were spread, in the expected order, around the center, but slightly to its right. By 1979 the whole electorate had moved further to the right in the pattern of the Great Moving Right Show, with the least partisan groups moving most sharply of all. However, the rightward drift was modest—in reality, a case of a Minor Moving Right Show. Moreover, by 1983 the whole electorate had reversed direction, each group locating itself further to the left than its original position in October 1974. Presumably this shift was partly in reaction to the actual cuts in benefits imposed between 1979 and 1983, but it is notable that committed Conservatives, few of whom depend on the reduced benefits, moved to the left at the same pace as everyone else. Mrs. Thatcher may have triumphed in 1983, but Samuel Smiles did not.

Nor has the new Conservatism converted the electorate to a low-tax, minimal-service economy. Here our evidence is restricted to frequency distributions from the opinion polls (see table 9.9). Asked to choose between tax and service cuts or tax and service increases, the public was evenly divided, 37 percent apiece, when the Conservatives first came to office in May 1979. By 1983 service increasers outnumbered tax cutters by 52 to 24 percent, and by 1986 by the even greater margin of 63 to 17 percent. Similarly, the proportion agreeing that "the Conservatives want to cut back too much on health, education and other services" has consistently been 75 percent or more since August 1983 and over 80 percent since 1985 (Gallup, 1985:23).

Trade Unions

The postwar history of Conservative–trade union relations is one of growing hostility. The Conservative governments of the 1950s treated trade unions as an estate of the realm, entitled to legal immunities and, increasingly, to formal consultation on matters of economic and social policy. However, by the early 1970s this sort of corporatism was losing support among backbenchers adhering to Thatcherite values (see table 9.4). They increasingly looked unfavorably upon trade union

Table 9.9.   Thatcherism's Economic Priorities: Taxes vs. Social Services.

Question: "People have different views about whether it is more important to reduce taxes or keep up government spending. How about you? Which of these statements comes closest to your view?"

Cut taxes, even if this means some reduction in government services such as health, education, and welfare.

Things should be left as they are.

Government services such as health education and welfare should be extended, even if it means some increases in taxes.

Month/year	Cut taxes	No change	Extend services
10/78	29	26	45
5/79	37	26	37
3/80	25	27	47
3/81	22	25	53
2/82	22	27	52
2/83	24	23	52
———————————————————————————————(1983 general election)			
10/83	18	23	53
5/84	15	27	58
11/84	13	26	62
2/85	17	19	63
2/86	17	20	63

Source: Gallup Political Index.

leaders and their rights to consultation. Edward Heath's government continued to incorporate trade unions in tripartite decisionmaking bodies, but its attempts to impose a statutory incomes policy and a tighter legal framework over industrial relations were thwarted by strikes, precipitating an early general election in February 1974, which the government lost.

Chastened by the February 1974 defeat, the Conservative party's proposals in 1979 were, on the face of it, less sweeping: a review of the law of picketing, especially secondary picketing; the protection of individuals expelled or excluded from a closed shop; public funds for the holding of secret ballots; and, in a veiled reference, the withdrawal of (nontaxable) supplementary benefits from strikers. But these piecemeal changes masked a sea change in attitudes. The Heath administration regarded trade unions as a legitimate national institution in need of reform. Thatcherites regarded trade unions as "the enemy within" whose powers needed to be cautiously but ruthlessly stripped. Thus, the Thatcher governments not only carried out their manifesto proposals but denied trade unions access to Whitehall and refused to intervene or compromise even in the most prolonged and damaging of disputes, such as the miners' year-long strike of 1984–85.

Two points may be established about the connections between Thatcherism and public attitudes to trade unions. On the one hand, Thatcherism followed rather than created the public's conviction that trade unions had become too powerful. The public's widespread belief that trade unions are overmighty reached its peak in 1974, after the miners' successful strikes of 1972 and 1974. Fully 80 percent said the unions had too much power, an increase of 18 percent from the 63 percent who gave the same response in 1963. This figure did not advance after Mrs. Thatcher took over the Conservative leadership. Her specific proposals for reform were strikingly popular,[4] again because the party moved closer to public opinion, not vice versa: another case of "Thatcherites in Marble." On the other hand, Thatcherism has failed in its more ambitious aim of persuading the electorate that trade unions are undesirable or unnecessary institutions (i.e., illegitimate organizations). One set of evidence is provided by Gallup's annual question of thirty years' standing: "Generally speaking, and thinking of Britain as a whole, do you think that trade unions are a good thing or a bad thing?" As table 9.10 shows, a majority have always answered positively, and although the size of the majority fell in the 1970s, it has clearly risen during Mrs. Thatcher's tenure as prime minister.

Law and Order

The Conservative party has, of course, traditionally been the party of law and order. Long before Mrs. Thatcher became leader, vehement calls for the return of capital (and corporal) punishment were a ritual at the annual Conservative party conference; and opinion polls show that the electorate has always preferred the Conservative party to others on penal issues. Nonetheless, under Mrs. Thatcher's leadership the party has spoken even more often and stridently on these issues. Its 1979 manifesto promised a renewed debate on the death penalty

Table 9.10.   Standing of the Trade Unions.

Question: "Generally speaking, and thinking of Britain as a whole, do you think that the trade unions are a good thing or a bad thing?"

Government	Dates	Good thing	Bad thing	Don't know
Eden/Macmillan	1954–59	62	18	20
Macmillan/Home	1960–64	62	19	19
Wilson	1965–70	61	23	16
Heath	1971–73	59	25	16
Wilson/Callaghan	1974–79	54	31	15
Thatcher	1980–83	60	28	12
Thatcher	1984–	63	27	10

Note: Figures are the annual mean for each period. Periods correspond to successive governments.

(albeit on a free, i.e., unwhipped, vote) early in the new Parliament, a stronger and better paid police force, and the establishment of a new type of detention center in which juvenile offenders would be taught a "short, sharp shock." The current Parliament has passed a new Police and Criminal Evidence Act that shifts the balance of power and rights toward the police at the expense of the accused and has held a repeat debate on the death penalty. Although the call for restoration of capital punishment was again defeated, Mrs. Thatcher, as before, voted in favor as did most of the newly elected Conservative backbenchers. Mr. Heath and most of his former associates voted against. More significantly, the present Conservative leadership has redefined a number of issues and problems as being purely matters of law and order, notably militant strike action in the coalfields and elsewhere, and unrest in the racially mixed and jobless inner cities. After the riots in Handsworth and Tottenham, for example, the government refused to order an enquiry into the causes, wholly attributing them to human wickedness.

With regard to the electorate's position on these two issues (combined), in 1979 and 1983 the electorate was located on common ground well to the right of center. There was almost no differentiation between the party groups, although committed Conservatives were, predictably, furthest to the right and committed Labour supporters closest (but not close) to the center. Unfortunately, exactly comparable data are not available for 1974. However, there are two grounds for inferring that the electorate's right-of-center position in 1979 did *not* represent a shift to the right since 1974. First, the proportion in favor of restoration of the death penalty was even greater in 1966 (82 percent) and 1970 (81 percent) than in 1979 (75 percent). And second, the electorate moved slightly to the left between 1974 and 1979 on a related issue (for which the question was, alas, not repeated in 1983). Asked what they felt about "people challenging authority," the proportion answering that it had gone "too far" fell from 82 percent in 1974 to 65 percent in 1979. Among these, the proportion saying "much too far" fell from 49 percent to 32 percent. The balance of evidence is therefore tipped against the view that the years 1974 to 1979 marked a resurgence of tough-minded authoritarianism among the public. It has always been present to a considerable degree.

On issues of law and order, therefore, there was no Great Moving Right Show. The electorate had moved there long before Mrs. Thatcher's Conservative party did. Thatcherites in Marble describes the situation better. The party abandoned the previous bipartisan understanding that politics should be kept out of law-and-order issues and that appeals to the public's easily aroused punitive instincts were somehow cheap and nasty. In so doing it struck a responsive chord, although not one that was converted into many additional votes in 1979 (Sarlvik and Crewe, 1983:169–70). The change between 1979 and 1983, moreover, defies all three scenarios. The entire electorate shifted to a slightly less authoritarian position, while remaining firmly right of center. Unlike the government, it did not react to the rash of urban riots in 1981, or to the alleged growth of violent crime, by calling for even tougher sentencing policies. This facet of Thatcherism has always had majority opinion on its side, but the majority was slimmer after four years of office than before.

Immigration and Racial Equality

The Conservative party has always been formally committed to equality before the law and equality of opportunity for all citizens, irrespective of ethnic origin. However, Mrs. Thatcher and her close supporters are associated with a hard line on black immigration and relative indifference to discrimination and prejudice against black minorities. On January 30, 1978, following a surge in the National Front vote at local elections, Mrs. Thatcher had this to say on Granada Television's

"World in Action": "You know, the British character has done so much for democracy, for law, and done so much throughout the world, that if there is a fear that it might be swamped, people are going to react and be rather hostile to those coming in. So, if you want good race relations, you have got to allay people's fears on numbers." These remarks gained widespread publicity. They established Conservatives in the eyes of the electorate as the anti-immigration party and implied that blacks were a threat to the British character, to the law, and to democracy. The 1979 manifesto promised much tighter restrictions on immigration, including dependents of those already settled in Britain. This was implemented in the 1979–83 government and when, in 1984, the law was declared contrary to the European Convention of Human Rights (to which Britain is a signatory) because wives could join husbands but not vice versa, the government announced that it would make the law more, not less, restrictive.

The Conservatives' new hard line on immigration undoubtedly moved it closer to the overwhelming (and intensely held) majority view of the British electorate that "too many immigrants have been let into this country."[5] In this sense the party discerned Thatcherites in Marble. However, it is a mistake to infer, as is commonly done, that Thatcherism mobilized a popular and authoritarian racism between 1974 and 1983. As table 9.11 shows, support for the repatriation of immigrants, which never commanded a majority, *fell* between 1974 and 1979, especially among Conservatives. And support for the principle of equal opportunity for blacks (more accurately, denial that it has "gone too far"), remained the same between 1974 and 1979 and rose slightly by 1983, again mainly among Conservatives. On matters of racial equality the British electorate remained moderate, edging gradually to a more liberal position, during the Thatcher years.

Permissiveness

The Conservative governments of Mrs. Thatcher have not attempted to identify themselves with the reaction against "permissiveness" in a way that matches their capture of law-and-order issues. They have been content to leave such issues as abortion, divorce, and obscenity to backbench initiatives and free votes. The Moral Majority's counterparts in Britain, such as the antiabortion movement and Mary Whitehouse's National Viewers and Listeners' Association (concerned

Table 9.11.   Attitudes to the Repatriation of Immigrants, 1974 and 1979.

Question and index: "What is your view about sending colored immigrants back to their own country?"

Very important that it should be done.	(scores 1)
Fairly important that it should be done.	(scores 2)
It doesn't matter either way.	(scores 3)
Fairly important that it should not be done.	(scores 4)
Very important that it should not be done.	(scores 5)

I.e., low score is conservative, high score is liberal.

	Percentage supporting repatriation		Index score	
	October 1974	1979	October 1974	1979
Committed Conservatives	43	34	2.82	3.24
Uncommitted Conservatives	32	22	3.04	3.47
Liberals	30	31	3.20	3.36
Uncommitted Labour	38	29	3.05	3.37
Committed Labour	36	29	2.91	3.26

with pornography, especially on television), cannot muster anything approaching the equivalent electoral forces. Nor does their influence in the Conservative party compare with the Moral Majority's in the Republican party.

Nonetheless, a connection between the breakdown of social order and the "permissive society" is commonly made by Thatcherites. Norman Tebbit, chairman of the Conservative party and ideologically close to Mrs. Thatcher, has recently attributed the violent riots in London to the liberalizing legislation on abortion, homosexuality, divorce, censorship, and capital punishment ushered in during the Labour governments of 1964 to 1970. Mrs. Thatcher's famous celebration of Victorian values mainly referred to economic self-sufficiency within the family but certainly referred to those of traditional sexual probity as well. The prohibition of obscene magazines, it may be recalled, was fairly strongly associated with the Thatcherism index among MPs and candidates (Gamma = 0.22) (see table 9.5).

It is therefore worth tracing changes in attitude toward two

Thatcherite indicators of permissiveness between 1974 and 1983, abortion and pornography. Table 9.12 suggests that attitudes have remained static on pornography and become slightly more liberal on abortion between 1979 and 1983. This is corroborated by answers to a Gallup question on whether the law should make legal abortion easier, more difficult, or be left as it is: the proportion saying "more difficult" (excluding don't knows) was 41 percent in 1970, 42 percent in 1973,

Table 9.12.   Attitudes to Pornography and Abortion

Questions and index: "Would you say that the right to show nudity and sex in films and magazines/the availability of abortion on the National Health Service

has gone much too far	(scores 1)
has gone a little too far	(scores 1)
is about right	(scores 2)
has not gone quite far enough	(scores 3)
has not gone nearly far enough	(scores 3)

(In 1983 the only answer categories were gone too far/is about right/not gone far enough.)

	Index Score			
	1974	1979	1983	Change 1974–1983
Pornography				
Committed Conservatives	1.33	1.33	1.35	+0.02
Uncommitted Conservatives	1.39	1.43	1.52	+0.13
Liberals	1.41	1.41	1.41	—
Uncommitted Labour	1.51	1.63	1.50	−0.01
Committed Labour	1.44	1.39	1.37	−0.07
All respondents	1.42	1.37	1.40	−0.02
Abortion				
Committed Conservatives	1.61	1.66	1.76	+0.15
Uncommitted Conservatives	1.78	1.75	1.91	+0.13
Liberals	1.79	1.71	1.74	−0.05
Uncommitted Labour	1.79	1.64	1.82	+0.03
Committed Labour	1.75	1.67	1.85	+0.10
All respondents	1.72	1.68	1.81	+0.09

and 36 percent in 1980. Once again, social conservatism in the electorate has preceded rather than followed the triumph of Thatcherism in
the Conservative party. It would be in keeping with Thatcherism to
campaign on such issues—seeking, again, to sculpt Thatcherite voters
out of the marble—but so far the party has refrained from doing so.

CONCLUSION AND SPECULATION

Mrs. Thatcher's ideological crusade poses problems for political scientists brought up on the assumptions that party leaders formulate
ideologies and policies in line with public opinion. Similarly, voters
are expected to reward parties whose policies are close to their own
and to punish parties whose policies are distant. How, then, did Mrs.
Thatcher persuade a party celebrated for its electoral pragmatism and
distaste for dogma to abandon the postwar policy consensus in favor
of minority doctrines? And having done that, why was she not penal-
ized at the polls either in 1979 or, more significantly, after four years of
"ideological" government in 1983?

It is, of course, a simple matter to invent explanations. The rise of
Mrs. Thatcher and Thatcherism can, at a pinch, be accounted for in
electoral terms. But it is not a plausible account. Mrs. Thatcher did
not win the leadership for electoral (or ideological) reasons but because
she was the best instrument at hand for defeating an unpopular and
failed incumbent. Thatcherism was not formulated out of an amalgam
of private opinion poll findings on what the public thinks it wants. It
arose from Mrs. Thatcher's long-held personal convictions, with some
refinements from Conservative thinkers and policy institutes. And it
was not its electoral attractions that made it acceptable to the parliamentary Conservative party but its origins in preexisting elements of
Conservative ideology. Thatcherism's success within the party arose
from its linking of *two* minority traditions—Liberal Whiggery and
Traditional Toryism—into a new broad coalition. It was not a freshly
minted minority doctrine imposed on the party (although the preroga-
tives of the party leader helped) but a new combination of old Conservative values.

Why was the new Conservatism rewarded—or at least not punished—in the 1979 and 1983 elections? Did Mrs. Thatcher's ideological crusade convert the electorate as well as the party, or were voters
Thatcherite before the party was? There is no neat and tidy answer. On

issues connected with the core Thatcherite values of strong government and discipline—immigration control, trade union reform, the death penalty, crime, pornography—the electorate held Thatcherite positions before the Conservative party did. On all these issues the electorate has been characterized by a cross-party consensus, a right-wing populism, since 1974 and beyond. By appealing on these grounds Mrs. Thatcher served her party, as Disraeli did a century earlier, by discerning potential supporters as the sculptor discerns an angel in a block of marble.

On issues connected with the third Thatcherite value, free enterprise, the ideological position and development of the electorate is much less clear. Between 1974 and 1979 the electorate did drift rightward on the issues of nationalization, welfare benefits, and the trade-off between social services and taxation. It also endorsed a free-enterprise rather than state-directed strategy for reducing unemployment. But this amounted to much less than a full-blooded conversion to Thatcherism; the move to the right was modest and the electorate was dispersed across a spectrum running from the center to the center right. Moreover, by 1983 all groups within the electorate, including committed Conservatives, had reversed direction on these issues, moving to the left of their 1974 position. The 1979–83 government failed to convert the electorate to a minimal welfare state or the general undesirability of trade unions. Nationalization provides the one exception to this pattern. This is the only issue on which the electorate's shift to a Thatcherite position was consolidated rather than weakened by 1983. So far it is the single clear-cut victory in Thatcherism's crusade.

The Conservative party was reelected in 1983 despite the leftward drift of the electorate away from most key Thatcherite positions. Mrs. Thatcher's triumph was not an electoral triumph for Thatcherism. Nonetheless, we make in conclusion a speculative point about Thatcherism's electoral appeal. So far we have treated Thatcherism as a distinct ideology that can be decomposed into specific policy positions. But we may also think of Thatcherism as a style of leadership, as distinctive in manner as much as matter. In support of established values, Thatcherites are self-assured, aggressive, and explicit where their predecessors were hesitant, defensive, and mealymouthed.

Thatcherism is combative and resolute where earlier Conservatism was diplomatic and conciliatory.

Lacking comparable data for the 1974, 1979, and 1983 elections, we cannot know for certain how much of Thatcherism's electoral appeal lies in its style rather than its substance, and whether this appeal grew

Table 9.13.   Thatcherism and Vote Switching, 1979–83.

	Thatcherite			Anti-Thatcherite	
	Very	Fairly	Intermediate	Fairly	Very
Voted Conservative in 1979 and stayed Conservative in 1983	95%	88%	86%	74%	59%
defected to Alliance	5	9	14	19	29
defected to Labour	—	3	—	7	12
	100%	100%	100%	100%	100%
(N)	(411)	(496)	(156)	(357)	(151)
Voted Labour in 1979 and stayed Labour in 1983	53%	65%	69%	65%	75%
defected to Alliance	18	20	19	29	24
defected to Conservatives	29	15	12	6	1
	100%	100%	100%	100%	100%
(N)	(75)	(254)	(143)	(348)	(462)
Voted Liberal in 1979 and stayed Alliance in 1983	78%	79%	67%	74%	80%
defected to Conservatives	20			9	
defected to Labour	2		33	17	
	100%		100%	100%	
(N)	(44)	(77)	(36)	(92)	(94)

Source: BBC TV/Gallup survey, June 8–9, 1983. The question wording is given in the text.

between 1979 and 1983. But there is evidence that Thatcherism as a style of government contributed to the Conservative victory in 1983 (see appendix B on construction of the Thatcherism-style scale). The British electorate was not overwhelmingly Thatcherite in this stylistic sense. In fact, the antistylistic Thatcherites (48 percent) outnumbered the stylistic Thatcherites (41 percent). But the significance of Thatcherism as a style of government lay in its relation to vote-switching between 1979 and 1983 (see table 9.13). For example, only 5 percent of very stylistic Thatcherite ex-Conservatives defected, all to the Alliance, whereas 41 percent of the very antistylistic Thatcherite ex-Conservatives (a one-in-ten minority) switched. The equivalent pattern occurred among Labour's 1979 supporters, but with greater impact. Most were antistylistic Thatcherite (63 percent), and, of these, 29 percent defected, almost all to the Alliance. But a quarter were stylistic Thatcherites, and of these 38 percent defected. And among the small minority who were very stylistically Thatcherite, fully 47 percent changed sides, the majority moving directly to the Conservatives.

Such was the effect of Thatcherism as a style of government at one election. Whether it reflected no more than the extraordinary but short-lived events of the Falklands War or signified a more profound change in the mood of the electorate awaits the results of future elections. In the meantime it is a reminder that electorates as well as politicians respond to quality and style of leadership as well as to policies, and that this needs to be incorporated into our theories about ideology and voting behavior.

NOTES

1   Although we are primarily interested in the first principal component, an inspection of the complete factor analysis presents a rather flaccid picture: a varimax rotation recovers eight dimensions with eigen values above 1.00, which together explain only 69 percent of the variance.

2   Its strength compared to the second factor is somewhat more impressive than that found with the Whigs. Again, however, the overall structure is relatively weak with seven factors with eigen values above 1.00 explaining together only 62 percent of the variance.

3   When Mrs. Thatcher was returned to power in May 1983, the most recent elections in Australia, Austria, Canada, France, Greece, the Irish Republic, Norway, Portugal, Spain, Sweden, the United States, and West Germany had turned out the government.

And in Finland, Italy, and Japan the most recent elections had recorded the lowest support for the permanent party of government in generations.

4   In answer to Gallup's annual question, "Do you approve or disapprove of the Government's plans to reform trade union law?," approvers outnumbered disapprovers by 64 percent to 36 percent over the five years from 1979 to 1983. Support for specific proposals was even greater. For example, a MORI survey in August 1980 (when the government's overall standing was relatively low) found the following proportions agreeing with the government's reform proposals (the proportion of trade union members agreeing is in parentheses):

> 86% (84%) on compulsory postal ballots on whether to strike
> 77% (72%) on limit to number of pickets at any one place
> 76% (67%) on ban on secondary picketing
> 60% (62%) on government-paid postal ballots for union officials
> 54% (44%) on taxing social security benefits to strikers' families

Numerous other surveys confirm this pattern of opinion. For another example, see "A sweeping disapproval of flying pickets," *The Times*, January 21, 1980.

5   The proportions taking this view (with the proportions feeling "very strongly" about it in parentheses) were:

> 1964:   83%   (42%)
> 1966:   81%   (44%)
> 1970:   85%   (44%)
> 1979:   86%   (41%)

APPENDIX A. QUESTIONNAIRE ITEMS IN
TABLES 9.5 AND 9.6

The items below include all those presented in the study's mailback questionnaire. The other entries in tables 9.5 and 9.6 are based on either salience rankings or coding of transcribed discussions.

1   Profitable sectors of nationalized industries should be denationalized.
2   Trade union organizations do not have an automatic right to be consulted about the making of policies which affect their interests.
3   Business organizations do not have an automatic right to be consulted about the making of policies which affect their interests.
4   To compromise with political adversaries is dangerous because it normally leads to the betrayal of one's own side.
5   The Government ought to prohibit the sale of adult magazines which are obscene.
6   Social service benefits and exemptions ought to be provided only to the really poor rather than to all low wage earners.
7   The death penalty should be re-introduced for the murder of police officers.
8   Criminals convicted of violent crimes should be given longer prison sentences and fewer paroles.

APPENDIX B. CONSTRUCTION OF
"THATCHERISM STYLE" SCALE

The scale is constructed from answers to the following five questions (frequency distributions are given in parentheses).

1   When dealing with political opponents, what is better—sticking firmly to one's political beliefs (50 percent) or trying to meet them halfway (39 percent)?
2   In difficult economic times, what is better—for the government to be caring (46 percent) or for the government to be tough (34 percent)?
3   When governments make decisions about the economy, what is better—to involve major interests like trade unions and business (60 percent) or to keep them at arm's length (28 percent)?
4   It is sometimes said that no government of any party can in fact do much to create economic prosperity, that it is up to people themselves. Do you agree (48 percent) or disagree (37 percent)?
5   In its relations with the rest of the world, what is better—for Britain to stick resolutely to its own position (30 percent) or for Britain to meet other countries halfway (58 percent)?

Respondents were awarded a score of +1 for each Thatcherite response, 0 for a neutral response (e.g., "neither," "both," "don't know") and −1 for an anti-Thatcherite response. They were categorized on the Thatcherism Style scale according to their total score, as follows:

	Score on Thatcherism style scale	Percentage of respondents
Very Thatcherite	+4, +5	15
Fairly Thatcherite	+1 to +3	26
Intermediate	0	11
Fairly anti-Thatcherite	−1 to −3	26
Very anti-Thatcherite	−4, −5	22
		100

REFERENCES

Alt, James, Bo Sarlvik, and Ivor Crewe. 1976. "Partisanship and Policy Choice: Issue Preference in the British Electorate, February 1974." *British Journal of Political Science* 6: 273–90.
Beattie, Alan. 1979. "Macmillan's Mantle: The Conservative Party in the 1970s." *Political Quarterly*, pp. 273–85.
Beer, Samuel H. 1965. *British Politics in the Collectivist Age*. New York: Alfred A. Knopf.
Behrens, Robert. 1980. *The Conservative Party from Heath to Hatcher*. London: Saxon House.
Bulpitt, Jim. 1986. "The Discipline of the New Democracy: Mrs. Thatcher's Statecraft." *Political Studies*, pp. 19–39.

Gallup Poll. 1985. *Political Index*, no. 296.

Hall, Stuart. 1979. "The Great Moving Right Show." *Marxism Today*.

———, and Martin Jacques, eds. 1983. *The Politics of Thatcherism*. London: Lawrence and Wishart, pp. 19–39.

Leonard, Dick. 1975. *Paying for Party Politics: The Case for Public Subsidies*. London: Political and Economic Planning, vol. 41, broadsheet no. 555.

Lipset, Seymour M. 1983. "The Economy, Elections and Public Opinion." *Working Papers in Political Science* (Hoover Institution), no. P-83-1.

Norton, Philip, and Arthur Aughey. 1981. *Conservatives and Conservatism*. London: Temple Smith.

Pinto-Duschinsky, Michael. 1984. "Trends in British Political Funding, 1979–1983." *Parliamentary Affairs*, pp. 328–47.

Rokeach, Milton. 1968. *Beliefs, Attitudes and Values*. San Francisco: Jossey-Bass.

———. 1973. *The Nature of Human Values*. New York: Free Press.

———. 1979. *Understanding Human Values: Individual and Societal*. New York: Free Press.

Sarlvik, Bo, and Ivor Crewe. 1983. *Decade of Dealignment*. Cambridge: Cambridge University Press.

Searing, Donald D. 1978. "Measuring Politicians' Values: Administration and Assessment of a Ranking Technique in the British House of Commons." *American Political Science Review*, pp. 65–79.

Utley, T. E. 1978. "The Significance of Mrs. Thatcher." In Maurice Cowling, ed., *Conservative Essays*. London: Cassell, pp. 41–51.

Wapshott, Nicholas, and George Brock. 1983. *Thatcher*. London: Macdonald.

10. The Resurgence of Conservatism in British Elections After 1974

MARK N. FRANKLIN

INTRODUCTION

In the general election of 1979 the British Conservative party won what was widely regarded as a landslide victory, with a swing in terms of votes that was greater than in any election since 1945. And in 1983 the landslide was repeated, with Mrs. Thatcher winning a majority of over 160 seats. So in terms of simple political party indicators it is tempting to talk of a resurgence of conservatism in Britain over the past decade. Much the same is true if we look at public opinion. In terms of casual observation of the modes of discourse in the press and on television, it seems clear that there has been a swing to the right in terms of attitudes on political issues. This can be confirmed by indicators derived from postelection studies conducted in 1974 and 1979.[1] In those studies, eighteen attitude questions were asked in virtually identical form, and if we compare the percentage of respondents who felt the more conservative position on these issues to be fairly important or very important in 1974 with the same percentages in 1979, we see consistent increases in conservatism in seventeen of the eighteen issues (see figure 10.1). Curbing communists was the only issue to register less conservatism in 1979, although this was the most conservative of all the issues to begin with.

But first impressions can be misleading. The landslide swing of 1979 resulted in an electoral majority of only forty-three seats, and the landslide majority of 1983 was won despite a decline in the number of Conservative voters (the anti-Conservative vote was of course split

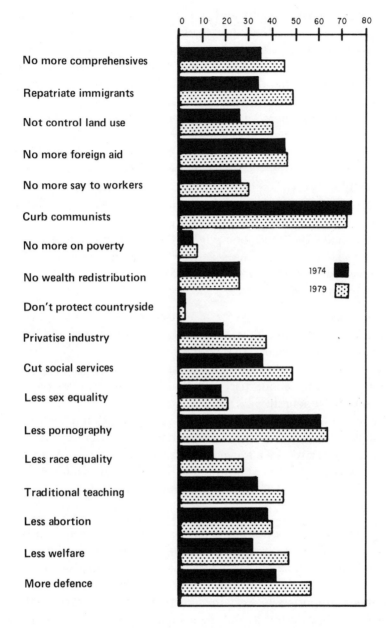

Figure 10.1. Percentage of Respondents Feeling Certain Positions to Be Very or Fairly Important, 1974 and 1979.

two ways, between Labour and Alliance candidates): Moreover, the undoubted increase in the extent to which conservative sentiments are expressed in the media and by individuals could as easily be the consequence of a conservative regime in Whitehall as its cause, since the government of the day commands immense power to shape the terms in which political discourse is carried on.

Even the propensity of voters to record pro-Conservative stances on political issues may not be quite what it seems. Issue preferences can as easily result from a voting decision as cause it, and if voters supported Mrs. Thatcher because in their eyes "there was no alternative" (Miller, 1984), such a decision would certainly be reflected in subsequent expressions of issue preference, as the well-known "coloured spectacles" inseparable from identification with party (Cambell et al., 1960) did their work on new Conservative supporters.

At least three hypotheses can be advanced to account for the changes in party support and issue preference that have occurred during the past ten years.

1 There has been a resurgence of conservatism in Britain, bringing with it increasing numbers of Conservative supporters, and increasing support for conservative policies.
2 There has been a decline of socialism in Britain, bringing disillusion with the Labour party so that the Conservative party has benefitted by default.[2]
3 There has been a rise in the importance of issues not traditionally associated with either the Conservative or the Labour parties, and the Conservatives have proved themselves better able to adapt to the new climate of political opinion, gaining support from voters who are voting for Mrs. Thatcher despite her conservatism rather than because of it.

These hypotheses are not mutually exclusive, and more than one of them might of course be confirmed at the same time. The first is the conventional explanation given by Conservative supporters to explain their party's success. The second is the conventional explanation given by Labour supporters to explain their party's failure. The third is an explanation that deserves careful consideration as an alternative to the first two, because it arises from an analysis of the nature of the fundamental changes that have occurred in the basis of British voting choice over the past twenty years.

The purpose of this essay is to show how changes in British electoral politics are compatible with the hypothesis that the British electorate has not so much moved to the right on the traditional left-right spectrum, but rather moved in a quite different direction that does not register on that spectrum at all ("up," perhaps, as distinct from "down," rather than "right" as distinct from "left"). This suggestion derives from an analysis of the manner in which issues have come to dominate the process of electoral choice in Britain, at the expense of group loyalties that used to be far more important.

THE DECLINE IN THE SOCIAL GROUP BASIS OF BRITISH ELECTORAL CHOICE

It is now a commonplace of political analysis that class does not dominate British electoral choice to the extent that it once did (Crewe, Sarlvik, and Alt, 1977; Franklin, 1984). Franklin (1982, 1985b) has shown that, when various contaminating features are taken into account, the decline turns out not to have been a gradual process, but one that largely occurred in a single step between 1966 and 1970. Heath, Jowell, and Curtice (1985) identify the same step, but deny that there has been a decline of class voting partly because they view the word "decline" as implying a sustained progression.[3] Whatever we call it, the drop has had the effect of changing the basis upon which electoral choice in Britain is made. Franklin (1985a, 1985b) has shown how changes in class voting have been mirrored by changes in issue voting over a twenty-year period, with the dominance of class loyalties at the start of the period giving way to a situation in which issues were roughly twice as important as class by the end of the period.

The move was from what Huckfeldt (1983) describes as a *social group* basis for electoral choice to what he calls a *behavioral contagion* basis. An electorate whose choices are based largely on issue preferences is one with no long-run equilibrium party balance. Any party can gain votes in such a system, and no party is safe from large-scale losses in electoral support. The consequences have been most evident in British elections since 1974, with dramatic gains for the Liberal and

Social Democratic parties, dramatic losses for the Labour party, and dramatic gains followed by equally dramatic losses for the Scottish Nationalist party.

THE END OF THE "COLLECTIVIST AGE"?

But what are the issues that now drive the electoral choices of British voters? How have they changed from the issues that dominated when British electoral choice was characterized by class voting? The best description of the issues that dominated during the period before class voting declined is given by Samuel Beer in his *Modern British Politics* (1965). Beer contrasts the issue basis of postwar Britain with that of an earlier era by showing how both major parties had been agreed since 1950 on a collectivist approach to political problems. Political debate was couched in terms of what the state should do in order to increase material well-being. In this context there was no room for issues that had been an important part of British political discourse in earlier years, such as those dealing with civil liberties and the quality of life (see Greenleaf, 1973:182). This restrictive political debate was a tribute to the success of the Labour party in placing the issue of material well-being squarely at the top of the political agenda and in forcing the Conservative party to compete for power on this basis. Because of the redistributive features of Labour's program, the political debate led to a polarization of issue positions along class lines, and it is clear in retrospect that the resulting group basis for voting choice in turn reinforced the dominance of collectivist issues on the political agenda of the 1950s and early 1960s.

By the late 1960s the dominance of collectivist issues was already under challenge. The question of whether Britain should join the European Economic Community cut across party and class lines, as did some of the major legislative proposals of the 1966 Parliament: divorce reform and abortion reform among others (Richards, 1970). Moreover, the growing problem of colored immigrant communities in British cities, though kept out of Parliament by tacit agreement of the parties, became a "hidden" issue of major importance. Finally, nationalist sentiment in Scotland and Wales, and religious conflict in Northern Ireland, came to seem more important to many inhabitants of those British peripheries than the increasingly sterile political debate within the collectivist mold.

In the election of 1970 these new issue concerns played little overt role. The election was dominated by conventional appeals by the two major parties,[4] and these two parties gained the bulk of votes as in earlier years. But careful analysis can show that the basis of electoral choice was nevertheless quite different in 1970 from that which had been evident in earlier elections. Members of social groupings that had previously shown great loyalty to the party of their class abandoned that loyalty in unprecedented numbers to vote for the other major party (Franklin, 1982, 1985b); and Miller (1980) has suggested that the Tories may well have won the 1970 election on the basis of working-class votes cast on the "hidden" issue of race.

THE PARTICULARIZATION OF VOTER CONCERNS

By 1974 the old collectivist mold of British politics could no longer contain the diversity of issue concerns of importance to British voters. For the first time since the war Labour and Conservatives gained the allegiance of less than half of those eligible to vote. Some of their losses were attributable to lower electoral turnout, but far more important were gains by the Liberal party and by nationalists in Scotland and Wales. Indeed, after the October 1974 election Scotland emerged with a three-party system, with the Scottish Nationalist party commanding a third of Scottish votes.

But the 1974 election did not constitute a realignment. In part this became evident only in retrospect, when the nationalist and Liberal successes of 1974 were not repeated in 1979; but in part it was evident even in 1974. The challenge to collectivism was too diverse to serve as a basis for realignment. Scottish nationalists had little in common with Welsh nationalists (apart from a desire to be rid of the English) and nothing in common with Northern Irish bigots. Liberal supporters had little in common with any of the other minor parties. Moreover, there were other issues of importance in 1974 that did not fall within the purview of existing political parties, but these issues did not provide a basis for new political parties either. Race and the Common Market remained issues of this kind; and women's issues had by then begun to be important too. What happened in Britain between the mid-sixties and the mid-seventies was very similar to what happened in the United States in the same period. Turkel and Tejera (1983) have described American developments in terms of the "particularization" of voting choice in that country, with different voters reacting to different particular concerns, and British developments can be characterized in similar terms. Sometimes (as in 1970 and 1979) the particular concerns of greatest salience may have benefited the Conservatives, but at other times (as in 1974 and 1983) minor parties may have gained from the salience of particular concerns that the traditional parties did not cater to.

These various concerns define groups of voters who hold similar views on particular sets of issues. Table 10.1 illustrates this point by showing the interrelationships (Pearson's r) among twelve issues chosen as representative of all of those measured in the postelection survey of 1983.[5] The relationships are not in general very strong ones,

Table 10.1.   Clusters of "Conservative" Attitudes Based on Intercorrelations (Pearson's r) Between Selected Attitude Variables, 1983.

	CM	TC	PM	PI	W	H	L&O	SE	RE	A	PP
Common market	New right										
Tax cuts	.121										
Private medicine	.108	.158									
Privatize industry	.228	.228	.279								
Welfare*	.136	.199	.186	.263	Old right						
Handouts*	.027	.141	.170	.165	.284						
Law and order	.004	.102	.095	.157	.137	.170					
Sex equality*	.036	.115	.064	.093	.156	.136	.111				
Race equality*	−.092	.126	.091	.082	.182	.176	.152	.276			
Abortion*	.018	.029	.021	.037	.107	.070	.084	.143	.088	Nonpermissive right	
Police powers	−.053	.048	.133	.047	.104	.233	.253	.076	.191	.125	
Pornography*	−.015	−.018	.040	.038	.114	.135	.111	.052	.093	.246	.165

*These variables are coded in the negative, so that positive values correspond to respondents who are against state welfare benefits, state handouts, race equality, sex equality, pornography, or abortion.

emphasizing the particularistic nature of these concerns, but the correlations such as they are do fall into three clear clusters. Within each cluster, all variables are connected by correlations of at least 0.1 in contrast to generally lower correlations with variables in other clusters.[6] These clusters have been characterized in the table as "new right," "old right," and "nonpermissive right." The last of these appears to represent issues that constitute a reaction to the permissive society: abortion, pornography, and the limitations on police powers associated with contemporary concerns for human rights. We will see below that traditional prison sentencing procedures also fall within this group, so that it might well have been termed an "authoritarian" cluster. The central group consists of variables that are traditional components of conservative orthodoxy: a stress on law and order, dislike of state handouts, and suspicion of sexual or racial equality. This was labeled the "old right" cluster in table 10.1, but it might as well have been termed a "paternalistic" cluster. Finally, the left-most group of concerns has been labeled "new right" and contains issues concerned with privatizing industry, promoting private medicine, cutting taxes, and supporting the European Economic Community.

The particular clusters distinguished in the table are somewhat arbitrary. Not only do they appear to shade into one another (antiwelfare belongs in two clusters as already mentioned, and police powers could almost as readily have been placed in the "old right" cluster); but they could also be further subdivided (a line could easily be drawn between order and sex equality, for example, if a correlation of 0.12 rather than 0.1 were to be required as a minimum prerequisite for inclusion in a cluster).

CLEAVAGES AND DIMENSIONALITY
OF THE ISSUE SPACE

Each of the clusters illustrated in table 10.1 contains an implicit cleavage separating those who take a conservative viewpoint from those who take the alternative view. Thus each variable could have been coded in the negative to pick out those respondents who were against the Common Market, in favor of welfare, against arbitrary police powers, and so on. But there is also a second cleavage inherent in table 10.1. This separates variables at the top of the table from those at the bottom. Careful inspection of the correlations shows that the different clusters are not equally distinct but fall into a clear hierarchy, with the first and second clusters being generally positively related, as are the second and third; but relationships between the first and third clusters are generally close to zero and sometimes negative. The gradient involved in this ordering of clusters is not a steep one, and it is an open question whether it would turn out to be sufficient in practice to distinguish supporters of "new" political concerns from others.

The question can be put to the test by placing the policies in relation to each other within a two-dimensional space defined by factor analysis.[7] Figure 10.2 illustrates the possible outcomes of such a test. In the absence of a genuine second dimension, the cleavage structure inherent in the clusters identified in table 10.1 will dominate and leave new issues at opposite poles, old issues at opposite poles, and issues relating to the permissive society at opposite poles, as illustrated in figure 10.2A. Only if there really is a true attitude dimension underlying the ordering of clusters noted in table 10.1 will the attitudes be placed in the manner illustrated in figure 10.2B, with new issues of both left and right placed on the same side of old issues of both left and right. The placement of nonpermissive views at the bottom of figure 10.2B has been parenthesized to indicate that their placement in the presence of a new-old dimension is not (strictly speaking) defined. Permissiveness might very well constitute a third attitude dimension, and the manner in which differences within such a third dimension turn out to project themselves within a two-dimensional space is not critical to our argument.

A TWO-DIMENSIONAL VIEW
OF THE BRITISH ISSUE SPACE

Factor analysis has been employed before to study the issue structure of the British electorate, and four or five clusters of variables have generally been identified as corresponding to different factors (Whiteley, 1983; Chapman, 1985); but if there really are two cleavages underlying the clusters picked out in table 10.1 it will be possible to represent these clusters in terms of only two underlying dimensions: a traditional left-right dimension that corresponds to the political conflict of the collectivist era, and a second dimension that distinguishes collectivist concerns from those of more recent vintage. Figure 10.3 displays such a view of the issue space that existed at the time of the 1983 election,[8] and the placement of issues clearly has more in common with figure 10.2B than with figure 10.2A. Leaving aside two issues that fall close to the center-point of the left-right dimension ("fight wage rises" and "keep troops in Northern Ireland"), the issues of the right fall clearly into the same three clusters that were picked out in table 10.1. On the left, only two clusters are evident, with no clearly delineated group of antipermissive concerns.[9] But it has already been pointed out that no particular significance attaches to the placement of antipermissive issues. What is important is that issues of the new left are placed at some vertical distance *above* collectivist concerns, as are issues of the new right.

The manner in which the cleavages inherent in table 10.1 have been distorted through the presence of the vertical dimension is worthy of close attention. The desire to spend public money on poverty, pensions, and the health service correspond to three issues that fall well down into the old left quadrant, but an issue that might have been seen as a polar opposite to these three ("cut welfare") does not appear in the opposite quadrant but is displaced downward as a consequence of its lack of connection with new right concerns. "No handouts" (a more intemperate version of the same issue position) falls even further

Figure 10.2. Possible Arrangements of Three Attitude Cleavages Within a Two-dimensional Issue Space.

(a) in the absence of a new-old dimension

Permissive Left	New Right
Old Left	Old Right
New Left	Nonpermissive Right

(b) in the presence of a new-old dimension

New Left	New Right
Old Left	Old Right
(Nonpermissive Left)	(Nonpermissive Right)

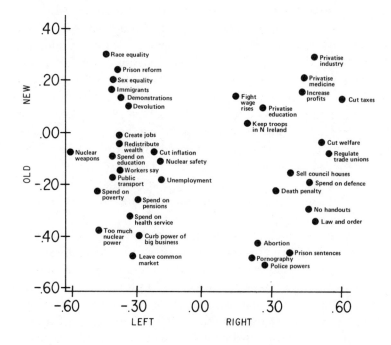

Figure 10.3. The Issue Space of the British Electorate in 1983, Represented in Two Dimensions Defined by Factor Loadings.

down toward the foot of the old right quadrant—ironically even closer to public spending than is "cut welfare." This is not because those who oppose handouts are more likely to spend on poverty than those who would cut welfare payments, but because those who oppose handouts are so much more at odds with those who would privatize industry. What we see in figure 10.3 are differences *within* the left and right that rival in intensity differences *between* the left and right.

Precisely how the vertical dimension should be characterized is not of fundamental importance to this study. By labeling it a "new-old" dimension I hope to be able to focus on its properties rather than its identification. Nevertheless, it is worth pointing out that on the left, at least, the dimension appears to correspond to a cleavage between those who are concerned about civil liberties and those who are not. Although the distinction between old right and new right is not generally thought of in such terms, it is noteworthy that when Mrs. Thatcher lost her bill to remove present restrictions on Sunday trading, as a consequence of a rebellion by no fewer than sixty-eight Tory back-benchers who voted against their government, Mr. Ivor Stanbrook MP commented that "Conservatives are not libertarians" (*Economist*, April 19, 1986: 25). On the other hand, issues at the top of the page also appear to have much in common with the "new populism" mentioned by Samuel Beer in *Britain Against Itself* (1983). In many ways it may be preferable to think of these "new" issues in terms of particularistic concerns, since this characterization covers both the above interpretations, and others as well.

THE ISSUE SPACE BEFORE 1983

That a new-old dimension should be evident in the 1983 issue space lends support to our hypothesis without confirming it. The structure of the 1983 issue space could as well be a consequence as a cause of Mrs. Thatcher's regime. In order to discover whether Mrs. Thatcher's victory in 1979 was due to new issues rather than old it is necessary to establish first that the issue space in 1979 was analogous to that in 1983, and second that within that issue space the increased appeal of the Conservative party was due to policies of the new right rather than of the old. Implicit within this requirement is the need to establish that the same issue space also existed in 1974, so that changes in party support between then and 1979 can be related to policy concerns.

Luckily the British postelection studies of 1974 and 1979 were conducted by the same group of investigators at the University of Essex and contain many questions that are identical in both wording and response coding. In particular (as already indicated), eighteen questions about the respondents' stance on specific issues were asked in identical terms in both surveys. These were subjected to the same form of analysis already reported for 1983, and the results are presented in figure 10.4. There we see an issue space recognizably similar to the one seen in figure 10.3 for 1983 and, more importantly, one that shows only minor changes between the two election years. The number of variables defining the issue space is much reduced, and certain issues that appear high on the right and low on the left-hand side of figure 10.3 are notable by their absence. However, enough variables are similar in both illustrations to suggest that the issue space had changed substantively by 1983 in minor respects. In particular, privatization of schools and industry were not new right policies in 1974, although both variables register quite large movements between then and 1979 in the direction of the locations they are seen to occupy in 1983. Clearly, the new right was in the process of distinguishing itself from the old right during the decade in question, whereas the new left was already well-established.

Figure 10.4. The Issue Space of the British Electorate, 1974 and 1979, Represented in Two Dimensions.

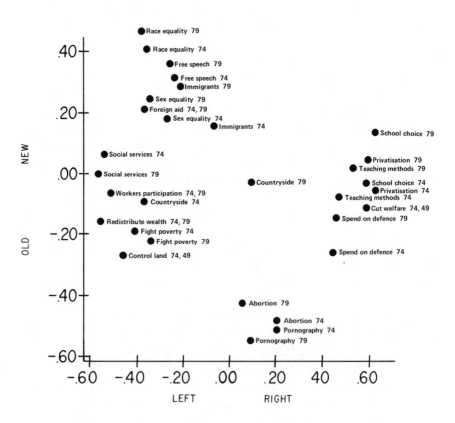

A CRITICAL TEST OF THE SOURCES OF SUPPORT
FOR MRS. THATCHER

Despite minor evolutions, the issue space seems stable enough for us to proceed to the critical question of where in that space did Conservative votes come from in 1979. To recapitulate, our hypothesis requires that the Tory party received increasing support from new right and new left voters compared to their support in 1974, rather than increasing support from the older wings of both parties. In order to provide a direct (if somewhat crude) test of this hypothesis, voters were placed in one of four categories depending on their factor scores on the left-right and new-old dimensions.[10] The proportion of new left, new right, old left, and old right voters giving their support to each party at each election was then determined by cross-tabulation, and changes in these proportions between 1974 and 1979 are presented in table 10.2. There it can be seen that Conservative gains were on average almost three times as great among voters of the new left and new right quadrants as among voters of the old left and old right quadrants. Moreover, the Conservative party actually *lost* support among voters of the old right: abundant proof that Mrs. Thatcher's victory was not a victory of the right as conventionally conceived.

The nature of Conservative ideological support in 1979 is further clarified if we consider the changes that occurred in 1983. Table 10.3 is arranged in the same manner as table 10.2, and again the changes in support that affected the Conservatives can be seen to be concentrated in the new left and new right quadrants. Indeed, on average Conservative voting saw no change among old left and old right supporters. The major battlefield appears to have been the new left quadrant, which is where the Alliance of Liberals and Social Democrats made its greatest gains (in comparison with Liberal votes in 1979) and which is where Conservative support saw its greatest losses. The implication is that Mrs. Thatcher was in competition with the leaders of the Alliance for voters of the new left. In 1979 this was the only quadrant that saw Liberal gains, but Mrs. Thatcher had more appeal to these voters in 1979 (see table 10.2). This reinforces our suggestion that her victory in that election was due rather to a resurgence of particularistic concerns than to a resurgence of conservatism.

All this will become much clearer if we place the parties and their leaders within the issue space defined in previous sections.

MOVEMENT OF PARTIES AND LEADERS WITHIN
THE ISSUE SPACE

The calculations presented in tables 10.2 and 10.3 are somewhat crude. By dichotomizing respondents into those who are members of a particular quadrant and those who are not, one loses all sense of distinctions between locations *within* each quadrant. Thus a respondent barely over the borderline between left and right counts for as much in those tables as one in the ninety-fifth percentile on the left-right factor. One way of placing the parties within the issue space in a more sensitive fashion is to correlate party support with each of the two issue factors and to employ the resulting coefficients as coordinates defining the points in the issue space at which supporters for those parties fall.[11] Figure 10.5 illustrates the results of such an analysis both for groups of respondents defined by their support for particular parties and also for groups defined by their preference for particular leaders.[12] Supporters of parties and leaders are located in 1974, 1979, and 1983, with arrows showing the direction of movement of these groups from one election to the next.

Two caveats need to be made about figure 10.5 before we turn to its interpretation. In the first place it should be noted that while changes in the locations of groups between 1974 and 1979 are strictly interpretable since the issue space in each year is based on an analysis of identical issue variables, changes between 1979 and 1983 should be

Table 10.2.   Changes in the Percentages of Voters in Each Quadrant Giving Support to Major Parties and the Liberals between 1974 and 1979.

	Left	Right	Average
New	Con +7.7 Lib +2.0 Lab −10.7	Con +15.5 Lib −8.1 Lab −5.0	Con +11.6 Lib −8.7 Lab −7.8
Old	Con +8.4 Lib −3.5 Lab −4.6	Con −0.4 Lib −3.0 Lab +5.2	Con +4.0 Lib −3.3 Lab +1.0

Table 10.3.   Changes in the Percentages of Voters in Each Quadrant Giving Support to Major Parties and the Alliance* between 1979 and 1983.

	Left	Right	Average
New	Con −6.6 All +17.2 Lab −11.2	Con −3.5 All +8.7 Lab −3.8	Con −10.1 All +25.9 Lab −16.0
Old	Con −0.9 All +14.8 Lab −14.0	Con +0.9 All +4.2 Lab −5.7	Con +0.0 All +18.8 Lab −19.7

*Liberals in 1979. See note 14.

regarded as no more than indicative since the 1983 issue space, while it appears rather similar to that of earlier years, is derived from an analysis of quite different variables. In the second place it should be noted that two sorts of change are being registered from election to election: both change in the composition of groups supporting parties and leaders, and change in the opinions of continuing members of each group. To the extent that the attitudes of individuals remain constant, the movements we see in figure 10.5 represent changes in the size and composition of electoral support groups. To the extent that the same individuals continue to populate the same support groups, movements represent changes in the issue preferences of those individuals. For our present purposes it is not necessary to distinguish between these two sources of movement.

The first thing to notice about the findings displayed in figure 10.5 is that changes in the attitudes of the supporters of various leaders are much greater than changes in the attitudes of party supporters.[13] Such a contrast is possible because not all supporters of a party necessarily give high ratings to that party's leader. Among party supporters, Labour and Conservative voters show relatively little change in attitude from election to election as compared to Liberal supporters, for whom the greatest movement occurred when they joined with Social Democrats in 1983 to form the Alliance.[14]

But the most interesting feature of figure 10.5 from the viewpoint of the present study is the manner in which the supporters of Mrs. Thatcher, alone among the groups represented there, appear to move progressively in the same direction from election to election; and that

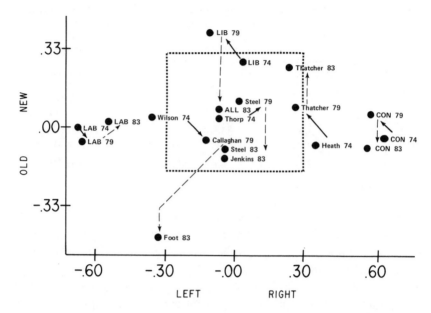

Figure 10.5. Movement of the Supporters of Various Parties (Upper Case) and Leaders (Lower Case) Within the Issue Space Between 1974 and 1979, with Relative Movements to 1983 (broken lines). The 1974 and 1979 issue spaces are comparable, but the 1983 space is not comparable to the other two. Thus positions in 1983 are meaningful in relation to other 1983 positions, but comparisons with earlier years should be regarded as no more than suggestive. Figure 10.6 is on a larger scale than figure 10.5, and the box outlines the area of figure 10.6 in order to make comparisons easier.

direction is upward. It is Mrs. Thatcher, rather than the Conservative party, whose supporters are identifiably members of the new right quadrant of our issue space; and, indeed, while Conservative supporters followed her lead a short distance in 1979, this movement appears to have gone into reverse in the following election when the distance between supporters of Mrs. Thatcher and voters for the Conservative party seems to have increased considerably.

These findings serve to flesh out the bones of the electoral developments that were sketched by means of tables 10.2 and 10.3. The swing to the Conservatives in 1979 did not occur in the old right quadrant. On the contrary, the position of Callaghan's supporters, just across the center line in the old left quadrant, appears to represent a movement by some of the old right away from support for the Conservatives. By contrast, the location of Mrs. Thatcher's supporters of the new right and new left appears to correspond to the major increase in Conservative votes in 1979, which came at the expense of the Liberals in the new right and of Labour in the new left. The increasing distance between Thatcher's supporters and supporters of the Conservative party strongly suggests that many of the voters she attracted to that party did indeed vote for her despite her conservatism rather than because of it.

The change in the ideological complexion of Thatcher's supporters in 1983, by contrast, is not linked to any corresponding increase in Conservative votes. On the contrary, Thatcher lost votes in the new quadrants precisely at the same time as her supporters appear to have become more concentrated there. Of course, changes in support for major parties in 1983 were due mainly to the intervention of the new political alliance between Liberals and Social Democrats; but Alliance gains were mainly at the expense of Conservatives in the new quadrants, in contrast to their inroads into Labour support in the old quadrants (see table 10.3). The essential ambiguity of the Alliance position is seen in the central location of their supporters in figure 10.5.

These developments have contradictory implications for the future of Conservative support. On the one hand, Mrs. Thatcher's supporters are shown to have become increasingly distant from the main body of Conservative voters, who were as close in ideological space to Steel and Jenkins in 1983 as they were to Thatcher. If "Conservatives are not libertarians" to the extent of finding attractions in an alternative platform, traditional conservatives could easily be lost to a more middle-of-the-road appeal (although the libertarian tradition in the Liberal component of the Alliance makes such a development less likely than if the Social Democrats had occupied the central ground alone). On the other hand, the developments of 1983 have left Mrs. Thatcher in virtually sole command of the upper quadrants of the issue space. If she can defend her back (as it were), avoiding deposition and containing defection by adherents to old right values, then she would be in an excellent position to attract back voters of the new right and new left, while Labour and the Alliance slug it out for control of the remaining quadrant.

Such speculations can be made more concrete by examining the positions of various social groups within the issue space.

MOVEMENT OF SOCIAL GROUPS WITHIN
THE ISSUE SPACE

Figure 10.6 is subject to the same caveats as figure 10.5; changes in position between 1979 and 1983 should be regarded as indicative rather than as definitive, and movements involve both changes in the opinions of individuals and changes in the composition of groups. However, in this case, the small amount of change in group composition possible when groups are defined by social characteristics rather than by political preferences implies that most movements have to represent changes in opinion. One new caveat has to be made before the findings displayed in figure 10.6 can be discussed. The scale of the illustration is twice as great as that of previous figures. This enlargement was made necessary by the need to include descriptive titles of each group on the chart and was made possible by the fact that the groups were much less widely dispersed within the issue space than were groups of party supporters. This is clear from the fact that the whole of figure 10.6 fits within the outline box that is superimposed upon figure 10.5. In practice, what this means is that movements illustrated in figure 10.6 are only half as great as shown, in relation to movements illustrated in figure 10.5. So no change in the position of any social group was as great as the movement from Liberal support in 1979 to Alliance support in 1983 (see figure 10.5); and the distance within the issue space moved by young men between 1979 and 1983 is roughly equivalent to the distance moved by Thatcher supporters in the same period.

This illustration is the one upon which orientation of the issue space was based. As mentioned in an earlier footnote, the location of the axes in factor space is quite arbitrary; and, rather than simply accepting the solution that came from the analysis, it was decided to orient our issue space in a more intuitively satisfactory fashion. As a starting point, it was felt that a Conservative or Labour political orientation inherited from parents would provide a baseline running from left to right, from which deviations effected by more recent events could be expected to be random within each group. In fact, when the

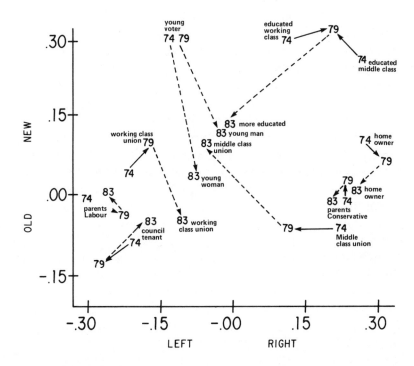

Figure 10.6. Movement of Various Groups of Respondents Within the Issue Space Between 1974 and 1979, with Relative Movements to 1983 (broken lines). See note to figure 10.5.

axes of measurement were orientated so that the group of those whose parents were Labour was located as far to the left as possible in 1974, the group with Conservative parents were found to take up a corresponding position on the right of the issue space. Moreover, this orientation turned out to give appropriate positions for groups currently supporting major parties, as shown in figure 10.5[15]

Figure 10.6 adds considerable detail to our understanding of the nature of support for Thatcher and conservatism. At the top right of the illustration we clearly see the convergence in 1979 of those with more than a minimum education, whether middle class or working class, to a position of maximum support for new right values. On the left-hand side of the illustration we find an almost equivalent position occupied both in 1974 and in 1979 by voters who entered the electorate in 1964 or later.[16] The position of young voters in the upper left of the issue space strongly suggests the presence of Inglehart's "post-bourgeois" values, which were supposed to be held primarily by those brought up during the affluent postwar era (Inglehart, 1971, 1977). If this is the interpretation we make of the new left quadrant, however, it is clear that Inglehart's "silent revolution" was only part of a more general redefinition of the issue space in Britain: post-bourgeois values constitute only one theme in the particularization of British voting concerns. At all events it appears to have been the young (and especially the better-educated among the young) who provided the bulk of the converts to Thatcherism in 1979. Equally, the large change in the location of these groups within the issue space by 1983 suggests that Thatcher suffered her greatest losses in that year within precisely the same groups.

All this is very much as might have been expected, given what we already know about changes in the basis of British voting choice since 1964. It was mainly among young voters that class characteristics first declined as basic determinants of voting choice, and so it was the young voters who provided the bulk of those who abandoned class loyalties in 1970 (Franklin, 1985b:168–170). These were the voters least immunized against change, and these are still the voters showing the most flexibility in their political attitudes. The founding of the Social Democratic party and its alliance with the Liberals provided a new focus for political choice in Britain, and it is hardly surprising that those least immunized against change should have been those most attracted by new programs.

So the convergence of the young and the better-educated (who will in any case tend to be the same individuals, given the vast expansion of the British higher educational system since World War II) to the vicinity of Alliance support (compare figure 10.6 with figure 10.5) was only to be expected. What is much less expected is the extensive migration (over a longer period) of middle-class union members to the same general position. We saw in table 10.3 that the Alliance did make gains from among voters in the old right quadrant, and it seems clear from figure 10.6 that the greatest proportion of these converts will have come from members of middle-class unions. Since this is the group on the right of the issue space most distant from support for Thatcher, their migration toward the position of Alliance voters would tend to support our earlier suggestion that Mrs. Thatcher was vulnerable to defection by members of the old right who no longer felt close to her particularistic concerns. On the other hand, union members may well be the middle-class group most immediately threatened by Mrs. Thatcher's economic policies, and the migration of middle-class union members may thus reflect a concern for pocketbook rather than ideology. On either interpretation, right-wing union members must have had the most collectivist of right-wing concerns, and their estrangement from their original position at the heart of the old right quadrant is the clearest indication we have yet seen of the change in the nature of Tory appeals under Mrs. Thatcher.

SOCIAL GROUPS AND SUPPORT FOR PARTIES IN 1983 AND BEYOND

Viewed in more general terms, the change in the placement of social groups within the issue space between 1974 and 1983 is worthy of careful attention. In 1974 and 1979 social groups were well differentiated, with some groups finding themselves at each of the four corners of the issue space. In 1983, by contrast, groups had become much more concentrated and had moved away from the extremes of new left and new right. In the old left quadrant, council tenants and working-class union members formed a cluster so tight that the groups concerned were placed virtually within sampling error of each other on the basis of their policy preferences. Voters with Labour parents constituted another group whose attitudes were quite close by. On the right side of the issue space, a corresponding cluster linked homeowners with those whose parents had been Conservative. In the new left, but very close to the center of the issue space, a third cluster of social groups consisted of the young, the better-educated, and the middle-class union members already discussed. Essentially the location of social groups had taken on a triangular configuration much closer to the midpoint of the issue space.

We cannot tell whether this triangular configuration will still characterize the locations of groups within the issue space at the time of the next election. The decline of class voting in Britain has freed the members of social groups to change their concerns rapidly in response to new events and new political stimuli. Past experience would lead us to expect the central cluster of groups, at the apex of the triangle, to prove the most fickle.[17] From this point of view the apparent strategy of Alliance leaders in contesting the Labour party for the allegiance of old left voters may well be a sound one. On the other hand, as already mentioned, such a strategy leaves Mrs. Thatcher in virtually sole control of the remaining three quadrants within the issue space. Unless her exposed position loses her further support within the old right this could give her a decisive advantage in a future election.

Unfortunately, the insights that we gain by viewing the British attitude space in two dimensions bring us no closer than we ever were to an ability to predict the future. These insights may, however, help us to make sense of that future when it arrives.

BRITISH POLITICS IN
THE POSTCOLLECTIVIST ERA

Our investigations make it clear that the revival of Conservative fortunes in 1979, and the continuation of Conservative ascendancy in 1983, owe little to the traditional position of the Conservative party at the right of a spectrum of collectivist values. Indeed, the "swing to the right" was no such thing, but a swing upward to a new position on a different dimension. What we call this swing is a matter of no great substantive concern. We can call it a "resurgence of conservatism" if we like, redefining conservatism to encompass the concerns of the new right as we do so. However, such a sleight of hand appears more than somewhat misleading, since resurgence implies the restoration of something that previously existed, whereas Conservative gains in 1979 came primarily from individuals whose concerns were quite different from those of Conservatives in what Samuel Beer called the "collectivist age." Of course, it can be argued that these new values are not new at all, but constitute modern forms of values that conservatives have held in centuries gone by (Norton and Aughey, 1981:30); however, while it is always useful to see contemporary developments in historical perspective, there is little to be gained from knowing that "plus ça change, plus c'est la même chose."

The new dimension in British politics can be characterized in at least three different ways. In the first place it bears a strong resemblance to the "libertarian-collectivist" dimension stressed by Greenleaf

(1973) in his description of the evolution of Tory ideology in this century. In the second place it is clearly linked to the distinction drawn by Ronald Inglehart between bourgeois and post-bourgeois values. In the third place the collectivism of earlier years can be contrasted with a new individualism both of left and right, whose left-wing adherents espouse post-bourgeois values, but whose right-wing adherents are more concerned with economic freedom and business style than personal freedom and self-actualization.[18]

In this chapter we have ducked the question of what to call the new dimension by characterizing it as having to do with particularistic concerns, thus bringing within its purview nationalists and feminists, free-marketeers and libertarians, without having to specify what these groups might have in common. That they have something in common is clear from the fact that members of the new left are attracted by new right policies, and vice versa. So to simply label these concerns as particularistic is to understate their coherence. Even if that coherence rests only in a common opposition to collectivist values, this deserves to be brought out more specifically than is implied by the word "particularist" (which is a horrid word, anyway). "Post-collectivist" is not much better from a euphonious point of view, but at least it implies a degree of coherence missing from the other term, and at least the words make clear its interim status until future research can clarify the nature of this postcollectivist era.

NOTES

1 Studies of the British general elections of October 1974 and of 1979 were conducted at the University of Essex by Ivor Crewe, Bo Sarlvik, James Alt, and David Robertson, and made available by the ESRC Data Archive at that university.

2 The effects of this decline can be viewed either in terms of a failure of the Labour party to stick to socialist principles, or in terms of a failure of the Labour party to realize how far the electorate has moved away from such principles.

3 These authors also raise the question as to whether what we observe is a decline from a previous high level of class voting, or whether the 1964 and 1966 elections were high points in a trendless fluctuation. Since we have no election studies prior to 1964, it is impossible to answer this question with certainty. However, the expectation we have from prior research is not of decline from a plateau of class voting in the years before 1966, but rather a decline that followed a gradual rise that peaked in 1966. Butler and Stokes's (1974) analysis of the evolution of electoral support during the previous fifty years makes it clear that only in 1964 did the Labour party

finally begin to reap the benefit of demographic movements in its favor.

4   Although Heath did propose to take Britain into the Common Market, Labour could not convincingly take issue with this proposal, since Wilson had tried to do the same thing a few years earlier.

5   The data are taken from the 1983 election study conducted at Oxford by Anthony Heath, Roger Jowell, and John Curtice, and made available by the ESCR Data Archive at the University of Essex. The questions were recoded where necessary to ensure that responses would constitute ordinal scales, and inverted where appropriate to ensure that positive values corresponded to a conservative orientation.

6   With some 3,500 cases in this survey, correlations well below 0.1 are highly significant, but not of much substantive interest.

7   Other analyses might have been thought more suitable. Smallest space analysis and multidimensional scaling both impose less structure on the space they identify. However, the structuring properties of factor analysis are precisely such as to make it more difficult for the outcome associated with our hypothesis to manifest itself. So, if successful, the test will be particularly definitive. Moreover, factor analysis provides us with useful tools for subsequent analysis, in the shape of factor scores, for which no analogues exist in smallest space analysis or multidimensional scaling.

8   The variables in table 10.1, together with all other available issue variables treated in a similar manner, were subjected to factor analysis employing the SCSS Conversational Statistical System (Nie, Hull, Franklin, et al., 1980). In such an analysis the orientation of the axes and location of variables at one end or other of each axis are quite arbitrary. Factor analysis will rotate its axes until the dominant factor is aligned as closely as possible with the largest number of variables. Introduce a different mix of variables, and the axes will be oriented differently, even though the same variables are placed in the same positions relative to each other. In the present instance the factor solution with varimax rotation was subjected to further manipulation in which the axes were reoriented manually in such a way as to ensure that the first (left-right) dimension distinguished traditional collectivist concerns on an axis that ran horizontally across the page (the precise considerations that determined the extent of reorientation will be described below), and on this dimension variables were placed on the side corresponding to the weight of opinion expressed in the survey. Thus "cut welfare" is represented as a right-wing concern, rather than being represented in terms of "increase welfare" on the left, because more respondents sought cuts than increases. "Spend on poverty" is represented on the left of the page for analogous reasons. Issues that correspond to postcollectivist concerns are represented at the upper end of the second factor no matter what was the weight of opinion in their regard (many particularistic concerns gain little support, but are no less "new" for that). Antipermissive concerns were coded so as to appear in the lower quadrants. Clearly, the placement of issues is still somewhat arbitrary; and it is important to bear in mind that any issue can be represented in the negative at the same coordinates in the opposite quadrant of figure 10.3.

9   This may be due to the fact that few such issues have yet been defined. "Curb power

of big business" is arguably the only such issue represented in figure 10.3, and it is noteworthy that it is placed well down on the left.

10   Before conducting this computation the factors were reoriented to match the reorientation of figures 10.3 and 10.4 by adding 0.3 (New) to the left-right factor and 0.3 (Right) to the old-new factor: quantities calculated to displace the factors anticlockwise by approximately 30 degrees (in 1983 the constant employed was 0.4, designed to yield a reorientation of approximately 40 degrees for reasons that will be described below). The resulting measures were not again normalized, so that the number of respondents in each quadrant varies slightly from election to election; but this does not appear to affect the findings.

11   In order to place groups of respondents in this fashion, members of some group (Conservative voters, for example) are coded 1 on a variable representing that group, and all others are coded 0. Employing correlations between such variables and the factors defining the issue space then constitutes an identical procedure to the one employed in figures 10.3 and 10.4, since correlations between issue position and each factor provide precisely the loadings that were employed to place the issues within each space. By analyzing the relationships after the factors have been established, however, we avoid contaminating the issue space with cleavages between the groups that interest us. Had group variables been included in the factor analyses along with issue variables, relationships among the groups would have contributed to the structuring of the space. A factor space based both on group cleavages and issues would not have constituted an issue space properly so called.

12   Note that the status of the leadership support groups is not quite the same as that of the party support groups, since it is possible to favor a leader without voting for him or her (and, indeed, to favor more than one leader at a time).

13   Indeed, changes in the locations of Labour and Conservative party supporters are so slight as to fall virtually within the bounds of sampling error. The placement of Conservative and Labour supporters at the far right and left of the issue space should be regarded as confirmation that the correct degree of reorientation was applied to the axes of the issue space, although the extent of reorientation was in fact determined by other considerations (see below).

14   It is not possible to meaningfully distinguish Liberal voters as a separate group in 1983, since Liberal identifiers were asked to support Social Democratic candidates where no Liberal candidate was standing. Moreover, many Alliance supporters were unable to recall whether the candidate they voted for was in fact a Liberal.

15   The additional reorientation given to the 1983 issue space in order to place groups defined by parental party support in positions comparable to those occupied by the same groups in earlier years turned out also to minimize the sum of movements between 1979 and 1983. So the placement of 1983 group (and party) positions relative to those of 1979 is optimal in two respects. The minimizing of movement between 1979 and 1983 serves to provide some confidence that movements registered by broken lines in figure 10.6 are real.

16   The choice of cutting point to differentiate young voters from others is based upon analysis conducted in Franklin (1975b: chapter 7). There it was found that three

cohorts could be clearly distinguished within the British electorate after 1970: those who came of age before Labour's rise to major party status, those who came of age during the years of Labour's ascendancy, and those who came of age after the election of 1959. By 1983 very few of the first group (born before 1906) remained in the electorate, and to simplify our discussions they have been ignored in this analysis.

17 Not only do these consist largely of the young, but also we know that those who have recently changed their opinions are those most liable to future change.

18 In the American context the contrast would be between Flower Children and Yuppies, and the fact that some of the former have turned into the latter may be easier to understand in the context of a two-dimensional view of value change.

REFERENCES

Beer, S. H. 1965. *Modern British Politics*. London: Faber.

———. 1983. *Britain Against Itself*. London: Faber.

Butler, D. E., and D. Stokes. 1974. *Political Change in Britain: The Evolution of Electoral Choice*, 2nd ed. London: Macmillan.

Campbell, A., P. E. Converse, W. E. Miller, and D. E. Stokes. 1960. *The American Voter*. New York: John Wiley and Sons.

Chapman, J. 1985. "Marital Status, Sex, and the Formation of Political Attitudes in Adult Life." *Political Studies* 33: 592–609.

Crewe, I., B. Sarlvik, and J. Alt. 1977. "Partisan Dealignment in Britain 1964–1974." *British Journal of Political Science* 7: 129–90.

Franklin, M. N. 1982. "Demographic and Political Components in the Decline of British Class Voting." *Electoral Studies* 1: 195–220.

———. 1984. "How the Decline of Class Voting Opened the Way to Radical Change in British Politics." *British Journal of Political Science* 14: 437–62.

———. 1985a. "Assessing the Rise of Issue Voting in British Elections Since 1964." *Electoral Studies* 4: 36–55.

———. 1985b. *The Decline of Class Voting in Britain: Changes in the Basis of Electoral Choice 1964–1983*. Oxford: Oxford University Press.

Greenleaf, W. H. 1973. "The Character of British Conservatism." In R. Benewick, R. Berki, and B. Parkeh, eds., *Knowledge and Belief in Politics: The Problem of Ideology*. London: Allen and Unwin, pp. 177–212.

Heath, A., R. Jowell, and J. Curtice. 1985. *How Britain Votes*. Oxford: Pergamon Press.

Huckfeldt, R. R. 1983. "The Social Context of Political Change: Durability, Volatility, and Social Influence." *American Political Science Review* 77: 929–44.

Inglehart, R. 1971. "The Silent Revolution in Europe: Inter-generational Change in Post-Industrial Societies." *American Political Science Review* 65: 991–1017.

———. 1977. *The Silent Revolution: Changing Values and Political Styles Among Western Publics*. Princeton, N.J.: Princeton University Press.

Miller, W. L. 1980. "What Was the Profit in Following the Crowd? The Effectiveness of Party Strategies on Immigration and Devolution." *British Journal of Political Science* 10: 15–38.

————. 1984. "There Was No Alternative: The British General Election of 1983." *Parliamentary Affairs* 37: 364–84.

Nie, N., C. H. Hull, M. N. Franklin, et al. 1980. *A User's Guide to the scss Conversational System.* New York: McGraw-Hill.

Norton, P., and A. Aughey. 1981. *Conservatives and Conservatism.* London: Temple Smith.

Richards, P. 1970. *Parliament and Conscience.* London: J. M. Dent.

Turkel, P. S., and F. Tejera. 1983. "Changing Patterns in American Voting Behavior, 1914–1980." *Public Opinion Quarterly* 47: 143–302.

Whiteley, P. 1983. *The Labour Party in Crisis.* London: Methuen.

11. Conservatism in Canada: The Ideological Impact of the 1984 Election

ROGER GIBBINS

On September 4, 1984, the Progressive Conservative party swept to power in Canada by capturing 211 of the 282 seats in the House of Commons, a national landslide almost unprecedented in Canadian political history.[1] The event was significant not only because of the magnitude of the Conservative win but also because of the rarity with which governments change hands in Canada. In the fifty years preceding the 1984 election, for example, the Liberal party held national office for all but seven years, winning eleven of fifteen general elections. A single Liberal leader, Pierre Trudeau, was prime minister for all but nine months between 1968 and 1984, a period during which the United States experienced the presidencies of Lyndon Johnson, Richard Nixon, Gerald Ford, Jimmy Carter, and Ronald Reagan.[2] When one considers that each of these presidents, with the possible exception of Ford, has been associated with a distinctive episode in American political life —one can talk, for example, of the "Nixon years" or the "Carter presidency"—it is clear that political change in Canada proceeds at a much slower rate than it does in the United States.

The 1984 election thus enables us to address an elementary question, yet one that has been elusive in Canada given the rarity of electoral change. Simply put, do political parties matter?[3] More specifically, are changes in government associated with significant changes in the direction of public policy, or are modern governments so constrained that little policy change is to be expected in the wake of electoral change? Given the policy constraints imposed by the international environment (e.g., interest rates in the United States and world oil prices) that apply with particular force in the Canadian case, the inertia of established public policies (e.g., Medicare, family allowances, and basic Social Security programs), the widely assumed although difficult to demonstrate bureaucratic resistance to change,[4] the political opposition to change by entrenched groups identified with existing public policies, and the financial limitations imposed by an escalating national debt, it is reasonable to ask whether parties can be expected to steer the ship of state or merely go along for the ride, bailing frantically when holes appear and hoping that fortune will smile when reefs are approached.

To put the same question in somewhat different terms, we might ask which adjustment is the greater: the adjustment of governments and their related public policies when a new party assumes the reins of power, or the adjustment that parties themselves must undergo when moving from the wilds of the opposition to the corridors of power. The thesis here is that the more pronounced change associated with the 1984 election was in the nature of the federal Progressive Conservative party rather than in the nature of Canadian public policy. To the extent that the change in government was associated with a significant shift in public policy, that shift reflected changes in the national political agenda that had been set in motion several years earlier by the proclamation of the Constitution Act on April 17, 1982.

This analysis incorporates two principal components. The first looks at changes in public policy that can be associated with the 1984 election. Here the analysis is a broad one that looks at changes in the national political agenda rather than at more specific policy initiatives. The second component deals with changes that have occurred in the Progressive Conservative party itself, changes that both predate and stem from the 1984 election. In both cases, it must be stressed, my focus is on the federal Progressive Conservative *party;* a more philosophical discussion of conservatism in Canada falls largely beyond the scope of this analysis and certainly beyond the competency of the author.

CHANGES IN THE NATIONAL
POLITICAL AGENDA

By the fall of 1987 the Progressive Conservative party had been in office for over three years. One might expect then that enough time has elapsed for the policy profile of the new government to emerge. In fact, however, it is very difficult to get a policy "fix" on Brian Mulroney's Conservative government. Rather than moving dramatically to reshape Canadian public policy, the government has exercised a degree of caution, even timidity, somewhat at odds with the Conservatives' overwhelming electoral mandate.[5] During the first two years of its mandate the government seemed to be repeatedly derailed by minor disputes and crises, of which the tempest-in-a-chowder-bowl over tainted tuna fish was only one.

Inadvertently or not, the personal style of Prime Minister Mulroney has played an important role in obscuring the policy thrust of the new government. In the 1984 campaign Mulroney emphasized the politics of national reconciliation in an understandable although by no means unusual attempt to draw all groups under the Tory umbrella. Since the campaign, ideological purity has been shunned whenever it threatens elements of the new Tory coalition, a situation that provides the rule rather than the exception. Mulroney's approach, moreover, has been felt within his party as much as it has been felt within the broader political arena. Mulroney has not moved to impose any particular ideological vision on his party, caucus, or cabinet, leaving conservative hard-liners, political moderates, and Red Tories to jockey for positions and influence. There has been at best a modest shake-up in the public service, and thus at best a modest infusion of new ideas and initiatives. New recruits to the prime minister's inner circle, including such figures as Senator Norman Atkins, Senator Lowell Murray, and former PC party president Dalton Camp, have been primarily political fixers and electoral strategists rather than torchbearers for any ideological crusade.

It should also be noted that the Progressive Conservative government has worked vigorously to keep the previous Liberal government, or at least the sins of that government and its leader, before the public. While this strategy may have useful electoral payoffs, it again blurs public perceptions of the new government and its policy perspectives.

Our attention is focused more on what the Liberals did wrong than on what the Conservatives might be doing differently and right.

The budget introduced by the Progressive Conservatives in February 1986 illustrates the problems that arise in trying to chart the policy course of the government. The 1986 budget can best be described as an incrementalist document that stayed well clear of dramatic policy change. The growth of the federal deficit was cut, but the cut was a modest and perhaps even illusionary one that may not be realized if the government's rather optimistic projections on interest rates and oil prices are not met. Taxes were raised, but only at the margins. Spending cuts, although not deep cuts, were imposed on departments, but few details were released in the budget, and the cuts were imposed across the board in a way that did not signal any significant adjustment in the government's spending priorities. Major social programs were left untouched, and reform of the tax system was not addressed, although it appears to be the subject of ongoing study within the government. All this, it should be stressed, is not to suggest that the budget was necessarily a bad one; I am more than happy to leave evaluations of the budget to others.[6] The budget, however, provides little evidence that the course of national public policy has departed significantly from that followed by the previous Liberal administrations.

Given these difficulties, one might conclude that the Progressive Conservatives have done little to change the course of public policy, and thus that the basic question posed by this analysis can be readily answered—a change in party does not lead to substantive changes in public policy. Such a conclusion, however, would be premature, for the Conservatives have played an important although not decisive role in recasting the Canadian political agenda.

The Liberal National Agenda

From the mid-1960s through the early 1980s the Canadian political agenda was dominated by four *interrelated* issues or sets of issues:

- National unity or, more specifically, linguistic conflict and the place of Quebec within the Canadian federal state.
- Intergovernmental conflict between the federal and provincial governments, conflict expressed through the developing institutions of executive federalism and brought to a climax in the search for a new

constitutional framework for the Canadian federal state.
- Regional conflict between the central Canadian heartland and the regional peripheries to the west and east, conflict that centered on but which was by no means limited to the ownership and control of natural resources.
- Canadian-American relations and the reaction of Canadian nationalists to the intrusion of American economic and cultural influence in Canada.

During the Trudeau years these issues did not exist in isolation but wrapped around one another like eels in a barrel. Together, they formed a "Liberal national agenda" that set Canada apart from other Western democracies and, to a significant degree, isolated the Canadian political system from ideological currents that were loose in Britain and the United States.[7]

Whether this agenda was to some degree imposed on the country by the Liberal party to its own electoral advantage, or whether it was the inevitable result of institutional deficiencies and structural change, is not an issue that can be satisfactorily addressed here. While I would argue that it is too harsh a judgment to conclude that the Liberals fanned the flames of national discord in pursuit of victory at the polls, the issue remains a contentious one. Much less contentious is the conclusion that the Liberal agenda, and in particular its stress on national unity, posed a major electoral hurdle to the Conservative party. It was difficult, and indeed ultimately impossible, for the Conservatives to find a national unity position on Quebec that was distinguishable from that of the Liberal party and its leader, Pierre Trudeau.[8] (It also proved difficult for the Conservatives to agree among themselves on national unity issues.) Thus as long as national unity dominated the national agenda, the Conservatives labored under an electoral disadvantage, forced to offer support, no matter how reluctantly, to the language policies and constitutional position of the Liberal government.

The Liberal national agenda was brought to a head in the eighteen months between the June 1980 Quebec referendum on sovereignty association and the November 1981 constitutional accord reached between the federal government and nine of the ten provinces. During that time Canadians experienced intense political debate over what can best be seen as a distinctive and even idiosyncratic set of national issues. (Patriation of the constitution, for example, was an issue that Americans would be unlikely to comprehend much less follow.) However, with the defeat of the Quebec sovereignty association referendum and the proclamation of the Constitution Act, that debate tailed off dramatically. While the act did little to resolve underlying structural conflicts and institutional deficiencies within the political system, did not except by its silence address the place of Quebec within the constitutional framework of the Canadian federal state, and did little if anything to shore up western Canada's position within the national community (Gibbins, 1983:119–32), it nevertheless fundamentally altered the tone and substance of political debate in Canada.

Wearied by the prolonged constitutional conflict leading up to the act, both governments and citizens turned their attention to an increasingly distressed Canadian economy. For the moment at least, the national unity issue had been successfully addressed, intergovernmental conflict decreased once constitutional negotiations had been laid to rest,[9] and, somewhat paradoxically, regional conflict in the west was eased by the growing concern of westerners about an acute downturn in the regional economy that took some of the wind out of the sails of an assortment of embryonic separatist organizations. Here it should also be noted that the Charter of Rights and Freedoms gave a new prominence to a host of issues—gender equality, aboriginal rights, minority language rights, the rights of the handicapped, Sunday closings, etc.—that, prior to 1982, had played a much more modest role in Canadian political life. In short, then, the Constitution Act *set in motion a fundamental transformation of the national political agenda*, a transformation that was accelerated by the landslide election of the Mulroney Conservatives in September 1984.

The New Progressive Conservative National Agenda

The new Progressive Conservative government, and the new Conservative leader in particular, made a concerted effort to move away from the Liberal agenda of the last two decades, an agenda that had posed a serious obstacle to the Conservatives at the polls. Prime Minister Mulroney moved quickly and successfully to improve the tone of intergovernmental relations, a move that was facilitated initially by the presence of Conservative governments in seven of the ten provinces and the total absence of Liberal provincial governments.[10] The Conservatives also moved to dismantle those aspects of the National Energy Program that had particularly disturbed western Canadians and to put in place an offshore energy agreement with Newfoundland, moves that signaled a heightened sensitivity on the part of the national government to the concerns of the regional peripheries. Unfinished constitutional business—Senate reform and Quebec's refusal to recognize formally the Constitution Act of 1982—slid down and, at least in the former case, off the government's agenda.

The only component of the old agenda that was retained intact by Mulroney was the prominence that had been assigned to Quebec in the national scheme of things, although even here the previous concern over national unity had been greatly reduced by the referendum defeat and the constitutional settlement and was reduced even further when the Parti Quebecois government was swept from office by the provincial Liberals in late 1985. One prime minister from Quebec—Pierre Trudeau—had been replaced by another prime minister from Quebec —Brian Mulroney—with the two individuals differing at the margins if at all in their orientations toward Quebec, bilingualism, and the basic parameters of the Canadian federal state and political community. Whereas in the early 1980s the federal government's sensitivity to Quebec had been assured by the presence of seventy-four Quebec Liberal MPs on the government side of the House, that sensitivity was assured in the mid-1980s by the presence of fifty-eight Progressive Conservative MPs from Quebec on the government benches. In this case, then, the orientation of the national *government* to Quebec and Quebec-related issues was not changed by the 1984 election. The fundamental transformation has occurred instead *within* the Progressive Conservative party, which for the first time since 1958 has a sizable contingent of Quebec MPs, and which for the first time ever has a Quebec leader. The Progressive Conservative party has been brought into line with the Liberal experience, rather than the national government having to adjust to a party that, until 1984, had lacked a significant French-Canadian and Quebec component.

In the 1984 election campaign the Progressive Conservatives paid lip service to a number of issues that can best be seen as arrows in the quiver of any opposition party, arrows that are used in opposition but discarded when in office. Thus, for example, the Conservatives pledged to increase defense spending and to strengthen Canada's military contribution to the Western Alliance, pledges that to this point have borne no fruit. The patronage practices of the Liberal government came under harsh attack but have been replaced by indistinguishable Conservative practices. The escalating national debt was attacked, but, as noted above, the efforts of the Conservative government to curtail the deficit have been less than vigorous. The size of the federal bureaucracy was attacked on the campaign trail, but to date that bureaucracy has been pruned not with a machete but with tweezers. Prior to the election the Conservatives attacked what they saw as the excessive influence of the prime minister's office and the "presidentialization" of national politics, but since the election the P.M.O. has been expanded even further and Mr. Mulroney's dominance over his cabinet and caucus colleagues easily rivals that of Mr. Trudeau. In these respects, then, the Progressive Conservatives were not seeking any fundamental transformation of the national political agenda but were rather employing the standard electoral tools used by opposition parties since time immemorial, charging that the incumbent Liberals were too corrupt, too careless with the public's money, too mired in bureaucratic red tape, too dominated by the prime minister and his minions, and too lax about international threats.

A more important transformation came with the Conservatives' attempt to move economic issues to the top of the national agenda. Correctly sensing that the Liberals had done well in the past by concentrating on noneconomic issues, such as those entangled in the question of national unity, but had performed poorly on the economic front, the Conservatives tried to restructure the national agenda so as to move traditionally "Liberal issues" down the agenda while at the same time elevating economic issues on which the Liberals had performed poorly and on which, hopefully, a Progressive Conservative government would perform well. Thus we had Mulroney's stress on "jobs, jobs, and jobs." This shift in emphasis was particularly well received by Conservative MPs from the west who, perhaps more than any other group of parliamentarians, had chaffed under the Liberals' emphasis on "national unity" and their near avoidance of economic concerns.

It is important to stress, however, just which economic issues the Progressive Conservatives have tried to move up the political agenda. As noted above, the government has *not* launched any sweeping attack on the national debt. Canada's social security net has been declared a "sacred trust" by Mr. Mulroney, and even the more radical elements within the Progressive Conservative caucus have shown little inclination to significantly alter the web of programs and public expenditures that make up the Canadian welfare state. Nor has the government embraced the economic neoconservatism that has marked the Thatcher and Reagan administrations in Britain and the United States. There has been no major push toward economic deregulation, tax reform, the selling of crown corporations, or the privatization of social services. While there may have been modest incremental moves in these directions, they fall well short of providing any firm evidence that the Mulroney Conservatives have jumped, or have any intention of jumping, upon the neoconservative bandwagon that has been rumbling through Britain and the United States.

It is free trade that has come to be *flagship of the new Conservative national agenda*.[11] This is not to say, of course, that the Progressive Conservative free trade initiative is unprecedented. Free trade initiatives by first the Liberal opposition and then by the Liberal government of Sir Wilfrid Laurier played a central role in the 1891 and 1911 general elections, and the pros and cons of free trade have been a staple of academic analysis and political discourse for decades. In 1985 the Macdonald Royal Commission on the Economic Union and Development Prospects for Canada, a commission appointed by Liberal prime minister Pierre Trudeau, strongly endorsed free trade with the United States.[12] Indeed, the Macdonald recommendations can be seen as the final step in a general Liberal retreat from the economic nationalism of the 1970s, a retreat that reflected a growing Canadian reliance on bilateral trade with the United States despite repeated attempts to strengthen trade with Europe and the Pacific rim, the decline of American direct investment in Canada to the point where American ownership of the Canadian economy waned as a political concern, and the general weakening of the Canadian national economy during the recession of the early 1980s. Thus when Mulroney declared, shortly after the 1984 election, that Canada was once again "open for business" and that American investment would be welcome, he was riding with rather than in opposition to the policy tide in Canada. When the Conservative government turned the Foreign

Investment Review Agency into Investment Canada, and changed its mandate from that of screening foreign investment to encouraging foreign investment, the government was completing a gutting of FIRA that had been well under way during the final years of the Trudeau government.

However, with respect to the free trade initiative, the Mulroney government has clearly broken with the economic policies of the previous Liberal government by formally launching free trade negotiations with the United States. While the Liberal and Conservative governments may have been responding to the same economic imperatives, only the latter has nailed the free trade colors to the mast of the Canadian ship of state. In this sense, the Mulroney government stands apart from its predecessor. Yet I would argue that the free trade initiative and, in a more general sense, the quest for a closer relationship with the United States are less radical departures for the government of Canada than they are for the Progressive Conservative party. To demonstrate this point, we must turn to a more detailed look at the Progressive Conservative party and the impact of the 1984 election on that party.

CHANGES IN THE PROGRESSIVE
CONSERVATIVE PARTY

The Conservative party[13] was initially forged by Sir John A. Macdonald to serve as a barrier to American political influence in Canada. Macdonald, who led the Conservatives from their pre-Confederation birth in the 1850s through to his death in 1891, and who was the leading actor on the Canadian political stage throughout that period, was noted for his articulate and effective opposition to American political influence. When free trade with the United States was proposed by the Liberals in the 1891 election campaign, it was Macdonald who championed opposition to free trade and, in so doing, led the Conservatives to victory. An essential component of Macdonald's argument in that campaign was that free trade posed as much a political threat to Canada as it did an economic threat. Free trade, it was argued, would erode Canada's British connection and thus launch the country down the slippery slope toward assimilation into the larger and not necessarily better society to the south. This was a course that Macdonald rejected, declaring that "a British subject I was born and a British subject I will die."

The Macdonald Conservatives, it should be stressed, did not oppose American economic investment in Canada. Indeed, in 1879 the Conservatives fashioned the high tariffs of the National Policy that were designed in part to encourage American investment and that laid the foundations for the modern branch-plant economy in Canada. To the Conservatives, and to Canadians more broadly at the time, the ownership of industry was of little consequence compared to its location north or south of the American border. Thus the National Policy was designed to protect Canadian jobs by providing tariff protection to industries located north of the border, be they Canadian-owned or American branch plants. It is the tariff legacy of Macdonald's National Policy that the Mulroney free trade initiative seeks to erase.

The identification of the Conservatives with opposition to American influence did not end with Macdonald. When free trade was again proposed prior to the 1911 general election, this time by the Liberal government of Sir Wilfrid Laurier, it was the Conservatives once more who rallied opposition to free trade under the banner of "No Truck or Trade with the Yankees" and who defeated the Liberals at the polls. Here it should be noted that the Conservatives' opposition to free trade soured that party's relationship with the western Canadian agrarian community, which enthusiastically supported free trade. The prairie west was to remain an electoral wasteland for the Conservatives until Saskatchewan's John Diefenbaker swept the west and the nation for the Tories in 1958. Diefenbaker, however, who was noted for both his Macdonald-like anti-Americanism and his abrasive relationship with American President John F. Kennedy, who with less than affection described Diefenbaker as "that bastard," won the west despite his orientation toward the United States rather than because of it.

While Canadian party politics defy most sweeping generalizations, it seems fair to say that until recent years it has been the Conservatives that have acted as the main counterweight to American influence in Canadian political life, while the Liberals have been more prone to endorse a continentalist approach.[14] However, the role played by such Conservative leaders as Macdonald and Diefenbaker has been emphatically rejected by the current leader of the party and prime minister of Canada. In breaking with both his own party's past and the legacy of the Trudeau government, Mulroney has moved boldly to improve Canadian-American relations and to establish a close personal working relationship between himself and the American president. The contrast between Trudeau's rather abrasive relationship with American presidents and that of the current prime minister is dramatic and has been emphasized by Mulroney who has made every effort to alert the American president to shifts in Canadian public policy, to offer prompt support for American foreign policy initiatives, to offer sympathy and condolences for American misfortunes, and to enhance the personal relationship between the two governments. The contrast was underscored by the 1985 "Shamrock Summit" in Quebec City where Prime Minister Mulroney and President Reagan shared the stage to sing Irish melodies. It is hard, indeed impossible, to imagine a similar scene occurring between Trudeau and Reagan or, for that matter, between any past combination of Canadian prime ministers and American presidents.

The roots of Mulroney's shift toward the United States are undoubtedly complex and open to considerable speculation. The shift may reflect Mulroney's corporate background with the multinational Iron Ore Company and, within that background, the impact of frequent, sociable, and profitable transactions across the international border. (In a crude sense, free trade may be seen as the Iron Ore Company experience writ large.) It may also reflect an effective electoral exploitation of a Liberal weakness, for there is little question that Canadian-American relations were abrasive during much of the Trudeau period. It should also be noted that Canadian nationalism reached a peak during the late 1960s and early 1970s. As I have written elsewhere:

> It was not coincidental . . . that Canadian nationalism bloomed when the American society was experiencing deep distress. Looking south at racial conflict, a spiraling crime rate, deteriorating cities, student unrest, and the horror of the Viet Nam war, and drawing upon radical American critiques of the American society, Canadians could objectively and somewhat smugly conclude that it was better to live in Canada than in the United States. Canada

looked good and Canadian nationalism was strong because things looked so much worse in the United States.[15]

By the mid-1980s, however, the American society had regained much of its vitality and the American economy was enjoying robust health. Canada no longer fared as well in Canadian-American comparisons, and the rationality of Canadian nationalism came into question. Finally, we should not neglect the possibility that free trade negotiations were seen as a necessity given the evolution of world trade patterns and the growth of protectionist sentiment in the United States, a possibility that is supported by the research findings and recommendations of the Macdonald Royal Commission.

From the perspective of this analysis, however, the interesting point to note is how little Mulroney was constrained by the historical traditions of his party. There are a number of reasons for this lack of constraint. First, Mulroney's own roots in the Progressive Conservative party, or at the very least in the parliamentary wing of that party, are relatively shallow. He assumed the party's leadership in 1983 and only subsequently was elected to the House of Commons. Second, the 1984 Conservative landslide swept into office a large number of neophyte Conservative MPs who, like their leader, have shallow roots within the party.[16] Third, the most experienced bloc of MPs within the Conservative caucus were those from western Canada, MPs who were the most removed in geography and spirit from the early ideological roots of the Conservative party among the United Empire Loyalists of Upper Canada. Fourth, the Tory legacy of the past few decades, a legacy marked by electoral failure and intraparty conflict, has been a tempting one for contemporary Tories to put aside. Fifth, and perhaps of greatest importance, Mulroney's party roots are planted in Quebec where the philosophical soil of Tory tradition has been shallow in the extreme.

This last point should not suggest that small-c conservatism has been absent from the Quebec political scene. In fact, conservatism has had a rich philosophical, religious, and literary tradition in Quebec and has found forceful political articulation through pre-1960s nationalist movements and, in the electoral arena, through the Union Nationale. That conservatism, however, failed to find expression in, or to shape, the Conservative party per se. In part this has been because, since the mid-1930s, there has not been a provincial Conservative party to shape.[17] Federally, the Conservative party was all but shut out of Quebec since the conscription crisis of the First World War, although the 1958 election provided a brief respite. As a consequence, there was no party conduit through which the currents of Quebec conservatism could contribute to the broader stream of Conservative/conservative thought in Canada. The ideological foundations of the national Conservative party, such as they were, were shaped almost exclusively by the English Canadian political experience.

Mulroney's Quebec background, then, did not expose him to the Conservative traditions of Macdonald and Diefenbaker. He was unconstrained by his party's past because, in the Quebec setting, his party had no past. He was thus able to fashion the Conservative party in his own image without reference to party norms and traditions. Nor was he constrained by his fellow Conservative MPs from Quebec whose roots within the party were even shallower than his own and whose exposure to English Canadian Conservatism and conservatism was even briefer. In short, then, the combination of Mulroney's leadership and the results of the 1984 election cast the Progressive Conservative party adrift from whatever ideological moorings its past and traditions had provided.

FUTURE DIRECTIONS

If the Progressive Conservatives have indeed been cut loose from the traditions and values that, if ever so gently, guided their party in the past, it is appropriate to ask where the party might find a new set of moorings. One possibility is that they may be found in the neoconservative thought and practice that have been so manifest in both Britain and the United States.

Certainly in the past the Progressive Conservatives have been open to British experience, and the current free trade initiative would appear to throw open the doors to ideological influence from the United States.[18] As noted above, however, there has been little evidence to date that the Progressive Conservatives have embraced neoconservatism, that the ideological spectrum has shifted to the right,[20] or that the terms of political debate are much different than they were in the sunset years of the Trudeau government. While one can sift through the first two years of Conservative government and find some evidence of movement toward deregulation and privatization, the steps have been both modest and hesitant. Interestingly, it appears that Mulroney himself may be the major barrier to the influx of neoconservative thought from the United States and Britain. Mulroney's leadership style—his relentless search for the political center, national reconciliation, and public acceptance—is ill-suited for ideological warfare. There is also little in Mulroney's leadership style or political background to indicate any strong interest in ideological or philosophical issues. In a sense, and in the best sense, Mulroney can be seen as Canada's new William Lyon Mackenzie King, albeit with more personal style and attractiveness than King was able to muster.

There is little likelihood that the Progressive Conservative government will adopt the aggressive international posture that has been characteristic of the conservative administrations of Margaret Thatcher and Ronald Reagan; a Canadian-style Falklands War or midnight raid on Libya is difficult to imagine. International saber rattling has not been the Canadian style or indeed a Canadian option in the past, and it appears to have no attraction to the incumbent prime minister who, in the Commonwealth debate over sanctions for South Africa, has followed the same diplomatic highroad trod by Canadian prime ministers before him. More practically, Mulroney's free trade initiative precludes a more aggressive stance toward the United States, although here it should be noted that the Conservative government has been quietly resistant to American border claims in the Alaska panhandle. In short, a more bellicose international stance is ruled out by Canada's geographical location, by her traditional diplomatic style, by her middle-power status within the international community, and, by all indications, by the personal inclination, values, and style of the prime minister.

Thus the argument that I would make, and an argument that appears to be supported by the actions and inactions of the Progressive Conservative government to date, is that Mulroney is unlikely to emerge as the neoconservative standard-bearer in Canadian political life. Given the tight control that he has been able to exert over his own party, his reluctance to play this role makes it unlikely that the party itself will become the ideological vessel of neoconservatism on the Canadian scene.

If the Progressive Conservatives fail to find ideological moorings in neoconservative thought emanating from Britain and the United States, then perhaps the party may drift toward regional moorings instead, staking its electoral fortunes on the defense of regional interests. However, this is a difficult and potentially suicidal role for a national party to play. The Progressive Conservatives, moreover, lack a regional heartland. While Atlantic Canada has provided strong electoral support for the party, it lacks sufficient demographic weight to moor a national party. The newfound Conservative support in Quebec appears to be an uncertain commodity, and the continued courtship of Quebec may be a source of internal strain in a party still unaccustomed to straddling the linguistic divide. Ontario could provide a heartland of sorts, but the recent success of the provincial Liberals in Ontario and the historical volatility of the Ontario electorate make the province an insecure anchor.

Since 1958 the Canadian west has provided the Conservative heartland and, in the short run at least, this role may continue. It is more likely, however, that the longer-term impact of the 1984 election will be that the west will have gained greater influence in the national government while at the same time having seen its influence in the national Progressive Conservative party decline, that the west may have gained a government but lost the Conservatives as a regional champion. In the four federal elections held between 1972 and 1980, western Canadian MPs constituted 44 percent of the federal Tory caucus, while following the 1984 election this proportion dropped to only 27 percent.[20]

It may be the case that the Conservatives will not need an ideological or regional mooring, that the Progressive Conservatives can mimic the Liberal success of old by appealing to a broad regional and ideological cross-section of the Canadian electorate, that they can become all things to all people. If, however, the Conservatives do become the new Liberal party, this brings us back to the opening question of this analysis — do parties matter? Did the 1984 election have a greater impact on the government of Canada, faced as it was with a new set of partisan masters, or did it have a greater impact on those new masters, forced to adjust their party to a new governmental and electoral reality?

The tentative conclusion must be the latter, that the changes stemming from the 1984 election have been more pronounced within the Progressive Conservative party than they have been within the government of Canada or for Canadian public policy. There is no question that the 1984 election fundamentally changed the political face of Canada—the Conservatives are now the dominant political force on the national stage, the once-dominant federal Liberals are in disarray while their provincial counterparts are enjoying an unexpected revival, and a new national agenda is shaping political discourse. However, the 1984 election did not dramatically change the face of Canadian public policy. It was without question a landmark election, but not because it signified the resurgence of conservatism in this particular Anglo-American democracy.

NOTES

1   By winning 208 seats in 1958 the Progressive Conservatives captured a greater proportion of the seats in a somewhat smaller House of Commons.

2   The tenure of provincial governments has been equally impressive. To cite but a few examples, the Conservative party held office in Ontario from 1941 to 1985, the Social Credit party has held office in British Columbia for all but three years since 1952, and Alberta has experienced only a single change in government since 1935, and only three changes since the province was created in 1905.

3   Needless to say, this is not an original question. For an answer that reaches far beyond the constraints of this analysis, see Richard Rose, *Do Parties Make a Difference?*, 2d ed. (Chatham, N.J.: Chatham House, 1985).

4   For a discussion of this point in the Canadian context, see Glen Edward Armstrong, *Senior Public Servants and Government Transition in Canada*, unpublished M.A. thesis, University of Calgary, 1986.

5   It might be argued, however, that the size of the Conservative landslide encouraged the new government to move cautiously. Given the party's apparently overwhelming mandate and the fact that the Liberal party was all but shattered by the election results, ministers in the new government apparently could look ahead to an extended term of office. If this was in fact the calculus that dictated caution, it is one that has been severely challenged by recent public opinion polls indicating broad public dissatisfaction with the national government and a resurgent Liberal party on both the federal and provincial fronts.

6   From the Conservative perspective, perhaps the most appropriate analogy for the 1986 budget exercise can be drawn from *Gulliver's Travels*. The Mulroney government, pinned down as it was by the constraints of existing program commitments and the financial limitations of the national debt, was denied the maneuverability needed to pursue a new policy course.

7   For an extended discussion of this point, see Roger Gibbins, "Free Trade in Political Ideologies: The Impact of Reduced Trade Barriers on Canadian Political Life," paper presented to the Canadian Studies Section, Western Social Sciences Association annual meetings, Reno, Nevada, April 25, 1986.

8 Under the leadership of Robert Stanfield, the Progressive Conservatives adopted a "special status" option for Quebec in which the Quebec provincial government would be able to exercise legislative responsibilities denied to other provincial governments. This option failed to satisfy Quebec nationalists, attracted the wrath of other provincial governments, opened up cleavages within the Conservative parliamentary caucus, and was intellectually savaged by Trudeau.

9 Section 37 of the Constitution Act set in motion an ongoing series of First Ministers' Conferences on aboriginal constitutional issues. These conferences, however, have not provided a showcase for federal-provincial conflict in part because the issues under discussion are of little salience to the national or provincial electorates, and in part because the major lines of cleavage have been between the aboriginal and nonaboriginal representatives at the conferences rather than between the federal and provincial governments themselves.

10 Since that time Liberal governments have been elected in Ontario, Prince Edward Island, and Quebec.

11 This is not to deny the possibility that free trade could turn out to be a new *arena* within which the regional, intergovernmental, and nationalist elements of the old Liberal national agenda are once again brought into play.

12 For the commission's economic analysis of free trade issue, see John Whalley, Research Coordinator, *Canada-United States Free Trade* (Toronto: University of Toronto Press in cooperation with the Royal Commission on the Economic Union and Development Prospects for Canada, 1985).

13 Prior to 1942 the Progressive Conservative party was simply the Conservative Party of Canada. The *Progressive* was added when the Progressive premier of Manitoba, John Bracken, was recruited as party leader in an ill-fated effort to enhance the party's electoral prospects in western Canada.

14 For a discussion of this point, see W. Christian and C. Campbell, *Political Parties and Ideologies in Canada*, 2d ed. (Toronto: McGraw-Hill Ryerson, 1983).

15 Roger Gibbins, *Conflict and Unity: An Introduction to Canadian Political Life* (Toronto: Methuen, 1985), p. 216.

16 This is particularly true of the fifty-eight Conservative members from Quebec, of whom only Roch Lasalle has had any significant parliamentary experience.

17 In the mid-1930s the provincial Conservatives were absorbed in the coalition that created the Union Nationale. With the success of the latter party in the 1936 election, the Conservatives ceased to exist as a provincial party and have not fielded candidates in provincial elections.

18 For an expanded discussion of this point see Gibbins, "Free Trade in Political Ideologies."

19 For the contrary argument that there has indeed been a rightward shift in the ideological spectrum, see Michael J. Prince, ed., *How Ottawa Spends, 1986–87: Tracking the Tories* (Toronto: Methuen, 1986), pp. 1–60.

20 For an expanded discussion of this point, see Roger Gibbins, "Alberta: Looking Back, Looking Forward," in Peter M. Leslie, ed., *Canada: The State of the Federation, 1985* (Kingston: Institute of Intergovernmental Relations, 1985), p. 126.

REFERENCES

Armstrong, Glen Edward. 1986. "Senior Public Servants and Government Transition in Canada," unpublished M.A. Thesis, University of Calgary.

Christian, W., and C. Campbell. 1983. *Political Parties and Ideologies in Canada*, 2d ed. Toronto: McGraw-Hill Ryerson.

Gibbins, Roger. 1983. "Constitutional Politics and the West." In Keith Banting and Richard Simeon, eds., *Had No One Cheered: Federalism, Democracy and the Constitution Act*. Toronto: Methuen, pp. 119–32.

Gibbins, Roger. 1985. *Conflict and Unity: An Introduction to Canadian Political Life*. Toronto: Methuen, p. 216.

Gibbins, Roger. 1985. "Alberta: Looking Back, Looking Forward." In Peter M. Leslie, ed., *Canada: The State of the Federation*. Kingston: Institute of Intergovernmental Relations, p. 126.

Prince, Michael J., ed. 1986. *How Ottawa Spends, 1986–87: Tracking the Tories*. Toronto: Methuen, pp. 1–60.

Rose, Richard. 1985. *Do Parties Make a Difference?* 2d ed. Chatham, N.J.: Chatham House.

Whalley, John. 1985. *Canada-United States Free Trade*. Toronto: University of Toronto Press.

12. Canada's Tory Tide: Electoral Change and Partisan Instability in the 1980s

ALLAN KORNBERG AND HAROLD D. CLARKE

INTRODUCTION

The evening of September 4, 1984, was not a pleasant one for John Turner, erstwhile crown prince of the Liberal party, and Canada's recently anointed prime minister. It grew worse as it wore on as the electoral returns from the Atlantic provinces suggested, and those from Quebec confirmed, that the Liberals might be in for a defeat as great as the one they suffered in 1958 when their party won only 34 percent of the popular vote and 18 percent of the then 265 parliamentary seats. Although by gaining 50 percent of the vote and 75 percent (211 of 282) of the parliamentary seats the Brian Mulroney-led Progressive Conservatives virtually duplicated their 1958 victory (see figures 12.1 and 12.2), the initial focus of political cognoscenti was more on the "whys" of the Liberal defeat than on the "hows" of the Conservative victory. Most of their explanations centered on tactical errors committed by Mr. Turner, as, for example, his agreement to a number of high-level patronage appointments foisted on him by his predecessor, long-time Prime Minister Pierre Elliott Trudeau; his midcampaign dismissal of top operatives and their replacement by some of the old guard associated with his predecessor; his agreement to a nationally televised debate in *French* with the fluently bilingual Mulroney; and his gaffe in patting the derriere of the president of the national Liberal party organization. (The lady was not amused!)

More systematic analyses indicated that neither the magnitude of the Liberal defeat nor the Conservative victory could be fully explained

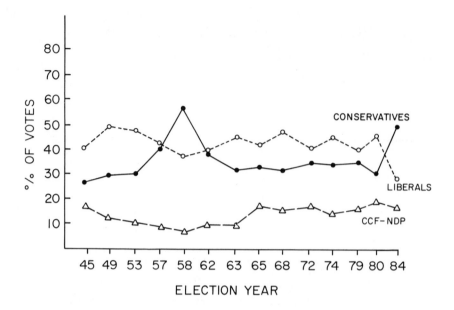

Figure 12.1. Percentage of Votes Won by Liberal, Conservative, and CCF/New Democratic Parties in Federal Elections, 1945–1984.

by those or other tactical errors Turner may have committed. For one thing, only in Quebec was his party more highly regarded by the electorate than he was. For another, for the first time in history the Conservatives won the largest share of the popular vote in every province, from Newfoundland to British Columbia. Indeed, so great was their margin of victory among every major group in the country (see appendix A) that the question arises whether the 1984 election was "critical" in the sense of signaling a basic redistribution of partisan forces in Canada. That is the principal question addressed in this chapter.

We begin by considering the two principal short-term forces influencing voting decisions in the 1984 election and indicate how the constellation of those forces strongly favored the Conservatives. We then discuss the properties of psychological identification with a political party, the principal long-term force influencing the vote in Canada as in Britain and the United States. Our chief data sources are two studies of the national electorate, the first conducted in the autumn of

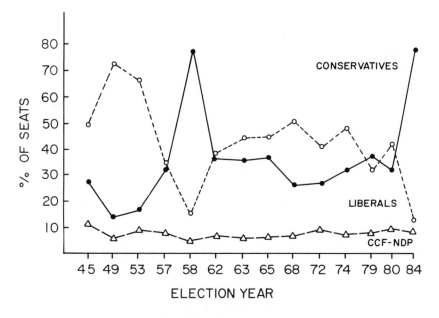

Figure 12.2. Percentage of Seats Won by Liberal, Conservative, and CCF/New Democratic Parties in Federal Elections, 1945–1984.

1983, the second immediately following the 1984 federal election.[1] We also will employ data derived from previous studies of national elections as well as panel data embedded in the 1980, 1983, and 1984 studies.[2] It will be argued that outcomes of federal elections in the past twenty years have been strongly influenced by short-term forces. And, despite the overwhelming Conservative victory, the 1984 election was no different. Moreover, the results of a national survey conducted a year afterward strongly suggest that the electorate currently is "up for grabs" and that the outcome of the next election will depend largely on whether the constellation of short-term forces at the time favors the present Conservative government or the Liberal opposition.

LEADER AND ISSUE ORIENTATIONS

Data derived from our 1984 postelection study of 1,928 respondents reveal that in the struggle for the hearts and minds of the Canadian public, Mr. Mulroney and the Conservatives won in a walk. With respect to their hearts, "feeling" thermometer scores[3] revealed that the average Canadian had a much higher regard for Brian Mulroney and his party than for the Liberal and New Democratic parties and their respective leaders, John Turner and Edward Broadbent. Mulroney ran 5 percentage points ahead of the New Democratic party leader and 14 points ahead of the Liberal leader. His party did even better, topping the NDP by 14 points and the Liberals by 13 (see table 12.1). As noted above, only in Quebec did Mr. Turner run behind his party. However, he did not run far enough ahead in other areas of the country to justify the hopes invested in him by the hundreds of Liberal insiders who for years had treated him as a kind of "emperor in exile" and who had pleaded with him to enter the leadership fight when Mr. Trudeau announced his intention to return to private life. Those Liberal insiders and their counterparts in the Conservative party seemed convinced that the public was so disaffected from both Pierre Trudeau and Joe Clark that neither party might win an election if they remained at the helms. Table 12.1 indicates the Conservatives gained far more from their change of leaders than did the Liberals. Nationwide, Mulroney was fully 14 percentage points more popular than his predecessor. In sharp contrast, Turner actually ran slightly behind Trudeau, even though Trudeau—then at the nadir of his popularity after some fifteen years as prime minister—was regarded as a veritable prince of darkness in the western half of the country.

In a previous study (Clarke and Kornberg, 1985) we demonstrated

Table 12.1.   Party and Party Leader Affect by Region, 1984.

	Atlantic	Quebec French	Quebec other	Ontario	Prairies	BC	Canada	eta
Turner	50	45	45	47	49	51	47	.10*
Liberal party	50	48	48	44	40	42	45	.15*
Mulroney	61	62	60	61	63	58	61	.07
Conservative party	59	60	57	61	62	58	60	.08
Broadbent	55	51	54	60	54	56	56	.15*
NDP party	49	47	47	46	45	46	46	.06
Trudeau	54	58	62	47	38	40	49	.26*
Clark	47	48	45	46	53	49	48	.13*

*$p \leq .05$.

that the economy was very much on the minds of average Canadians long before the 1984 election. More specifically, in a study conducted in the autumn of 1983 we found that half the public felt the government's handling of the economy left much to be desired; 36 percent said the government had done a "poor job," and an additional 15 percent stated it had done a "very poor job." Only 3 percent credited the government with doing a "very good job" of managing the economy. People were just as critical of the *condition* of the economy. In response to the question, "How well is the economy doing these days?," 54 percent said "not very." And, in answer to the question, "On the whole do you think the economy generally has gotten better, worse, or stayed about the same over the last three or four years?," 48 percent said it was worse, whereas only 23 percent felt it had improved.

The long periods of Liberal government since World War II (i.e., 1945–57, 1963–79, and 1980–84) and structural factors such as a Westminster-model parliament and cohesive parliamentary parties make it a virtual certainty that large numbers of Canadians would associate the federal government with the Liberal party. As a consequence, not only did a majority of the public feel the "economy" was the most important issue in the campaign and that the Conservatives were closest to them on that issue, most of those making this judgment probably also blamed the Liberal party qua government for the economy's impoverished state.

As if that were not enough, table 12.2 indicates—except for "social" and "human rights" issues—that a majority of the public stated the Conservatives were closest to them on each major category of issues mentioned. Moreover, even on social and human rights issues the Conservatives were more often seen as "closer" than either the Liberals or New Democrats. It seems clear, therefore, that the overwhelming Conservative victory in 1984 was firmly grounded in two principal short-term factors—orientations toward issues and party leaders.

PARTISANSHIP AND VOTING

Each of the last three federal elections has produced a turnover of government; a 1979 minority Conservative government holding 48 percent of Parliament's seats gave way the following year to a majority

Table 12.2.   Party Closest on Most Important Issue, 1984 Federal Election
(in percentages).

Issue category	Most important issue**	Party closest				
		Liberal	Conservative	NDP	Other	None
Economic +	60	14	53	21	x	12
Confederation (New Constitution, National Unity)	2	9	53	3	18	16
Resource	1	11	70	9	5	6
Social	2	30	39	15	0	16
Other:						
Leaders, leadership	3	17	58	11	0	14
Parties, electoral change	10	4	77	10	0	9
Human rights, womens' rights	3	14	44	31	0	12
Honesty in government	1	10	61	16	5	8
Miscellaneous	3	*	*	*	*	*
None, don't know	22	—	—	—	—	—
All issues		13	55	18	1	12

x less than 0.5 percent.
* varies by specific issue.
+ includes unemployment—31, state of the economy—22%, deficits and currency—
5%, inflation—1%, taxes—1%.
** multiple response, $N = 1,928$.

Liberal administration with 52 percent of the seats, which was turned
out four years later when voters elected 75 percent of the Conservative
candidates offered them. These simple facts alone suggest that a model
of voting behavior in contemporary Canada should give pride of place
to short-term forces. Research conducted over the past decade bears
this out (e.g., Clarke et al., 1979, 1984; Clark and Stewart, 1985, 1987).
Both electoral choices and more general orientations toward political
parties are subject to considerable individual-level instability strongly
associated with feelings about party leaders and evaluations of party
performance on salient issues. These findings have important implications for how one conceptualizes partisanship in Canada, and, in turn,
how one constructs a model of the vote.

Introduced as a concept in the 1950s (Belknap and Campbell,

1952), initial studies of party identification conducted in the United States (Campbell et al., 1954, 1960) indicated that it was a powerful, long-term force determining electoral choice. However, subsequent studies in non-American settings questioned both the generality of those findings and the cross-national applicability of the concept itself (e.g., Budge et al., 1976). In Canada, 1965 and 1968 national election surveys conducted by John Meisel and associates indicated that the correlation between partisan attachments and the vote was extremely strong: indeed, so strong as to raise the possibility that responses to the party identification questions were simply alternative reports of current voting intentions.[4] Relatedly, questions about prior partisan ties revealed that many voters (upward of one-third of the electorate) recalled changing their federal party identification one or more times. Their findings led Meisel (1975: 67) and others to seriously question whether party identification in Canada is characterized by high levels of inter- and intragenerational stability.

The ensuing debate on the properties of partisanship in Canada (see Sniderman et al., 1984; Jenson, 1975, 1976) was hampered by a lack of panel data with which to accurately measure the stability of party identification. Such data are now available and they confirm that partisan instability is indeed widespread (e.g., LeDuc et al., 1984; Clarke and Stewart, 1985). The data on the distribution of federal party identifications in the 1980−83 and 1983−84 panels are illustrative.[5] Between 1980 and 1983, 15.6 percent of a national panel of voters changed their federal party identification; 13.7 percent either stopped being or became nonidentifiers; 66.9 percent maintained their identifications; and the remaining 3.8 percent were stable nonidentifiers (see table 12.3).[6] The electorate was even more volatile in the 1983−84 interval, indicating that Meisel and his colleagues were correct in arguing that for many Canadians the reality of party identification contrasts sharply with the model of stable intra- and intergenerational partisan ties depicted in the early American studies.

There are reasons to believe, however, that for a sizable proportion of the Canadian electorate party identifications *do* represent something more than current vote intentions. Evidence for this assertion comes from two sources. One is the results of political socialization studies (e.g., Kornberg, Smith, and Bromley, 1969; Kornberg, Smith, and Clarke, 1979: chap. 2; Van Loon and Whittington, 1981: 120−134)

Table 12.3.   Patterns of Federal Party Identification, 1980–83 and 1983–84.

A. *1980–83 Panel*

1983 party identification	1980 party identification				
	Liberal	Conservative	NDP	SC	None
Liberal	32.3	1.1	2.0	0.0	1.6
Conservative	6.9	26.2	2.3	0.3	3.9
NDP	0.6	0.7	8.1	0.0	0.4
SC	0.4	0.7	0.3	0.3	0.0
None	3.5	1.7	1.8	0.8	3.8/100*

V = .51, p≤.001.

B. *1983–84 Panel*

1984 party identification	1983 party identification				
	Liberal	Conservative	NDP	SC	None
Liberal	27.2	4.0	0.7	0.1	1.7
Conservative	6.1	29.0	1.1	1.1	3.4
NDP	2.3	2.3	7.2	0.2	2.3
SC	0.0	0.1	0.0	0.2	0.4
None	1.4	2.4	0.8	0.2	5.7/100*

V = .48, p≤.001.
*All percentages computed in terms of total panel N's: 1980–83 = 834, 1983–84 = 1,294, missing data and "other" parties excluded.

which indicate that a majority of Canadians form party attachments during childhood or adolescence, in many cases before developing an awareness of or interest in other aspects of political life. Although a substantial proportion of persons in these studies reported one or more subsequent changes in party identification, others stated that they always had identified with the same party. This latter finding is consistent with the results of similar questions asked in a series of national election studies. Although there are problems involved in using recall data to generate precise estimates of partisan stability over the life cycle, the magnitudes of the percentages of "recalled stable identifiers" are large enough to make us reasonably confident that a substantial minority of Canadians *always* have identified with the same party. Relatedly, although the available panel studies obviously cover only a segment of the life cycle, their data on rates of partisan stability reveal that a majority of the electorate are stable identifiers over a period of several years. Although this evidence is not definitive, it indicates that the orientations of many Canadians toward political parties are reasonably durable and long-standing.

The second piece of evidence is that the correlation between party identification and the vote, although always strong in each of several national election surveys, is imperfect and varies in predictable ways. In 1984, for example, short-term issue and party leader forces strongly favored the Conservatives (see above). If there is a long-term component to party identification, therefore, one would expect voting defection rates to be notably greater among Liberal and NDP identifiers than among Conservative partisans. This, in fact, is the case. As table 12.4 indicates, only 6 percent of 1984 Tory identifiers failed to vote for their party in 1984. Comparable percentages for NDP and Liberal identifiers were 16 percent and 37 percent, respectively (see table 12.4). This is precisely the pattern one would expect in an electoral context in which short-term forces were running strongly against one party (the Liberals) and strongly in favor of another (the Conservatives). Party identification in Canada, then, although sensitive to short-term forces, also has a longer-term component.

Still another property of party identification in Canada is its inconsistency across levels of the federal system. Survey data repeatedly have documented that large numbers of voters fail to identify with the same party in federal and provincial politics (e.g., Clarke et al., 1979, 1984; Kornberg and Clarke, 1982; Clarke and Stewart, 1987). Some people have an identification at one level only; others identify with party "A" at the federal level and party "B" at the provincial level. Again, the 1984 data are typical. They show that 59 percent identified with the same federal and provincial party, 11 percent identified at one level only, and 24 percent were directionally inconsistent (i.e., "split" identifiers). In addition, 6 percent were nonidentifiers at both levels. Moreover, although patterns of party identification at the two levels varied across provinces, in every case there were sizable numbers of voters whose identifications differed across levels. Research indicates that this kind of partisan inconsistency influences the stability of party identification and electoral choice (e.g., Clarke et al., 1979; Clarke and Stewart, 1987) and that a model of federal or provincial voting

Table 12.4.   Vote in 1984 Federal Election by Federal Party Identification.

1984 vote	Party identification, 1984*				
	Liberal	Conservative	NDP	Other	None
Liberal	63%	2%	3%	4%	16%
Conservative	26	94	12	24	57
NDP	11	2	84	9	21
Other	1	2	1	63	6
(N)	(515)	(661)	(246)	(26)	(116)

$V = .64$, $p \leq .001$.
*1984 national cross-sectional sample.

behavior should incorporate information about the distribution of partisan identifications at both levels of the federal system.

Clearly, then, a model of federal voting behavior in 1984 should include variables capturing such short-term forces as orientations toward important issues and party leaders as well as measures of federal and provincial party identifications. The likelihood that identifications both influence and are influenced by issue and leader effects complicates the construction of such a model, however. One approach might be to develop a nonrecursive model comparable to those proposed by Jackson (1975) or Page and Jones (1979) in their studies of American voting behavior. However, the estimation of the linkages in such a model would be problematic, because it is difficult to specify theoretically meaningful and statistically powerful exogenous variables (Fiorina, 1981: 188; Beck, 1986: 261). A convenient alternative would be to employ our panel data and hypothesize that the 1984 vote was a function of federal and provincial party identifications measured earlier (i.e., in 1983), as well as issue and leader orientations measured in 1984. By so doing the two identification variables would become summary measures of long- and short-term forces operating at earlier points in time. This use of party identification data would be consistent with the assumption that partisanship in Canada has both long- and short-term components and would be analogous to the conceptualization of party identification proposed by Fiorina in his influential "retrospective voting" theory of electoral choice (1981: 90). For Fiorina, party identification in the United States can be modeled as follows:

$$PID_t = PID_{t-1} + \Sigma bRE_t + u_t$$

where: PID_t = party identification at time t

PID_{t-1} = party identification at time t−1

RE_t = retrospective evaluations of government performance at time t

u_t = error term

In the analyses that follow we will treat retrospective evaluations of governmental performance as one component of a larger set of forces influencing party identification.

The full model of the vote, then, may be stated as:

$$V_t = a + b_1 FPID_{t-1} + b_2 PPID_{t-1} + \sum_{i=3}^{k} b_i IS_t + \sum_{i=k+1}^{n} b_i LE_t + u_t$$

where: V_t = vote for Liberals, Conservatives, or NDP at time t

a = constant

$FPID_{t-1}$ = federal party identification at time t−1

$PPID_{t-1}$ = provincial party identification at time t−1

IS_t = issue orientation variable(s) at time t

LE_t = leader orientation variable(s) at time t

u_t = error term

As noted above, we measured affect for party leaders with 100-point "feeling" thermometers. In addition to entering measures of affect for Mulroney, Turner, and Broadbent in each of the analyses, in one instance we also included a measure of feelings about the former Liberal leader, Pierre Trudeau. We did so largely because feelings about him were so varied and intense, and his departure from political life so recent, that it was reasonable to assume they had a significant impact on the vote.

Issue orientations were measured in two ways. The first was whether a respondent stated unemployment or another economic issue was "most important." The second was a measure of a respondent's perception of which party, if any, was closest on the issue judged most important, with the measure weighted for its perceived importance in his/her voting decision.[7] The use of the first "unmediated" economic measure is consonant with the reward-punishment theory of voting, arguing that in times of economic adversity macroeconomic issues will work *against* governing and *for* opposition parties. The use of the second was prompted by Butler and Stokes's specification (1976) of the conditions under which issue voting occurs: namely, that even salient issues must be linked in the voters' minds with a particular political party. We have employed a probit analysis because the dependent variables are dichotomies (e.g., voted Conservative, voted for another party). The results (see table 12.5) indicate that a majority of the predictor variables performed as expected. In all nine cases federal party identifications exerted significant effects, and (except in the Conservative case) *provincial* party identifications also were significant.

Party leader effects also were pervasive, with fully twenty-seven of the thirty leader variables entered in the nine analyses achieving statistical significance. In every case the direction of the effect was consistent with expectations. Thus, for example, in the analysis of Liberal voting, feelings about the current Liberal leader, Turner, were positively associated with the likelihood of a Liberal vote, whereas those about Mulroney and Broadbent were negatively related. Similarly, positive affect for Trudeau had a significant positive impact on Liberal voting and a negative impact on Conservative voting, but had no effect on NDP voting.

Table 12.5.   Probit Analyses of Voting in 1984 Federal Election.

A. *Including economic issues*

| | 1984 Vote | | |
	Liberal	Conservative	NDP
Constant	−.96*	−.72*	−.67*
Federal party identification, 1983	.32*	.31*	.31*
Provincial party identification, 1983	.14*	−.00	.13*
Party leader affect:			
Turner	.03*	−.02*	−.01*
Mulroney	−.02*	.05*	−.03*
Broadbent	−.01*	−.02*	.04*
Economic issue mentioned:			
Unemployment	−.03	−.02	.09
Other	.05	−.14	.12
Estimated R^2	.65	.69	.63
rho	.60	.63	.57
% correctly predicted	86	82	88

B. *Including party closest most important issue*

	Liberal	1984 Vote Conservative	NDP
Constant	−.79*	−.58*	−.78*
Federal party identification, 1983	.27*	.24*	.25*
Provincial party identification, 1983	.13*	−.00	.11*
Party leader affect:			
Turner	.03*	−.02*	−.00
Mulroney	−.01*	.04*	−.02*
Broadbent	−.01*	−.02*	.03*
Party closest, most important issue	.37*	.35*	.33*
Estimated R^2	.71	.76	.68
rho	.68	.72	.69
% correctly predicted	88	86	91

C. *Including party closest most important issue*
and Trudeau affect

	Liberal	1984 Vote Conservative	NDP
Constant	−1.48*	−.27	−.81*
Federal party identification, 1983	.18*	.18*	.25*
Provincial party identification, 1983	.10*	−.00	.11*
Party leader affect:			
Turner	.03*	−.02*	−.00
Mulroney	−.01*	.04*	−.02*
Broadbent	−.01*	−.02*	.03*
Trudeau	.02*	−.01*	.00
Party closest, most important issue	.36*	.35*	.33*
Estimated R^2	.74	.78	.68
rho	.72	.73	.69
% correctly predicted	90	87	91

*$p \leqslant .05$.

Note: 1983−84 national panel; weighted $N = 1,126$.

As in previous studies of Canadian voting (Clarke et al., 1984; Clarke and Zuk, 1986) unmediated economic variables did not have significant effects, a seeming paradox given their claimed importance by voters, but supportive of previous research which indicates that economic issues—however important—do not "speak for themselves." Instead, they must be linked to parties. When they were, they and other issues had strong effects, indeed. In every case, voters who preferred a particular party on an issue they regarded as most important were more likely to vote for that party, net of all other considerations (see table 12.5, panels B and C). Consequently, the Conservatives' commanding lead on economic and other issues enabled them to translate these *individual-level* effects into handsome *aggregate* gains.

The impact of issues can be further clarified if we construct a scenario in which we assign plausible values to other predictor variables. In this scenario we will assume that a voter identified "fairly strongly" at both levels of government (in 1983) with the party whose vote is being analyzed. Substantively, this amounts to assuming that prior (long- and short-term) forces predispose a person to vote for that party. We also will assume that a voter's feelings about the three current party leaders and the former Liberal leader are "typical" of the electorate as a whole (i.e., the leader variables are set equal to their means). Given these values, we can determine how the probabilities of voting for the three parties were influenced by changes in party-issue linkages and variations in the perceived importance of issues on the vote decision.

In all three cases the likelihood of voting for a party increased markedly as the issue variable changed (see table 12.6). The Conservative case is illustrative. The probability of voting Conservative in 1984 was slightly less than .5 if a voter either was unable to select a party closest to him/her on a most important issue or failed to recognize the existence of such an issue. However, if the voter selected the Conservatives and believed the issue was very important in deciding for whom to vote, the probability of voting Conservative increased to .84. In contrast, for voters selecting *another* party on the most important issue, the probability of a Tory vote was well under .5 and fell to only .14 if the issue was judged very important in the voting decision. As table 12.6 reveals, Liberal and NDP vote probabilities are roughly comparable to those just described. In both cases, however, the vote probability was well over .5 (.59 for the Liberals, .64 for the NDP) *if* the voter was "neutral" toward issues, and rose to .75 or greater if the party in question was closest on a most important issue. The problem for both

Table 12.6.   Voting Probabilities Given Various Assumptions About Party
Closest on Most Important Election Issue.

Evaluation of party and most important issue	Probability of voting		
	Liberal	Conservative	NDP
Favor party, issue very important for vote	.92	.84	.91
Favor party, issue not very important for vote	.75	.61	.76
Do not favor any party or no important issue	.59	.48	.64
Favor other party, issue not very important for vote	.48	.34	.52
Favor other party, issue very important for vote	.22	.14	.27

Note: Probabilities have been calculated assuming voter identifies "fairly strongly" with
party in question at federal and provincial levels and has levels of party leader affect
equal to mean for all voters.

the Liberals and the New Democrats was that in 1984 the electorate
contained precious few such voters!

A similar exercise can be conducted for leader effects. Consider a
scenario in which a voter identified with the Liberal party "fairly
strongly" at both levels of government, favored the Conservatives on
the most important election issue but discounted the importance of
the issue in his/her voting decision, and had average affect for Mulroney
and Turner (i.e., thermometer scores of 61 for Mulroney and 46 for
Turner). Under those conditions, the probability of a Liberal vote was
.48 (see table 12.6). If, however, the scores for Mulroney and Turner
were reversed, the probability of voting Liberal increased to .70 and
the probability of voting Conservative dropped from .61 to .28.

These changes in vote probabilities under varying assumptions
about party leader popularity suggest the potential influence of leader
effects in Canadian federal elections. They tempt one to conclude that
if only the voters had found Turner more appealing, the outcome of
the 1984 election might have been different. Undoubtedly, a stronger
showing by their new leader would have helped the Liberal cause.
One must remember, however, that the scenario above assumes the
voter was a "fairly strong" Liberal identifier: a valid assumption
throughout the 1965–80 period when the party had a large plurality
of federal party identifiers, but no longer the case in 1984 (see table 12.7
below). Consequently, it is doubtful that even a highly regarded John
Turner would have been sufficient, by himself, to stem the Tory tide.

Table 12.7.   Direction of Federal Party Identification in Canada, 1965–85.

Party identification	1965[a]	1968[a]	1974[a]	1979[a]
Liberal	43%	50%	49%	42%
Conservative	28	25	24	29
NDP	12	11	11	13
SC/Creditiste	6	5	3	3
No identification	11	9	13	13
(N)[d]	(2,615)	(2,706)	(2,411)	(2,604)

[a] National Election Study data.
[b] Social Change in Canada data.

PROPERTIES OF PARTISANSHIP REVISITED

Prior to the early 1980s time series data on federal party identification in Canada presented a portrait of impressive aggregate stability. To be sure, panel data documented that underlying the very modest inter-election fluctuations in the proportions of identifiers for each party were sizable *individual-level* shifts in partisan affiliations. Overall, however, these shifts did not seem to matter much since they were largely self-canceling. In fact, as late as 1981 the percentages identifying with the Liberal and Conservative parties were identical to what they had been sixteen years earlier, and the proportions of both New Democratic identifiers and nonidentifiers had changed only slightly (see table 12.7). Perhaps the most marked trend was the slow erosion of Social Credit support. Since the party had enjoyed the support of only 6 percent of the electorate at the time of the first national survey in 1965, however, its demise went largely unnoticed.[8]

Between 1981 and 1984 substantial aggregate changes did occur; the percentage of Liberal identifiers decreased by 11 percent, whereas the percentage of Conservative identifiers increased by 13 percent (NDP strength was largely unchanged). Taken in conjunction with the massive Conservative victory in the 1984 election, one is tempted to interpret this shift as a major realignment of partisan forces. If, however, the concept "realignment" is intended to denote a basic and enduring change, we believe such an interpretation is incorrect. Rather than a realignment, the 1981–84 shifts in party identifications signified a conjunction of short-term forces that produced a strong but *temporary* swing to the Conservatives. In the post-1984 period these forces again

1979[b]	1980[a]	1981[b]	1983[c]	1984[a]	1984[c]	1985[c]
41%	45%	45%	37%	34%	32%	33%
26	28	28	36	41	40	30
13	15	13	10	14	15	16
4	1	2	2	1	1	1
16	10	13	15	9	12	20
(2,837)	(1,761)	(2,792)	(2,013)	(2,965)	(1,876)	(1,660)

[c] Political Support in Canada data.
[d] Missing data and "other" party identifiers removed.

have changed so that the current electorate is characterized by weaker party ties, perhaps the weakest in recent Canadian history.[9]

The transitory nature of the shift to the Conservatives also can be inferred from trends in recent public polls that reveal a steady and marked decrease in Conservative popularity after November 1984 and a corresponding increase in Liberal support.[10] By November 1985, a little more than a year after the election, levels of support for the two parties were virtually identical. Such sizable shifts in party popularity are not consistent with a realignment hypothesis. Rather, they characterize an electorate in which the partisan orientations of many voters are weak and subject to the vicissitudes of transient political forces.

A national survey we commissioned in November 1985 provides more direct evidence on the transitory nature of the 1984 shift in partisanship.[11] These data reveal that only fourteen months after the 1984 election the percentage of Conservative federal identifiers had decreased by 11 percent, but despite the Liberals' rise in the aforementioned party popularity polls the percentage of Liberal identifiers (33 percent) was essentially unchanged from what it had been at the time of the election. Similarly, NDP strength had increased by only 2 percent. Other than the pronounced Tory slippage, therefore, the only other major change was the sharp increase in the percentage of nonidentifiers. Fully one-fifth of the electorate did not have a federal party identification, a figure approximately twice what it had been in 1984 and the largest recorded in eleven national surveys conducted over a twenty-year period (see table 12.7).

The large but temporary surge in Conservative identification in

Table 12.8

A. Patterns of Partisanship, Various National Panels

	74–79	79–80	80–83	83–84	80–84
Stable identification	62.3%	72.2%	66.9%	63.6%	62.6%
Switched parties	16.1	12.0	15.6	18.1	21.3
To/from nonidentification	16.2	11.8	13.7	12.6	11.7
Stable nonidentification	5.4	4.0	3.8	5.7	4.4
(N)	(1,299)	(1,690)	(834)	(1,294)	(600)

B. Patterns of Partisanship, 1974–79–80 and 1980–83–84
National Panels

	1974–79–80	1980–83–84
Pattern	%	%
Stable identification:		
Liberal	34.6	24.5
Conservative	18.3	23.2
NDP	6.5	6.4
SC	0.5	0.2
Total	59.9	54.3
Stable nonidentification	2.6	2.8
Unstable identification:		
switched parties	22.1	29.8
to/from nonidentification	19.7	18.4

Note: 1974–79–80 national panel, N = 865, missing data, N = 38, removed; 1980–83–84 national panel, N = 601, missing data, N = 3, removed. Percentages do not total 100 because of multiple patterns of partisan instability.

the early 1980s is consistent with the substantial instability in Canadians' party identifications. A comparative analysis of this phenomenon using data from several adjacent panel surveys is presented in table 12.8, panel A. These show that the percentages of unstable partisans in the 1980–83 and 1983–84 panels were quite similar to those for earlier ones. Panel B of the table, which compares the 1974–79–80 and 1980–83–84 panels, indicates that although there was somewhat more instability between 1980 and 1984, the difference clearly was one of degree (see table 12.8).

What did differentiate the more recent period was the advantage the Conservatives gained from the movement to and from various parties. It will be recalled that during the 1980–83 period changes in party identifications resulted in a net gain of 9.2 percent for the Conservatives; 13.4 percent of the electorate became Conservative identifiers and 4.2 percent stopped identifying with the party (see table 12.3). Although the amount of partisan shuffling was slightly greater between 1983 and 1984 the net gain for the Tories was much smaller—2.8 percent. Nonetheless, the Conservatives' net gain in identification over the 1980–84 period was a very impressive 12.0 percent.

The data presented in tables 12.1 and 12.2 indicate why Conservative partisanship should have surged during this period. Mulroney was far more popular than either Turner or Trudeau, and the Conservatives enjoyed a wide edge in popularity on most issues including those pertaining to the economy. Students of American voting behavior have argued that public judgments about the economy have a significant impact on party support. They have distinguished between judgments about one's personal economic condition, which, for convenience' sake, may be labeled "egocentric," and judgments about the condition of the economy, which have been labeled "sociotropic" (e.g., Kinder and Kiewiet, 1981; Kiewiet, 1983). Fiorina (1981) and others (e.g., Whiteley, 1984; Miller and Wattenberg, 1985) have suggested that time itself is an important factor in such judgments, and thus they have distinguished retrospective from contemporaneous and prospective evaluations. We have employed our 1983 and 1984 surveys to capture these distinctions.[12]

A principal components analysis reveals that Canadians' thinking about the economy and its management by the federal government has an underlying structure with three distinct factors. The first reflects past and present judgments about the economy as a whole; the second, future-oriented judgments about both the condition of the economy and one's own economic status; and the third, judgments about one's own past and present condition. We used the 1980–83 panel data to assess effects of these three types of judgments on federal party identification.

In the probit analysis below, strength and direction of federal party identification in 1983 is the dependent variable.[13] The independent variables include factor scores for the three economic factors and the three 100-point thermometer scales measuring party leader affect. We also used measures of federal and provincial party identifications in 1980 as independent variables so that we could evaluate the impact of the economic and party leader predictors net of prior partisan attachments. The results indicate that feelings about party leaders and evaluations of the government's economic performance both influenced 1983 federal party identifications. Regarding party leaders, people who identified with the NDP in 1983 were influenced by their varying degrees of affection for all three national party leaders at the time, Messrs. Broadbent, Mulroney, and Trudeau. However, people who identified with the Liberal and Conservative parties in 1983 were influenced only by their feelings for Trudeau and Mulroney (see table 12.9).

The effects of economic judgments vary. In every case judgments

Table 12.9.   Probit Analysis of 1983 Federal Party Identification.

	Liberal	Conservative	NDP
Constant	2.08*	1.80*	1.73*
Federal party identification, 1980	.30*	.31*	.24*
Provincial party identification, 1980	.11*	.14*	.13*
Party leader affect:			
Trudeau	.01*	−.01*	−.01*
Mulroney	−.02*	.02	−.01*
Broadbent	−.00	−.00	.01*
Economic evaluation:			
Judgments about the economy based on past and present	.15*	−.08*	−.11*
Judgments about the economy and personal condition based on future prospects	.04	.06	−.10*
Judgments about personal economic condition based on past and present	−.02	−.04	.03
Estimated R^2	.60	.57	.41
Estimated rho	.76	.73	.62
% correctly predicted	41	39	41

*$p \leqslant .05$.

Note: 1980–83 national panel; weighted $N = 765$.

about the economy in general were significant. By way of illustration, positive evaluations of the then-governing Liberals' economic performance increased the likelihood that a voter would be a Liberal identifier and decreased the probability of his being a Conservative or New Democratic one. In contrast (pace commonsense assumptions about the importance of "pocketbook" voting), people's evaluations of the extent to which the government's economic performance influenced personal well-being did *not* affect the strength and direction of their federal party identifications. Nor did judgments about the government's *prospective* impact on the economy and personal well-being significantly affect identifications with the two old-line parties. However, such judgments did influence New Democratic identifications, for voters who were optimistic about future economic prospects were less likely to identify with the NDP. Lastly, it appears that orientations toward federal and provincial parties were not hermetically sealed; identifications at one level "spilled over" so that prior federal *and* provincial party identifications both exerted statistically significant effects on current federal identifications.

Probit estimates of the determinants of federal party identification in 1984 (using the 1983–84 panel) were very similar to those just described. Again, it appears that the strength and direction of party identification were functions of party leader affect and judgments about the condition of the economy as well as previous federal and provincial party identifications. Once more, other types of economic evaluations were of little or no consequence, at least in any direct sense. These results suggest that the Tory tide in the early 1980s was at least partially a product of the electorate's reactions to economic adversity in a country where governments are held responsible for macroeconomic performance and partisan orientations are endogenous to other forces at work in the political arena.

This is not to suggest that a kind of "conversion" process took place during the 1980–84 period. The term "conversion" connotes that a new distribution of partisanship will have considerable durability. However, the 1985 survey indicates that fourteen months after the 1984 election the Tories had lost fully 10 points of the 12 percent increase in party identification they had gained over the previous four years, and the number of nonidentifiers had increased by 10 percent since 1980.

This newly swelled cohort of nonidentifiers might represent the culmination of a long-term, but hitherto unnoticed, trend toward partisan *dealignment*. However, there is no evidence of such a trend. As table 12.10 shows, average levels of strength of party identification were virtually constant between 1965 and 1984. Relatedly, the percentages of persons with different levels of intensity of party identification varied erratically within a very limited range over this period, with the 1984 figures being almost exactly the same as those for 1965. It is only in 1985 that a sharp decrease in the strength of partisan attachments is discernible.

The data in table 12.10 also suggest that the decreased strength of party identification in the 1985 survey cannot be explained by some variant of a "replacement" theory. The latter posits that partisan change is the product of alterations in the composition of an electorate such as might occur because of natural demographic processes, changes in voter eligibility criteria, the entry of a new group of nonpartisan voters into the electorate, or cataclysmic events such as wars and depressions. However, if such a replacement mechanism had been at work in the 1980s, the decline in strength of party identification would have assumed the characteristics of a trend, and a weakening of partisan ties would have been evident in pre-1985 surveys. In fact, this is not the case (see table 12.10). Instead, the 1985 decline in partisan strength appears to represent the operation of a "period" effect that influenced the entire electorate.

Table 12.10.   Strength of Federal Party Identification, 1965–85.

Strength of party identification	Year (in percentages)							
	1965	1968	1974	1979	1980	1983	1984	1985
Very strong	24	26	27	26	31	23	25	17
Fairly strong	43	43	40	42	42	39	43	34
Weak/leaning	22	23	20	19	17	23	20	29
No identification	11	9	13	13	10	15	12	20
(N)	(2,615)	(2,706)	(2,411)	(2,624)	(1,761)	(2,037)	(1,892)	(1,660)
Mean strength of party identification	1.8	1.8	1.8	1.8	1.9	1.7	1.8	1.5

*Strength of party identification scored: very strong = 3, fairly strong = 2, weak/leaning = 1, no identification = 0.

In support of this argument we may note the average levels of strength of party identification across several age groups in the 1974, 1979, 1984, and 1985 surveys (see table 12.11). Prior to 1985 the strength of party identification generally increased across various age groups in a fashion predicted by Converse (1969, 1976) in his well-known life-cycle interpretation of the dynamics of partisanship. One may observe this process in table 12.11 by tracing changes in partisan strength for various groups in the 1974, 1979, and 1984 surveys as these groups increased in age over the ten-year period. (The groups are joined by diagonal lines in the table.) It does not appear that the youngest cohorts of voters in the 1984 electorate were appreciably less partisan than their counterparts were a decade earlier. In 1985, however, the average intensity of partisanship decreased for every age group, and there is no indication that such decreases were especially pronounced among younger as compared to older voters.[14] Such a "nonpattern" across age groups is exactly what one would expect if a period effect were operative.

What is presently unknown, of course, is how long this period will last. The 1985 results may signify a "ratcheting up" of the weakness of federal party identification, or perhaps the beginning of a trend toward a profoundly dealigned, and hence, extremely volatile electorate. A second possibility is that the 1985 data simply represent the temporary disillusionment of an electorate whose high hopes for the new Tory government had been dampened considerably by its perceived ineptitude during its first year in office. If so, there could well be a return to the balance of partisan forces that prevailed before the Conservative surge in the early 1980s. A third possibility has been long predicted by NDP partisans: a realignment along left-right ideological lines, with the New Democrats and the Conservatives the two major parties in federal politics (Alford, 1963; Horowitz, 1966; Wilson, 1968) and the Liberals reduced to a minor center party much like the British Liberals prior to their rebirth through an alliance with the SDP.

Although the demonstrated volatility of the Canadian electorate makes prediction a risky business, there already is limited evidence to suggest that the second scenario—a return to the status quo is more realistic. As noted, the Gallup and other public opinion polls have documented a resurgence of Liberal strength, a marked decline in Tory popularity, and some gains for the NDP. The results of provincial elec-

Table 12.11.   Mean Strength of Federal Party Identification
by Age Group, 1974, 1979, 1984, 1985.

Age group	1974 $\overline{X}$	1979 $\overline{X}$	1984 $\overline{X}$	1985 $\overline{X}$
18–23	1.71	1.66	1.68	1.39
24–29	1.72	1.63	1.69	1.40
30–34	1.75	1.79	1.77	1.44
35–39	1.75	1.81	1.70	1.48
40–44	1.70	1.84	1.80	1.44
45–49	1.84	1.82	1.84	1.58
50–54	1.90	1.87	1.81	1.48
55–59	1.84	1.94	1.91	1.69
60–64	1.97	1.81	2.00	1.43
65–69	1.81	2.00	2.01	1.48
70–74	1.92	2.01	2.02	1.57
75 and over	2.17	1.96	2.13	1.73
Everyone	1.80	1.81	1.81	1.48
eta =	.12	.12	.14	.09
p≤	.001	.001	.001	n.s.

Note: Strength of party identification scored: very strong = 3, fairly strong = 2, weak/
leaning = 1, no identification = 0.

tions also suggest that Liberal fortunes may again be on the rise. In
Quebec the Liberals have regained power from the Parti Quebecois
after a nine-year hiatus; in Ontario the party has formed a minority
government after some four decades in the political wilderness. Since
partisan orientations at one level of the federal system influence partisanship at the other, these two victories in provinces containing approximately two-thirds of parliament's seats are not inconsequential.

Further, a comparison by region of federal party identifications in
1984 and 1985 indicates that the Liberals have regained much of the
ground they lost in Ontario and, equally important, did not suffer an
erosion of party identification in Quebec comparable to their massive
loss of votes in 1984 (see table 12.12). Notwithstanding this improvement, as of November 1985, then, the percentages of Liberal and Conservative identifiers in Ontario were 38 percent vs. 29 percent, and in
Quebec the comparable figures were 40 percent and 20 percent, respec-

tively. Moreover, Tory losses in central Canada had not been offset by appreciable gains elsewhere. Indeed, in the Prairies and British Columbia the Conservatives had lost substantial numbers of identifiers, many of whom evidently had retreated (perhaps temporarily) to the status of nonidentifiers. As for the NDP, although opinion polls have lent some credence to its claims to be the "real opposition," there is no evidence in any region of a prospective surge in New Democratic identifications.

In sum, despite uncertainties engendered by a large number of nonidentifiers and the sensitivity of partisan attachments to transient political forces, it appears that predictions of the Liberals' imminent demise and of an era of Tory dominance—perhaps accompanied by a realignment of the federal party system along left-right lines—were greatly exaggerated in the first instance and problematic in the second. To be sure, "plus ça change" is not an especially exciting prediction, but it is consonant with the data on party support and our knowledge of the properties of partisanship in contemporary Canada.

ON PARTISANSHIP AND
DEMOCRATIC GOVERNANCE

The principal question we have addressed is whether the overwhelming Conservative victory in the 1984 national election signaled a basic realignment of partisan forces in Canada. The 12 percent net gain in

Table 12.12.   Federal Party Identification, 1984 and 1985 by Region.

Federal party identification	Atlantic		Quebec		Ontario		Prairies		BC	
	1984	1985	1984	1985	1984	1985	1984	1985	1984	1985
Liberal	37%	35%	42%	40%	33%	38%	18%	22%	26%	20%
Conservative	37	40	29	20	40	29	61	43	39	27
NDP	15	7	10	7	15	18	14	18	27	28
SC	0	0	1	1	0	x	1	2	1	4
None	12	18	18	32	12	15	6	15	7	21
(N)	(162)	(134)	(498)	(426)	(677)	(611)	(319)	(293)	(220)	(195)

x less than 0.5 percent.
1984 V = .15, p≤.001.
1985 V = .17, p≤.001.

Conservative identifications in the interim between the 1980 and 1984 elections and the fact that in the latter election the party, for the first time in history, won the largest share of the popular vote in each of the country's ten provinces pointed to such a possibility. However, realignment implies that changes in partisan forces will be relatively permanent. The data we have examined indicate this has not been the case; fourteen months after the election, other than in the Atlantic provinces, the 1980–84 Conservative gains in identification largely had dissipated. Moreover, the 1985 data revealed that party identifications were weaker and the incidence of nonidentification was greater than at any time during the past twenty years.

The weakening of party ties generally and the erosion of Tory identifications in particular suggest, despite the magnitude of the Conservatives' 1984 victory, that in the next election campaign a concatenation of short-term forces largely will determine who will govern the country. Such an outcome would be consistent with those of other recent national elections. Research indicates that in each of those, short-term issue and leader effects not only determined whether and for whom an individual would vote, but they also influenced the direction and intensity of his/her partisan ties. In the 1984 election short-term forces overwhelmingly favored the Conservatives. More specifically, the high regard in which Mr. Mulroney was held, the congruence between voters' positions on issues they deemed most important and those they ascribed to the Conservatives, as well as their negative judgments about the Liberal administration's handling of the economy not only helped the Conservatives win office, but they also influenced people to identify with the party during and prior to the 1984 election. However, disenchantment with the Tories that in part can be attributed to the end of the traditional "honeymoon" period any new government enjoys and in part to a series of scandals that tarnished the image of the Mulroney administration, coupled with revived Liberal fortunes in provincial politics, produced the conditions noted above.

One interpretation of the events we have chronicled is that democracy is alive and well in Canada; that the late V. O. Key's bottom-line conclusion that American voters are not stupid also applies to their Canadian cousins.[15] From a systemic perspective the periodic alternation of political parties in office is fully in accord with democratic norms. So too is basing individual voting choices on a comparative evaluation of the content of party platforms, current issues, and the past performance of parties and their leaders. Clearly, a substantial proportion of the Canadian voting public seems to behave in a way in which citizens in a democratic society are supposed to behave. That is the up side. The down side, it can be argued, is that even if millions of voters do make rational voting choices on the basis of their assessments of short-term forces, in many parts of the country the effective range of those choices in federal elections is a narrow one both ideologically and substantively.

Average Canadians see little ideological distance between and among the four national parties[17]—especially between the Liberals and Conservatives—the only two parties to have held national office in the past. It is alleged that one of the reasons voters are unable to discern significant differences between and among parties is that in their campaigns the parties tend to stress "leadership," to point to problems rather than offer solutions, to "fuzz" issues, to fail to offer issues that transcend regional differences, and to focus on valence rather than positional issues: in short, to practice a "politics of ambiguity."[18] It is not surprising, therefore, that political participation, affect for parties, their leaders, and the key institutions of the political regime are low, and political inefficaciousness, distrust, and disinterest are high (Kornberg et al., 1982: chap. 3; Clarke et al., 1984: chap. 2).

Implicit in the complaint about the lack of effective choice available to Canadian voters is that the Liberals and Conservatives—indeed, all the federal parties—have failed to perform the integrative function that is important in any democratic political system and critically important in the Canadian system given the country's deep-seated regional cleavages. One of the few Canadian party scholars to make the linkage between inter- and intraparty differences explicit is John Meisel, who in a series of thoughtful essays (1973:183–252; 1979:119–35) argued that the inability or unwillingness of Canadian parties to perform the integrative function—to bring people *together* before they *divided* them in elections—adversely affected the parties' ability to perform other basic functions. In particular, it had a negative impact on their ability to formulate and adhere to clearly defined policy positions that transcended provincial and regional interests. Not knowing what the parties stood for, people did not know what they were about.[19]

Meisel laid much of the blame for the condition of the party system in the mid-1970s at the doorstep of the federal Liberals and the media. The excessive influence of the bureaucracy over both the formulation and administration of public policy during the post-World War II period he attributed to successive Liberal governments who seemed to have an affinity for bureaucrats and vice versa. The media were indicted for ascribing to themselves the role of "official opposition" to all parties: a kind of "plague on all your houses" posture that contributed to the negative images many Canadians had not only of the parties but of the democratic political process itself. In addition, the media, with the active connivance of the several party leaders (but particularly of Liberal leaders), were blamed for trivializing the political process generally and the electoral process in particular. They did this by representing elections to the public as quasiathletic contests in which the personalities and tactical brilliance (or lack thereof) of the star players (i.e., the party leaders) were the principal, indeed, the only things that mattered.

One can argue with Meisel about the extent to which the party system was in crisis in the mid-1970s and the relative contributions to the crisis of the media, the Liberal party, and other major players (e.g., interest group leaders, senior federal and provincial bureaucrats). What cannot be argued about, however, is the extent to which the Liberals dominated politics in the generation after World War II. Whether they will do so again, whether they and Conservatives will alternate in national office as they have in the past three elections, whether the NDP will break into the winner's circle, or whether the Tory tide of 1984 will continue to roll is presently unknown. Canada's federal political parties long have sailed on a sea of public support in which the currents of short-term forces are often unpredictable and occasionally treacherous. The present analyses strongly indicate that this situation will obtain for the foreseeable future and that the parties will continue to confront a restless electorate that makes successful political navigation a fascinating, if hazardous, enterprise.

Appendix A.   Vote in 1984 Federal Election by Sociodemographic Variables (horizontal percentages).

| | | 1984 vote | | | |
		Liberal	Conservative	NDP	Other
Region:	Atlantic	34	49	17	0
	Quebec-French	27	57	13	3
	Quebec-Other	30	50	14	6
	Ontario	24	53	22	1
	Prairies	14	62	20	4
	British Columbia	14	56	27	3
	V = .12, p ⩽ .001				
Family income:	<$10,000/year	26	48	22	3
	10,000–19,999	25	52	20	3
	20,000–29,999	22	51	24	4
	30,000–49,999	22	59	17	2
	50,000 & over	21	60	18	2
	V = .06, p = n.s.				
Education:	Elementary or less	26	57	16	1
	Some secondary	23	56	19	3
	Completed secondary	21	55	21	4
	Some college or university	21	57	19	3
	Completed college or university (B.A. or more)	28	49	21	2
	V = .05, p = n.s.				
Occupation:	Professional	23	51	24	2
	Owner, manager	22	57	13	7
	Sales	22	62	16	0
	Clerical	28	48	22	2
	Skilled labor	14	60	22	4
	Unskilled labor	23	56	20	2
	Farmer	22	64	9	5
	Housewife	30	52	16	2
	Student	25	50	25	1
	Retired	27	54	17	2
	Unemployed	15	63	20	3
	V = .11, p ⩽ .01				
Gender:	Male	20	57	19	4
	Female	27	52	20	1
	V = .13, p ⩽ .001				

Appendix A.   (Continued)

| | | 1984 vote | | | |
		Liberal	Conservative	NDP	Other
Age:	18–21 (1984)*	22	61	17	1
	22–27 (1979–1980)	23	47	25	4
	28–39 (1968–1974)	19	56	21	4
	40–51 (1957–1965)	15	65	19	1
	52–64 (1945–1953)	30	49	19	2
	65 & over (1940 or earlier)	33	50	16	1
	V = .11, p≤.001				

*election in which first eligible to vote

NOTES

1   The 1983 and 1984 studies were funded with a research grant to us from the National Science Foundation. The fieldwork was conducted by Canadian Facts Ltd. under the direction of Mary Auvinen, Senior Project Director. The weighted N's for the surveys are 2,107 and 1,928, respectively.

2   Weighted N's for various panels are 1980–83 = 834; 1983–84 = 1,294; and 1980–84 = 601. Information regarding the sample design, weighting scheme, and other aspects of the study are available from the principal investigators upon request.

3   When this measurement device is used, a respondent is either given a picture of a thermometer scaled from 0–100 with 50 designated as the neutral point or, in a telephone survey, asked to "think of" such a thermometer. The respondent is told that the warmer his/her feelings about an object or person named, the higher the score that should be given the object or person, and the cooler the feeling, the lower the score.

4   The 1965 and 1968 national election studies were funded with grants from the Canada Council. Principal investigators for the former study were Philip Converse, John Meisel, Maurice Pinard, Peter Regenstreif, and Mildred Schwartz; for the latter, John Meisel. The sample sizes are: 1965 = 2,729 (weighted) and 1968 = 2,769. These data are available from the Inter-University Consortium for Political and Social Research, University of Michigan. Neither the principal investigators nor the Consortium are responsible for the analyses and interpretations of the data presented here.

5   For all of the surveys employed in this chapter, except those by Meisel et al., the sequence of questions used to measure federal party identification is as follows: (a) "Thinking of federal politics, do you usually think of yourself as Liberal, Conservative, NDP, Social Credit, or what?" (b) "How strongly [party named] do you feel, very

strongly, fairly strongly, or not strongly?" (c) [If "refused," "don't know," "independent," or "none" in (a)] "Still thinking of *federal* politics, do you generally think of
yourself as being a little closer to one of the parties than to the others?" [emphasis
in original]. (d) [If "yes"] "Which party is that?" All respondents supplying a party
label to questions (a) or (c) were considered to have some degree of party identification. Persons declining to provide a party label in (a) but doing so in (c) were
classified as "weak" identifiers in the analyses of strength of party identification
below. A parallel sequence of questions was asked to ascertain party identification
at the provincial level. The 1965 and 1968 party identification questions are similar, except that the federal and provincial questions are integrated into one sequence.
For details on the latter consult the 1965 and 1968 elections study codebooks.

6   The term "nonidentifier" is used instead of "independent" because the latter term
     has very little currency in Canadian politics. Analyses show that only a handful of
     the survey respondents used the term in their responses to the party identification
     questions.

7   The construction of this variable varies depending on whether Liberal, Conserva-
     tive, or NDP voting is being analyzed. In the case of Liberal voting, for example,
     persons selecting the Liberals as closest on their "most important issue" are scored
     1, those selecting another party, –1, and those not selecting a party or not designating
     an issue, 0. These scores are weighted by multiplying them by a variable assessing
     perceived importance of the issue in the vote decision. The latter variable is scored:
     "very important" = 3; "fairly important" = 2; "not very important" or "no
     important issue" = 0.

8   The 1974, 1979, and 1980 Canadian national election and panel studies were
     funded by the Social Sciences and Humanities Research Council of Canada (princi-
     pal investigators: Harold D. Clarke, Jane Jenson, Lawrence LeDuc, and Jon H.
     Pammett). Information concerning the design of the 1974 survey may be found in
     Clarke et al., 1979, pp. 397–400. Those for the 1979 and 1980 surveys and the
     panel components therein are available from the principal investigators upon
     request. All the data sets are available from the Inter-University Consortium for
     Political and Social Research, University of Michigan. The weighted N's for the
     1974, 1979, and 1980 cross-sectional samples are 2,445, 2,670 and 1,786, respec-
     tively. The weighted panel N's are 1974–79 = 1,353; 1979–80 = 1,770; 1974–79–
     80 = 865. The "Social Change in Canada" data in table 12.7 are from the 1979
     (weighted N = 2,837) and 1981 (weighted N = 2,792) national surveys conducted
     by Tom Atkinson et al. Details concerning these surveys are available from the Insti-
     tute for Behavioural Research, York University. The "1984 National Election Study"
     data in the table (weighted N = 3,380) are from Kay et al. (1985). The analyses and
     interpretations of these several data sets are the responsibility of the authors.

9   These comparisons are with the data from the 1984 wave of our "Political Support
     in Canada" study (column 10 of Table 12.7). Comparisons with data from the 1984
     national election study conducted by Jerome Black et al. (column 9 of Table 12.7)
     yielded virtually the same results.

10   The Tory slide in public support is amply documented in the public opinion
     (Gallup) or the several polls conducted by Environics Research Group Ltd. Results

of the latter for the period from September 1982 to November 1985 are available in the *Globe and Mail*, December 21, 1985, pp. 1, 4.

11   The 1985 survey was conducted by the authors as part of their "Political Support in Canada" project. The weighted national sample N is 1,853.

12   On the construction of the six economic evaluation variables, see Clarke and Kornberg (1986).

13   The construction of the dependent variables depends upon whether Liberal, Conservative, or NDP identification is being analyzed. For example, for the Conservative analysis the dependent variable is: very strong Conservative = +3, fairly strong Conservative = +2, weak/leaning Conservative = +1, nonidentifier = 0, weak/leaning other party = −1, fairly strong other party = −2, very strong other party = −3. The Liberal and NDP dependent variables and the 1980 measures of federal and provincial party identifications are constructed in an analogous fashion.

14   In fact, the 1984–85 difference in average strength of party identification was somewhat greater among voters sixty and over, −.49, as compared to −.29 for younger groups.

15   It will be recalled that many of the critics of the findings of American voting studies during the 1950s/1960s were both chagrined and appalled because they indicated that the most important determinant of whether and for whom the majority of Americans voted was a psychological identification with party symbols—an identification that occurred early in life for largely nonrational reasons. Moreover, that same identification also appeared to act as a kind of conceptual screen through which a voter's judgments about issues and candidates were filtered and formed. As indicated, subsequent studies have questioned these findings and tried to demonstrate that Key's judgment, in fact, was a valid one.

16   Probably the classic statement about the lack of effective voter choice is one by Gad Horowitz (1967:55–74).

17   People more often view the parties along government-opposition and major-minor, French–non-French dimensions (Kornberg, Mishler, and Smith, 1975).

18   A concise synthesis of these and other criticisms of party and electoral politics in Canada is contained in Kornberg, Mishler, and Clarke, *Representative Democracy*, chaps. 4 and 5; and Clarke et al., *Absent Mandate*, chap. 8.

19   That not knowing what political parties are about, in turn, may affect party identification and its several properties noted above is a point we need not labor here.

REFERENCES

Aitkin, D. 1977. *Stability and Change in Australian Politics*. New York: St. Martin's Press.

Aldrich, J. H., and F. D. Nelson. 1984. *Linear Probability, Logit, and Probit Models*. Beverly Hills: Sage Publications.

Alford, R. R. 1963. *Party and Society*. Chicago: Rand McNally.

Alt, J. 1984. "Dealignment and the Dynamics of Partisanship in Britain." In R. Dalton,

S. Flanagan, and P. A. Beck, eds., *Electoral Change in Advanced Industrial Democracies*. Princeton, N.J.: Princeton University Press.

Anderson, K. 1979. *The Creation of a Democratic Majority 1928–1936*. Chicago: University of Chicago Press.

Beck, P. A. 1976. "A Socialization Theory of Partisan Realignment." In R. G. Niemi and H. F. Weisberg, eds., *Controversies In American Voting Behavior*. San Francisco: W. H. Freeman.

———. 1984. "The Dealignment Era in America." In R. G. Dalton, S. C. Flanagan, and P. A. Beck, eds., *Electoral Change in Advanced Industrial Democracies*. Princeton, N.J.: Princeton University Press.

Belknap, G., and A. Campbell. 1952. "Political Party Identification and Attitudes Toward Foreign Policy." *Public Opinion Quarterly* 15: 601–23.

Berelson, B., P. F. Lazarsfeld, and W. N. McPhee. 1954. *Voting*. Chicago: University of Chicago Press.

Blake, D. E. 1982. "The Consistency of Inconsistency: Party Identification in Federal and Provincial Politics." *Canadian Journal of Political Science* 15: 691–710.

Brodie, M. J., and J. Jenson. 1980. *Crisis, Challenge and Change: Party and Class in Canada*. Toronto: Methuen.

Budge, I., I. Crewe, and D. Farlie, eds. 1976. *Party Identification and Beyond*. New York: John Wiley and Sons.

Butler, D., and D. Stokes. 1976. *Political Change in Britain*, 2nd college ed. New York: St. Martin's Press.

Campbell, A., G. Gurin, and W. E. Miller. 1954. *The Voter Decides*. Evanston, Ill.: Row, Peterson.

Campbell, A., P. Converse, W. Miller, and D. Stokes. 1960. *The American Voter*. New York: John Wiley and Sons.

———. 1966. *Elections and the Political Order*. New York: John Wiley and Sons.

Clarke, H. D., J. Jenson, L. LeDuc, and J. Pammett. 1979. *Political Choice in Canada*. Toronto: McGraw-Hill Ryerson.

Clarke, H. D., and M. C. Stewart. 1984. "Dealignment of Degree: Partisan Change in Britain, 1974–83." *Journal of Politics* 46: 689–719.

Clarke, H. D., J. Jenson, L. LeDuc, and J. Pammett. 1984. *Absent Mandate: The Politics of Discontent in Canada*. Agincourt, Ont.: Gage.

Clarke, H. D., and M. C. Stewart. 1985. "Short-Term Forces and Partisan Change in Canada: 1974–80." *Electoral Studies* 4: 15–35.

Clarke, H. D., M. C. Stewart, and G. Zuk. 1986. "Politics, Economics and Party Popularity in Britain, 1979–83." *Electoral Studies* 5: 123–41.

Clarke, H. D., and G. Zuk. 1986. "The Politics of Party Popularity: Canada 1974–79." *Comparative Politics* 19: 299–315.

Clarke, H. D., and A. Kornberg. 1986. "Public Reactions to Economic Performance and Political Support in Canada." Paper presented at the Canadian Political Economy in Comparative Perspective: The 1980s and Beyond Conference, Blacksburg, Virginia, May 9–11.

Clarke, H. D., and M. C. Stewart. 1987. "Partisan Inconsistency and Partisan Change in

Federal States: The Case of Canada." *American Journal of Political Science* 31: 383–407.

Converse, P. 1969. "Of Time and Partisan Stability." *Comparative Political Studies* 2: 139–71.

———. 1976. *The Dynamics of Party Support.* Beverly Hills: Sage Publications.

Crewe, I., B. Sarlvik, and J. Alt. 1977. "Partisan Dealignment in Britain 1964–74." *British Journal of Political Science* 7: 129–90.

Downs, A. 1957. *An Economic Theory of Democracy.* New York: Harper and Row.

Enelow, J. M., and M. J. Hinich. 1984. *The Spatial Theory of Voting: An Introduction.* Cambridge: Cambridge University Press.

Englemann, F. C., and M. A. Schwartz. 1975. *Canadian Political Parties: Origin, Character, Impact.* Scarborough, Ont.: Prentice-Hall.

Fiorina, M. P. 1981. *Retrospective Voting in American National Elections.* New Haven, Conn.: Yale University Press.

Franklin, C. H., and J. E. Jackson. 1983. "The Dynamics of Party Identification." *American Political Science Review* 77: 957–73.

Gutek, B. 1978. "On the Accuracy of Retrospective Attitudinal Data." *Public Opinion Quarterly* 42: 390–401.

Hadley, C. D. 1985. "Dual Partisan Identification in the South." *Journal of Politics* 47: 254–68.

Himmelweit, H., P. Humphreys, M. Jaeger, and M. Katz. 1981. *How Voters Decide.* London: Academic Press.

Horowitz, G. 1966. "Toward the Democratic Class Struggle." *Journal of Canadian Studies* 1: 3–10.

———. 1979. "Conservatism, Liberalism, and Socialism in Canada." In Hugh Thorburn, ed., *Party Politics in Canada*, 2nd ed. Scarborough, Ont.: Prentice-Hall.

Jennings, M. K., and R. G. Niemi. 1966. "Party Identification at Multiple Levels of Government." *American Journal of Sociology* 72: 92–110.

———. 1974. *The Political Character of Adolescence.* Princeton, N.J.: Princeton University Press.

———. 1981. *Generations and Politics.* Princeton, N.J.: Princeton University Press.

Jenson, J. 1975. "Party Loyalty in Canada: The Question of Party Identification." *Canadian Journal of Political Science* 8: 543–52.

———.1976. "Party Strategy and Party Identification: Some Patterns of Partisan Allegiance." *Canadian Journal of Political Science* 9: 27–48.

Kay, B., S. D. Brown, J. Curtis, R. D. Lambert, and J. M. Wilson. 1985. "The Character of Electoral Change: A Preliminary Report from the 1984 National Election Study." Paper presented at the annual meeting of the Canadian Political Science Association, Montreal, May 31–June 2.

Kiewiet, D. R. 1983. *Macroeconomics and Micropolitics.* Chicago: University of Chicago Press.

———, and D. Rivers. 1984. "A Retrospective on Retrospective Voting." *Political Behavior* 6: 369–94.

Kinder, D. R., and R. Kiewiet. 1981. "Sociotropic Politics: The American Case." *British*

Journal of Political Science 11: 129–61.

Kornberg, A., J. Smith, and D. Bromley. 1969. "Some Differences in the Political Socialization Patterns of Canadian and American Party Officials: A Preliminary Report."
Canadian Journal of Political Science 2: 63–88.

Kornberg, A., W. Mishler, and J. Smith. 1975. "Political Elite and Mass Perceptions of
Party Locations in Issue Space: Some Tests of Two Positions." *British Journal of
Political Science* 5: 161–85.

Kornberg, A., J. Smith, and H. D. Clarke. 1979. *Citizen Politicians—Canada*. Durham,
N.C.: Carolina Academic Press.

Kornberg, A., W. Mishler, and H. D. Clarke. 1982. *Representative Democracy in the
Canadian Provinces*. Toronto: Prentice-Hall.

Lazarsfeld, P. F., B. Berelson, and H. Gaudet. 1948. *The People's Choice*. New York:
Columbia University Press.

LeDuc, L., H. D. Clarke, J. Jenson, and J. Pammett. 1984. "Partisan Instability in
Canada: Evidence from a New Panel Study." *American Political Science Review* 78:
470–84.

McKelvey, R. D., and W. Zavoina. 1975. "A Statistical Model for the Analysis of Ordinal
Level Dependent Variables." *Journal of Mathematical Sociology* 4: 103–20.

Markus, G. B., and P. Converse. 1979. "A Dynamic Simultaneous Equation Model of
Electoral Choice." *American Political Science Review* 73: 1055–70.

Markus, G. B. 1986. "Stability and Change in Political Attitudes: Observed, Recalled,
and 'Explained.'" *Political Behavior* 8: 21–44.

Martinez, M. 1984. "Intergenerational Transfer of Canadian Partisanships." *Canadian
Journal of Political Science* 17: 133–43.

Meisel, J. 1973. *Working Papers on Canadian Politics*, enlarged ed. Montreal: McGill-
Queen's University Press, pp. 183–252.

———. 1975. *Working Papers on Canadian Politics*, 2nd enlarged ed. Montreal: McGill-
Queen's University Press.

———. 1979. "The Decline of Party in Canada." In Hugh Thorburn, ed., *Party Politics in
Canada*. Scarborough, Ont.: Prentice-Hall, pp. 119–35.

Miller, A., and M. Wattenberg. 1985. "Throwing the Rascals Out: Policy and Performance Evaluations of Presidential Candidates, 1952–1980." *American Political
Science Review* 79: 359–72.

Miller, W. 1983. *The Survey Method in the Social and Political Sciences: Achievements,
Failures, Prospects*. London: Francis Pinter.

Monroe, K. 1984. *Presidential Popularity and the Economy*. New York: Praeger.

Niemi, R., R. Katz, and D. Newman. 1980. "Reconstructing Past Partisanship: The Failure
of the Party Identification Recall Questions." *American Journal of Political Science*
24: 633–51.

Page, B. I., and C. C. Jones. 1979. "Reciprocal Effects of Policy Preferences, Party
Loyalties and the Vote." *American Political Science Review* 73: 1071–89.

Sarlvik, B., and I. Crewe. 1983. *Decade of Dealignment*. Cambridge: Cambridge University Press.

Smiley, D. V. 1980. *Canada in Question: Federalism in the Eighties*, 3rd ed. Toronto:

McGraw-Hill Ryerson.

Sniderman, P., H. D. Forbes, and I. Melzer. 1974. "Party Loyalty and Electoral Volatility: A Study of the Canadian Party System." *Canadian Journal of Political Science* 7: 268–88.

Van Loon, R. J., and M. S. Whittington. 1981. *The Canadian Political System: Environment, Structure and Process*, 3rd ed. Toronto: McGraw-Hill Ryerson.

Weisberg, H. 1980. "A Multidimensional Conceptualization of Party Identification." *Political Behavior* 1: 33–60.

Whiteley, P. 1984. "Perceptions of Economic Performance and Voting Behavior in the 1983 General Election in Britain." *Political Behavior* 6: 395–410.

Wilson, J. 1968. "Politics and Social Class in Canada: The Case of Waterloo South." *Canadian Journal of Political Science* 1: 288–309.

13. The Economic Conservatism of the Reagan Administration: Notes for a Theory of Party Differences, Partisan Change, and Electoral Accountability

HENRY W. CHAPPELL, JR., AND WILLIAM R. KEECH

The Reagan administration is said to be uniquely conservative among American presidencies of the last half century. In part this is to be attributed to its partisanship. Ronald Reagan is only the third Republican to be elected president since Herbert Hoover. Yet his administration is seen as more conservative than those of the Eisenhower and Nixon-Ford presidencies, not to speak of the Democratic administrations in this period.

Some of this perception is due, no doubt, to President Reagan's open embrace of several of the goals of the "new right" on issues such as school prayer and abortion. Furthermore, all of the president's publicly stated goals, such as a stronger national defense and a constitutional amendment to require a balanced federal budget, are at least compatible with what is understood as conservatism, if not distinctly conservative. Indeed, Reagan has been the leading presidential contender of the conservative wing of the Republican party since 1968, when he won 14 percent of the delegate votes at the Republican convention. With these credentials the president may be seen as *defining* what conservatism is in the contemporary United States.

This chapter will analyze the conservatism of the Reagan administration from the perspective of theory about party differences, especially as this has developed in the study of macroeconomic policy and performance. While the president surely deserves his conservative

We would like to acknowledge the support of National Science Foundation Grants SES 8420122 and SES 8420709 and the helpful comments of Keith Archer.

credentials in many respects (see Lowi, 1984), we will argue that in some his performance is like that of an ordinary Republican, while in others he is not conservative at all.

ELECTING A CONSERVATIVE

The election and reelection of Ronald Reagan can be well understood without calling attention to his conservatism. But his election does illuminate some long-standing issues about the prospects of electing conservatives.

Retrospective Voting and the Elections of 1980 and 1984

The elections of Ronald Reagan in 1980 and 1984 need not be explained by any electoral shift toward conservatism. Carter's defeat and Reagan's reelection are readily explained in terms of the economic performance of the two administrations. These elections can be interpreted with the help of contemporary theories of retrospective voting, which explain votes in terms of the performance of incumbents in the period before the election (Fiorina, 1981). The performances of the Carter administration and of the first Reagan administration are not very different in terms of inflation and unemployment summed over the entire periods.

However, in the period just before elections, which counts the most for electoral purposes, the difference in performance is quite striking. Table 13.1 shows that the sum of the inflation and unemployment rates, sometimes known as the "misery index," was 11.7 in 1984, while it was 20.5 in 1980. Not only was Reagan's election year performance far better than Carter's by this standard, but Kiewiet and Rivers (1985: 69–72) show that it is comparable with that of other landslide reelections such as those of 1964 and 1972.

Numerous analysts have argued that the rejection of Carter and the choice of Reagan had much more to do with the latter's past performance on inflation and unemployment than with the electorate's perceptions of policy differences on those issues. For example, Markus (1982) argues from survey evidence that public opinion provided no clear guide as to desired priorities on a trade-off between the two, and the public had only the vaguest perception of a difference in the priorities of the two candidates on such a trade-off (1982: 543–45,

Table 13.1.   Macroeconomic Performance, 1977–1984.

	Inflation (CPI)	Unemployment	Misery index
1977	6.5	6.9	13.4
1978	7.7	6.0	13.7
1979	11.3	5.8	17.1
1980	13.5	7.0	20.5
Carter average	9.8	6.4	16.2
1981	10.4	7.5	17.9
1982	6.1	9.5	15.6
1983	3.2	9.5	12.7
1984	4.3	7.4	11.7
Reagan first-term average	6.0	8.5	14.5

Source: Economic Report of the President, 1986. Tables B35, B59.

549). "There is . . . no evidence to support the argument that Reagan's victory represented a mandate for either his ideological posture or his policy intentions" (1982: 558).[1]

Taft Was Right, but for the Wrong Reasons

In winning these two elections Ronald Reagan has put to rest a debate that has occupied the Republican party since the New Deal. Can a "true" conservative win the presidency? The candidacies of Thomas Dewey and Dwight Eisenhower reflected the view that moderates who accepted the basic shape of the post-New Deal welfare state were more electable than more outspoken conservatives such as Robert A. Taft. Supporters of the latter claimed that a "true" conservative candidate would win by bringing out conservative voters who were too alienated from the party by "me too" candidates to vote at all.

Barry Goldwater presumably provided a test for this theory in 1964 by offering "a choice but not an echo." His stunning defeat was a major setback for the view that the Republicans could do better by offering a distinctly conservative alternative, but the Reagan elections make clear that some of the earlier conclusions were hasty and too broad. The Goldwater candidacy showed that a self-consciously conservative stance was not sufficient for victory, but we now see that it did not mean that an avowed conservative must lose. Goldwater was a weak candidate running in a year in which conditions strongly favored the incumbent.

It is tempting in retrospect to conclude that the opposite was the case in 1980: that Reagan was a strong candidate running in a year in which conditions strongly favored the challenger. Only the second part of the statement is true. We documented above the fact that conditions favored the challenger, but Reagan was in 1980 a weak candidate who was actually more of a liability to the Republicans than an asset. Miller and Wattenberg (1985) have calculated the balance of positive and negative comments on the personal attributes of all presidential candidates from 1952 through 1980 as measured in the National Election Surveys. They find a balance for Reagan that is more negative than that for any other candidate in this period, including Goldwater and McGovern (1985: 368). Kelley found that Reagan had fewer "highly favorable" ratings as measured by the Gallup Poll than any other president elected in a period beginning in 1952 (1983: 171–73). The Republicans won in 1980 in spite of Reagan rather than because of him, though clearly perceptions of the president became markedly more favorable afterward.

The 1980 Reagan election shows that a "conservative" challenger can win if conditions are favorable, and the 1984 election shows that a "conservative" incumbent can win if performance is good. We may anticipate that both facts will enhance the prospects of conservatives in future Republican nominating conventions. So the Taft supporters were right in suggesting that an avowedly conservative candidate can win, but they were wrong in suggesting that the victory would be *because* of his conservatism. What is crucial for the reelection of a conservative or anyone else is that overall performance on fundamental issues of peace and prosperity be satisfactory. Beyond this, an incumbent has considerable freedom to pursue his own values and those of his clientele.

UNEMPLOYMENT, INFLATION, AND
THE DIFFERENCE BETWEEN REPUBLICANS
AND DEMOCRATS

The choices made by the Reagan administration about relative priorities in stabilizing the economy and achieving prosperity are consistent both with conventional wisdom and with the empirical study of party differences. In these respects the Reagan performance is comparable to that of a typical Republican administration.

That the Republican and Democratic parties have different goals with respect to inflation and unemployment has been well documented by Tufte (1978: chap. 4) and Schlozman and Verba (1979: chap. 11). The link between these publicly articulated goals and objective assessments of the interests of social and economic class groupings has been made by Hibbs (1977). Deeper analyses of the bases for party differences have been articulated by Black (1982).

While unemployment fell throughout most of the Carter administration, it has risen in the Reagan administration, consistent with predictions for a Republican (see Hibbs, 1977, 1986; Beck, 1982b), and in spite of the relatively high level when the Democrats left office. While there have been no studies of party differences in inflation comparable in sophistication to those on unemployment, low inflation is clearly a higher priority for Republicans than for Democrats. Consistent with this fact, while inflation rates rose during the Carter administration, they have fallen in the Reagan administration. (See table 13.1.)

Both patterns reinforce each party's reputation as the party best able to deal with unemployment or inflation. As such, they reinforce existing bases for policy-oriented as opposed to incumbency-oriented voting (see Kiewiet, 1981). That is, while much of voting behavior can be understood as a simple judgment about whether or not an administration has performed satisfactorily, there are elements of voting behavior that use information about the special commitments or strengths of the parties. For example, Kiewiet has shown that people who have been unemployed and people who see unemployment as the most important national problem are often more likely to vote Democratic (1983: 42–46, 96–100). This phenomenon is presumably due to the historic commitment of that party to concern itself with unemployment, and because of the fact that unemployment is generally lower under Democratic administrations.

The evidence of policy-oriented voting regarding inflation has been weak to nonexistent since 1960 (Kiewiet, 1983: 97–98), perhaps because the inflationary experiences of the Nixon-Ford administration eroded the Republicans' historic advantage in that regard. We expect that the sharp drop in inflation under the Reagan administration will serve to revitalize that Republican strength. Fiorina (1981) has suggested that party identification is in fact a "running tally of retrospective evaluations," and the Reagan performance can be expected to strengthen the Republican party among inflation-sensitive voters. In these respects the Reagan administration is typically Republican rather than uniquely conservative.

LINKING RETROSPECTIVE VOTING, PARTY DIFFERENCES,
AND ECONOMIC CONSTRAINTS FOR A THEORY
OF SHORT-TERM PARTISAN CHANGE

While retrospective voting models help explain electoral change by explaining the defeat of incumbents, the work on party differences has no explanation of partisan change. If parties control the instruments of policymaking and are fulfilling the preferences of their main supporters, why should they ever fail to be reelected? What accounts for the kind of performance that leads to rejection at the polls?

There are many possibilities. For example, supply shocks and shifts in world demand can have major impacts on inflation and unemployment rates (Alt, 1985), and voters might punish politicians for outcomes over which the politicians have little or no control. Moreover, one prominent stream of modern macroeconomics questions whether policymakers have any systematic control over real economic variables (Lucas, 1983). While this view is far from universal, there is no doubt that there are important limits on the combinations of inflation and unemployment that policymakers are able to achieve and sustain (see Friedman, 1977).[2]

At any point in time there is a "natural rate of unemployment" at which inflation rates are likely to be stable. If unemployment is pushed below the natural rate for electoral or other purposes, additional and lasting inflation will ensue. Unemployment above the natural rate will be associated with falling inflation. In this view, aggregate demand affects unemployment, which in turn helps determine whether inflation will be rising, falling, or stable. This model is a mechanism that may help explain electoral change.

We suggest that electoral turnover occurs in part because parties may make mistakes or misjudgments about what economic policies are feasible, and that the two parties are likely to make different kinds of mistakes. Arthur Okun (1973: 175) has observed that "when the chips were down, the Democrats have taken their chances on inflation and the Republicans on unemployment and recession. For a generation, every major mistake in economic policy under a Democratic president has taken the form of overstimulating the economy and every major mistake under a Republican president of overrestraining it."

Stabilization policy decisions may be mistakes because they overshoot or undershoot the natural rate of unemployment, and therefore have undesired and perhaps unexpected secondary consequences. This is understandable and does not imply that the parties are foolish or irrational. The natural rate of unemployment is a theoretical construct, and there is ample room for disagreement on exactly where it is, if indeed it exists at all. Given their clienteles, we suggest that Republicans tend to overestimate the natural rate (or act as if they did), risking economic slack but enjoying generally lower rates of inflation. Democrats, in contrast, tend to underestimate the natural rate, risking rising inflation but enjoying generally lower rates of unemployment (see Hibbs, 1986: 67–68). Thus the misjudgments of the different parties may be made in different directions.[3]

Some defeats of incumbent administrations may thus derive from "characteristic mistakes" that parties may make given their goal of fulfilling the needs of their clientele under the context of constraints that may or may not be well understood. We do not mean to imply that parties repeatedly, knowingly, and irrationally undertake actions that are expected to have consequences contrary to their own interests, such as electoral defeat. What appear to be systematic mistakes ex post may have resulted from rational calculation ex ante.

For example, suppose that Democrats and Republicans have different preferences regarding the losses attributable to cyclical fluctuations. Republicans attach greater weight to utility losses associated with unanticipated inflation than do Democrats, and Democrats attach greater weight to utility losses from unemployment in excess of the natural rate than do Republicans. If there is uncertainty regarding the value of the natural rate of unemployment, one would still expect the parties to make different choices in order to minimize expected utility losses, even if they agreed on the probability distribution for the natural rate. Because of the greater weight Democrats attach to recessions, they would rationally choose policies that would have them err on the side of having excessive stimulus (ex post), while the converse would be true for Republicans.

Similarly, suppose that the parties are fully aware of the natural rate of unemployment. Democrats still may prefer more temporary stimulus than Republicans because of distributive consequences that favor the Democratic clientele. However, there may be uncertainty about how much extra stimulus and inflation may be tolerated by voters. Ex ante, a party may rationally risk a somewhat greater probability of election loss in order to achieve gains for party members. Sometimes such a strategy will actually result in election loss, and thus it might in hindsight be considered a "mistake." This is so even though the behavior might have resulted from perfectly rational choices.

Thus in using the term "characteristic mistakes" we refer to actions and outcomes that, with the benefit of hindsight, parties might prefer to have altered. We do not imply that parties are unaware of or uninterested in their own electoral or policy interests. Indeed, it is the purposiveness of their actions that causes parties' "mistakes" to be characteristic.

While many other factors were relevant when the Democrats were turned out of office in 1952 and 1968, in each case the economy had been overstimulated due to war, with concomitant inflationary pressures. In 1980 Carter had moved toward restraint, but only after demand had expanded too fast, with associated inflationary pressures that were intensified by the oil shocks. Characteristic mistakes of the Republicans involve too much slack as a price of efforts to keep inflation down. And each time the Democrats replaced Republicans (in 1960 and 1976), the economy was coming out of serious recessions.

In this context the Reagan administration has been characteristically Republican in producing low inflation at the expense of unemployment that is just above a natural rate that is currently thought to be 6 or 7 percent. But the administration has not had a recession since 1982, and its performance since that year has avoided the "characteristic mistake" of Republicans.

CHARACTERISTIC MISTAKES AND POLITICAL
BUSINESS CYCLES

The above interpretation helps us understand the intriguing, once fashionable, and now discredited idea that incumbents seek to enhance their careers by manipulating the timing of economic events. While William Nordhaus (1975) explicitly linked the political business cycle idea to the natural rate hypothesis through a long-run Phillips curve, both he and Edward Tufte (1978) suggested that unemployment rates might be expected to rise early in an administration so they could be falling as election time approached.

Both of these analyses seem to have been inspired by the experience of the first Nixon administration. This is most explicit in Tufte (1978: chap. 2). Yet in our view it is no coincidence that the best examples of economic slack early in an administration combined with growth as election approached were the first administrations of Nixon and Reagan. Both were Republicans elected on the heels of Democratic administrations making their characteristic mistake of creating inflationary pressures in the economy.

In order to reduce inflation, slack is introduced into the economy, creating an early-term recession. The recessions give way to expansions that begin in time for the next presidential election. An apparent political business cycle is very similar to a characteristic Republican remedy to an economic situation created by a characteristic Democratic mistake. (See Chappell and Keech, 1986, for another reason why Republican administrations are more likely to *appear* to run political business cycles.)

Democrats, in contrast, have moved to stimulate the economy right away in both of the cases in which new Democratic administrations were elected since World War II. The Kennedy-Johnson administration initiated a long expansion that did not create inflationary pressures until wartime. The Carter administration sustained an expansion before previously established inflationary pressures were reduced, and unemployment fell to inflationary levels. This and its bad luck in experiencing major price shocks forced the Carter administration to abandon its expansionary goals and restrain the economy at the worst possible time from an electoral point of view. This experience has been characterized as running the political business cycle backward (Kiewiet and

Rivers, 1985). In fact, it was a characteristic mistake of a Democratic administration seeking to meet the needs of its core constituency but erring.

The Reagan administration came into office on the heels of this Democratic mistake, inheriting an overstimulated economy with inflationary pressures. Given its commitment to price stability, this administration continued the deflationary monetary policies that were instituted in October 1979, causing a deep recession in which unemployment rates topped 10 percent. According to our estimates of a monetary policy reaction function, Republicans normally have a more restrictive monetary policy, even taking into account different economic conditions. This is consistent with our characterization of them. We found, however, that the Reagan administration was if anything even more restrictive than a normal Republican administration (table 13.2), which may help account for the depth of the 1982 recession.

Table 13.2.   Monetary Policy Reaction Function, 1948–84.

$$M1 = -.0023 + .2818\ M1(-1) + .0070\ UN(-1) + .1784\ IN(-1)$$

	(.9683)	(.0794)	(.0022)	(.0725)

	$-.1724\ SUR(-1)$	$-.0022\ REP$	$-.0029\ REAGAN$
	(.0400)	(.0011)	(.0023)

$R^2 = .47$
$DW = 1.99$

M1	is the growth rate of the money supply.
UN	is unemployment divided by its natural rate as estimated by Robert J. Gordon.
IN	is the rate of inflation.
SUR	is the high employment surplus or deficit divided by potential output.
REP	is a dummy variable reading one when Republicans (including Reagan) hold the presidency and zero otherwise.
REAGAN	is a dummy variable reading one when Reagan is president and zero otherwise.

Numbers in parenthesis below coefficients are standard errors, and (-1) designates a one quarter lag.

As indicated above, this left time for both a dramatic drop in inflation and a recovery that was well under way by election time. As table 13.1 shows, the misery index had reached its lowest level in the two administrations by the election year of 1984. The pattern is very much like that which inspired the idea of the political business cycle, but there is an important difference. The expansion associated with the 1972 election took unemployment below the natural rate, exacerbating inflationary pressures that were disguised by the price controls then in effect. The favorable conditions at the 1972 election were not sustainable, hence raising suspicion of cynical manipulation. The favorable conditions of the 1984 election were sustainable because demand had not been overstimulated and unemployment had not been pushed below the natural rate.

The speed of the disinflation has been attributed by some to unique features of the Reagan administration, such as supply side economics or credibility effects. The evidence suggests, however, that the macroeconomic experience of the early 1980s is explainable by more conventional economic thinking. Earle and Kniesner (1984), for example, have estimated the relationship between price inflation, wage inflation, unemployment, and price shocks over a period from 1955 to 1980. Using this model, they forecast inflation for the first years of the Reagan administration using unemployment rates and price shocks of those years as predetermined values. They find little evidence that the behavior of inflation rates during that period were any different from what one might expect for a recession as deep as that of 1981–82. In a comparable analysis Stone and Sawhill argue that almost as much disinflation could have been achieved at substantially less cost in unemployment and lost output (1984: chap. 3).

While this finding may suggest that Reagan is somewhat more conservative than other Republicans, it is not a major difference. In general, the experience of the Reagan administration with respect to economic aggregates fits well with a pattern of "normal" differences between the parties.

A DISAVOWAL OF FINE-TUNING

The Reagan administration has disavowed Keynesian manipulation of the economy (*Economic Report of the President*, 1982:48–50), and in this respect it has returned us to the stance of an earlier era. The Kennedy administration was the first to take up the tools of Keynesian economic policy in such a way as to actively stabilize the economy, or to fine-tune it so as to achieve maximum employment, productivity, and growth (Heller, 1966). Subsequent experience has suggested that active stabilization policy can actually be destabilizing due to the difficulty of predicting the timing of economic events. Furthermore, the prescriptions of Keynesian stabilization policy may be applied asymmetrically, so that the deficits run in times of recession are not appropriately balanced by surpluses in times of prosperity (Buchanan and Wagner, 1977).

The Reagan administration has brought the economy to a stage of sustained growth at low inflation, but probably somewhat above the natural rate of unemployment. Macroeconomically it is a situation not unlike that of 1960, when inflationary expectations were low with moderate economic slack. Stein (1984: chap. 4) has criticized the Kennedy administration for raising expectations for economic performance beyond what the president had a clear program to deliver. Stein draws a parallel with the Carter administration, which sought to repeat the Kennedy success at "getting the economy moving again." But since Carter did not inherit the price stability that Kennedy did, his successes would be short-lived, as indicated above (Stein, 1984:216).

The Reagan administration may leave the economy better than it found it, in terms of a misery index or in terms of the sustainability of the macroeconomic situation. Such a state of affairs may be considered a conservative achievement and a favorable situation for the subsequent administration to inherit. Unless the Republicans win the 1988 election, it may ironically redound to the advantage of the Democrats, just as the price stability and economic slack of the Eisenhower years was exploited by the Kennedy administration (Stein, 1984: chap. 4).

Professional economists are very much less sanguine about the possibilities of active stabilization policy than they were in 1961. But Democrats are still likely to aspire to more growth and lower unemployment, which may risk active destabilization. President Reagan cannot run again, and retrospective voting counts for less in races in which incumbents are not running (Miller and Wattenberg, 1985). Ironically, then, continuing success in macroeconomic performance by the Reagan administration may be followed by the election of a Democrat who has not learned the lessons of the previous three decades.

BUDGET DEFICITS, LONG-TERM GROWTH, AND POLITICAL ACCOUNTABILITY

Ironically, the most lasting macroeconomic legacy of the Reagan administration may be something that is not conservative at all, and that makes things more difficult for many succeeding administrations. In 1980 candidate Reagan promised a package of achievements that was scoffed at by his opponents. Balancing the federal budget while cutting taxes yet increasing defense expenditures was said by George Bush to be voodoo economics, and by John Anderson to be doable "with mirrors." In practice, of course, these three goals have not been simultaneously achievable, and there is no doubt that a balanced budget has been the lowest priority of the three. Defense expenditures have been increased, and income tax rates have been cut, while deficits have skyrocketed.

The commitments to defense and to low taxes are compatible with traditional and conventional views of conservatism, but the budget deficits are not. The deficits reflect a present orientation that is at odds with the long view one normally associates with conservatism. In this sense the Reagan administration is either redefining conservatism or simply not conservative.

There is little doubt that the Reagan deficits are unprecedented, even after various adjustments are made in order to make them less misleading than raw nominal deficits sometimes are. (See Courant and Gramlich, 1986: chap. 1; for alternative views, see Eisner and Pieper, 1984; and Barro, 1974.) Paul Peterson (1985) has argued that the "new politics of deficits" reflects shifts in both elite and mass opinion in the direction of increased tolerance of unbalanced budgets. But the conventional wisdom still opposes deficits for a variety of reasons, not least of which is the "principle" that government budgets ought to balance by the same logic applied to household budgets. (This explanation of course ignores the fact that household budgets are commonly and regularly out of balance.) A second prominent reason is that deficits are said to cause inflation, which is surely possible (see Buchanan and Wagner, 1977). This can happen when the Federal Reserve "monetizes" the deficit by expanding the money supply at a sufficient rate, but the Reagan deficits have been associated with declining inflation, undermining this argument.

Yet deficits do have consequences. In the current context the main consequence is a shifting of savings away from investment in productive capital to government debt service. Since future consumption depends on the future capital stock, this shift undermines the basis for future well-being. Since government debt is largely paying for current consumption, these deficits essentially shift resources away from future toward present consumption. They have been described as a "great consumption binge" (Courant and Gramlich, 1986). Such behavior reflects a present orientation that we find uncharacteristic of conservatism.

Furthermore, this binge at the expense of future generations undermines a fundamental process of political accountability. The retrospective voting that we described above was part of a process of politics that had a certain rationality. So long as incumbent administrations meet basic performance standards, they are likely to be reelected, subject to the limitations of the Twenty-Second Amendment. They are free to pursue the partisan goals of their clienteles so long as they meet the basic and general goals of peace and prosperity broadly conceived.

Pursuit of these goals may lead to the "characteristic mistakes" we identified above, and to electoral defeat. In the context of stabilization policy most of these mistakes become apparent soon enough to allow punishment of the administration that made the mistakes. Moreover, Fair (1978) suggests that the mistakes of stabilization policy may be corrected in the course of a single administration, so that they do not lead to the electoral punishment of those not responsible for the problems.

The consequences of deficits are fundamentally different in timing, however. These deficits increase current consumption at the expense of the future. They imply more consumption during the periods of electoral accountability of the current administration. The question is how long can this go on? When will future consumption decline as a result of this shift in the direction of the present? Edward Gramlich (1984) has carried out some simulations designed to address just this question. He concludes that consumption will not actually decline as a result of current deficits for twenty or twenty-five years. If this is correct, those responsible for these deficits will not be available for a meaningful kind of electoral accountability. Future generations will enjoy a lower standard of living than they might have because of decisions made years before in the Reagan administration.

CONCLUSION

The Reagan administration is in the short term much like other Republican administrations in its macroeconomic policies, and if anything somewhat more conservative. Low levels of inflation with unemployment near the natural rate constitute a substantial achievement compared to recent decades. Moreover, the disavowal of fine-tuning stabilization policy is in the context of these decades a conservative innovation. However, when we take the longer view that is necessary to assess the consequences of massive budget deficits, it appears that the Reagan administration is not so conservative. Its presently oriented policies may leave the nation with problems that reduce the possibilities for future administrations of either party to maintain a high standard of living. As such, these policies may undermine not only economic welfare, but also a system of electoral accountability.

NOTES

1   See also Kiewiet and Rivers (1985), Abramson et al. (1982), and Hibbs (1982b). For alternative views, see Miller and Shanks (1982) and Ladd (1984).
2   We mean to take a rather agnostic point of view ourselves. We argue that policymakers have limited and imperfect control over unemployment in the short run, but that they cannot sustain unemployment indefinitely above or below the "natural rate." Given a variety of possibilities, including multiperiod labor contracts, this view is compatible with rational expectations, though it is consistent with other plausible views of economic reality as well.
3   We are not arguing that parties repeatedly make systematic mistakes without learning from them. They may take calculated risks under conditions of uncertainty about the consequence of their choices. The Democrats may be willing to risk inflation in order to reduce unemployment, and the Republicans may be willing to risk unemployment in order to reduce inflation. The risks may be seen as acceptable, given the value each party places on its preferred goal.

402   The Reagan Administration

REFERENCES

Abramson, Paul R., John H. Aldrich, and David W. Rohde. 1982. *Change and Continuity in the 1980 Elections.* Washington, D.C.: Congressional Quarterly Press.

Alt, James E. 1985. "Political Parties, World Demand and Unemployment: Domestic and International Sources of Economic Activity." *American Political Science Review* 79:1016–40.

Barro, Robert J. 1974. "Are Government Bonds Net Wealth?" *Journal of Political Economy* 82:1095–1117.

Beck, Nathaniel. 1982a. "Does There Exist a Political Business Cycle? A Box-Tiao Analysis." *Public Choice* 38:205–9.

———. 1982b. "Parties, Administrations, and American Macroeconomic Outcomes." *American Political Science Review* 76:83–94.

Black, Stanley W. 1982. "Strategic Aspects of the Political Assignment Problem in Open Economies." In Raymond Lombra and Willard Witte, eds., *The Political Economy of International and Domestic Monetary Relations.* Ames: Iowa State University Press.

Buchanan, James M., and Richard E. Wagner. 1977. *Democracy in Deficit.* New York: Academic Press.

Chappell, Henry W., and William R. Keech. 1986. "Party Differences in Macroeconomic Policies and Outcomes." *American Economic Review Papers and Proceedings* 76:71–74.

Courant, Paul N., and Edward M. Gramlich. 1986. *Federal Budget Deficits.* Englewood Cliffs, N.J.: Prentice-Hall.

Earle, John S., and Thomas J. Kniesner. 1984. "Inflation, Unemployment and the Reagan Administration." *Business Economics* 19:26–33.

Economic Report of the President. 1982. Washington, D.C.: U.S. Government Printing Office.

Economic Report of the President. 1986. Washington, D.C.: U.S. Government Printing Office.

Eisner, Robert, and Paul J. Pieper. 1984. "A New View of the Federal Debt and Budget Deficits." *American Economic Review* 74:11–29.

Fair, Ray C. 1978. "The Use of Optimal Control Techniques to Measure Economic Performance." *International Economic Review* 19:289–309.

Fiorina, Morris P. 1981. *Retrospective Voting in American Elections.* New Haven, Conn.: Yale University Press.

Friedman, Milton. 1977. "Nobel Lecture: Inflation and Unemployment." *Journal of Political Economy* 85:451–72.

Gramlich, Edward M. 1984. "How Bad Are the Large Deficits?" In Gregory B. Mills and John L. Palmer, eds., *Federal Budget Policy in the 1980s.* Washington, D.C.: Urban Institute Press.

Heller, Walter W. 1966. *New Dimensions in Political Economy.* Cambridge, Mass.: Harvard University Press.

Hibbs, Douglas A., Jr. 1977. "Political Parties and Macroeconomic Policy." *American Political Science Review* 71:1467–87.

———. 1982a. "The Dynamics of Political Support for American Presidents Among Occupational and Partisan Groups." *American Journal of Political Science* 26: 312–32.

———. 1982b. "President Reagan's Mandate from the 1980 Elections: A Shift to the Right?" *American Politics Quarterly* 10:387–420.

———. 1986. "Political Parties and Macroeconomic Policies and Outcomes in the United States." *American Economic Review Papers and Proceedings* 76:66–70.

Kelley, Stanley, Jr. 1983. *Interpreting Elections.* Princeton, N.J.: Princeton University Press.

Kiewiet, D. Roderick. 1981. "Policy-Oriented Voting in Response to Economic Issues." *American Political Science Review* 75:448–59.

———. 1983. *Macroeconomics and Micropolitics.* Chicago: University of Chicago Press.

———, and Douglas Rivers. 1985. "The Economic Basis of Reagan's Appeal." In John E. Chubb and Paul E. Peterson, eds., *The New Direction in American Politics.* Washington, D.C.: Brookings Institution.

Ladd, Everett Carll, Jr. 1984. "The Reagan Phenomenon and Public Attitudes toward Government." In Lester Salamon and Michael S. Lund, eds., *The Reagan Presidency and the Governing of America.* Washington, D.C.: Urban Institute Press.

Lowi, Theodore J. 1984. "Ronald Reagan—Revolutionary?" In Lester M. Salamon and Michael S. Lund, eds., *The Reagan Presidency and the Governing of America.* Washington, D.C.: Urban Institute Press.

Lucas, Robert E. 1983. *Studies in Business-Cycle Theory.* Cambridge, Mass: MIT Press.

Markus, Gregory B. 1982. "Political Attitudes in an Election Year." *American Political Science Review* 76:538–60.

Miller, Arthur H., and Martin P. Wattenberg. 1985. "Throwing the Rascals Out: Policy and Performance Evaluations of Presidential Candidates, 1952–1980." *American Political Science Review* 79:359–72.

Miller, Warren E., and J. Merrill Shanks. 1982. "Policy Directions and Presidential Leadership: Alternative Interpretations of the 1980 Presidential Election." *British Journal of Political Science* 12:299–356.

Nordhaus, William D. 1975. "The Political Business Cycle." *Review of Economics and Statistics* 42:169–90.

Okun, Arthur M. 1973. "Comments on Stigler's Paper." *American Economic Review Papers and Proceedings* 63:172–77.

Peterson, Paul E. 1985. "The New Politics of Deficits." In John E. Chubb and Paul E. Peterson, eds., *The New Direction in American Politics.* Washington, D.C.: Brookings Institution.

Schlozman, Kay Lehman, and Sidney Verba. 1979. *Injury to Insult.* Cambridge, Mass.: Harvard University Press.

Stein, Herbert. 1984. *Presidential Economics.* New York: Simon and Schuster.

Stone, Charles F., and Isabel V. Sawhill. 1984. *Economic Policy in the Reagan Years.* Washington, D.C.: Urban Institute Press.

Tufte, Edward R. 1978. *Political Control of the Economy.* Princeton, N.J.: Princeton University Press.

14. Religion and the Resurgence of Conservatism

MICHAEL GILLESPIE AND MICHAEL LIENESCH

Since the late 1970s the Anglo-American democracies have experienced a surprising resurgence of conservatism. This new conservatism has been concerned primarily with issues of economics and foreign policy. In the United States, however, it has also addressed issues of cultural and social policy, and as a result has taken on a moral or even moralistic cast.

In this chapter we consider the reasons for this American exceptionalism, concentrating on the role of religion in American public life. Beginning with a comparison of the respective relationships between religion and politics in the United States, Britain, and Canada, we will attempt to consider the peculiar place of religion in American politics in the larger context of Anglo-American experience. Second, we will examine the historical and theoretical role of religion in American politics. Third, concentrating on conservative Protestants, Catholics, and Jews, we will try to explain how and why religion has been influential in the new conservatism of the 1970s. Finally, we will consider larger theoretical implications, speculating on the future role of religion in American politics.

RELIGION AND POLITICS IN ANGLO-AMERICAN PERSPECTIVE

At first glance it might seem that religion is important in American politics for the simple reason that so many Americans are religious.

American religiosity is uncontestable: 95 percent of the population claim to believe in God; 80 percent believe that Jesus Christ is God; a surprising one-third believe in Satan, or a literal devil (Fowler, 1985: 1). Approximately 65 percent of Americans belong to an organized religious group, and about 40 percent attend church in any given week (Fowler, 1985: 2). These numbers are somewhat surprising when compared to Canada, where church members make up 60 percent of the population, and weekly church attendance is about 35 percent, but they are remarkable in comparison to Britain where church membership runs about 17 percent and weekly church attendance approximately 13 percent (Hastings and Hastings, 1983–84: 445; Brierly, 1983).

Recent surveys also indicate that Americans are more intensely religious than Canadians or Britons. A 1979 Gallup survey shows that 80 percent of those Americans queried felt that religion played either a very important (42 percent) or fairly important (38 percent) part in their lives (Gallup, 1980: appendix Q). Among Canadians only about 51 percent were willing to say that religion played any part in their lives at all (Canadian Gallup, 1980: 439A). Asked to rate the importance of religion on their lives on a scale of 1 (less) to 9 (more), only 18 percent of Britons responded in the 7 to 9 range (Hastings and Hastings, 1983–84: 445).

Even so, America's religious faith is deeply divided. In the United States only 50 to 60 percent of church members are found in mainline Protestant (Methodist, Presbyterian, Lutheran, Episcopal) or Roman Catholic denominations (Simpson and MacLeod, 1983: 7). In Canada, by contrast, 87 percent of the total religious membership is found in the Roman Catholic, United, and Anglican churches (Simpson and MacLeod, 1983: 6). In Britain membership in the four major denominations (Roman Catholic, Presbyterian, Church of England, Methodist) composes 88 percent of the total religious population (Brierly, 1983: 14–15). John Simpson and Henry MacLeod have pointed out that in the United States it takes the combined membership of twenty-one independent denominations to reach a similar percentage (1983: 6).

Sectarianism is a hallmark of American religion. In the United States Baptists alone constitute 20 percent of the churchgoing population. Another 20 to 30 percent are members of non-mainline churches, including independent fundamentalists, evangelicals, and pentecos-

406 Religion and Conservatism

tals, along with Jehovah's Witnesses, Mormons, Seventh-Day Adventists, and others (Simpson and MacLeod, 1983: 6). Among Canadian churchgoers, on the other hand, Baptists, pentecostals, and sectarian Protestants together make up only 9 percent of the total population, and in Britain sectarianism is even more unusual, constituting a mere 2–3 percent of the population (Simpson and MacLeod, 1983: 6; Brierly, 1983: 18–22).

In addition, with the exception of a few regionally restricted denominations such as the Southern Baptists, the American religious population is drastically dispersed. This is in clear contrast to Britain, where religion is regionalized, with Episcopalians and Methodists in England, Presbyterians in Scotland, and Baptists in Wales (Brierly, 1983: 16–20). In Canada as well churches are territorially dispersed. The domination of Roman Catholicism in Quebec, contrasted to the large Protestant majorities in the other provinces, suggests the basic bipolarity of Canadian religious politics (see O'Toole, 1982: 3–4).

The American political system is also a factor. Within the framework set forth by James Madison in Federalist 10, American religious groups have the same voice as members of other interest groups. In this pluralist system the denominations are forced to compete for political visibility, both among themselves and with other nonreligious groups. Moreover, in seeking political power they must make alliances, compromising principles in order to build coalitions. In Britain and Canada, on the other hand, there is no strong tradition of interest-group politics. Simpson and MacLeod have described the absence of interest-group activity among Canadian churches. They write: "Rather there is a tradition of interests and issues being dealt with through what, in other circumstances, would be called 'diplomatic channels' or, perhaps, 'back-door representations'. Thus, the major denominations have always been, more or less, well-connected with governments as a matter of course" (1983: 9).

The American party system mirrors this pluralism. Though a few denominations, notably Catholics and Jews, have traditionally been allied with one of the major parties, the recent tendency has been to dispersal. The situation is far different in the other Anglo-American democracies, where the connections between religion and party have historically been quite close. In England, the Anglican church has been described until quite recently as "the Tory party at prayer." In

Canada as well, the Catholic, United, and Anglican churches have historically acted in close cooperation with the majority parties, serving, as Simpson and MacLeod (1983:9) put it, as "the conscience of the state." Moreover, the ties between William Aberhart's Prophetic Bible Institute and the Alberta Social Credit party, and (to a lesser extent) the link between the Canadian Social Gospel movement and the Co-operative Commonwealth Federation in Saskatchewan, suggest that the connections are not limited to the major parties.

Above all, there is the fact that in the United States religion is disestablished. In this regard the American churches would seem to be condemned to political powerlessness. The presence of American Baptists alone, with their deep historical commitment to the separation of church and state, is crucial here, as is the presence of other even more fiercely apolitical sects such as the Jehovah's Witnesses. By contrast, the Church of England has profited vastly over the centuries from its establishment (Hinchliff, 1966). While there has been no established church in Canada since 1854, the power of the major denominations within their provinces has been so great that some Canadian sociologists of religion have argued that these churches have attained "quasi-established" status (Simpson and MacLeod, 1983: 8).

Yet the effects of religious establishment are quite complicated. In America, where no established church exists, religious involvement in politics has been both intense and pervasive. In Britain, on the other hand, the Church of England has played a subdued and often ambivalent part in public life. Indeed, in the 1960s, tensions between church and Parliament spawned a successful movement to free the church from parliamentary authority over ecclesiastical appointments (Hinchliff, 1966: 153−72). In Canada the very power of the quasi-established churches in their respective regions has led to an atmosphere of accommodation, and the result has been both religious and political toleration. According to Simpson and MacLeod (1983:8), the Canadian churches "do not underwrite a singular notion of Canadian nationhood. There is no way to participate through religious practice in a symbolic unity called Canada."

Thus we are faced with the paradox that the United States, with its broad but divided and dispersed religiosity, its pluralistic political system, its interest-based, self-consciously secular parties, and its sectarian tradition of free exercise, relative religious tolerance, and separation of church and state, may well be the regime in which religion has the greatest effect on politics. To explain this paradox, we turn to a consideration of the role of ideology, for it is in American political thought that we find explanations for the complicated interconnectedness between American religion and American politics. Our treatment considers the three major manifestations of religion in America: Protestantism, Catholicism, and Judaism. Here our intention is not to be comprehensive, but to be broadly representative. Our discussion is historical and theoretical. We begin with Protestantism.

PROTESTANTISM AND POLITICAL CONSERVATISM

The peculiar relationship between American Protestantism and American politics begins with covenant theology. As described by Perry Miller (1953: 414–15), seventeenth-century Protestants considered themselves to be inheritors of the Abrahamic covenant, according to which America stood as the last in the long line of the descendants of Abraham, the modern "chosen nation" or the "New Israel." As such, they saw themselves as unique, not only specially favored by God, but also peculiarly responsible for founding a Christian commonwealth that would be a model for the rest of mankind. Robert Bellah (1975: 1–35) has singled out this concept of "chosen people," replete with the themes of persecution and exile, wandering in the wilderness, and founding a new "promised land," as crucial not only to American Protestantism, but also to American nationalism, to what he calls America's "myth of origin." Transformed even in the seventeenth century into a covenant requiring that Americans retain their original religious mission while also pursuing the secular ends of prosperity and progress, the concept of the covenanted nation has remained prominent in numerous versions of American nationalism, including Henry Luce's "American Century," John Foster Dulles's identification of America with the "free world," and Ronald Reagan's 1976 vision of America as the "shining city on the hill" (see Bellah, 1975: 39).

Equally essential to the relationship between Protestantism and politics is the theme of the "errand into the wilderness." At least from the mid-seventeenth century, according to Miller (1956: 1–15), American Protestants have seen themselves as engaged in two missions, one requiring that they save the Old World by establishing a "saving remnant," the other requiring that they save themselves by creating their own Christian commonwealth out of a new and often forbidding land. By confronting and taming the western wilderness, Protestants could convince themselves of their special chosen status. Miller (1956) has shown how this particular calling can be seen as planting the seeds of American expansionism and continental empire. At the same time Sacvan Bercovitch (1978: 3–30) has described how the idea of the errand was transformed in the eighteenth century into a crusade to establish Christian civilization and an early form of commercial capitalism, creating in America an environment where, in the words of one early Puritan, "religion and profit jump together" (cited in Bercovitch, 1978: 34). Nevertheless, the reconciliation of faith with commerce was problematic, for early American Protestants were encouraged to pursue success, but never at the cost of salvation. In other words, American Protestantism has almost from the beginning assumed an ambivalent attitude toward commerce, demanding that America be both Christian and capitalist. Moreover, as Bellah (1975: 61–86) has shown, from Samuel Sewall to Norman Vincent Peale the ambivalence has remained in the continuing Calvinist commitment to pursue a gospel of "salvation and success" (see also Cawelti, 1965).

Third and related, American Protestantism has influenced American politics through the medium of millennialism. From the earliest Puritan "Fifth Monarachists," who saw the New World as the fifth and final empire promised in the Book of Revelation, Protestants have believed they were playing a millennial role (see Maclear, 1971). America was not simply a refuge, it was a new beginning, the site of the "New Jerusalem." Ernest Tuveson (1968: 52–73) has described how the theme became peculiarly important in the mid-eighteenth century, as theologians led by Jonathan Edwards and Joseph Bellamy applied biblical eschatology to current events and set in motion a millennial politics that would culminate in the apocalyptical fervor of the American Revolution. Yet as Tuveson (1968: 73–90) has also shown, the theme of the "redeemer nation" has retained its vitality from that time, becoming manifest in the millennial expectation of the pre-Civil War period ("Mine eyes have seen the glory of the coming of the Lord"), the hopes of the First World War (the "war to end all wars"), and the more complicated mixture of postatomic hopes and fears that have led Americans to believe not only that God was "on our side," but also that in their hands lay "the fate of the world."

With these themes providing ideological underpinning, Protestantism faced the more troublesome task of reconciling itself to liberalism. Here the crucial connection was provided by the egalitarian and individualistic impulse of evangelicalism (see Ahlstrom, 1975: 656–58). Inspired in part by the revivalism of the Second Great Awakening, which swept back and forth across America in the first two decades of the nineteenth century, Protestantism became a democratic faith, with circuit riders and camp meeting preachers holding forth from stump stages and baptizing in rain barrels, in what Alan Heimert (1966: 19) has called the "democratization of the Deity." Equally, because the evangelical message was so intensely personal, focusing on individual conversion as opposed to social conformity, Protestants of the period found themselves practicing a more individualistic faith (see Heimert, 1966). Strengthening antinomian and dissenter tendencies, Protestantism became both more diverse and, ironically, less sectarian (see Hudson, 1961: 33–49). The result was an extraordinary proliferation of churches, in which a largely monolithic Congregational faith became a hodgepodge of independent denominations. Sidney Mead (1975: 41–42) has shown how this religious pluralism fit well with the constitutional pluralism of the new nation, as Protestant churches adopted principles of religious and political toleration, opposing the establishment of a state church while demanding the free exercise of their own denominational faith.

At the same time, as Protestant evangelicals adopted these liberal tenets, they began to see themselves as protectors of liberal society. Grant Wacker (1984b: 24) has shown how nineteenth-century evangelicals took up the role of what he calls "custodians" of American culture, committing themselves to the twin tasks of propagating piety and maintaining public morality. Entering into a kind of crusade to protect America from perdition, they set out across a broad front, taking up causes from abolition and world peace to public hygiene, elimination of prostitution, and temperance (see Hudson, 1961:84; Marty, 1970: 89–99). Pervading these efforts was a mixture of moralism and social activism that transcended terms such as "liberal" or "conservative." Whether abolishing slavery or passing blue laws, advocating women's rights or attacking Masonry, evangelicals saw themselves as champions of what Booth Fowler (1985:31) has called "civic piety," Christian soldiers battling to save American society, and to save its Christian soul.

With the Civil War, however, and in its aftermath, evangelicalism became polarized. As early as the 1830s, efforts to create a continuing coalition of Protestant reformers, what the Jacksonian cleric Ezra Stiles Ely would call a "Christian Party in Politics" (see Handy, 1971: 57), would founder on the issue of slavery. Alienating North from South, splitting Baptists, Episcopalians, Presbyterians, and other denominations, slavery was only the first of a long line of issues that would divide and disperse the religious reform impulse (see Hudson, 1961: 103–9). But especially in the 1880s and 1890s, as Protestants faced the twin specters of immigration and urbanization, the old alliance of moralism and social activism became strained (see Fowler, 1985: 18–19). With the creation of the Social Gospel movement, reform became controversial, as liberals in the Federal Council of Churches undertook to bring Christian commitment to the cause of the poor and the oppressed in the new industrial order, and conservatives looked on in dismay.

By the early twentieth century the strains between liberal and conservative Protestants had resulted in schism. With the publication from 1910 to 1915 of *The Fundamentals*, a series of paperback volumes written by an array of American and British scholars, conservatives rediscovered not only a theological identity, but also a religious mission. Emphasizing personal piety, denouncing the "isms" (Russelism, Eddyism, Mormonism, Modern Spiritualism, and, most important, "modernism"), the "fundamentals" recalled conservatives to the standards of biblical inerrancy, miraculous revelation, and millennial eschatology. Moreover, as George Marsden (1980: 120) has shown, they served as a rallying point for conservatives to take the offensive in reasserting their role as cultural custodians, defenders of traditional rural and small-town values, champions, as Billy Sunday would put it, of "decency, patriotism, and manliness" (cited in Hudson, 1961: 148).

The roots of contemporary Protestant conservatism lay in this early twentieth-century fundamentalism. By the 1920s custodial conservatives could be found attempting to ban the teaching of evolution in the public schools, confiscating pornography, and passing blue laws. Fundamentalists took up temperance with a vengeance, turning a moralistic concern for public health and welfare into a "symbolic crusade" to assert "American" values (Gusfield, 1963). By the 1940s Protestant conservatives such as Gerald L. K. Smith had extended the crusade into an all-out assault on Franklin D. Roosevelt and the New Deal. In the 1950s Billy James Hargis's Christian Anti-Communist Crusade strongly supported Senator Joe McCarthy and Congressman Richard M. Nixon in their efforts to search out communists in high places. Protestant conservatives of the 1960s continued the campaign, seeking to counter the influence of the civil rights movement and to impeach Earl Warren (see Ribuffo, 1980). In short, the line from fundamentalist antimodernism to the anticommunism and antiliberalism of the midcentury Christian conservatives was clear and direct, leading sociologists of the postwar period to describe the continuing influence of what they would call the "radical right" (Bell, 1963).

Protestant conservatives of the 1980s are inheritors of this legacy. Yet while tapping the tradition of anticommunism and antiliberalism, the contemporary religious right stands far removed from its early fundamentalist origins. Theologically, Protestant conservatism has changed its character dramatically, moving from a closed and suspicious sectarian fundamentalism on the one hand, and a complacent and highly conventional evangelicalism on the other, toward a more aggressive, more dynamic fundamentalist evangelicalism. The result has been an extraordinary resurgence of conservative religion in the United States, so that a 1979 Gallup Poll (1979: 14) could find that thirty million Americans considered themselves to be born-again "evangelicals," while another twenty million were willing to call themselves sympathetic to or supportive of this evangelicalism. In the 1970s, while mainline churches lost some two million members, fundamentalist and evangelical churches gained some ten million more (Kelley, 1978: 165–72). Symbolic of this revived religious conservatism are television preachers such as Jerry Falwell, Pat Robertson, Jimmy Swaggart, and others, several of whom boast of audiences in the tens of millions and pledges amounting in some cases to over $1 million per week (see Hadden and Swan, 1981). When one also considers the economic power of the conservative arms of the Christian publishing, broadcasting, and recording industries, this new-style "old-time religion" seems particularly formidable.

Contributing to this theological transformation is a significant sociodemographic realignment. The new Protestant conservatism can be seen as the product of a long postwar process of modernization and secularization (Guth, 1981: 1). With its blend of piety and traditional morality, it has commonly been described as an attempt to shore up established values in the face of rapid social change and to reclaim Victorian lower-middle-class values, centering especially on the home and family (see Fairbanks, 1981: 3–7; Wacker, 1984a: 311). Demographic data appear to support this view, since the new conservativism is largely a product of the New South, following the Southern Rim which runs from Pat Robertson's Virginia Beach and Jerry Falwell's Lynchburg, Virginia, through Kentucky and Tennessee, across Arkansas and Oklahoma, touching the major metropolitan areas of Texas and ending in traditionally conservative Southern California (Wacker, 1984b: 25–26). In these areas of rapid population growth, rural and small-town Protestants find themselves gravitating to the smaller and middle-sized cities, where conservative churches provide a means to ease the transition from the old to the new society (see FitzGerald, 1981: 72–73).

It follows that Protestant conservatives are most militant in the cause of morality. As Wacker has argued, the neo-Victorianism of the Protestant right is closely tied to the perceived breakdown of social and especially sexual mores. Thus writers like Tim LaHaye in his *Battle for the Family* can make the case not only against abortion and birth control, but also against feminism, homosexuality, and an ill-defined "sexual liberation," including everything from pornographic movies to sex education in the schools (see Wacker, 1984a: 307). Closely related is the concern with "secular humanism," an ill-defined combination of atheism, liberalism, modernism, and socialism. LaHaye, for example, believes that there exists a cadre of some 250,000 secular humanists who conspire together to control the basic institutions of American society. More important, however, is secular humanism's indirect influence, and especially its use of the media to indoctrinate unsuspecting Americans in "adultery, fornication, perversion, abomination, and just plain *sin*" (cited in Wacker, 1984: 307). In this setting Protestant conservatives feel both alienated from and responsible for

America's moral decline. Their response is a revivalistic return to cultural custodianship, a commitment to, in the words of Jerry Falwell, "decency, the home, the family, morality, the free enterprise system, and all the great ideals that are the cornerstone of this nation" (Falwell, 1980: 244; see also Lienesch, 1983: 83–85).

Equally in economic terms, the new Protestant conservatives can be seen as the product of the change to a postindustrial economy. Far from the stereotype of backwoods hillbillies, these new-style conservatives tend to be small businessmen, lower-level white-collar workers, and service personnel. Largely white, moderately well-educated, adequately skilled, they are an economically marginal population, insecure enough to want to protect what they have, successful enough to desire more (see Fitzgerald, 1981: 99).

Thus these Protestant conservatives are eager to emphasize the connections between capitalism and Calvinist morality. Typical is Christian businessman Rich DeVos, founder of Amway Corporation, who contends in his autobiographical self-help manual *Believe!* that economic profit is a sign of inner grace. Poverty, by contrast, suggests not only financial but also moral failure (see Lienesch, 1983: 74–76, 88–90). Indeed, Protestant conservatism compounds its Calvinism with a healthy dose of Social Darwinism, so that many can argue that the best and most moral businessmen are rewarded, and the worst, "the inefficient and infirm," are "weeded out" (cited in Lienesch, 1983: 90). This leads to an abiding attachment to free market economics, and especially to its supply-side and trickle-down versions. Complementing this commitment to relatively unrestricted capitalism is a deep distrust of democratic social programs. "Nowhere at any time did Christ mention a government welfare program," Senator Jesse Helms has asserted (cited in Lienesch, 1983: 76). His words are echoed by the Reverend Mr. Falwell, who has argued that all public assistance programs should be returned to the church (see Lienesch, 1982: 414).

Ideologically, Protestant conservatism is not far removed from earlier versions of Christian anticommunism. Some of the most prominent figures in today's religious right were associated in the 1950s with organizations such as the John Birch Society and the Christian Anti-Communist Crusade. Throughout Protestant conservatism, patriotism runs deep. Notable about the recent Protestant right, however, is its millennialism. To many in the movement, communism represents the new Antichrist. America, by contrast, is the organizing point for the Christian armies of light. In this bipolar view of the world, conflict is inevitable. Indeed, to Protestant conservatives, the coming conflict has already been prophetically foreseen in the millennarian books of the Bible. The final battle, or Armageddon, will be for the survival of Israel. (Hence the Protestant conservative fascination with events in the Middle East, as well as its uncompromising commitment to the state of Israel.) But Armageddon will in turn bring on the millennium, the thousand years of peace. Hence Protestant conservatives such as Falwell are fairly blithe fatalists, who seem almost eager to predict the coming nuclear catastrophe. Says Falwell: "If God is on our side, no matter how superior the Soviet Union is, they could never touch us. God would miraculously protect America" (cited in Lienesch, 1983: 93).

Finally, it can be said that the new religious conservatism has been instrumental in the creation of a new kind of conservative American politics. In the last ten years alone, fundamentalists and evangelicals have shown a remarkable increase in political participation. In ten studies based on data from 1950 to 1974, evangelicals were found to express more disapproval of political action than any other religious group; after 1976, seven national and three local studies found them to be the most politically involved of all the groups studied (Latus, 1982: 10). As fund-raisers, Falwell and the conservative television preachers are well-practiced professionals (Hadden and Swan, 1983). As backroom politicians, their political operatives, many of them veterans of the Christian school lobby, have been surprisingly skillful (Keller, 1980). In terms of electoral power, especially in national elections, Christian conservative influence has proven hard to measure and even harder to predict (see Lienesch, 1982:403–5). But in the broader context, considering their involvement with local school boards, town councils, party caucuses, and lobbying campaigns and mass protests at virtually all levels, Christian conservatives have demonstrated remarkable political power. Moreover, their activism has tended to be self-perpetuating, with increasing interest and involvement begetting even greater levels of participation (see Lienesch, 1982: 415–21).

Yet it should be noted that this combination of morality and movement politics has not been limited to Protestant conservatives. In the last two decades church leaders and congregations of almost every denomination and political persuasion have taken up political causes. Among the most important of these have been American Catholics, to whom we turn now.

CATHOLIC CONSERVATISM

Since its introduction into the British American colonies in 1634, Roman Catholicism has been a minority religion, whose theological authoritarianism placed it at odds with Protestantism. Throughout the pre-Revolutionary period Catholicism was a persecuted religion in all of the colonies except Pennsylvania and Maryland, where it was a religion of refugees (Tavard, 1969: 13). Although American Catholicism was much more liberal than European Catholicism, Protestant prejudice and persecution remained, especially among Puritan Congregationalists, those inheritors of the English Reformation who felt that Catholicism was fundamentally authoritarian and thus antagonistic to the spirit of religious and political freedom.

The American Revolution, however, helped integrate Catholics into America's "Christian Israel." Almost without exception, Catholics supported the Revolution, as did the Catholic kings of Spain and France (see Moore, 1956:3). In addition, the Revolution had a profound impact within Catholicism, for after 1783 American Catholics began to restructure their faith along the Protestant model of the layman's church. This movement, called trusteeism, and based originally on lay ownership of church property, became influential in the 1780s and 1790s, with trustees increasingly laying claim to the right to appoint and dismiss pastors without interference from superior ecclesiastical authorities (Carthy, 1964:47; Moore, 1956:3). Here the relative autonomy of the American church was a factor, for in this early period distance alone made it difficult for Rome to exercise its authority in any but the most superficial way. In 1790 the Vatican recognized this reality, granting authority to American Catholics to elect their own bishop.

The place of Catholicism in American politics was largely shaped by the democratic forces of the nineteenth century, and in particular by the competing strains of ethnic assimilation and nativist persecution. With Irish and German immigration in particular, the number of Catho-

lics increased, while their social status fell (see Gleason, 1970: 13 ff.).
The Protestant reaction that followed, which Ray Allen Billington (1938: 322–44) has called the "Protestant Crusade," inspired the Know-Nothing movement and the widespread anti-Catholic riots of the mid-1850s (see also Reichley, 1985: 185).

The Protestant nativism of the antebellum period united Catholics and drove them into the Jacksonian Democratic party (Reichley, 1985: 183). This was especially true of Irish Catholics, who bore the brunt of the nativist attack because they remained mostly in the cities where they competed with the white Protestant labor force for jobs (see Odegard, 1960: 117). In the long run, however, the most crucial effect of nativism was that it accelerated assimilation on the part of Catholics. Indeed, by the close of the century, nativist attacks would often be led by assimilated Irish and Germans who, styling themselves "true" Americans, acted to hold back the tides of eastern and southern European immigrants.

Following the Civil War, this process of assimilation accelerated, as liberals within the church tried to show that Catholicism was not only compatible with American democratic society and nationalism, but that American liberalism was divinely sanctioned (Tavard, 1969: 102; Ellis, 1952: II, 1–80; Maynard, 1941: 489–521). Bishop John Ireland, a leading liberal, turned to Protestant millennialism in declaring America the providential nation: "Even as I believe God reigns over men and nations, so do I believe that a divine mission has been assigned to the republic of the United States. That mission is to prepare the world by example and moral influence for the universal reign of human liberty and human rights" (cited in Tavard, 1969: 71). Yet resistance to liberalization within the church was strong. In 1864 Pope Pius IX had included liberalism among the heresies meriting condemnation in his "Syllabus of Errors" (Moore, 1956: 4). This reaction to secular liberalism reached its zenith in 1870 with the declaration of papal infallibility (Carthy, 1964: 54; Moore, 1956: 5). In addition, "Americanism," or the trend toward assimilation within the American church, soon came under fire, and was condemned in 1899 by Pope Leo XIII's *Testem Benevolentiae*. The results of this declaration were devastating to the American church, leading to greater subordination to Rome and an increasing conservatism and mediocrity within the American Catholic hierarchy.

The rejection of "Americanism" came simultaneously with a new wave of anti-Catholicism. Ironically, by drawing a line between Catholicism and liberalism, the church itself had played a role in dividing Catholics from Protestants. But Protestant nativists needed little encouragement for their anti-Catholicism. By 1884, Catholics had become identified as the party of "Rum, Romanism, and Rebellion" and the target of strong anti-Catholic attacks by the American Protective Association and the Ku Klux Klan (Moore, 1956: 9; Greely, 1977: 10). Anti-Catholic nativism culminated in 1928 when Protestant Republicans and Democrats alike argued that the election of Al Smith would mean the subordination of Washington to Rome, while Billy Sunday characterized Smith supporters as "damnable whiskey politicians, bootleggers, crooks, pimps and streetwalkers," and Senator Tom Heflin of Alabama argued from the floor of Congress that all Catholics should be deported from the country (cited in Menendez, 1977: 41).

The failure of "Americanism" left Catholics as ambivalent and often alienated supporters of American politics. Although they were part of the New Deal coalition, they had little influence on policy and were equivocal about many reforms. While recognizing the necessity of active government to confront the problems of the Great Depression, many Catholics feared that big government endangered Catholic institutions such as the parochial schools and charitable institutions (Gleason, 1970: 101–14). Catholic social reformers such as Peter Maurin and Dorothy Day of the Catholic Worker Movement, drawing on Catholicism's ancient suspicion of individualism and materialism, condemned the liberal reformism of the New Deal and offered a socialist communitarian alternative (Tavard, 1969: 89; Reichley, 1985: 222). More commonly, Catholic critics confronted the Roosevelt reforms from the right with a uniquely Catholic conservatism that had proponents in Father Charles Coughlin and Father Francis Talbot, editor of *America*, who declared that Catholics were the last group resisting un-American progressivism and adhering "to the Constitution and the traditional Americanism that made our country what it was before 1914" (cited in Gleason, 1970: 106).

This Catholic conservatism continued to be a strong current beneath the mainstream postwar liberalism of American politics. With rising levels of education and income, urban ethnics could be found moving in large numbers from the cities to the suburbs and from blue-collar to white-collar occupations. Thus while Catholics remained among the most traditionally "liberal" voting groups, they began to edge somewhat to the right, at least on economic issues. At the same time Protestant prejudice seemed to wane, as signified by the election of John F. Kennedy in 1960. Ironically, by effectively foiling Protestant fears, Kennedy's secular progressivism also weakened traditional Catholic loyalties and had the long-term result of encouraging Catholic conservatives to move beyond the boundaries of Democratic party liberalism. The cold war was also crucial to this increasingly influential Catholic conservatism, as anticommunists like Cardinal Francis Spellman supported American involvement in Korea and Vietnam and denounced critics of American foreign policy.

On the whole, however, the greatest single factor in the creation of contemporary Catholic conservatism was Vatican II, which in a sense institutionalized the very "Americanism" that had been condemned as heresy in 1899. While Vatican II gave birth to an age of liberal reform, it also evoked conservative reaction. As Andrew Greely (1977: 126–51) has shown, the Vatican II reforms resulted in a marked increase in the religious participation of liberal Catholics. At the same time conservative Catholic resentment began to grow. Exacerbating this trend was the decentralization of policymaking, leading to a more activist clergy and a more involved laity. The cumulative effect of these changes was that conservative laymen for the first time began to question liberal positions within the clergy on issues such as civil rights, social welfare, and the Vietnam War. Finally, following John XXIII's *Mater et Magistra*, which legitimized social and political activism, Vatican II prepared the way for a reconciliation of Catholicism with socialism and revolutionary reform under the auspices of liberation theology. While Paul VI's *Octogesima Adveniens* drew a sharp distinction between historical movements and philosophical teachings, enabling Catholics to join socialist parties while rejecting socialist ideology, the distinction was often lost on conservatives.

Augmenting this trend toward a more conservative Church was Pope Paul VI's encyclical on birth control and reproductive rights, *Humanae Vitae*, which led to widespread disillusionment among liberals. Greely (1977:93) estimated that the encyclical led to a 50 percent decline in religious practice among Catholics, and that most of the decline was drawn from the church's most liberal members. Moreover, even among conservatives *Humanae Vitae* seemed to augment the trend toward a more restive laity. Finally, the ascension of Pope John Paul II was crucial, for Catholic conservatives found in him a champion of traditional values, a supporter of market capitalism (in *Laborem Exercens*), and an uncompromising anticommunist.

The issue that mobilized conservatives most was abortion. Here the turning point was the 1973 Supreme Court decision *Roe v. Wade*. The antiabortion movement that followed not only motivated some Catholics to become intensely involved politically, but also impelled them to form alliances with Protestant conservatives. Indeed, as Paul Weyrich, one of the founders of the new right and a devout Eastern Rite Catholic, has described it, the issue of abortion has been instrumental in bridging the ancient enmity between rural fundamentalist Protestants and urban ethnic Catholics (see Conaway, 1983). Here Vatican II played a surprising part as well, in that its ethos of ecumenism and religious toleration calmed anti-Catholic fears among conservative Protestants. In any case, the early success of this coalition in promoting passage of the Hyde Amendment (1980) and in working against pro-choice candidates in the 1980 election added even more impetus to this revived Catholic conservatism.

More recently, conservatives have taken up the issues of economics and economic justice. In the response to the recent Bishop's Letter on the Economy, for example, conservatives led by Michael Novak, Alexander Haig, William E. Simon, and others have reiterated their support for capitalism as a religiously rooted system. America, they argue, is a symbol of both Christianity and capitalism. Inherent in each of these legacies is freedom, including free enterprise. In his "The Theology of the Corporation," Novak continued to update Calvinism by arguing that the modern corporation could best be understood in religious terms, offering, as he put it, "metaphors for grace, a kind of insight into God's ways in history" (cited in McCarthy, 1983). In fact, while Catholic conservatives like Novak stop short of arguing that capitalism is God's gift (Falwell makes the point explicitly), they come at times very close. Although "no political economy dares to pretend that it measures up to that Kingdom [of God]," Novak concludes in his *The Spirit of Democratic Capitalism*, "democratic capitalism does welcome judgment under that Kingdom's clear light" (1982: 359).

Finally, these contemporary Catholic conservatives are Christian anticommunists, whose views on foreign policy sometimes seem to presuppose a millennial mission. Indeed, the response of the conservative laity to the bishops echoes those early Fifth Monarchists who saw America as the savior of the world: "We cannot but believe that a singular mission is assigned to America, glorious for itself and beneficent to the whole race. . . . With our hopes are bound up the hopes of the millions of the earth. . . . The world is in a throes; a new age is to be born" (*Toward the Future*, 1984: 14).

The politics of the new Catholic conservativism exhibits considerable diversity. Paul Weyrich, for example, a member of the Greek Catholic church, which he joined after deeming the Roman Catholic church too liberal, is not only a founder of the new right, but a devout Christian ideologue who has stated that the purpose of Christian conservative politics is to "Christianize America" (see Conaway, 1983). Novak, by contrast, considered by some a "neoconservative," prefers to call himself a "neoliberal" (McCarthy, 1983). Others, such as Haig and Simon, prefer a more conventional Republican conservatism. All, however, share characteristics that distinguish them from earlier Catholic conservatives. First, theirs is a lay politics, independent of the church, relying instead on a surprisingly secular structure of lay organizations such as the recent Lay Commission on the Economy, foundations like the Institute on Religion and Democracy, and media, including magazines such as *This World*. In terms of political strategy the new conservatives practice single-issue politics, as illustrated by the antiabortion or pro-life movement. Finally, the new conservatives are ideologically far from the "throne and altar" Catholics of earlier times and are in many ways far more sympathetic to the capitalist economy than older Catholic conservatives.

In short, the new Catholic conservatism is similar in certain respects to the new Protestant conservatism. Despite differences, the potential exists for alliances and political cooperation between these groups. Yet in many ways the new Catholic conservatism has even more in common with Jewish neoconservatism, to which we now turn.

NEOCONSERVATISM AND THE JEWS

Though relatively few in numbers, Jews have played a significant part in the story of America's faith. Early America provided a welcome refuge for small numbers of Jews, most of whom were Sephardic and Orthodox. Beginning in the second quarter of the nineteenth century, however, German Ashkenazim, generally Reformed in their religious beliefs, began to arrive in America in large numbers and by 1850 constituted a majority of the Jewish population. By the end of the century a third and uniquely American form of Judaism had come into being, a synthesis of orthodoxy and reform. This Conservative Judaism, committed on the one hand to a return to the traditional liturgy and a reaffirmation of the Zionist hope for a restored Israel, and on the other hand to a faith in toleration and progressive reform, was in many ways characteristic of American Judaism as a whole (Reichley, 1985: 232). For regardless of particular practices, American Jews of all kinds have considered themselves to be both Americans and Jews. As a result, Jews have found themselves living a dilemma: residents of the New World, citizens of the New Israel, seekers for the New Jerusalem, they have also felt an obligation to keep alive an ancient faith, a time-honored set of laws, and an abiding hope of ultimate return.

The dilemma has been made more difficult by the anti-Semitism that became a serious problem after 1850 due to the influx and concentration of Jews in the northeastern cities and to their lower economic standing and consequent competition with Gentiles for jobs (Reichley, 1985: 233). Like Catholics, Jews confronted this prejudice by assimilation and by organization. Assimilation was so successful that by the early twentieth century it seemed likely that Jews would follow the path of the Catholics before them, toward a more or less complete Americanization (see Reichley, 1985: 234).

With respect to organization, the case was different, for before the Second World War Jews played only a marginal role in politics. In large degree their political loyalties were defensive. For example, it was the perceived nativism of the pre-Civil War Whigs that was most important in inspiring Jews to participate in the Democratic party. Following the war, the same fears, this time of Catholic anti-Semitism, helped move Jews into the Republican party. In the 1920s and 30s, largely for economic reasons, they began to be attracted to the Demo-

cratic party again, though the Catholicism of Al Smith proved something of a deterrent (Reichley, 1985: 231). In any case, prior to the New
Deal Jews had little influence on national politics (see Fowler, 1985:
166).

Nazism and the Holocaust wrought a fundamental transformation
among Jews, inspiring a rebirth of Jewish self-consciousness and inten-
sifying the dedication of Jews to a left-liberal politics. Both of these
were essentially compatible with Zionism, especially after the birth of
the state of Israel in 1948, along with the establishment of an Israeli
Labor party. For American Jews of all kinds, Israel became a unifying
force. The extreme congregationalism of Judaism and the variety of
ethnic backgrounds had always presented an obstacle to Jewish unity.
Nativism, anti-Semitism, and especially Nazism had fostered a kind
of defensive and self-protective spirit. After 1948, however, Jews had a
positive point of cultural and religious identification. Thus they found
themselves for the first time undertaking a more uniquely Jewish role
in American politics. While still deeply opposed to anti-Semitism,
and to ethnic and racial prejudice of all kinds, and strongly committed
to civil and social rights, Jews no longer confined themselves to supporting assimilationist goals. The survival of the state of Israel was
now also a factor.

During the 1950s and 1960s Jews remained loyal to the liberal
wing of the Democratic party. In fact, President Eisenhower's support
of Egypt in 1956, in contrast to the continued strong support for Israel
within the Democratic party, reinforced the view among Jews that
liberal Democrats were their best friends abroad as well as at home.
This faith was shaken, however, by the Six-Day War and the Arab oil
boycott of the early 1970s. The increased power of the Arab states
seemed to imperil Israel, and some liberal Democrats began to question whether long-term American interests were not better served by a
realignment of alliances in the Middle East. The perceived tilt in the
Democratic party toward the Arabs, along with the unwillingness of
liberal Democrats to press the Soviet Union on Soviet Jewish emigra-
tion, opened an ever-widening chasm between Jews and their erstwhile liberal allies.

Domestically as well, Jews became restive. With postwar prosperity,
large numbers had attained very high levels in education and in the
professions. Thus while they had supported the civil rights move-

424   Religion and Conservatism

ment, Jews were increasingly unenthusiastic about affirmative action and were angered by the introduction of racial quotas, in part because of the perceived anti-Semitism among urban blacks.

These dissatisfactions with domestic policies were reinforced by the rise to power of the conservative religious parties in Israel. Many American Jews found it increasingly difficult to reconcile their own perceptions of Israel, the Israel of David Ben-Gurion and Golda Meir, with the realities of the new Israeli government headed by Menachem Begin and Ariel Sharon. Forced to choose between their liberal ideals and the conservative reality, most chose conservatism. Having made the choice, however, it seemed equally logical to support conservatism at home, especially when many Republican conservatives were claiming that they were now Israel's most faithful friends.

Hence in the 1970s Jews found themselves increasingly drawn toward neoconservatism. The change has been somewhat equivocal. According to traditional criteria, Jews still remain the most liberal group in American politics, but polls increasingly indicate a deep ambivalence, as Milton Himmelfarb (1985) has pointed out. Philosophically, Jews seem to remain faithful to liberal principles. However, when asked to voice support for specific policy alternatives, their responses are often conservative, especially on issues tied to Israel and the world Jewish community. Adding to this change is the prominence of Jewish neoconservative intellectuals such as Irving Kristol, Norman Podhoretz, Seymour Siegel, and others. In magazines like Commentary and the New Republic, conservative Jews have found a voice. Indeed, a few have even sought out alliances with Protestant conservatives, who have been seen as among the surest supporters of Israel (see Bernstein, 1983).

In the 1980s the trends have continued. While most Jews continue to profess and practice liberal politics, as seen by their strong support for Walter Mondale and other liberal Democrats, a growing minority has become self-consciously conservative (see Himmelfarb, 1985). One factor here may be the recent renewal of interest in Orthodox and Conservative Judaism, as well as continuing concern for the fate of Soviet Jewish dissidents, a concern that has soured many American Jews on détente. Also important were anti-Semitic statements made by the Reverend Jesse Jackson during the 1984 election campaign, along with the anti-Semitism of the Reverend Louis Farrakhan. Far more critical may be developments in Israel, including the continuing controversy over the annexation of the West Bank. Whether such factors culminate in a strong conservative commitment among large numbers of American Jews remains to be seen. Nevertheless, at least for the present, conservative Jews, like their Protestant and Catholic counterparts, have become a factor in the complex calculus that links American religion and American politics.

CONCLUSION

In this essay we have sought to show that religion has not only played a role in the resurgence of conservatism in the United States but also has given this conservatism a moralistic character that is lacking in its Canadian and British cousins. This moralism has been most evident in the concern that America's religious conservatives have shown for social reform, as demonstrated in debates over abortion, creationism and evolution, school prayer, sex education, pornography, and the like. But it has been present in the realms of economic and foreign policy as well. Whatever the economic strategies of conservatives in the Anglo-American democracies, only in the United States are these policies legitimated by references to the Protestant ethic, let alone the Holy Bible. Moreover, while Anglo-American democracies may agree in considering the USSR a threat, it is only in America that this confrontation is transformed into a religious drama featuring an apocalyptic confrontation between the American children of light and the Antichrist, the Russian "evil empire." Much of America's conservatism, for better or worse, is moralistic, and it is, we contend, religion that helps make it so.

Our analysis suggests that the influence of American religion on American politics has its origins in the ideological affinity between America's liberalism and its faith. We have tried to show that, from the beginning, Americans have sought both liberty and religious liberty, and that the two have been closely connected. Democracy and denominationalism have gone hand-in-hand. Progress has meant both social and moral reform and has required, in the phrase so commonly used by Progressive reformers, both "efficiency and uplift." Throughout, freedom has been complemented, controlled, sometimes contradicted by biblical faith and millennial hope. Tocqueville may have put it best when he observed that while it "never intervenes directly in the government of American society," religion is for Americans "the first of their political institutions" (1969 ed.: 292).

As to recent manifestations, our analysis is more complex. Our historical examination suggests that religion has long been involved in American politics, and its appearance now should come as no surprise. Yet in at least one sense the situation is different. From the time of Madison the American political system has attempted to channel the religious reform impulse. With denominational pluralism, faith has come to be treated as one element in an ever-expanding universe of groups and interests. In this Madisonian system, moral issues have no special standing. Indeed, much of the success of Madisonian pluralism has been a result of its ability to channel moral concerns through institutional structures, making possible compromise and eventually some shaky consensus. With slavery and prohibition these channels failed, and the result was conflict and dislocation.

In the 1970s and 1980s this Madisonian system seems once again on the edge of collapse. The decline of strong party identification (along with the increase of independent voting), the apparent dissolution of the Roosevelt coalition, and the demise of the postwar consensus on economic and foreign policy have all been factors in the creation of a new kind of American politics. This new-style politics relies on independent foundations, political action committees, and direct mail operations; it prefers single-issue campaigns and intensive behind-the-scenes lobbying; and it is strongly, often uncompromisingly ideological, a politics of principle.

In this setting religion would seem likely to play a continuing and influential part in American politics. Less predictable is its conservative character. Here we should keep in mind that religious involvement has historically flourished on the left as well as on the right, as examples like abolitionism, the civil rights movement, and the Catholic bishops' stand against nuclear weapons testify. Maybe most significant, our review of earlier examples of religious politics strongly suggests that traditional ideological alignments are often brought into question in religious reform. Today, for example, it is quite possible to find Catholics who are strongly opposed to both abortion and nuclear proliferation, and who think of themselves not as liberals or conservatives, but in other terms altogether.

As to political strategy, our review would suggest that while a conservative religious coalition is possible, it must be tenuous. Areas of agreement are few, with the possible exception of abortion and school prayer, along with the survival of Israel, and the building of conservative religious coalitions has proven difficult. If nothing else, denominational differences, along with the constantly changing character of single-issue politics, must continue to make such common efforts problematic.

All told, we believe that while religion will continue to influence American politics, there is no reason to think that its influence will be exclusively conservative. Alienated, angry, committed to change, these conservative religious reformers are less like traditionalists than millennialists. In contradistinction to Britons and even Canadians, they are the product of a tradition that rejects the past in favor of progress and an ever-improving future. Thus these American conservatives may well prove in the end to be much more American than conservative.

REFERENCES

Ahlstrom, S. 1975. *A Religious History of the American People*. Garden City, N.Y.: Doubleday.

Bell, D., ed. 1963. *The Radical Right*. Garden City, N.Y.: Doubleday.

Bellah, R. 1975. *The Broken Covenant*. New York: Seabury.

Bercovitch, S. 1978. *The American Jeremiad*. Madison: University of Wisconsin Press.

Bernstein, R. 1983. "Evangelicals Strengthening Bonds with Jews." *New York Times*, February 6, 1983.

Billings, W. 1980. *The Christian's Political Action Manual*. Washington, D.C.: National Christian Action Coalition.

Billington, R. 1938. *The Protestant Crusade*. New York: Macmillan.

Brierly, P. 1983. *U.K. Christian Handbook*. London: Evangelical Alliance Bible Society.

Canadian Gallup Poll, June 1980.

Carthy, M. P. 1964. *Catholicism in English-speaking Lands*. New York: Hawthorne Books.

Cawelti, J. 1965. *Apostles of the Self-Made Man*. Chicago: University of Chicago Press.

"The *Christianity Today*–Gallup Poll: An Overview." 1979. In *Christianity Today*, December 21, 1979.

Conaway, J. 1983. "Righting the Course." *Washington Post*, March 22, 1983.

Ellis, J. 1952. *The Life of James Cardinal Gibbons*, 2 vols. Milwaukee: Bruce Publishing.

Fairbanks, J. D. 1981. "The Evangelical Right: Beginnings of Another Symbolic Crusade?" Paper presented to the American Political Science Association, New York.

Falwell, J. 1980. *Listen, America*. Garden City, N.Y.: Doubleday.

Fitzgerald, F. 1981. "A Disciplined, Charging Army." *New Yorker*, May 18, 1981.

Fowler, B. 1985. *Religion and Politics in America*. Metuchen, N.J.: American Theological Library Association.

Gallup, G. 1980. *The Search for America's Faith*. Nashville, Tenn.: Abingdon.

Gleason, P., ed. 1970. *Catholicism in America*. New York: Harper & Row.

Greely, A. 1977. *The American Catholic*. New York: Basic Books.

Gusfield, J. 1963. *Symbolic Crusade*. Urbana: University of Illinois Press.

Guth, J. 1981. "The Politics of the Evangelical Right: An Interpretive Essay." Paper presented to the American Political Science Association, New York.

Hadden, J., and C. Swan. 1981. *Prime-Time Preachers*. Reading, Mass.: Addison-Wesley.

Handy, R. 1971. *A Christian America*. New York: Oxford University Press.

Hastings, E., and P. K. Hastings, eds. 1983–84. *The Index to International Public Opinion*. Westport, Conn.: Greenwood Press.

Heimert, A. 1966. *Religion and the American Mind*. Cambridge, Mass.: Harvard University Press.

Himmelfarb, M. 1985. "Another Look at the Jewish Vote." *Commentary* (December 1985).

Hinchliff, P. 1966. *The One-Sided Reciprocity*. London: Darton, Longman, & Todd.

Hudson, W. 1961. *American Protestantism*. Chicago: University of Chicago Press.

Keller, B. 1980. "Evangelical Conservatives Move from Pews to Polls." *Congressional Quarterly Weekly Report*, September 6, 1980.

Kelley, D. 1978. "Why Conservative Churches Are Still Growing." *Journal for the Scientific Study of Religion* 17 (June 1978): 165–72.

Latus, M. 1982. "Mobilizing Christians for Political Action: Campaigning with God on Your Side." Paper presented to the Society for the Scientific Study of Religion, Providence, R.I.

Lienesch, M. 1982. "Right-Wing Religion: Christian Conservatism as a Political Movement." *Political Science Quarterly* 97 (Fall 1982): 403–25.

———. 1983. "The Paradoxical Politics of the Religious Right." *Soundings* 66 (Spring 1983): 70–99.

McCarthy, C. 1983. "The Crossing of the Bishops." *Washington Post*, May 11, 1983.

Maclear, J. 1971. "The Republic and the Millennium." In E. A. Smith, ed., *The Religion of the Republic*. Philadelphia: Fortress Press.

Marsden, G. 1980. *Fundamentalism and American Culture*. New York: Oxford University Press.

Marty, M. 1970. *Righteous Empire*. New York: Dial Press.

Maynard, T. 1941. *The Story of American Catholicism*. New York: Macmillan.

Mead, S. 1975. *The Nation with the Soul of a Church*. New York: Harper & Row.

Menendez, A. 1977. *Religion at the Polls*. Philadelphia: Westminster Press.

Miller, P. 1953. *The New England Mind: From Colony to Province*. Cambridge, Mass.: Harvard University Press.

———. 1956. *Errand into the Wilderness*. Cambridge, Mass.: Harvard University Press.

Moore, E. 1956. *A Catholic Runs for President*. New York: Ronald Press.

Novak, M. 1982. *The Spirit of Democratic Capitalism*. New York: Simon and Schuster.

Odegard, P. 1960. *Religion and Politics*. New Brunswick, N.J.: Oceana Publications.

O'Toole, R. 1982. "Sacralizing National Identity: Notes on Religion and Power in Canada." Paper presented to the Society for the Scientific Study of Religion, Providence, R.I.

Reichley, A. J. 1985. *Religion in American Public Life.* Washington, D.C.: Brookings Institution.

Ribuffo, L. 1980. "Liberals and That Old-Time Religion." *Nation,* November 29, 1980.

Simpson, J., and MacLeod, H. 1982. "The Politics of Morality in Canada." Paper presented to the Society for the Scientific Study of Religion, Providence, R.I.

Tavard, G. 1969. *Catholicism U.S.A.* New York: Newman Press.

Tocqueville, A. 1969. *Democracy in America,* ed. J. P. Mayer. New York: Doubleday.

Toward the Future: Catholic Social Thought and the U.S. Economy. A Lay Letter. 1984. New York: Lay Commission on Catholic Social Teaching and the U.S. Economy, American Catholic Committee.

Tuveson, E. 1968. *Redeemer Nation.* Chicago: University of Chicago Press.

Wacker, G. 1984a. "Searching for Norman Rockwell: Popular Evangelicalism in Contemporary America." In L. Sweet, ed., *The Evangelical Tradition in America.* Macon, Ga.: Mercer University Press.

———. 1984b. "Uneasy in Zion: Evangelicals in Postmodern Society." In G. Marsden, ed., *Evangelicalism and Modern America.* Grand Rapids, Mich.: Eerdmans.

15. The Reagan Years: Turning to the Right or Groping Toward the Middle?

MORRIS P. FIORINA

In the presidential election of 1984 Ronald Reagan obliterated his opposition. The Democratic candidate carried only his home state, and that by the narrowest of margins. An electoral victory of this magnitude fuels speculation that something fundamental has happened in American politics. In this instance that tendency was reinforced by a lack of excuses such as those accompanying Reagan's narrower but still impressive 1980 victory. In 1980 it could be said that Reagan was fortunate to run against the sorry record of a hapless Jimmy Carter. But in 1984 Reagan faced an experienced, well-regarded Democratic politician. In 1980 it could be said that the Democratic party was deeply wounded by Senator Edward Kennedy's attempt to wrest the nomination from a sitting president. But in 1984 the Democratic party was reasonably united following a spirited nomination contest. In 1980 Republican capture of the Senate could be discounted as largely the result of serendipity and idiosyncratic factors (Fiorina, 1983). But in 1984 attempts to explain away continued Republican control sounded more like sour grapes.

Basking in the afterglow of 1984, conservative commentators had apparent reason to believe that the American electorate had not veered from the right turn it took in 1980. Democratic politicians, meanwhile, had apparent reason to believe that there was something fundamentally wrong with their party—that it was committed to outdated "statist" approaches, that it could not integrate the demands of selfish constituency groups, that it lacked a vision. As parties customarily do following resounding defeats, the Democrats occupied themselves with retreats and reexaminations.

Academics, who generally have more historical perspective than either journalists or politicians, are characteristically skeptical of claims about electoral transformations. But a number of the changes and events of recent years are sufficiently noteworthy that even the customary academic skepticism has lifted. A generation ago scholars wrote of the Democratic bias in the electoral college. With their strength in the South and the industrial North the Democrats needed only to hold their base and make modest additions of states outside it in order to win the presidency. Now commentators contrast the number of N^2 FR^2 states—those carried by Nixon twice, by Ford and by Reagan twice —with HMC^2M states—those carried by Humphrey and McGovern, by Carter twice, and by Mondale. The first category contains twenty-three states with 202 electoral votes, only sixty-eight votes shy of a majority. The second category contains no states. In less than a generation the South has gone from Democratic territory to Republican in presidential politics, and most of the rest of the states from Democratic or competitive to competitive or Republican. The result, as so many observers have noted, is that the Republicans have won six of the past nine presidential elections and four of the past five. In the face of these simple facts even the most skeptical academic must admit that major changes in the electoral system have occurred over the course of the past two decades.

Interpretations of the electoral politics of the 1980s fall into two general categories, each containing a variety of subtypes differing in emphasis. The first position (generally taken behind a shield of caveats and with all flanks covered) is that, yes, a realignment has taken place, though it differs in various more-or-less important ways from preceding realignments and from our theoretical understanding of the realignment process. The second, more skeptical position claims that recent electoral changes reflect myriad interacting processes that are perfectly comprehensible without recourse to realignment arguments. After surveying these differing interpretations of American electoral politics in the 1980s, I will discuss some puzzles and inconsistencies that make choosing among these interpretations difficult. Then I consider the phenomenon of ticket-splitting in national elections, arguing that recent elections reveal an electorate far from committed to the Republican party, an electorate not yet given the evidence it needs to make such a commitment. In the final section of the chapter I offer some speculations about elections beyond Reagan, and the likelihood that an era of Republican or conservative hegemony has arrived.

ALTERNATIVE INTERPRETATIONS

The purported periodicity of electoral realignment (Beck, 1974) has kept some political scientists in a holding pattern since the mid-1960s. For these patient waiters there are encouraging signs in the patterns of recent elections. The classic realignment perspective developed by Key (1955) and Burnham (1970) is rooted in changes in mass electoral behavior. And a number of such changes underlie the Republican electoral successes of the 1980s.

If realignment is conceived of as durable alterations in the alignment of social groups with parties (Petrocik, 1981), then the defection of the white South to the Republicans, the continued difficulties of the Democrats with Catholics, the demise of black Republicanism, and a variety of smaller changes constitute evidence of realignment. "By the standard of shifting group alignments, realignment has certainly occurred" (Ladd, 1986: 24).

From a less group-oriented perspective, lasting change in the distribution of individual party allegiance indicates realignment. Here, too, the evidence seems more than suggestive. Group voting shifts such as those mentioned above reflect changes in party identification among individual group members (Petrocik, 1986). And evidence from some commercial polls indicates that for the first time in a half century young voters are moving toward the Republicans (Norpoth, 1986). The gradual increase in political independence over the past two decades appears to have reached a plateau, and perhaps even begun to decline. "If the current trends persist into 1988, one would probably be justified in declaring that a realignment—not one as decisive as that of the 1930s but one of a second order of magnitude—had occurred" (Cavanagh and Sundquist, 1985: 42–43).

Some scholars have argued that realignment theory should not be based entirely on shifts in mass electoral behavior. Voting behavior changes for a reason, generally thought to be the emergence of a new cleavage that supersedes or cross-cuts the existing basis of political competition (Sundquist, 1983). However unlikely it may be, one can imagine the emergence of a new issue that entirely changes the basis of political competition but leaves the parties identically placed vis-à-vis supporting groups. Then research would find no indication of changed electoral behavior, but in a very basic sense the politics of the system would have changed. Thus, some analysts emphasize changes in the political agenda as essential concomitants of realignment processes (Sundquist, 1983; Ginsberg, 1972; Brady and Stewart, 1982). Here too the evidence seems clear. No longer does one hear about national health insurance or other social welfare initiatives; one hears only the question, can domestic programs be cut back any further? For five years politicians did not debate whether defense spending should rise or fall, only its rate of increase. Inflation, which dominated the late 1970s agenda, is gone. For better or worse, the deficit has taken its place. More than any administration since the New Deal, the Reagan presidency altered the political agenda of the nation (Shefter and Ginsberg, 1986).

Given such evidence, why are many academic analysts reluctant to accept the fact of electoral realignment? Two reasons underlie their hesitation. First, the present realignment has been "secular" (Key, 1959), proceeding gradually over time, rather than "critical" (Key, 1955), occurring as a sudden break with the past. One of the two major parties did not disintegrate and disappear, as did the Whigs in the 1850s. A tragic economic depression did not threaten the constitutional order, as in the 1890s and 1930s. Moreover, the secular realignment has been dragged out over a longer period than it would have been except for the occurrence of a unique event—the Watergate scandal—that interrupted the pro-Republican drift (Phillips, 1982). From this perspective, the 1974 and 1976 elections should be dismissed as aberrations. When that is done, 1968–1972–1980 constitute a realigning sequence analogous to, if weaker than 1928–1932–1936.

A second reason analysts have been needlessly reluctant to accept the conclusion of realignment is the existence of institutional "frictions" not present in earlier realignments. The most notable of these is the continued Democratic hold on the House of Representatives as a function of the incumbency advantage that developed in the mid-1960s. To quote William Schneider (1984: 20) yet one more time, "If the government had passed a decree prohibiting incumbents from running for reelection, the Republican Party would probably have gained control of both Houses of Congress. . . ." On the subnational level, after 1984 the Republicans held only one-third of the state governorships, and in 1984 they gained only a trivial number of seats in state legislatures. But only a third as many states hold their elections concurrently with presidential elections today as in 1932. Thus, the subnational impact of presidential coattails is structurally more limited than was the case a generation ago. Moreover, in the aftermath of the Australian ballot reforms, split-ticket voting became easier than it was at the time of the realignment of the 1890s (Rusk, 1970). In view of institutional variations like these, one cannot hope to find as clear an electoral picture of realignment as that presented by earlier realigning eras. At present the United States may have a "split-level realignment" (Phillips, 1985), or "half a realignment" (Schneider, 1984b). But whether House-presidential and national-subnational differences persist indefinitely, or eventually converge, is not critical for identifying realignment. In a highly institutionalized political system realignment will not take the same form as in a less institutionalized system (Chubb and Peterson, 1985).

Despite such arguments, some scholars remain unconvinced. This continued skepticism rests in large part on puzzles and inconsistencies of both an empirical and conceptual-theoretical nature. On the empirical level there have been numerous analyses of changes in party identification. Unfortunately, their results have been anything but consistent. For example, one of the major stories of 1984 was the shift of American youth to the Republican column. Relying on *New York Times/* CBS polls, Norpoth (1986: 11) concludes "unlike the 1950s and late 1960s, when prospects of a Republican realignment remained unfulfilled, the 1980s provide a number of clues that such a realignment is now underway. What is new is that the younger cohorts profess a marked loyalty to the GOP." But after analyzing data from Market Opinion Research, Petrocik (1986: 12) observes that "there is, in short, no evidence that the current GOP success has depended upon the volatility of youth. This realignment is not a new cohort phenomenon." Moreover, based on the 1984 NES/CPS data Miller (1986: 7) contends that "there is no evidence that the national shift favoring the Republicans was supported, to say nothing of impelled, by the observed changes in the youngest generation."

Subgroup change aside, even the national aggregate figures have shown a surprising volatility both over time and across different survey organizations.[1] After examining the panoply of available data some scholars have begun to suspect that party identification no longer means what it once did. Perhaps Shively (1979) was correct in suggesting that increasing education and mass communication would render party identification obsolete. When respondents answer the party identification question today, are they simply reporting their vote choice? Or perhaps the data reflect a notion of party ID as a running tally of retrospective evaluations (Fiorina, 1981). Following the

Table 15.1.   Turn to the Right.

"Government should see that every person has a job and a good standard of living."

Year	Yes	No
1956	57%	27%
1960	59	24
1964	31	43
1968	31	47
1972	27	39
1976	24	39
1980	26	41

"Government should see to it that white and black children are allowed to attend the same schools."

Year	Yes	No
1962	52%	33%
1964	41	39
1968	38	44
1972	37	45
1976	24	39
1978	27	41

Source: NES.

disappointing presidencies of Johnson, Nixon, Ford, and Carter, American party identification would likely be in a weakened state. The perception of a good performance by Reagan would be enough to tilt some weak identifiers and independents in a Republican direction. But if so, a poor performance, or a good performance by a Democrat, could tilt them right back. Whatever the meaning of party ID in contemporary politics, its measurement leaves the cautious analyst unsure of what to conclude.

Another area of inconsistency surrounds direct attempts to identify the United States' supposed shift to the right. A resurgence of traditional values coupled with public disaffection with government intervention in the economy allegedly left the Democratic party too far to the left of the mainstream. Without going into extensive detail, suffice it to say that the evidence is mixed at best. For a few issues one can find seemingly strong evidence of a rightward drift in public opinion in the years preceding the election of Ronald Reagan (table 15.1). But on most issues no clear trend is apparent, and on a few issues there are suggestions of leftward drift (table 15.2). As for trends during the first Reagan administration, Miller (1986: 10) observes "whatever changes occurred in ideology-tinged policy preferences between 1980 and 1984, the nation as a whole moved in a liberal direction rather than in the direction of increased support for conservative policy preferences. On all but one of the questions on public policy assessed both in 1980 and 1984 by the National Election Studies, there was a perceptible drift to the left." Similarly, commercial polls indicate no change or some leftward movement between 1980–81 and 1985 (CBS/ New York Times Report, January 1986).[2]

Of course, mass attitudes toward public policy issues have long been known to be ill-formed and unstable (Campbell et al., 1960: chap. 8; Converse, 1964), so looking for clear trends in public opinion data may be too demanding a test. Perhaps an examination of more general orientations, such as self-identified ideology, is more revealing. But it isn't. Gallup polls show no trend over the period from 1976 to 1986 (Sussman, 1986). Likewise, Harris figures show a marked stability over the past two decades. The more detailed NES/CPS data show nothing in the way of interesting change (table 15.3). Again one can question the evidence. Many people may not understand the meaning of the concepts well enough to place themselves accurately. More-

Table 15.2.   Turn to the Left.

Whites have right to preserve "neighborhood homogeneity"

Year	Yes	No
1964	26%	57%
1968	22	68
1972	16	76
1976	8	85

Equal Role for Women?

Year	Equal role	Neutral	Traditional role
1972	47%	19%	29%
1976	50	18	24
1980	58	16	19

Source: NES.

Table 15.3.   Ideological Self-Classification.

NES

Year	Very liberal	Liberal	Neutral	Conservative	Very conservative
1972	9%	10%	27%	15%	12%
1976	8	8	25	12	13
1980	7	8	18	13	14
1984	8	11	25	17	13

Harris

Average	Liberal	Middle of the road	Conservative
1968–1983	17%	40%	34%
1984	18	40	36

over, liberalism and conservatism are multidimensional, so placements on an oversimplified one-dimensional scale are suspect (Maddox and Lillie, 1984). While such caveats are valid, one would think that a major change in the opinion climate would show up *somewhere* in the

data. But the simple fact is that numerous academic researchers, relying on a variety of data, consensually reject the interpretation of 1980s
elections as revealing a turn to the right (Schneider, 1980; Hibbs, 1982;
Miller, 1986; Ferguson and Rogers, 1986).[3]

Apostate politicians changing parties typically protest that they
haven't left the party, but that the party has left them. Similarly, it is
possible that public opinion only appears to have moved right when
viewed from the standpoint of those who have moved left. Wilson
(1986) argues something of this sort in interpreting the 1984 election
as the culmination of a process of dealignment in the mass electorate
and realignment—in the sense of polarization—among party activists. To a Democratic party turning left, an electorate driving straight
ahead might appear to be turning right.

The preceding possibility aside, the bottom line is that no one has
built a convincing case for one of the principal components of a realignment process: a major shift in the views of the electorate or the emergence of a new cross-cutting issue. Regarding the latter, it is important
to remember that the so-called social issue emerged in the mid-1960s
and was a major part of the 1968 elections. And the Democrats have
always been on the wrong side of that issue complex. Scammon and
Wattenberg (1970) warned the Democrats of their vulnerability three
elections before pundits announced that the "San Francisco Democrats" had problems in the realm of traditional values. The Democratic advantage on economic issues enabled them to survive their
nonoptimal position on social issues for a considerable time. Only
when they dissipated their New Deal economic capital in the late
1970s stagflation and suffered an array of foreign policy misadventures
did their electoral prospects plummet.

In sum, those who doubt that the 1980s will appear in retrospect
as a period of significant realignment point to inconsistent and incon-
clusive data that make it difficult to discern precisely what has been
occurring electorally in recent years. As for the broad fact of Republican presidential success, a number of known processes are sufficient
explanations. These include (1) demographic change that has advan-
taged the Republican-leaning sunbelt relative to the Democratic-leaning
frostbelt; (2) a continuous process of dealignment reflecting various
social and technological developments that eroded the base of Democratic party identification; (3) a Democratic party that presided over

traumatic times in the mid-1960s, and then, when handed a second chance, compiled a miserable record when it had full control of the federal government from 1976 to 1980. Following that sorry performance, the American electorate followed its standard practice of throwing the rascals out (Schneider, 1980; Miller and Wattenberg, 1981). Whether this will lead to a performance-based realignment (Wattenberg, 1986) or leadership-based realignment (Miller, 1986) remains to be seen, but there is ambiguous evidence for and little explanatory need for classical conceptions of realignment.

THE CONTEMPORARY AMERICAN VOTER

As a student of American national elections, my understanding of the most recent ones falls closer to the second interpretation sketched above. In twenty years we may look back and say that, yes, there was a realignment in the 1980s, but at the present time the inconsistency of the empirical evidence suggests that skepticism is the most appropriate academic stance. I concede that on an intuitive level the empirical evidence seems somewhat out of line with the gut feeling that conservatism is ascendant and liberalism in retreat. But there are reasonable explanations for such seeming contradictions. For one thing citizens can turn against government activity in a particular policy area, say welfare, because they decide that existing programs are ineffective and wasteful, not because they have become niggardly conservatives. They can take a harder line on crime and drugs, not because they have grown more callous, but because experience teaches that present rehabilitation regimes are worthless. They can demand a stronger national defense not because of the growth of a "Rambo" mentality, but simply because they want a country capable of protecting American citizens and interests. The seeming rejection of "liberalism" may actually be a rejection of failed programs and policies championed by the liberal party.

Moreover, as suggested above, the country has always been further "right" on various social and racial issues than the policies actually adopted by the government. The Democratic party relied on the bureaucracy and the courts to implement social and racial policy that could not win popular approval.[4] Whatever one's view of the moral merits of this strategy, the empirical fact is that it corroded the image of the party as the representative of middle America. In the realm of social and racial issues the Republicans capitalized not so much on a popular turn to the right as on the continued positioning of the Democrats on the left.

In sum, there is little doubt that conservative elites are brimming with self-confidence while liberal elites are full of doubt and disillusion. And there is certainly no arguing with the fact that Republican electoral fortunes are the brightest in a generation. But there is good reason to believe that recent years have seen considerably more change on the elite level than in the mass electorate. There is always some information in the electoral signals, but it typically is overinterpreted and misinterpreted by overreactive elites.

Beyond skepticism about a general resurgence of conservatism, I am also not convinced that an apparent "split-level" realignment is best interpreted as a natural feature of an institutionalized political system. Rather, I think it may indicate a reasonably sophisticated voter adaptation to the disorganized and contradictory state of contemporary American politics. Scholars now realize that American citizens are more informed and sophisticated than they were given credit for two decades ago (Nie et al., 1976). Moreover, because the decline in turnout has occurred disproportionately at the lower end of the SES distribution (Burnham, 1982), the active electorate is more sophisticated and informed than the citizenry as a whole. Observing the presidencies of the late 1960s and 1970s this electorate saw little to convince it that either party had much of an idea about how to deal with contemporary issues—either the reemergence of traditional economic issues or the newly emergent social issues. When the late 1970s Democratic party achieved a modern low in cohesion and national vision, and suffered some bad luck besides, the country turned with both hesitation and trepidation to the Republicans.

The issue/ideological implications of the 1980 presidential victory were greatly overinterpreted, as discussed above. And the more-or-less accidental 1980 Senate victory was nearly devoid of ideological implication (Fiorina, 1983). But whatever the reality, the electoral outcomes and perceptions of why they occurred governed national politics as Reagan took the helm. The Republican administration believed it knew what to do (or at least projected that image) and demonstrated the determination and capacity to do it. By 1984 the country enjoyed peace, prosperity, and, on a less tangible level, confidence. Even if disgruntled Democrats attributed all of this to luck, who cares? The American voter can hardly be blamed for preferring a lucky president to an unlucky one. Walter Mondale stood no more chance than George McGovern did in 1972. By the best available evidence—reality—Ronald Reagan had performed very well, and the electorate judged that he would be likely to perform better over the next four years than Walter Mondale.

But the same electorate that gave the bulk of its vote to Ronald Reagan preferred that defense spending not be increased any further, opposed national policies that could get the country involved in Central American conflicts, and feared the continued growth of the federal deficit. Young voters and yuppie voters attracted to Reagan for other reasons were at odds with the views of the religious right, an important component of the Reagan core coalition. Numerous election analysts noted contradictions such as these. But what should a voter do when the choice is between two imperfect alternatives? Many voters simply weighted performance judgments more heavily than issue fears. Others voted for Democratic congressmen.

More than a quarter of the national electorate split their tickets between the presidential and congressional levels. This resulted in an anomolous situation like that of 1972; in both years 44 percent of all the congressional districts in the country gave pluralities to the presidential candidate of one party and the House candidate of the other. Three-quarters of these split decisions listed a preference for Reagan and a Democratic representative, resulting in a net difference of almost 10 percent in the Republican vote at the presidential and congressional levels.[5]

The falloff in Republican support as one moves from the presidential to the congressional levels is generally attributed to incumbency, or, more exactly, the complex of advantages incumbency confers —visibility, money, a noncontroversial image based on constituency service, and so forth. Certainly the disproportionate number of Democratic House incumbents must explain some portion of the ticket-splitting. But a suggestion that incumbency is not the whole story lies in the figures for congressional contests in open seats. If incumbency were of overriding importance, one would expect to see a pattern of the highest ticket-splitting rates in districts held by incumbents of the party opposite the victorious presidential candidate, and the lowest rates in districts held by incumbents of the same party as the victorious presidential candidate, with open seat rates falling in between.[6] Table 15.4 shows no such general pattern, and in 1980 specifically, ticket-splitting rates in open seats are not significantly different from rates in seats with Democratic incumbents. By definition incumbency cannot explain voting behavior in open seat contests. Something else then must account for ticket-splitting in such districts, and by extension may account for some of the ticket-splitting in incumbent-contested districts as well. One possibility is that consciously or unconsciously, some small but important portion of the electorate is engaging in a kind of sophisticated ticket-splitting that permits them to register a preference for a middle course between two parties, neither of which they fully trust to govern.

Calculated Ticket-Splitting: A Simple Model

The logic of the argument is most comprehensibly developed via a simplified model. Assume that voters have a rough understanding of the American constitutional order, at least to the extent they understand that the president and Congress together determine national policy. Specifically, voters expect national policy (P) to be a compromise between the positions of the president and the Congress. We represent this compromise as a weighted average or linear combination:

$$P = q \text{ (presidential position)} + (1-q) \text{ (congressional position)} \quad (1)$$
where $0 < q < 1$

Given the realities of American politics at least since the time of Franklin Roosevelt, it seems reasonable to assume that $q > \frac{1}{2}$, that is, that the presidency is the more powerful institution in determining national policy. Assume further that votes are simply expressions of preference —the pattern of votes registers a desire for a Republican president and Congress (RR), Republican president and Democratic Congress (RD), Democratic president and Republican Congress (DR), or Democratic president and Democratic Congress (DD).

Figure 15.1 lays out the elements of the argument more formally. The Democratic party is at D, the Republican party at R, and voter i at v_i. The assumption of a single policy dimension is purely one of

Table 15.4.   Ticket-Splitting by Incumbency Status of District.

Year	Democratic incumbent	Republican incumbent	Open seat	Total
1956	18%	12%	14%	15%
1960	14	12	7	13
1964	11	20	9	14
1968	18	17	16	17
1972	30	18	22	25
1976	26	27	15	24
1980	29	24	24	27
1984	28	18	18	24

Source: NES.

expositional convenience. The discussion that follows does not depend on the assumption of unidimensionality.

To get a better grip on the elements of the model, one could imagine that the policy dimension under consideration is the social issue. Then D represents the "San Francisco Democrats," the party of gays, blacks, pro-choice activists, and secular humanism. R represents the Reagan Republicans, the party of the Moral Majority, populist bigotry, pro-life activists, and traditional values. For voter 1, a liberal activist, the choice is clear—a straight-ticket vote (DD) for the Democratic presidential and congressional candidates, reflecting her preference for position D. Analogously, for voter 4, a new right zealot, the choice is clear—a straight-ticket vote for (RR), reflecting his preference for position R. But what about voters 2 and 3? These voters are tolerant of their fellow citizens but do not believe that deviant sexual practices

Figure 15.1. Basic Model.

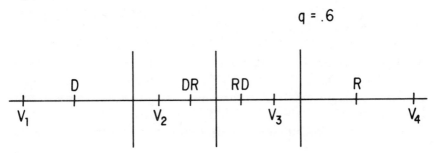

should be enshrined in the Constitution, consider abortion a troubling issue not appropriately dealt with by simple constitutional amendments, and appreciate traditional morality but do not believe that the federal government should be the enforcement arm of fundamentalist Christianity.

Alternatively, the policy dimension might be defense and national security. Position D represents "blame America" and high motives over sound policy. Position R represents liberating Nicaragua and preparing for Armageddon. For the guilt-ridden liberal, v_1, and the divinely inspired conservative v_4, the choice is clear. But what of voters 2 and 3, who favor an adequate defense, negotiation over confrontation, and policies based on traditional American principles?

Or finally, the policy dimension might be government intervention in the economy. Position D represents high taxes, regulation, and protection. Position R represents low taxes, deregulation, and free trade. For a New Deal liberal like voter 1 and a libertarian conservative like voter 4, an enthusiastic straight-ticket vote is reasonable. But what of citizens like voters 2 and 3, who want low inflation, a healthy environment, a cushion for economic losers, and sound fiscal practices?

These whimsical examples should make the point clearly. Voters 2 and 3 are everyman, the ordinary, moderate, reasonably open-minded American citizen who is not in close agreement with the package of stands taken by either party (table 15.5). Perhaps their state of cross-pressures will be so severe that they will decline to vote. Or perhaps they somehow resolve their cross-pressures and throw in with one party or the other. Or perhaps they decide to split their tickets.

Assume voters believe that $q = .6$. Then the expected policy output of a Democratic president and Republican Congress is DR in figure 15.1. Similarly, the expected policy output of a Republican president and Democratic Congress is RD. Notice that voter 2 is considerably closer to DR, the position of a divided government with a Democratic president at its head, than to DD, the closer of the two unified government positions. Similarly, voter 3 is closer to RD, a divided government with a Republican at its head, than to an all-Republican government. If preference varies directly with closeness, each of these voters will cast a split ticket, though they will split it in opposite ways.

Assuming voter preferences are symmetric we can partition the

Table 15.5.   Voter Policy Positions Compared to Perceptions
of Party Positions (Averages on 7-Point Scales).

Policy	Democratic position	Citizen position	Republican position
Liberal-conservative ideology	3.1	4.3	5.1
Government provision of public services	5.3	3.8	2.9
Aid to minorities	3.0	4.2	4.6
U.S. involvement in Central America	4.5	4.5	3.0
Defense spending	3.2	4.0	5.4
Aid to women	3.1	3.9	4.6
Cooperation with USSR	3.2	4.1	4.9
Government responsibility for jobs and living standards	3.1	4.4	4.9

Source: 1984 NES.

policy space in figure 15.1 into four regions differentiating two types
of straight-ticket and two types of split-ticket voters. The vertical lines
in the figure demarcate the four regions.[7] Without going into any technical analysis, visual inspection of figure 15.1 and its variations suggests several propositions of substantive interest.

P-1: Those ticket-splitters who vote Democratic for Congress are closer
to the Republicans, while those ticket-splitters who vote Republican for Congress are closer to the Democrats (all other things
equal).

This proposition is a direct consequence of the assumption that
the contemporary presidency is a stronger determinant of public policy than the contemporary Congress ($q > .5$). Given a valid measure
of "closeness," survey data in principle can provide a test of this
proposition.

P-2: Other things equal, when the parties are close together, there is
less split-ticket voting.

positions are much farther apart than in the bottom panel. Note how the convergence of the parties in the bottom panel "squeezes" the area in which ticket-splitting is the voter's preferred behavior. Proposition 2 is in general accord with trends in U.S. national elections.[8] Rates of ticket-splitting began to rise in the late 1960s following capture of the Republican party by the Goldwater wing, and the increased promi- nence of the New Politics wing of the Democratic party. The fact, however, that the parties did not and generally will not move simulta- neously and/or symmetrically suggests another question to which prop- osition 3 provides the answer.

P-3: Other things equal, if party distance increases because one party moves while the other holds its position, straight-ticket voting for the stable party will increase, straight-ticket voting for the

Consider figure 15.2. In the top panel the Democratic and Republican

Figure 15.2. Effect of Party Polarization.

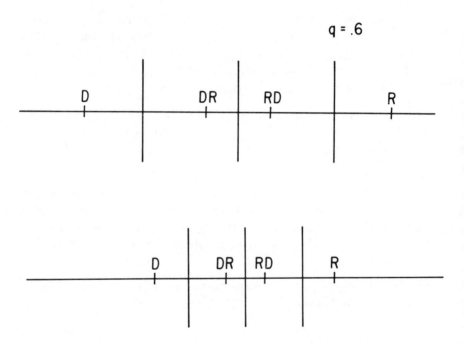

moving party will decrease, and split-ticket voting may increase or decrease depending on the shape of the voter distribution.

Figure 15.3 depicts the situation. The party that moves away (Republicans to the right in the bottom panel) contract their own straight-ticket region and expand the opposition's. Though the length of the split-ticket region increases, whether more voters fall in that region will depend on the shape of the voter distribution. Thus, proposition 3 suggests that Republican straight-ticket voting should have declined in 1964 (it did), and Democratic straight-ticket voting should have declined in 1972 (it did). Such evidence is ambiguous, however, because of the difficulty of ascertaining whether other things— principally the distributions of voter preferences—are in fact equal. The turnout rate declined during this period, and there is evidence (Nie, Verba, and Petrocik, 1976) that the shape of the voter distribution changed steadily through the 1960s and early 1970s. These departures from our ceteris paribus condition provide alternative interpretations for variations in straight- and split-ticket voting.

One additional factor can produce variations in the rate of split-ticket voting. The parameter, q, represents the relative power of the presidency vis-à-vis the Congress. Changes in this parameter will change the split-ticket voting region. The situation is similar to that in figure 15.2. An increase in q will expand the DR region to the left and the RD region to the right. Interpreting these expansions,

P-4: Other things equal, a relative increase in the power of the presidency will increase the rate of split-ticket voting.

Evidently, this proposition too is consistent with broad trends in contemporary American elections. Ticket-splitting rates rose in the same era that we began to hear talk of the imperial presidency and reached 25 percent in 1972 when the perception of congressional power was at a modern low. Rates stabilized as Congress reasserted itself in the late 1970s and have remained at about 25 percent since then, a level 10 percent higher than the pre-1964 figure. Of course, there are other plausible explanations for variations in straight-ticket voting, but the simple model of rational ticket-splitting is at least consistent with the broad outlines of recent electoral trends.

Circumstantial evidence aside, the voting pattern sketched in fig-

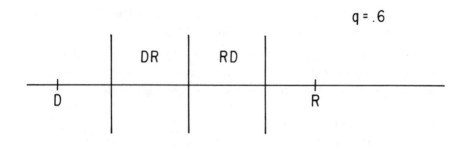

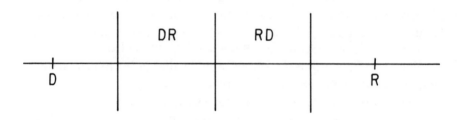

Figure 15.3. Effect of Asymmetric Shift.

ure 15.1 is susceptible to a test using existing survey data. Moreover, the fundamental behavioral postulate of the model—equation 1—is also susceptible to a very crude, indirect test. If the data are consistent with the basic postulate and its logical implications, we have some basis for using the model to interpret the 1984 election and to specu-late about its aftermath.

Calculated Ticket-Splitting: A Preliminary Test

Since 1968 the American National Election Studies have included various issue scales that ask citizens to place themselves, the candi-dates, and the parties along a seven-point scale running between two extreme positions on an issue. For example, the 1984 defense spend-ing scale appears as follows:

Some people believe that we should spend much less money for defense. Others feel that defense spending should be greatly increased.

Where would you place yourself on this scale, or haven't you thought much about this?

greatly decrease						greatly increase
1	2	3	4	5	6	7

Beginning in 1980 the election surveys also asked the respondents to place the federal government on some of the scales. This seems anomalous inasmuch as the government is a corporate entity that cannot be said to have a position in the same sense as Jimmy Carter or even the Democratic party. But fortunately for our purposes, most citizens obligingly make an effort to place the government on the scales.[9] Now recall that the fundamental behavioral postulate of our model asserts that citizens estimate the expected policy of the national government to be a weighted average of the positions of the president and the Congress. If this is so, the correlation between the citizen's placement of the president and the federal government should be higher when the presidency and Congress are controlled by the same party (e.g., 1980) than when control is divided (e.g., 1984). Four issue scales were asked in both years.[10] Correlations between placements of the president and the federal government are as follows:

	1980	1984
Aid to minorities	.51	.44
Jobs and living standards	.56	.47
Women's role/status	.49	.46
Defense spending	.59	.62

Although the differences are not large, three of the four 1980 correlations are greater than the corresponding 1984 ones, consistent with the model's basic postulate. The one contradictory observation, defense spending, involves a highly salient presidential priority where the president arguably imposed his position on the rest of the government.

So far so good. Citizen responses to survey questions do not contradict the assumption that they collectively appreciate the consequences of a separation of powers system for the shape of government policy. But does such an appreciation of the consequences of institutional structure inform their voting decisions? To bring systematic evidence to bear on that question we can examine the voting patterns illustrated in figure 15.1. Patterns of straight- and split-ticket voting should accord with relative closeness to the perceived positions of the Democratic and Republican parties and institutional combinations thereof.

Of course, we must take account of other important factors such as the party identification of the voter, whether the congressional candidate is an incumbent, and what the voter thinks of Ronald Reagan's performance as president. The policy distance considerations analyzed in the model are not the only important factors and in all likelihood are not even the most important factors. Thus, a multivariate statistical procedure is necessary for a sensible analysis of the data.

Without going into the technical detail at great length, the analysis assumes that voter choice accords with a random utility model (McFadden, 1974), where proxies for voter utility are closeness to the parties (summarized here by perceptions of party liberalism-conservatism), party identification, satisfaction with presidential performance, and, in the case of congressmen, incumbency.[11] The plausibility of the split-ticket model represented by (1) can be examined by comparing a model that incorporates it to more traditional specifications that incorporate the same variables. Thus, column 1 of table 15.6 reports a model that predicts the 1984 presidential vote and column 2 does the same for the congressional vote. Column 3 reports a model that treats both votes as jointly determined. All the included variables are significant in all equations, testifying to their general importance for contemporary American voting behavior. The presidential vote equation correctly predicts 90 percent of the Reagan-Mondale decisions, while the congressional vote equation correctly predicts 80 percent of the congressional decisions. Both figures are quite representative for voting models of this sort (Fiorina, 1981: chaps. 8, 9). Upon first examination these results appear far superior to the 74 percent figure achieved by the split-ticket voting model. But, to perform a valid comparison one must ask how many voters have *both* their votes correctly predicted by the separate presidential and congressional models. Cross-tabulating the percentage correctly predicted by the two

Table 15.6.   Alternative Models of 1984 Voting.

		Presidential vote	Congressional vote	Joint decision
Net Reagan preference		−3.44**	—	−4.00**
Net congressional preference		—	−2.40**	−2.58**
Reagan job rating:				
Presidential effect	approve strongly	5.00**	—	5.88**
	approve	3.28**	—	3.69**
	disapprove	.44	—	.99*
Congressional effect	approve strongly	—	2.74**	2.98**
	approve	—	2.41**	2.59**
	disapprove	—	1.24**	1.38**
Party identification:				
Presidential effect	Republican	2.37**	—	2.65**
	Independent	1.51**	—	1.92**
Congressional effect	Republican	—	1.48**	1.43**
	Independent	—	.67**	.64**
Policy distance		−.19**	−.007*	−.25**
Incumbency		—	1.50**	1.49**
q		—	—	.74
N		1,024	885	861
% correctly predicted		90.9	80.9	74.2

**$p<.01$.
*$p<.05$.

equations gives an answer of 74 percent, the same as the 74 percent figure achieved by the calculated split-ticket voting model (column 3).

In a statistical sense there is no basis for choosing between the traditional model of separate decisions on the one hand and the split-ticket joint-decision model on the other. The traditional and alternative analyses estimate the same number of coefficients, and their predictive success is identical. But these preliminary results are at the least highly suggestive. A model that enters policy distance considerations in the specific form posited by equation (1) does as well as one that imposes no constraints on the estimates of policy distance considerations in presidential and congressional voting. Moreover, the joint-decision model provides an estimate of an additional parameter, q, the electorate's implicit judgment of the importance of the president vis-à-vis the Congress. The .74 estimate suggests that the electorate in 1984 viewed the president as three times as important as the Congress (74:26) in determining national policy, a piece of information not yielded by the traditional analyses.[12]

Summary

After the 1984 election results were in, various commentators complained that the American people voted for Reagan despite greater agreement with Mondale on the issues. Unhappy Democrats attributed such seemingly schizophrenic behavior to Reagan's affability—a benighted citizenry supposedly voted for "Doctor Feelgood" despite their misgivings about the doctor's prescriptions. More disinterested observers noted that a weak relationship between issue positions and votes is characteristic of a performance-based election. The analysts of 1972 also found that McGovern did more poorly than he should have done based on the citizenry's issue positions (Popkin et al., 1976). When citizens have the hard evidence provided by four years on the job, they are inclined to discount rhetoric and promises in favor of the hard evidence. Thus, according to this interpretation, the citizenry of 1984 believed rightly or wrongly that America was back, and they voted accordingly.

Undoubtedly both Reagan's affability and his performance explain why many citizens supported him in spite of their disagreement with many of his positions, though I think that the affability factor is overrated. The theory of calculated split-ticket voting adds still a third explanation for why Reagan's electoral support exceeded attitudinal support for his issue stances. Even if the citizenry did not care to go as far as Ronald Reagan on many issues, they did want to go in the *same direction* as he did, and they knew that a Democratic House would limit the distance he could go. Some of them decided that the point at which the weight of Congress would drag Reagan to a halt was preferable to the apparent alternatives.[13]

The theory of calculated split-ticket voting also helps to explain the emergence of the "split-level realignment." The simple fact of Democratic incumbency undoubtedly generates a good portion of the divergence between presidential and congressional voting in 1980 and 1984. But a model of policy calculation appears to explain some ticket-splitting that benefits Democratic congressmen above and beyond that explained by incumbency.

Two loose ends need attention before concluding. First, in no way do I mean to argue that policy calculation is the sole explanation for ticket-splitting. As stated repeatedly, congressional incumbency and Reagan's popularity and performance undoubtedly go a long way toward explaining the interesting features of recent elections. But as noted earlier, there are some features of recent elections not completely explained by such factors. These features can be explained as the result of some portion of the citizenry behaving in accord with a simple model of calculated ticket-splitting.

A second loose end concerns the role of the Senate in this argument. For purposes of keeping the model simple, I have assumed a unicameral legislature, but regrettably the Congress is bicameral. Is there any reason why citizens might focus more on the House as a means of moderating the actions of the executive? The most obvious one is that only one-third of the Senate is up for election at each presidential election. Thus, while every voter has an opportunity to split a president-House decision, two-thirds (more-or-less) of them have no opportunity to split a president-Senate decision. Again, institutional structure creates and constrains behavioral opportunities.

BEYOND REAGAN

All things considered, this chapter concludes that the resurgence of conservatism in the United States may be a liberal fear and a conservative hope, but it is not an empirical fact. At least, no disinterested analysis has yet marshaled convincing evidence of such a resurgence. Despite the gyrations of elites, the noteworthy policy changes of the past six years, and the electoral success of Ronald Reagan and Republican senatorial candidates (prior to 1986), there is no strong or even consistent empirical evidence that the citizenry has made a right turn or embraced the Republican party in significant and lasting numbers.[14] No features of recent elections appear to exceed the combined explanatory reach of (1) the ineptitude and bad luck of the late 1970s Democratic administration, (2) the competence and good luck of the Reagan administration, (3) House incumbency, and (4) calculated ticket-splitting. Perhaps there is some as yet unmeasured turn to the right and/or electoral realignment lurking beneath all this, but it appears to be both empirically elusive and theoretically redundant.

To be sure, the Republican party had and probably still has the *opportunity* to create a realignment. Increasingly, scholars are recognizing that realignments occur when large elements of the electorate are up for grabs and a united party in power seizes the opportunity by dealing with the problems or otherwise resolving the issues that loosened voters from their traditional moorings (Clubb et al., 1980; Brady, 1987). In 1980 the domestic and international situation, the collective state of mind of the citizenry, and the disarray of the majority party probably interacted to create a realignment opportunity. In reducing inflation and strengthening the U.S. position in the world, Reagan unquestionably provided some undecided citizens with serious food for thought. But there is good reason to believe that the Republicans are incapable of capitalizing on their opportunity, and that they have squandered some of it.

The Republican party cannot take full advantage of the realignment opportunity because of internal incompatibilities within it. No single issue or issue complex such as slavery or a depression has created the realignment opportunity; rather, the Democrats foundered on *all* the existing issues. Beginning in the mid-1960s Democratic racial and social policy began to alienate important parts of the Democratic coalition. As the 1970s wore on, economic conditions suggested that Democratic economic policies no longer were efficacious, whatever their value in the past. And the bad luck of the Iranian hostage crisis contributed to the impression that Democratic foreign and defense policy was similarly bankrupt. In light of this background, Democratic disarray poses no puzzle.

But what positions can Republicans stake out in an attempt to drive the final nails into the Democratic coffin? The new right social agenda repels the yuppie middle class otherwise attracted to the low tax and free trade Republican program. Conversely, the populist-conservative attraction to the new right social agenda stands at odds with free trade, everyone-for-themselves economic policies, a problem already noted by various new right leaders. On the international front Reagan machismo and saber rattling conjure memories of Vietnam, memories intense enough to override the economic self-interest of the yuppies. Conversely, the young cohorts attracted to Reagan's strong leadership are not equally attracted to the exhortations of the evangelicals, nor do they find much attraction in Republican policies in the realms of education and employment. If any one issue complex were notably more important than the rest, the Republicans would not face so large a problem, but at the present time all the issues seem important in American politics. Thus far the Republicans have done well by paying lip service to the social issues, speaking loudly and carrying a small stick, and concentrating on economic issues. But if economic conditions turn poor, Republican strategists will face a series of "heads we lose, tails they win" choices.

As for squandering what opportunities they have had, the reasons are the usual—hubris and ideology. The 1980 election provided no mandate. It indicated only that the American public had lost confidence in Democratic economic policy or what passed for it, and that the public was frustrated by international humiliations like the taking of the hostages in Teheran. Out of sheer desperation the populace turned to Reaganomics—could it be any worse than what already existed? Similarly, the citizenry demanded that the United States do what must be done to insure respect for American interests in the world.

The Reagan administration overplayed its hand by creating a structural deficit likely to create problems for Reagan's successors, and by equating strength of national defense with dollars poured into the defense industry, thereby giving new meaning to the old term "welfare queen." In both cases the reaction has set in, and it undermines prospects of a realignment that would enthrone the Republicans as the majority party.

What then should we expect when Ronald Reagan passes from the electoral scene? There are too many uncertainties to permit any firm predictions, but in politics you don't beat something or someone with nothing or no one, and as yet the Democrats have nothing and no one. Their major hope would appear to be an economic or foreign policy catastrophe that could be laid at the feet of the Republicans. Although such an unfortunate development for the country would prolong the realignment opportunity, the Democrats are probably less capable of capitalizing on it than the Republicans. If bets must be placed, bet on the Republican presidential candidate in 1988, but also bet that in

1994 political scientists will still be puzzling over their data, scratching their heads, and trying to make sense of the 1988 and 1992 outcomes—and still arguing about whether a realignment has taken place or is in progress.

NOTES

Inspiration for this essay comes from a variety of people, five of whom deserve explicit mention. First, for many years I have kibitzed Randall Calvert's and John Ferejohn's continuing (never-ending?) research project on presidential coattails. Second, in his Caltech doctoral dissertation Ken McCue characteristically got half of the critical insight. Finally, John Chubb's and Paul Peterson's ingenious, provocative, but ultimately unconvincing arguments as editors of a Brookings volume to which I contributed forced me to think more deeply about the subject of this essay.

1   For example, polls taken in late 1985 reported Democratic identifications ranging from 33 percent to 48 percent. Reported movements during the first half of the 1980s are equally at variance. See "Opinion Roundup," Public Opinion (October 1985): 22–23.

2   Of course, when examining opinion change over time one must be aware that a changing status quo can hide true change and/or produce the appearance of change when none is present. For example, when Reagan took office polls indicated that three-quarters of the citizenry believed that more should be spent on defense. By 1985 three-quarters believed that enough was being spent on defense. Given the huge amounts spent in the intervening five years, it would be dangerous to conclude that the citizenry had gotten more dovish. In all likelihood, their responses reflected a greatly changed status quo, as well as, if not more so, than revelations of waste, fraud, and abuse and concern about Reagan's bellicose approach to foreign policy. Fortunately, on few issues was the Reagan administration able to effect as significant a change in the status quo as on defense. Thus, most issues do not pose such a severe interpretative difficulty.

3   Miller and Shanks (1982) are a lone exception to this generalization. But their findings about the importance of ideology reflect their inappropriate postulation of a recursive voting model estimated via a stepwise regression procedure that enters ideology as the second variable (after party identification). Their conclusions in large part restate their assumptions.

4   Weissberg (1986) provides an in-depth discussion focusing on busing and affirmative action.

5   Immediately following the election there were suggestions that differential turnout in Democratic and Republican congressional districts, reapportionment, an unfavorable seats-votes relationship, and other factors underlay the divergent presidential-congressional results. While such variables always have some impact, analysts soon realized that the brute fact of greatest importance was the 9 percent lower support for Republican congressional candidates than for Ronald Reagan.

6   Take 1984, for example. Republican incumbency should reinforce the effects of
the pro-Reagan tide while Democratic incumbency should retard it. Open seats
presumably would have ticket-splitting rates not augmented or diminished by
incumbency.

7   To explain, the vertical line midway between positions D and R separates those
positions closer to one party than the other. All voters to the left will vote for a
Democratic presidential candidate, while all to the right will vote for a Republican. The vertical line midway between D and DR separates those positions closer to
the unified control position, DD, from those closer to the divided control position,
DR. The situation on the right is analogous. This analysis simply reflects equation 1
and the assumption of symmetric preferences (closeness equates to preference).

8   Proposition 2 conflicts, however, with the predictions of psychological theories of
ticket-splitting, which generally predict that as party differences lessen, ticket-
splitting will rise because voter cross-pressures will increase.

9   It is somewhat surprising to find that in a period of divided government more
citizens (50–150) can place the federal government than either of the two parties
on every seven-point scale included in the 1984 NES Study. Less surprisingly, more
citizens can place the Republicans than the Democrats on every scale, though the
differences are smaller.

10 Unfortunately, the women's scale differed across the two surveys. In 1980 it referred
to women's role (equal vs. traditional), while in 1984 it referred to federal government responsibility for women's socioeconomic status. Comparing the correlations
is obviously an iffy matter.

11 I am indebted to R. Douglas Rivers for pointing out the suitability of McFadden's
random utility model for testing the theory proposed in this chapter. Rivers also
provided the estimates that follow, a valuable check given his initial skepticism
about the voting model. In collaborative research now under way we are examining
straight- and split-ticket voting patterns in much of the postwar period.

12 The research with Rivers will enable us to determine whether temporal variation in
q parallels the rise of the imperial presidency in the late 1960s and the congressional resurgence of the mid-1970s. Preliminary estimates put the presidency/
Congress ratio for 1980 at about 2:1, compared to the approximately 3:1 ratio for
1984. Certainly it is plausible that citizens saw the presidency as more powerful
after the first Reagan administration than after the Carter administration.

13 For a theoretical analysis that focuses on movement relative to the status quo, see
Grofman (1985).

14 Except Southern whites, as noted above.

REFERENCES

Beck, Paul Allen. 1974. "A Socialization Theory of Partisan Realignment." In Richard G.
     Neimi, ed., The Politics of Future Citizens. San Francisco: Jossey Bass, pp. 199–219.
Brady, David. 1987. Forthcoming book on Congress and electoral realignment.
———, with Joseph Stewart, Jr. 1982. "Congressional Party Realignment and Transfor-

mations of Public Policy in Three Realignment Eras." *American Journal of Political Science* 26: 333–60.

Burnham, Walter Dean. 1970. *Critical Elections and the Mainsprings of American Politics.* New York: W. W. Norton.

———. 1982. *The Current Crisis in American Politics.* New York: Oxford University Press.

Campbell, Angus, Philip E. Converse, Warren E. Miller, and Donald E. Stokes. 1960. *The American Voter.* New York: John Wiley and Sons.

CBS/New York Times Report. 1986. January.

Cavanagh, Thomas E., and James L. Sundquist. 1985. "The New Two-Party System." In John E. Chubb and Paul E. Peterson, eds., *The New Direction in American Politics.* Washington D.C.: Brookings Institution.

Chubb, John E., and Paul E. Peterson. 1985. "Realignment and Institutionalization." In John E. Chubb and Paul E. Peterson, eds., *The New Direction in American Politics.* Washington, D.C.: Brookings Institution.

Clubb, Jerome, William Flanigan, and Nancy Zingale. 1980. *Partisan Realignment: Voters, Parties and Government in American History.* Beverly Hills: Sage Publications.

Converse, Philip E. 1964. "The Nature of Belief Systems in Mass Publics." In David Apter, ed., *Ideology and Discontent.* New York: Free Press, pp. 206–61.

Ferguson, Thomas, and Joel Rogers. 1985. "The Myth of America's Turn to the Right." *The Atlantic* 257, no. 5: 43–53.

Fiorina, Morris P. 1981. *Retrospective Voting in American Elections.* New Haven, Conn.: Yale University Press.

———. 1984. "The Presidency and the Contemporary Electoral System." In Michael Nelson, ed., *The Presidency and the Political System.* Washington, D.C.: Congressional Quarterly Press, pp. 204–26.

Ginsberg, Benjamin. 1972. "Critical Elections and the Substance of Party Conflict: 1844–1968." *Midwest Journal of Political Science* 16: 603–25.

Grofman, Bernard. 1985. "The Neglected Role of the Status Quo in Models of Issue Voting." *Journal of Politics* 47: 230–37.

Hibbs, Douglas A., Jr. 1982. "President Reagan's Mandate from the 1980 Elections: A Shift to the Right?" *American Politics Quarterly* 10: 387–420.

Key, V. O., Jr. 1955. "A Theory of Critical Elections." *Journal of Politics* 17: 3–18.

———. 1959. "Secular Realignment and the Party System." *Journal of Politics* 21: 198–210.

Ladd, Everett Carll. 1986. "Alignment and Realignment: Where Are All the Voters Going?" *The Ladd Report #3.* New York: W. W. Norton.

McFadden, Daniel. 1974. "Conditional Logit Analysis of Qualitative Choice Behavior." In P. Zarembka, ed., *Frontiers of Econometrics.* New York: Academic Press.

Maddox, William S., and Stuart A. Lilie. 1984. *Beyond Liberal and Conservative.* Washington, D.C.: Cato Institute.

Miller, Arther H., and Martin P. Wattenberg. 1981. "Policy and Performance Voting in the 1980 Election." Paper presented at the American Political Science Association convention, New York.

Miller, Warren E. 1986. "Party Identification and Political Belief Systems: Changes in Partisanship in the United States, 1980–1984." Manuscript.

————, and J. Merrill Shanks. 1982. "Policy Directions and Presidential Leadership: Alternative Interpretations of the 1980 Presidential Election." *British Journal of Political Science* 12: 299–356.

Nie, Norman H., Sidney Verba, and John R. Petrocik. 1976. *The Changing American Voter.* Cambridge, Mass.: Harvard University Press.

Norpoth, Helmut. 1986. "Party Realignment in the American Electorate: Overdue and Underway?" Paper presented at the 41st annual meeting of the American Association for Public Opinion Research.

Petrocik, John R. 1974. *Party Coalitions: Realignment and the Decline of the New Deal Party System.* Chicago: University of Chicago Press.

————. 1985. "The Post-New Deal Party Coalitions and the Election of 1984." Paper presented at the annual meeting of the American Political Science Association.

Phillips, Kevin P. 1982. *Post-Conservative America.* New York: Random House.

Popkin, Samuel, John W. Gorman, Charles Phillips, and Jeffrey A. Smith. 1976. "Comment: What Have You Done For Me Lately? Toward an Investment Theory of Voting." *American Political Science Review* 70: 779–805.

Rusk, Jerrold G. 1970. "The Effect of the Australian Ballot Reform on Split Ticket Voting: 1876–1908." *American Political Science Review* 64, no. 4: 1220–38.

Scammon, Richard M., and Ben J. Wattenberg. 1970. *The Real Majority.* New York: Coward, McCann & Geoghegan.

Schneider, William. 1981. "The November 4 Vote for President: What Did It Mean?" In Austin Ranney, ed., *The American Elections of 1980.* Washington, D.C.: American Enterprise Institute.

————. 1984. "Half a Realignment." *New Republic,* December 3, 1984, pp. 19–22.

Shefter, Martin, and Benjamin Ginsberg. 1986. "Institutionalizing the Reagan Regime." In Benjamin Ginsberg and Alan Stone, eds., *Do Elections Matter?* New York: M. E. Sharpe.

Shively, W. Phillips. 1979. "The Development of Party Identification Among Adults: Exploration of a Functional Model." *American Political Science Review* 71: 1039–54.

Sundquist, James L. 1983. *Dynamics of the Party System.* Washington, D.C.: Brookings Institution.

Sussman, Barry. 1986. "What's the Evidence for This Shift to the Right We Hear About?" *Washington Post National Weekly Edition,* July 21, p. 37.

Weissberg, Robert. 1986. "The Democratic Party and the Conflict Over Racial Policy." In Benjamin Ginsberg and Alan Stone, eds., *Do Elections Matter?* New York: M. E. Sharpe.

Wilson, James Q. 1986. "Realignment at the Top, Dealignment at the Bottom." Manuscript.

Index

About the Contributors

James E. Alt, professor of political science at Harvard University, is the author of *The Politics of Economic Decline* and *Political Economics* (with Alec Chrystal). He also is editor of *Advances in Quantitative Analysis* and coeditor of *Cabinet Studies*. A past president of the British Politics Group of the American Political Science Association, he has contributed numerous articles to scholarly journals including the *American Political Science Review*, the *American Journal of Political Science*, and the *British Journal of Political Science*.

William James Booth is assistant professor of political science at Duke University. His publications include *Interpreting the World: Kant's Philosophy of History and Politics* (University of Toronto Press, 1986) as well as articles on Aristotle and Kant. At present he is working on a book about Marx's political philosophy. Before coming to Duke, he was a member of the Canadian Department of External Affairs, Middle East and USSR/ Eastern Europe Relations Bureau.

Henry W. Chappell, Jr., is associate professor of economics at the University of South Carolina. He has contributed numerous articles to such journals in economics and political science as the *American Economic Review*, the *Review of Economics and Statistics*, the *Journal of Finance*, and the *American Political Science Review*.

Harold D. Clarke is professor of political science at Virginia Polytechnic Institute and State University. He is the coauthor of *Political Choice in Canada*, *Representative Democracy in the Canadian Provinces*, and *Absent Mandate: The Politics of Discontent in Canada*. His articles have appeared in such journals as the *American Journal of Political Science*, the *American Political Science Review*, the *British Journal of Political Science*, and the *Journal of Politics*. He currently is doing research on the dynamics of political support in Anglo-American democracies.

Barry Cooper is professor of political science at the University of Calgary. He is the author of *Merleau-Ponty and Marxism*, *Michel Foucault: An Introduction to His Thought*, *The End of History*, and *The Political Thought of Eric Voegelin*. He has translated books by Jean Baechler and Raymond Aron and has contributed articles to several journals including *Interpretation*, the *Canadian Journal of Political Science*, the *Journal of Canadian Studies*, and *Canadian Ethnic Studies*.

Ivor Crewe is professor of government at the University of Essex and coeditor of the

British Journal of Political Science. From 1974 to 1982 he was director of the ESRC Data Archive at Essex University and codirector of the 1974 and 1979 British Election Studies. In recent years he has coauthored *Decade of Dealignment* (with Bo Sarlvik) and *British Parliamentary Constituencies* (with Anthony Fox) and coedited *Electoral Change in Western Democracies* (with David Denver) and *Political Communications: The General Election Campaign of 1983* (with Martin Harrop). An election commentator for BBC-TV and the *Guardian*, he has contributed articles to, among others, the *British Journal of Political Science*, *Political Studies*, *Electoral Studies*, and *Comparative Politics*.

Morris P. Fiorina, professor of government at Harvard University, is the author of *Representatives, Roll Calls, and Constituencies*, *Congress—Keystone of the Washington Establishment*, *Retrospective Voting in American National Elections*, and coauthor of *The Personal Vote: Constituency Service and Electoral Independence*. He currently serves as chairman of the Board of Overseers of the National Election Studies.

Roy E. Fitzgerald is a graduate student in the department of political science at the State University of New York at Buffalo and is also a student at that university's law school.

Mark N. Franklin is senior lecturer in politics at the University of Strathclyde (Glasgow). He was a visiting professor at the University of Iowa in 1984–85 and at the University of Chicago in 1974–75 (where he was also senior study director at the National Opinion Research Center). He is the author of *The Decline of Class Voting in Britain* and of numerous articles on electoral and legislative behavior published in the *American Political Science Review*, the *British Journal of Political Science*, the *American Journal of Political Science*, *Political Studies*, *Legislative Studies Quarterly*, and *The Parliamentarian*.

Roger Gibbins is professor of political science at the University of Calgary. He is the author of *Prairie Politics and Society*, *Regionalism: Territorial Politics in Canada and the United States*, and *Conflict and Unity: An Introduction to Canadian Political Life*. He also has coauthored *Out of Irrelevance: An Introduction to Indian Affairs in Canada* and has contributed articles to such journals as *Canadian Ethnic Studies*, the *Canadian Journal of Political Science*, and *Canadian Public Policy*.

Michael Allen Gillespie is assistant professor of political science at Duke University. He is the author of *Hegel, Heidegger, and the Ground of History*. He also has contributed articles to the *Journal of Politics*, *Political Theory*, and other edited volumes.

Marilyn Hoskin is associate professor of political science and associate dean of social sciences at the State University of New York at Buffalo. She is the author of *The Political Involvement of Adolescents* (with Roberta S. Sigel) and has contributed articles to the *American Journal of Political Science*, *Comparative Politics*, *Political Psychology*, *International Migration*, and other journals and edited collections.

William Keech is professor of political science at the University of North Carolina at Chapel Hill. He is the author of *The Impact of Negro Voting*, *The Role of the Vote in the Quest for Equality*, and coauthor (with Donald R. Mathews) of *The Party's Choice*. His teaching and research interests are in the theory and practice of representative government.

Allan Kornberg is professor and chairman of the department of political science at

Duke University. He is the author of *Canadian Legislative Behavior, Influence in Parliament: Canada* (with William Mishler), *Citizen Politicians—Canada* (with Joel Smith and Harold Clarke) and *Representative Democracy in the Canadian Provinces* (with Harold Clarke and William Mishler). He is also coauthor and editor of *Legislatures in Developmental Perspective, Legislatures in Comparative Perspective*, and *Political Support in Canada: The Crisis Years*. He has contributed numerous articles to such journals as the *American Political Science Review*, the *British Journal of Political Science*, the *Canadian Journal of Political Science*, and the *Journal of Politics*.

Michael Lienesch is associate professor of political science at the University of North Carolina at Chapel Hill. He has written widely in the field of American political thought, concentrating recently on the role of religion in American politics. His articles and essays have appeared in the *Journal of Politics*, the *Western Political Quarterly*, *American Politics Quarterly*, the *Review of Politics*, *History of Political Thought*, *Political Science Quarterly*, *Soundings*, and other journals. At present he is completing a book on the American religious right.

William Mishler is professor and chairman of the department of government and international studies at the University of South Carolina. A specialist in empirical democratic theory, he is the author of *Influence in Parliament: Canada* (with Allan Kornberg), *Political Participation in Canada*, and *Representative Democracy in the Canadian Provinces* (with Allan Kornberg and Harold Clarke). He also has contributed numerous articles on political representation and legislative behavior in Britain, Canada, and the United States to various professional journals. Currently he is at work on a theory of political performance.

F. L. Morton is associate professor of political science at the University of Calgary. He is the editor and coauthor of *Law, Politics, and the Judicial Process in Canada*, and he has contributed articles on civil liberties, judicial policymaking, and political theory to such journals as *Polity, Publius*, the *Canadian Journal of Political Science*, the *Canadian Human Rights Yearbook, Canadian Public Policy*, and *Osgoode Hall Law Journal*. In 1985 he was coauthor of a major report on the political impact of the Charter of Rights for the Royal Commission on the Economic Union and Development Prospects for Canada.

Neil Nevitte is associate professor of political science at the University of Calgary. He is contributing coeditor of *The Future of North America: Canada, the United States and Quebec Nationalism* and *Minorities and the Canadian State*. He also has published articles on political ideology in such journals as the *Canadian Journal of Political Science, Canadian Public Policy*, and *Social Compass*.

A. Kenneth Pye (B.A., University of Buffalo; J.D., LL.M., LL.D., Georgetown University; L.H.D., Belmont Abbey College) is president of Southern Methodist University. Previously he twice served as chancellor of Duke University and twice as dean of Duke's School of Law. He has been a visiting professor in Australia, India, and Canada where he was a member of the faculty of law of the University of British Columbia. He is the author of a book, several monographs, and more than fifty articles. Most recently Samuel Fox Mordecai Professor of Law at Duke, he is chairman of the Council for the International Exchange of Scholars.

Donald D. Searing is professor of political science and director of the program in European studies at the University of North Carolina at Chapel Hill. He writes on comparative politics and political behavior and has published numerous articles on these subjects in the *American Political Science Review,* the *British Journal of Political Science,* the *Journal of Politics,* and *Comparative Politics,* as well as other leading journals. His current research is reflected in his forthcoming book, *Roles in Parliament,* which is based on extensive interviews of members of the British House of Commons.

Joel Smith is professor of sociology at Duke University. He is coauthor of *Citizen Politicians—Canada, Restructuring the Canadian State,* and *Ecology and Demography,* and coeditor of *Legislators in Development.* He has written numerous articles for sociological and political science journals in both Canada and the United States.

Norman C. Thomas is Charles Phelps Taft professor of political science at the University of Cincinnati. He is the author of *The Politics of the Presidency* (with Richard A. Watson); *Education in National Politics; Rule 9: Politics, Administration, and Civil Rights; Your American Government* (with Frederick Stoerker); and *Congress: Politics and Practice* (with Karl A. Lamb). He has edited *The Presidency and Public Policy Making* (with George C. Edwards III and Steven A. Shull); *The Politics of the Federal Bureaucracy* (with Alan A. Altshuler); *The Presidency in Contemporary Context;* and *The Institutionalized Presidency* (with Hans W. Baade). He also has published articles in *Science,* the *Journal of Politics,* the *Midwest Journal of Political Science,* the *Western Political Quarterly, Comparative Politics,* the *Policy Studies Journal, Public Policy, Presidential Studies Quarterly, Parliamentary Affairs,* the *Virginia Law Review,* the *Rutgers Law Review,* and the *Cincinnati Law Review.*

Library of Congress Cataloging-in-Publication Data
The Resurgence of conservatism in Anglo-American
democracies.
(Duke Press policy studies)
Includes index.
1. Conservatism—Great Britain—History—20th
century. 2. Conservatism—United States—History—20th
century. 3. Conservatism—Canada—History—20th century.
4. Great Britain—Politics and government—1979–
5. United States—Politics and government—1981–
6. Canada—Politics and government—1980–
I. Cooper, Barry, 1943–   . II. Kornberg, Allan.
III. Mishler, William, 1947–   . IV. Series.
JA84.G7R47 1988   320.5'2   87-22270
ISBN 0-8223-0709-X
ISBN 0-8223-0793-6 (pbk.)